Inklings of Democracy in China

_____

Harvard East Asian Monographs 210

Inklings of Democracy in China

Suzanne Ogden

Published by Harvard University Asia Center
and distributed by Harvard University Press
Cambridge (Massachusetts) and London 2002

© 2002 by the President and Fellows of Harvard College

Printed in the United States of America

The Harvard University Asia Center publishes a monograph series and, in coordination with the Fairbank Center for East Asian Research, the Korea Institute, the Reischauer Institute of Japanese Studies, and other faculties and institutes, administers research projects designed to further scholarly understanding of China, Japan, Vietnam, Korea, and other Asian countries. The Center also sponsors projects addressing multidisciplinary and regional issues in Asia.

Library of Congress Cataloging-in-Publication Data

Ogden, Suzanne.
    Inklings of democracy in China / Suzanne Ogden.
        p. cm. -- (Harvard East Asian monographs ; 210)
    Includes bibliographical references and index.
    ISBN 0-674-00856-1 (cloth : alk. paper) -- ISBN 0-674-00879-0 (pbk. : alk. paper)
        1. Democracy--China. 2. Democratization--China. 3. Political culture--China. I. Title.
    II. Series.

    JQ1516.O43 2002
    320.951--dc21   2002017171

Index by the author

♾ Printed on acid-free paper

Last figure below indicates year of this printing
12 11 10 09 08 07 06 05 04 03 02

For Peter, John, Miles, and JD

Acknowledgments

When I first went to China in 1979, I had a broad education in Chinese history, philosophy, language, and culture; but what I knew of China's political scene came almost entirely from printed documents, from meeting Chinese colleagues who had come to the United States or fled to Taiwan before 1949, from Chinese refugees who had escaped to Hong Kong after 1949, and from books written by China specialists who had a similar store of knowledge. At that time few Americans had traveled to, much less lived in, post-1949 China. Perhaps most important, the relentlessly anti-Communist policies of the Cold War period had shaped much of the writing, and even research, on what was usually called "Communist China."

Thus, it was gratifying to see those printed black and white documents at last turn into real people, each different from the next despite nearly uniform clothing and hair styles and despite a language encased in a rigidly Marxist-Leninist-Maoist vocabulary and manner of thinking. Our inimitable China Travel guide welcomed our U.S.-China Friendship Delegation by saying, "It is hot in Beijing, and we are hot in our hearts for romance with America." And so it was.

Since 1979, my understanding of China's political development has been enhanced by regular travels to China and by living and working in China where, as a Fulbright scholar, I taught at the Foreign Affairs Ministry's College of Foreign Affairs (Waijiao xueyuan) about international relations and Sino-American relations. I may well have learned as much from my students as they learned from me. Just as important has been the large number of Chinese scholars, journalists, students, and party-state officials who have come to universities in the Boston area to study, do research, or give lectures and seminars at the Fairbank Center for East Asian Studies at Harvard University. These contacts have deepened my understanding of China's political culture and political development since 1949.

Thus, I am grateful to the Fairbank Center for providing me with an extraordinarily rich intellectual environment over many years. I have learned much from the numerous Chinese who have visited there, as well as from the Western Sinologists, government officials, lawyers, human rights advocates, and business people who have come there to share what they know about China. I am also indebted to the successive directors of the Fairbank Center, Ezra Vogel, Roy Hofheinz, Philip Kuhn, Roderick MacFarquhar, James Watson, and Elizabeth Perry, for giving me an office so that I could be in the thick of things.

In addition, I am deeply indebted to my wonderful colleagues in the Department of Political Science, Northeastern University. They are such a pleasure to work with and have been an integral part of my personal and professional life. As political scientists, they have given me important insights into issues of political culture, democratization, and political development. I would especially like to thank those with whom I discussed my manuscript or who critiqued sections of it, notably, Bill Crotty, Gerald Bursey, Minton Goldman, Eileen McDonagh, and Michael Tolley.

I would also like to thank Wolfson College, Cambridge University, for welcoming me as a Visiting Scholar and Fellow for my sabbatical year, during which I began research on this book. The President, Gordon Johnson, the faculty, and the Fellows of Wolfson College provided a nourishing and happy environment in which I could pursue my research. Thanks also to Hans Van der Ven, who invited me to be a Visiting Scholar in the Department of Oriental Studies while at Cambridge; and to the School of Oriental and African Studies in London, where I did some of the research.

Chinese colleagues and Western specialists on China likewise helped make this a far better book than it otherwise would have been by reading and critiquing the manuscript in whole or in part at various stages: I particularly thank Bernie Frolic, Richard Kraus, Lin Tongji, Richard Madsen, Andrew Nathan, Michael Puett, Wang Zhenmin, Zheng Shiping, and members of the Harvard University Asia Center Publications Committee, as well as the anonymous reviewers of the manuscript. Fang Cheng contributed greatly as a research assistant, and colleagues and friends in China helped me think through my ideas. I am particularly grateful to John Ziemer, who saved readers from English written with my sometimes unique syntax.

I dedicate this book to my husband, Peter P. Rogers and to John, Miles, and JD, who I hope will grow up in a world characterized by deep respect and a strong friendship between China and the United States.

S.O.
Northeastern University

Contents

Inklings of Democracy in China

Introduction

Liberal democratic theory, like Marxism or any other theory, defines the world through a conceptual structure. Hence, "historical progress" has a different meaning for a liberal democrat than it does for a Marxist. Similarly, many in the West cannot imagine a better government than a liberal democracy, but in China, whose major thinkers had a vision of a utopia, the Great Unity or Great Harmony (*datong*), long before the Chinese Communist victory in 1949, this is not the case.

The traditional Chinese vision of a better world still pervades thinking in China today. When China's intellectuals and leaders speak or write about their hopes for their nation's future, elements of the notion of the Great Unity are still strongly evident—in spite of fifty years of Marxist ideology. Indeed, even when Marxist thinking was dominant, its proponents justified class struggle as a method of achieving ever higher levels of synthesis and harmony and, in the end, the unity of all the people in one classless, harmonious society. This is not to suggest that the concept of the Great Unity is completely at odds with liberal democratic thought; rather, the point is that the Chinese have thought about the goal of governance along different lines for a long time.

Behind the belief that other countries should adopt a liberal democratic form of government is a fundamental assumption—that the form of government is the critical element in maintaining the health of a society. Although few would question the importance of the form of government, other factors may well be even more significant to a country's health at the beginning of the new millennium. Whether a government is liberal democratic or authoritarian may matter less than (or no more than), say, the speed of modernization, the level of social and economic development, the bureaucratization of the government, the size of the population, religion, the impact of environmental problems or resource limitations, national security issues, or the place of the country within the international system, especially the international economy.

Not only may the mix of factors that a country encounters at a particular time in its history be critical to the state of its health, but also it may shape the form of government. Minimally, these factors set boundaries on the types of options available, although there is, of course, always the possibility of breakthroughs or even completely revolutionary methods and institutions. When we combine a knowledge of such parameters with China's political culture, we have a more realistic basis for thinking about the type of political institutions most likely to succeed in the short run in China.

In examining the question, then, of "Why not liberal democracy for China?" such factors must be taken into account. They are not excuses for China's "failure" to implement democracy in its Western liberal democratic form. Indeed, this book is not intended to justify or excuse anything the Chinese Communist Party has done since 1949; rather, its intent is to ask a series of questions about the relevance of Western liberal democratic theory for China. Behind these questions is the notion that China may perhaps find a way, perhaps a uniquely Chinese way, to build a fair, just, and decent society that does not rely on either the theories or the rationales of Western liberal democracy. By no means is this to say that liberal democracy will never work in China. To the contrary, this book is an attempt to look at why many Chinese insist that liberal democracy is not appropriate for China, why Chinese liberals insist it is, what evidence supports or does not support their respective views, and why the party-state is adopting elements of liberal democracy despite its stated objections.

Unresolved issues in comparative politics concerning the relationships among culture, democracy, and development are at the heart of this book. The book does not adopt a cultural determinist perspective, but it does ask, Is a democratic political culture essential to the establishment of a democratic political system, or is it a consequence of democratization? Must a society be able to call on democratic themes and attitudes in its own culture to establish a liberal democratic government, or if it lacks these, must it break with its culture and, in essence, import those themes and attitudes? How far and how fast can a political culture evolve? What are the relationships among capitalism, development, decentralization, and democracy? What kinds of problems confront latecomers to democracy?

Democratization is more than an isolated political process; it inevitably involves social and economic factors. Socioeconomic theories help explain how contradictory impulses can co-exist within China, how democratization *is* happening within the context of a deeply authoritarian political culture. Democratization may, in short, have less to do with conscious choices by the people or their leaders than with socioeconomic forces. Thus, whether the Chinese people (or their leaders) are inclined toward democracy or not, the power of socioeconomic forces, such as the free market, economic development, urbanization, and commercialization, appear to be challenging their predilections.[1]

This is not to argue that there is a perfect correlation between economic development and democracy. Indeed, as is pointed out in this book, for a variety of reasons, members of China's entrepreneurial middle class (and even the bulk of China's intelligentsia and [employed] working class) have not pressed for greater democratization. Economic development has, in fact, also contributed to the deterioration in the conditions necessary for a more just society, especially for a portion of China's peasants and workers—the very people for whom the communist revolution was fought in 1949. As a result, both the positive and the negative effects of economic and social forces in China must be considered. In other words, even if the Chinese people were content with their authoritarian culture, socioeconomic forces have a transforming power. This may lead to a polarization of wealth, but it may also help create wealth and a middle class with self-interests and a demand for rule by law, important factors in the erosion of authoritarianism.

China's political culture is, I will argue, being forced not to embrace but to accommodate democratic ideas and institutions. At the same time, that culture is also shaping the form democratization takes. As a result, the China of today is a society riddled with the tensions generated by the democratizing power of socioeconomic forces in the context of an authoritarian culture. We have only to look at, say, Singapore, Taiwan, or Japan, to see that polities can and do live with such tensions.

This book focuses, then, on China's movement toward becoming a more pluralistic, just, and democratic polity since 1949 and what factors have influenced the path it has taken. As I hope to show, the Chinese people have been accumulating rights, including greater individual freedom, and China is characterized by a growing pluralization of associations that is contributing

---

1. See, e.g., Huntington, *The Third Wave*; and Przeworski, *Democracy and the Market*.

to the development of a civil society. I do not, however, argue that these trends are the same as democratization, the institutionalization of the government's accountability to the people.

Overall, I adopt a utilitarian perspective. I am interested in the *results*: whether China's policies, institutions, and processes contribute to the development of a fair and just society, whether there is distributive justice, and whether people's substantive rights are growing. In assessing these matters, the preferred measure is the greatest good for the greatest number of people. I also look at the advances China has made in procedural justice and liberty, an issue more in keeping with a libertarian perspective. Libertarians tend to consider procedural democracy and procedural rights important even if they have negative consequences for some groups and individuals or an adverse outcome for a fair and just society. The proposition of this book is that although procedural rights generally do more good than harm, given China's social, economic, and cultural characteristics, substantive rights are more likely to benefit larger numbers and result in the greater good, at least in the short-run.

In this respect, although the book acknowledges serious problems in China's authoritarian governance since 1949, it focuses on the other side of life in China today, the side those interested primarily in the plight of political dissidents tend to ignore: the greater freedom in daily life for almost all Chinese, the lively debates within intellectual circles, the vibrancy of the mass media, the increasing autonomy of interest groups and associations, the growth of pluralism, the increasingly democratic nature of institutions, such as a more assertive national legislature, and a growing number of truly democratic elections for leaders in China's 930,000 villages, as well as the development of a more equitable legal system.

At the same time, I examine why it may be misleading to conclude that individual Chinese feel oppressed based on how *we* might feel under similar levels of governmental control. I have tried to tread lightly between the extremes of viewing all criticism of the party-state as a sign of a desire to overthrow Communist Party rule, or of viewing the lack of serious criticism or demands for democracy as a sign of satisfaction (or even an indicator of a "nation of sheep"). Nor do I assume that if the Chinese seem to agree with their government's policies, they have been brainwashed or are afraid to disagree. The book encourages readers to see the Chinese government from a Chinese citizen's perspective and to understand that—depending on the issue and the circumstances—there may be significant popular support for the government. (This is not to suggest that there is just *one* perspective. At various points, the often differing perspectives of such groups as protesters, the middle class, women, students, intellectuals, entrepreneurs, villagers, and urban workers are presented.)

Although most observers would acknowledge that China's people, living in a developing country and a Chinese culture, see the world differently from those coming from another type of society, how does this affect their view of their own political institutions? If they think about it at all, is it possible that the Chinese are more likely to worry about the impact of democracy on development than about development's impact on democratization?

When we analyze the pace and style of the development in China of a more pluralistic, democratic, and just polity, it is important to look beyond the assumed evils of communist ideology and Chinese Communist Party rule.[2] The book tries to avoid the highly emotional rhetoric surrounding so many discussions of communism, democracy, and rights[3] and concludes by presenting a non-ideological basis for evaluating China's efforts to become a better society. Its focus on "human development" as one of the critical measures of China's achievements allows an evaluation of how much substantive freedom the Chinese actually have. Although the accumulation of "rights" does not necessarily add up to democracy, the book asks how they have contributed to human development—and, indeed, to development in every sphere.

I will argue that there are three major forces pushing China toward greater democratization: growing pluralistic interests (which are becoming increasingly institutionalized) as a result of economic development, the country's desire to be respected by and participate in the international community, and the government's conviction that one of the best ways to deal with the rampant corruption that is threatening to end the Party's rule is to have a more open and transparent society. Yet foreign involvement, internationalization, marketization, the emergence of a middle class, the

---

2. Most serious scholars of Chinese politics and society today have, in fact, done so.

3. As William Theodore de Bary (*Asian Values and Human Rights*, pp. 9–10) notes, "Questions of Confucianism and human rights can be clarified better than they have been so far, so as to move beyond the level of the shouting match. In the process one could hope to recognize both shared human values, significant cultural differences, and limiting economic factors that condition the effective realization of certain humane values."

growth of fully autonomous associations and institutions, and even the development of broader political rights may turn out to be far less important to China's democratic development than the ability of the Chinese state to maintain stability as the country undergoes relentlessly rapid economic and social change.

The book itself contains a number of paradoxical propositions. Although I argue that the Chinese do not accept Western standards for democratization and that those standards are themselves questioned in the West, I conclude that the party-state has taken some of these standards seriously and has changed policies in order to move closer to them. And, although arguing that China wants to become more democratic on its own terms, I propose that China has other values, such as economic development, stability, and fairness, as well as a desire to maintain its national cultural identity and dignity (sometimes in the form of a militant nationalism), that may often interfere in the short run with democratization.

The book concludes that China is moving at a fair pace along the continuum from a "totalitarian" to a "democratizing" regime, albeit one heavily influenced by Chinese culture. Although China's political system may never resemble that of a Western European liberal democratic regime, China appears to be working hard at becoming a fairer, more just society. Unfortunately, the Chinese Communist Party's introduction of market-oriented reforms has, even as it has created greater overall wealth for the Chinese people, introduced greater economic inequality and the return of many related social problems that are reversing China's successes in achieving the fundamental conditions essential to democratization.

Because democratization is the book's topic, I have made a conscious decision to focus on the relevant aspects of Chinese political culture and institutions, whether or not they are supportive of democratization. This book is not about human rights as such,[4] and so it does not address the derogation of human rights resulting from inadequate democracy. China does not, for example, emerge as a shining example of fairness, pluralism, or democracy in its policies toward minority populations, and certainly its treatment of dissident intellectuals has at times been appalling. The class struggle and mass

---

4. I have tried not to conflate "human rights" with democratization. Human rights have standing in international law, whereas many rights, procedures, institutions, and aspects of democracy do not.

movements of the 1950s, 1960s, and 1970s were often exercises in inhumanity. A weak legal framework underwrote injustice and allowed such things to happen.

Many sinologists, myself included,[5] have dealt with these topics, as have human rights advocates, including organizations such as Amnesty International, Human Rights in China, and Asia Watch. The purpose of *this* book is to look at the broader question of democratization and pluralization and to address the other side of the story, the "inklings" of democracy in China and the supports and impediments to their progress.

Finally, this book has not confronted questions such as, if China democratizes, will we necessarily like the results? If, for example, China were to democratize, is it possible that the growing nationalism of the Chinese people could lead to a more militant, nationalistic foreign policy? As long as China is preoccupied with nation-building, and China's leaders are able to keep the lid on popular nationalism, "Chinese authoritarianism is not necessarily threatening," but on the other hand, if popular nationalism spirals out of control, "Chinese democratization will not necessarily be benign."[6] The possibility that a democratic but nationalistic China might be a more dangerous China, and a China that resists being integrated into the international community, is a topic taken up at length by others and will not be dealt with here.[7] Nevertheless, I hope that readers will consider this question as well as the question whether, if China's approach to democratization is too rapid and leads to societal disintegration and the collapse of Chinese Communist Party rule and even to the fragmentation of China into several competing polities, this is in anyone's interests.

In short, what follows is intended to deepen our understanding of pluralization, rights, and democratization in China. Its purpose is to take a broad, inclusive approach to this large issue rather than to offer up the last word on any one aspect of it. It makes no pretense of being an irrefutable analysis. Instead, it hopes to provide new lenses through which to view China and, at the same time, to provoke considerable debate.

---

5. See, e.g., Ogden, *China's Unresolved Issues;* and Ogden et al., *China's Search for Democracy.*

6. Jianwei Wang, "Democratization and China's Nation Building," in Friedman and Mc-Cormick, *What If China Doesn't Democratize?*, p. 49.

7. Friedman and McCormick, *What if China Doesn't Democratize?*

1 How Do We Know What Democracy Is?

If explanation demands understanding, then how can we ever be confident that we have explained what goes on in another society? . . . And what gives us this right to declare that others are wrong about themselves?

—Charles Taylor

No people could live without evaluating; but if it wishes to maintain itself, it must not evaluate as its neighbor evaluates. Much that seemed good to one people seemed shame and disgrace to another: Thus I found. I found much that was called evil in one place was in another decked with purple honors. One neighbor never understood another: His soul was always amazed at his neighbor's madness and wickedness.

—Friedrich Nietzsche

WHO DEFINES DEMOCRACY?

Before we can study democracy in China, we must first understand what democracy is and how it comes into being. Like most ideals, such as those espoused by Christianity and communism, perfect democracies do not exist. They are always in a state of becoming; they are always the result of compromises. If, as Vaclav Havel, then president of the Czech Republic, put it, "Democracy is a discussion," then we are inevitably looking at snapshots not of the completed forms of democracies but of the *process* of democratization. Throughout the history of Western political thought, theorists have defined and redefined the specific characteristics of an ideal political system. And much that thinkers once considered desirable in a polity is now viewed with

EPIGRAPHS: Taylor, *Philosophy and the Human Sciences*, p. 130; Nietzsche, *Zarathustra's Discourses*, p. 60.

abhorrence, at least by some. Many of Plato's ideas concerning an ideal republic, for example, would be considered highly undemocratic and undesirable today. Plato believed that the arts—poetry, drama, music, painting—played a critical role in shaping citizens. He criticized poets (Homer especially) for not telling the "truth" and dramatists for presenting evil characters, because both the actors and the audience might absorb their evil qualities. Only *good* role models could be presented. For Plato, censorship was of the utmost importance to the moral health of a polity: the government had to control the form and content of the arts.[1]

Today, the list of characteristics of a liberal democratic political system usually includes free elections, multiple independent parties, a free press and the right to free speech, and an independent judiciary that treats everyone as an equal. Among its central purposes is to provide an institutional framework that protects the rights of individuals against the state and allows the opposition to express itself (although not necessarily to have a role in policy formation). Among other things, "liberal" refers to greater openness, fewer restrictions on trade and business, less centralized state control of society and the economy, and the protection of individual civil and procedural rights. These typically come into being as a country democratizes.

Of course, political actors, not political theorists, determine whether anything resembling democracy exists. Similarly, a polity determines its standards for governance in large part by assessing its internal conditions, its goals, and the means available to pursue them. As the world has become increasingly interdependent, each polity has had to take into account external conditions. Yet, to say "the polity" determines the scope and limits of permissible actions by a government is also misleading. Within a polity, it is more specifically those with power—a person, a committee or a group, an

---

1. Not that these ideas have disappeared in the West. The U.S. Congress, for example, cut funding to the National Endowment for the Humanities because it had supported an exhibit of Robert Mapplethorpe's homoerotic art, and New York Mayor Rudolph Giuliani tried to shut down an art exhibit at the Brooklyn Museum that he found decadent. In both cases, the argument was that public morality might be undermined by these exhibits. Those familiar with the Chinese Communist Party's efforts to utilize the arts to promote good role models and insistence that only the "truth" be presented may be surprised to learn that Plato apparently believed he knew the truth about the gods since he stated in *The Republic* (377–81) through the voice of Socrates that they were inherently good. Their portrayal by Homer and dramatists as doing evil things was, Plato believed, wrong and should be censored so that the people would only learn the truth or morally uplifting legends (discussions about Plato with Gerald Bursey, Northeastern University, 2000).

economic or social class, or even a party—who decide these things. It is they who determine the division of rights between the people and the government. In undemocratic or less democratic polities, those in power usually distribute a narrow range of rights to a narrow range of people, in such a way as to benefit largely themselves and to maintain themselves in power. More democratic polities usually distribute a broader range of rights to a broader range of people, but even democratic polities may try to distribute rights in a way that keeps a particular party or class in power.

In newly established democracies, the people who come to hold power are the "winners": they have won out against a system that was less democratic or even undemocratic. Further, each extension of democratic rights to a new group (for example, extending the right to vote to men without property, women, minority groups, criminals, or people who are illiterate) usually occurs against a background of substantial opposition by those already holding power. Those in power tend to believe that the enfranchisement of new groups will lead to the diminution or even elimination of their own power or that the newly enfranchised groups will vote for unpalatable policies and laws. (Indeed, rarely are new groups enfranchised until those already in power see it as furthering their interests to do so, or, perhaps the same thing, see that the costs of continuing to exclude these groups outweigh the benefits.)[2] The newly enfranchised group, such as women or minorities, in turn tends to believe other polities are truly democratic only if they extend rights to people such as themselves. In short, conflict continues to occur among groups *within* a society because of different understandings of what democracy means and because of each group's efforts to redistribute resources and power to benefit itself. These differences arise largely from differences in self-interest and experiences.

Which groups would, then, support democratization, even if it required a revolution? As Theda Skocpol and Ellen Kay Trimberger have pointed out, the bourgeoisie is willing to lead a revolution against an aristocracy, but it only reluctantly agrees to reforms, much less a revolution, that leads to its own dispossession. *"Revolutionary leadership has never come from those who con-*

---

2. For example, when the Thai government became paralyzed and was forced to resign in 1996, Thailand's military, which had mounted eighteen coups since Thailand became a constitutional monarchy in 1932, sat on the sidelines because military leaders saw a new round of elections as something that could actually benefit them (*Asiaweek*, October 4, 1996, p. 23).

trolled the means of production."[3] In short, only the class that does not control the means of production and is excluded from political power will want to carry out democratizing reforms that undercut the power of the ruling class. Exceptions to this occur when those holding both property and power, in a rational cost-benefit analysis, see the pursuit of democratization as benefiting themselves. As noted in later chapters, self-interest helps explain why the leadership of the Chinese Communist Party offered the Chinese people the "four freedoms,"[4] introduced local-level elections, carried out legal reforms, and encouraged the growth of associations and interest groups during the reform period that began in 1978–79.

DEMOCRACY AS A SOCIAL CONSTRUCT

Like such concepts as gender, the state, and class, which many social scientists in the post-modernist tradition consider mere abstractions, democracy may be viewed as a "social construct." "Social constructions of the past are crucial elements in the process of domination, subjugation, resistance, and collusion. Representation is an expression and a source of power."[5] "Social constructionists"[6] argue that democracy, too, is an invented concept. Unlike an automobile or housing, it is not something objective or concrete or tangible. Nor, unlike having enough to eat, is it an absolute good. A polity interested in being democratic may, then, define and redefine consciously and repeatedly what democracy is or ought to be at any particular time and place in history, according to its own needs, development, culture, values, and institutions.

The concept of democracy is, in short, highly subjective and fluid. Over time, moreover, both the definition and the practice of democracy have moved generally in the direction of reserving greater rights for individuals

---

3. Skocpol and Trimberger, "Revolutions and the World-Historical Development of Capitalism," p. 123. Italics added.

4. In 1978, Deng Xiaoping offered the Chinese people the "four freedoms" so that they could speak out against the leftists who had gained power during the Cultural Revolution. At that time, leftists held power in most institutions throughout China, and Deng wanted to remove them from positions of authority. He assumed—correctly—that the Chinese people would use their new freedom of speech to attack them. When the people went too far with the Democracy Wall posters and publications in 1978–79, he curtailed those freedoms.

5. Bond and Giliam, *Social Construction of the Past*, p. 1.

6. Berger and Luckmann, *The Social Construction of Reality*; Biersteker and Weber, *State Sovereignty as Social Construct*.

and diminishing the powers of the state over its citizens. This is not the same as diminishing the *responsibilities* of the state to its citizens. To the contrary, the responsibilities of the state have tended to grow in the form of the welfare state and the protection of the individual against groups with economic or other forms of power. At the same time, the trend has been to enfranchise a greater percentage of a society's population. Although the concept of democracy originated with the Greek city-states, by today's definition of democracy, the ancient Greeks did not have democracy, for many people were excluded from voting and participation.[7] But, although *access* to democracy was denied, the ancient Greeks did have the *institutions* of democracy, and so, according to the standards of that time, they did indeed have democracy.

The judgment that democracy is "good" or "desirable" is also subjective. It depends in part on what a polity's powerholders interpret to be the necessary conditions for making democracy work, for they may be genuinely convinced that under existing conditions (further) democratization would not improve living standards. Unless they are voted out of power or are overthrown, only they can make this critical decision. History provides examples of countries that theorists might argue had all the conditions for democracy—were in fact "democratic" to a degree, at least in terms of institutions—and yet in which democracy failed (for example, Germany before Hitler came to power). Indeed, the literature on ancient democracy suggests that it was "associated with mob rule and disorder which eventually finds itself replaced by tyranny."[8] There are also examples of countries with phenomena that might be considered inimical to democracy and yet in which the institutions of democracy have flourished (such as post–World War II Italy, which has had close to 60 rounds of elections and new governments since 1945). The remarkable variety of historical conditions, responses, and outcomes has led political theorists to attempt to discover and define the characteristics and conditions favorable for democratization. Most of these studies focus on the relationships between development and democracy, between culture and democracy, or among development, culture, and democracy.[9]

---

7. Levin, *The Spectre of Democracy*, pp. 36–38.

8. Ibid., p. 38.

9. My own work on China has focused on the interactions of development, culture, and the political system; see, e.g., Ogden, *China's Unresolved Issues*.

Because of the cachet that the term "democracy" has gained worldwide over the course of the twentieth century, all forms of governments—fascist, communist, and even dictatorial—have at times claimed to be democratic. In those polities that have defined themselves as democratic, the division of rights and responsibilities between the government and the people has varied considerably, but states have tended to view themselves and present themselves to others as within an acceptable range of democratic practice according to the standards for democracy prevalent at the time.

China has likewise viewed itself as seeking democracy and even as practicing "socialist" democracy. What is socialist democracy? It is whatever the Chinese Communist Party *says* it is. And, like other governments and political theorists, the Chinese continually redefine "democracy." In short, whether in China or in the Western liberal democracies, the meaning of democracy is continually evolving. The term does not have an objective, scientific definition agreed on by all peoples for all times.

DOMINANCE OF THE WESTERN LIBERAL DEMOCRATIC CONCEPT

How did the Western liberal democratic concept of democracy become the dominant one in the world today? In the nineteenth and twentieth centuries, liberal democratic states gradually gained predominant power within the international system. They did this not through the ballot box or some other democratic process operating at the international level but through victory in war and, in more recent times, through economic influence. Today these international powerholders are the countries that commend the liberal democratic system to others. They point to their own stable political systems or their successful economies as evidence of the superiority of the liberal democratic system. Rarely do they credit extraneous factors—the luck of the draw in terms of resources, the influence of geography on secure international borders, their ability to exploit resources in other countries, or the institutional, structural, and normative bias that they have built into the international system itself—as relevant to the success of their own political and economic systems.

Because history tends to reflect the values of the winners, in the twentieth century it was the liberal democratic states (notably, the United States, Great Britain, and France) that had the privilege of writing and rewriting the history of the development of liberal democratic political systems as if that was the natural and only proper course for politics. All other states were encouraged to follow their example and adopt a liberal democratic system. That is, those who are now among the most influential actors in the international system present the history that led to the establishment of liberal democratic states in large part as if it were a story of a higher morality or natural right rather than, say, superior economic and military power and victory in war. In the view of the "ruling class" within the international system, those states in the international system that hold non–liberal democratic values (especially if they are viewed as adversaries) have failed to gain predominant power because of the ethical inferiority of their political values, not because of, say, their lack of economic resources or their military unpreparedness.

The possibility remains, of course, that regardless of natural right or moral standing, a nondemocratic country might become one of the dominant states, might even become *the* dominant state. After all, not all states have considered liberal democracy a worthwhile goal, and when nondemocratic rulers have become powerful in the international system, they have attempted to remake the world in their own image. Such was the case, for example, with the Austro-Hungarian, Prussian, and Ottoman empires, as it was later with Hitler's Germany, imperial Japan in the first half of the century, and the Soviet Union. Had these empires or states been the dominant states at the end of the twentieth century, a different history would be cited today to show who had a rightful claim to be rulers and what form the best polity should take.

In short, certain individuals or states gain predominant power, and they then rewrite history in a way that accords with their vision, as if that were the natural and right course for history and politics. They *should* be and *are* the proper rulers.[10] In contrast, they consider powerholders with different values as illegitimate.

Most commentators would probably portray the Cold War as a contest between the United States and the Soviet Union for world domination, but it was rationalized on both sides as a competition between two different visions of the proper ethical and political system, with "socialist democracy" competing against "liberal democracy." And, although communist party rule and socialist democracy ultimately collapsed in the Soviet Union and its

---

10. Thomas Kuhn (*The Structure of Scientific Revolutions*) makes this same argument about science and the scientists who control the path science takes.

Eastern European satellites, China still adheres to a form of socialist democracy. Indeed, a vision of democracy at odds with Western liberal democracy remains within much of Asia today. Given the dynamic growth in Asia in the past few decades (in spite of Asia's economic difficulties at the end of the twentieth century) and its resourceful and talented peoples, it remains possible that one day the Asian, perhaps even the Chinese, vision of the best form of government will become the dominant vision.

ETHNOCENTRICITY OF THE WESTERN
DEFINITION OF DEMOCRACY

With the dominant players in the international system in a position to stipulate appropriate political systems, inevitably the definition of democracy in the final decades of the twentieth century took on an ethnocentric hue that reflected their own preferences. The lack of a worldwide consensus on the meaning of democracy is in large part due to different historical experiences and cultural differences—to the different "myths" that each country cherishes about itself. "Shared understandings about matters like rights and justice" also are important in creating a society or country.[11] As a result, countries reach different conclusions on the nature of an ethical and just political system. This is apparent in the assumptions of one prominent liberal democratic theorist of the late twentieth century, Francis Fukuyama:

It has been a common practice for socialist countries to press for the recognition of various second- and third-generation economic rights, such as the right to employment, housing, or health care. The problem with such an expanded list is that the achievement of these rights is not clearly compatible with other rights like those of property or free economic exchange. In our definition we will stick to Lord Bryce's shorter and more traditional list of [three] rights [civil rights, religious rights, and political rights], which is *compatible with those contained in the American Bill of Rights.*[12]

---

11. Henry Shue, *Basic Rights*, p. 179. Shue is also drawing on arguments of Walzer, *Spheres of Justice.*

12. Fukuyama, *Trust: The Social Virtues and the Creation of Prosperity*, pp. 43–44. Italics added. Henry Shue (*Basic Rights*, p. 179) notes the American "tendency to overmoralize international affairs." Shue's book offers an extended essay about which rights should be considered "basic rights" for peoples throughout the world and how deprivation of those rights occurs, as well as a critique of the United States' prioritization of political rights over economic

For an American liberal democrat, this is a convenient definition: it values those rights enjoyed by the people of the United States (some of them extended to minorities only in the past thirty years) and excuses the exclusion of rights enjoyed by the citizens of other countries. In turn, it derides the decisions of other governments such as China's to give priority to "second- and third-generation economic rights." It is a good example of ethnocentric thinking and of the tendency of the most powerful countries to tell others what to do. And it leads to suspicions in China and elsewhere in the developing world that the motives of the United States in pressing for its own style of democracy while refusing to ratify the 1966 International Covenant on Economic, Social and Cultural Rights[13] had little to do with a desire to ensure the rights of people in other countries and a great deal to do with the desire to spread American power and influence.[14] Today, the national constitutions of most liberal democratic states include welfare rights along with traditional civil liberties. The American Constitution remains anomalous in this regard.[15]

Fukuyama's definition also illustrates why democracy is a highly subjective concept that incorporates a country's historical experience—its national myth. The way a historical experience is presented to a nation becomes part of its national myth and profoundly affects its culture and self-perceptions. Thus, "any nation, even the United States, is held together by stronger cultural cement than reason. What appears to be politically rational behavior is actually driven by common stories about the origins and destiny of the na-

---

rights. Rights are "basic" for Shue "only if enjoyment of them is essential to the enjoyment of all other rights. . . . When a right is genuinely basic, any attempt to enjoy any other right by sacrificing the basic right would be quite literally self-defeating, cutting the ground from beneath itself. Therefore, if a right is basic, other, non-basic rights may be sacrificed, if necessary, in order to secure the basic right. But the protection of a basic right may not be sacrificed in order to secure the enjoyment of a non-basic right" (p. 19).

13. As of the end of 2001, the covenant had been signed but not ratified by the United States. It is the only liberal democracy not to have done so. China signed in 1997 and ratified it in March 2001.

14. Many developing countries "wonder how the US can promote human rights when it is very selective about the type of rights it wishes to promote" (Harvard Law School, East Asian Legal Studies Program and Human Rights Program, "Human Rights and Foreign Policy," p. 20). Although some governments might take this position as a way of excusing their internal repression, other governments are sincere.

15. Mary Ann Glendon, "Welfare Rights at Home and Abroad: A Learning Process," *Current*, Nov. 1994, pp. 12–15; in Myers and Parsekian, *Democracy Is a Discussion*, p. 12.

tion, about its place within the larger community of nations and within the process of history."[16]

An important part of America's myth concerning itself as a liberal democratic country has grown out of its originating ideas. Among the most important of these were religious freedom and the consent of the governed (as in "No taxation without representation"). Out of these seemingly simple ideas developed the concept of individual autonomy, the rights reserved to an individual against the power of the state. Americans do not, however, view this conceptualization of individual freedom as uniquely American, something socially constructed and based on the American experience and liberal assumptions, but rather as a universally applicable truth. For example, American church leaders and missionaries, charitable organizations such as the Ford Foundation, and universities engaged in academic exchanges with the Chinese since the early 1980s were by the late 1980s deeply disappointed at the Chinese inability to understand the universality of their values.[17]

Yet the conditions and ideas that so profoundly influenced the American revolution have no real equivalent in Chinese history.[18] Instead, until the end of the imperial system in the first part of the twentieth century, historical and philosophical ruminations saw the movement of Chinese history as cyclical, and the rise and fall of dynasties for over 2000 years was interpreted in terms of the morality of its rulers, a morality reflected in an emperor's proper performance of rites (*li*) and his ability to maintain order. According to prevailing Confucian thought, an emperor had the "Mandate of Heaven" (*tianming*) to rule, but only to rule properly. To the people was reserved the right to rebel (*qiyi*) or revolt (*zaofan* or *geming*—"to cut off the mandate") against an emperor who, by inappropriate behavior, had lost the mandate. But this is not how we in the West might today understand the term "revo-

---

16. Madsen, *China and the American Dream*, p. 81.

17. Ibid., pp. 92, 161.

18. The inability of the Chinese government to quash the Falungong's activities since 1999 and the physical violence against hundreds of tax collectors as well as the known murder of twenty of them between 1993 and 2000 because of the imposition of arbitrary taxes on China's citizens (or, perhaps, because of the perceived illegitimacy of any taxes after more than 30 years of "tax-free" Maoism) suggest, however, that "religious freedom" and "no taxation without representation" may well turn out to be the rallying cries for democratic change, if not revolution, in China. See www.cnd.org (*China News Daily*), Feb. 14, 2000, based on report in *Business Week*, Feb. 13, 2000. The other major likely cause would be corruption.

lution," even though the word *geming* is translated as such.[19] In China a *ge-ming* led to a change in the holder of the mandate and provided the context in which a new ruling house established itself. After assisting in the *geming*, the people would resume their submissive and obedient role within a patri-archal system in which it was important that China's rulers had *enough* power to govern well. Hence, Chinese history was cyclical, until the 1911 Revolution. This was a true revolution, in which the imperial system was overthrown and replaced with a "republic," in name if not in fact.

Even so, the 1911 Revolution was not motivated by a desire to establish in-dividual freedom. For the revolution's founding father, Sun Yat-sen, individ-ual rights were never important. Later, he even "dismissed them as inappro-priate for China."[20] Instead, the guiding principles of the 1911 Revolution, as articulated by Sun Yat-sen in the "Three People's Principles," were democ-racy, nationalism, and the "people's livelihood." Although Sun Yat-sen con-ceptualized democratic government as government responsive to the will of the people, he did not envision it as giving the people the right to weaken ef-fective centralized authority. And neither the Nationalist Party nor the Chi-nese Communist Party chose to interpret "democracy" as meaning individual freedom or "one-man-one-vote."[21] Instead, they were more interested in the concept of "equality" embodied in the term democracy, as will be dis-cussed below.

The Chinese Communists for their part have reinterpreted and rewritten over 2,000 years of Chinese history to incorporate a new mythology. Push-ing aside the cyclical view of history, Chinese Marxists argued for a linear view of history: the historically "inevitable" progression of society from slav-ery through feudalism, capitalism, socialism, and finally to communism. Ac-

---

19. The noted historian Wang Gungwu ("To Reform a Revolution," p. 74) has alluded to the way in which Sun Yat-sen, the inspiration for China's revolution that overthrew the Qing (Manchu) dynasty in 1911, used the word *geming* to advantage: "The ambiguity in the term *geming*, . . . remained between the traditional sense of overthrowing a dynasty that had lost its Heavenly Mandate and the modern meaning of replacing a political system that was no longer viable, by force of arms if necessary. For Sun Yat-sen . . . , this ambiguity was probably useful. . . . The vast majority of [his] followers were not ready to accept that their modern ideals were derived principally from studying Western political institutions. What most Chi-nese really understood was the idea that the Qing dynasty's mandate was near its end and therefore the time had come to replace it. Already, for practical reasons, there had begun the fudging of foreign ideas that needed to be explicated in Chinese terms."

20. Angle and Svensson, "On Rights and Human Rights," p. 6.

21. This idea is developed in Chapter 3.

cording to Marxist analysis, history's progression is "determined" by the "mode of production" and the ownership of the means of production. It is, in short, an interpretation of history in terms of class conflict, with class defined in economic terms.

This rewriting of history, although it never succeeded in completely eradicating the cyclical view of history, nevertheless profoundly reshaped how Chinese coming of age after the Communists' victory in 1949 understood their history. Moral authority rested in the hands of the "ruling class," which, in Chinese Communist Party parlance, was the 95 percent of the population that made up "the people." (The reactionaries or "counterrevolutionaries" who constituted the remaining 5 percent were not qualified to possess the rights of "the people.") China's real rulers were, however, members of the Chinese Communist Party, the representatives of the ruling class responsible for protecting and promoting the people's interests, while depriving counterrevolutionaries of any rights. Depending on the nature of their wrongdoings, the latter would either be executed or educated and transformed so that they could return to "the people."[22] Most of the Chinese people fell between the revolutionary and counterrevolutionary poles.

Of course, the Chinese view themselves as possessors of unique personal and cultural characteristics because of their history. From elementary school on, all Chinese children are told that they possess the virtues of being hardworking, diligent, brave, intelligent, and creative; that their ancestors were responsible for four great inventions (paper, gunpowder, the compass, and printing); and that their ancestors created a "glorious" culture, thought, and civilization over China's five thousand years of history.

China is internationally recognized as one of the great ancient civilizations, and the Chinese people take great pride in this. To use the Marxist terminology common in the People's Republic, China had developed a prosperous feudalism and unified, peaceful central kingdom, when most of the nations of Europe were mired in slavery (in Marxist thought, inferior to feudalism) and warring against one another. Further, the Chinese are taught that China is a "nation of politeness and justice" and that the Chinese people

---

22. The two ways of achieving the *datong*, or Great Unity, according to Chinese colleagues, are either to transform or to execute those who hinder it. The Nationalists shared the Chinese Communists' view that those who opposed them should not be allowed to participate in politics and act freely. For more on this topic, see Chapter 3.

work together in harmony. They prize moral virtue, which they believe is the force unifying China. Morality and ethics, not rule by law or force, unified the Chinese in the past and made them "civilized," and they continue to do so today. On the day Puccini's magnificent opera *Turandot* opened in Beijing in the fall of 1996, the newspapers took pains to explain that although the Beijing production would not alter Puccini's music, Turandot had been recast as a princess from a barbarian group because no Chinese princess would have acted in such a brutal and uncivilized manner.

The term "civilized" (*wenming*) is used by the Chinese Communist Party to praise virtually any type of behavior it wishes to promote, precisely because to be "civilized" is still an important cultural value. In such a context, the campaign in the 1990s for "civilized behavior" makes sense, for the Chinese are ever conscious of the greatness of Chinese civilization, and to act in a "civilized" way is considered important to their identity, whether they are being "civilized workers" ("Speak courteously"; "Don't spit or throw trash on the streets"; "Help others"), "civilized students" ("Don't talk in loud voices when others are studying"; "Don't steal books"; "Don't cheat"; "Make your bed"; "Keep the bathrooms clean");[23] or building a "civilized airport,"[24] or driving taxis in a "civilized" manner, or becoming a "civilized urban district." (As with so many uses of the term *wenming*, the Chinese usage of it is synonymous with being a "model" urban district, a "model" student, and so on.) China's urbanites tend to disdain their compatriots who live in the countryside because they are *not* civilized, a fact that presents a conundrum for those urban intellectuals who envision democratizing China but are not so sure their rather uncivilized compatriots ought to participate. Whatever the

---

23. Obviously, a campaign for civilized behavior implies that the Chinese have *not* been acting in a civilized manner. Like other work units, the Foreign Affairs College in Beijing, where I was teaching in 1996–97, held many meetings to define what "civilized behavior" for its students should include. For my part, I was unable to find anyone at the college—student, faculty member, or administrator—who could explain what the campaign for "civilized behavior" was all about in the cities. When asked, they would often burst into giggles, but the Foreign Affairs College (Waijiao xueyuan) leadership was required to take the campaign seriously. (The Foreign Affairs College is run by the Ministry of Foreign Affairs in order to train future diplomats. I taught courses in international relations and U.S.-China relations.)

24. In its efforts to modernize, Shanghai Hongqiao International Airport was concerned not only that its employees receive a technical education but also that they act in a civilized manner (Mary Comerford Cooper, "Implementing the 'Modern Enterprise System' in Chinese SOEs: Case Studies from Shanghai," paper presented at the Harvard East Asian Studies Conference, Apr. 7, 2001, p. 12).

views of their haughty urban cousins, country people have likewise been caught up in campaigns to be civilized. They illustrate the party-state's interest in using the concept of being "civilized" to promote traditional Confucian family and community values, carry out party policies, and make the people more scientific and modern. The "Ten Stars of Civilization" program, carried out in the countryside, illustrates the broad manner in which being "civilized" can be interpreted. Under this program, a village household received a star for each of the ten cardinal virtues it exhibited when the officials in charge judged the household had met the criteria for that virtue. Virtues ranged from respect for the law, sending all children to school, practicing a new life style (i.e., "avoiding feudal superstition, no extravagant weddings or funerals"), and practicing birth control, to maintaining family unity, bringing up children properly, practicing hygiene, and breeding animals scientifically.[25]

In addition to being highly civilized, the Chinese are told that China has never acted as an aggressive power. The Chinese believe that China's only age of large-scale conquests came during the Yuan dynasty, whose rulers were actually Mongols, an emerging minority group that had not yet assimilated Chinese culture.[26] Real Chinese rulers considered it shameful to expand the boundaries of its civilization or pursue its economic interests through force.[27] Chinese culture was open and absorbed rather than conquered foreign cultures. Indeed, a few of the dynasties so neglected military force that they were easily overthrown by minority tribes; sooner or later,

25. Thorgensen, "Cultural Life and Cultural Control in Rural China."

26. In terms of China's policy toward surrounding minority ethnic groups, the Chinese people are taught that military force was used only as a last resort and usually unsuccessfully and that the most effective means of gaining control over minority ethnic groups had been to marry a Chinese princess to the tribal chief and thus form a closer, friendly relationship. For example, they are taught that Wang Zhaojun in the Western Han Dynasty married the head of the Xiongnu barbarians, and Princess Wencheng in the Tang Dynasty married the leader of Tibet. Both the Western Han and Tang dynasties were powerful. These Chinese princesses relinquished living as Han Chinese in order to serve their empire's interest in stopping border wars. They also acted as cultural ambassadors by bringing with them a large number of technicians, intellectuals, books, and tools and greatly promoted local productivity and border trade (discussions with students in my international relations courses at the Foreign Affairs College, Beijing, in 1996–97).

27. Yan Xuetong, "Zhongguo anquan zhanlüe de fazhan qushi" (The trend in China's security strategy), *Liaowang*, 1996, nos. 8–9: 51–52; cited in Yongnian Zheng, *Discovering Chinese Nationalism in China*, p. 81. Yan is a political scientist trained at Berkeley.

however, these victors became converts to Chinese culture. Thus, when Westerners argue that China will become a threat to the United States in the twenty-first century, the Chinese reply that they do not understand China's history, national culture, or character and are projecting Western imperialist objectives onto them. They often dismiss Western criticisms as part of an anti-China tendency. The Chinese insist they are strengthening their country only because of the lesson they learned from the nineteenth and twentieth centuries: that a weak China will be invaded and destroyed by foreigners. Thus, the Chinese argue, it is because of their fear of being invaded and conquered, not because they want to conquer others, that they have worked so hard to make China rich and strong.[28]

Samuel Huntington's essay "The Clash of Civilizations?" which contended that Western civilization had promoted so much good in the world, including democracy and human rights, provoked some Chinese to respond by painting a quite different picture of what Western civilization had offered. In particular, they argued for China's "civilizational superiority" on the grounds that Confucian civilization had promoted peace and harmony with its neighbors, whereas the expansion of modern Western civilization, driven by a Social Darwinism that claimed only the fittest (that is, the best-armed) would survive, has led to international conflicts. China has developed nuclear weapons, then, because it has learned from the Western model that only the fittest will survive. But its nationalism is defensive and merely "reacts" to the international environment.[29] In the view of China's "cultural nationalists," because Confucianism is this-worldly and not focused on the world hereafter, it lacks a mission to "save" the world and is more appreciative of "rationality, peace, and the doctrine of the mean."[30]

---

28. Class discussions with students in my international relations courses, Foreign Affairs College, Beijing, 1996–97.

29. One such "cultural nationalist" is Sheng Hong, an economist in the Chinese Academy of Social Sciences, who has exerted significant influence within intellectual circles since he published two articles in the two most important forums for the new nationalism, *Zhanlüe yu guanli* (Strategy and management), and *Dong Fang* (The Orient): "Shenmo shi wenming?" (What are civilizations?), *Zhanlüe yu guanli* 1995, no. 5: 88–98; and "Jingjixue zenyang tiaozhan lishi?" (How does economics challenge history?), *Dong Fang* 1996, no. 1: 49–55; cited in Yongnian Zheng, *Discovering Chinese Nationalism in China*.

30. Xiao Gongqin, "Zhongguo minzu zhuyi de lishi yu qinjing" (The history of Chinese nationalism and its prospects), *Zhanlüe yu guanli* 1996, no. 2: 58–62; cited in Yongnian Zheng, *Discovering Chinese Nationalism in China*, p. 81.

Given this vast chasm in the interpretations of our respective histories and in our myths about our identity and values as individuals and nations, does it make sense for Western liberals to interpret China's history as a yearning for individual freedom, universal suffrage, and a strict division of rights between government and the people? How much importance will be accorded individual rights in a millennia-old culture founded on the belief that the "good" society is one that is well-ordered (and, if so, necessarily prosperous) and that a society is well-ordered if its people and leaders practice "humaneness" (*ren*), and "propriety" or "rites" (*li*)? How much importance will be accorded freedom in a society that continues to emphasize obligations over rights, believes that the most egregious behavior for a person is a lack of filial piety,[31] and combines this with the idea that the good society is egalitarian and therefore redistributes property to eliminate class exploitation? In short, we need to understand China's self-perceptions so that we can understand the values that have propelled China and shaped the understanding China's people and leaders have of their mutual rights and responsibilities.

CULTURAL RELATIVISM

To make the argument outlined above on the sensitive topics of democracy and freedom is to risk being accused of cultural or moral "relativism." Relativism does not, however, require that individuals deny their own standards for judging actions; rather, it means only that they understand the standards of others. Relativism "means the practice of putting yourself in [someone else's] shoes, not in order to wear them as your own but in order to have some understanding (far short of approval) of why someone else might want to wear them."[32] However threatening this may be to their own standards, relativists reject the notion that one can objectively judge other people's values and actions as inferior. To do so is merely an effort to assert one's own superiority. Relativists recognize that upbringing, culture, history, and even songs, foods, and customs affect who people become. They are the "parameters" or boundaries that constrain the behavior and thinking of individuals

---

31. Sun Baohong, "The Main Points of Ethics Among Youth in Pudong (Shanghai)," *Zhongguo qingnian bao*, Aug. 17, 1996. Filial piety is considered a critical aspect of being "civilized."

32. Stanley Fish, "Condemnation Without Absolutes," *New York Times*, Oct. 15, 2001, p. A23.

and of nations. Each individual, each nation, is "path dependent." Had an individual been brought up in a different place and had a different life, he or she would have other reasons for thinking and acting that are equally valid.[33]

The theory of path dependence also asserts that no state begins with a clean slate. The past and the type of regime and institutions that already exist set a course for the state and the members of a society and limits its options.[34] For example, some of the constraints involved in shaping China's path are problems left from the Maoist period, such as overpopulation, the extreme emphasis on egalitarianism, and a fully planned, centralized economy. Those conditions, regulations, and institutions, together with the social relations that have resulted from them, cannot simply disappear. "Indeed, even those most able to circumvent these institutions and rules must adopt modes of circumvention that themselves are marked by the old system."[35]

Labeling arguments as "relativist" is frequently used to discredit the refusal to judge intercultural differences; yet these differences are precisely what have fueled many of the serious political conflicts between the liberal democracies of the West and the "socialist democracy" of China. But it is difficult to eliminate miscommunication across boundaries, because neither side has the other side's experience of history and life. (Perhaps the more our lives converge through modernization, MacDonaldization, or the Internet, the less that differences growing out of historical experience will seem to matter). In *Getting to Yes*, Roger Fisher and William Ury contend that, to negotiate an end to a conflictual situation between two cultures, negotiators must get inside each culture and ask Why are they acting this way? How has their historical experience shaped their perceptions?[36] Only with such an understanding of intercultural difference can conflict be resolved.

---

33. Relativists might even adopt the Nietzchean attitude that a single standard for behavior is inappropriate even for oneself. Can an ideal be appropriate "only if it is *the ideal*"? Is there only one way of "getting it right"? (Scanlon, "Fear of Relativism," pp. 229, 231–32; italics in original). For more on relativism and objectivity in moral evaluation, see Walzer, *Spheres of Justice*; and idem, *Interpretation and Social Criticism*.

34. North, *Institutions, Institutional Change, and Economic Performance*.

35. Solinger, "The Floating Population in the Cities," p. 137.

36. For example, Roger Fisher and William Ury (*Getting to Yes*) argued during the Cold War that if the Americans would listen carefully to what the Soviets were saying and try to see the world from the Soviet perspective, they might conclude that the reason the Soviets

In China's case, the only experiential historical knowledge of "people in charge" (that is, the people as rulers)—the literal translation of the term *minzhu* (which is the Chinese translation from the Japanese of the English word "democracy")—is the chaos and cruelty of governance under the Republic of China (1912–49), and the mob rule of the Great Proletarian Cultural Revolution (1966–76). Until this experiential knowledge is modified by practices that bring China's experience of democracy closer to that of the West, the term will conjure up different images to each side.

The problem here is that the equivalences enshrined in bilingual dictionaries can sometimes conceal chasms of difference in culturally embedded meanings and assumptions. The categories used, for example, by Western social scientists to interpret what is happening elsewhere, such as "interest aggregation," "interest articulation,"[37] voting, or negotiation, embody assumptions about what is actually happening. This is misleading because the assumptions behind such terms vary significantly among societies.[38] A term such as "compromise," which many Western liberal democrats might see as a critical component of negotiation, for the Chinese bears the intersubjective meaning of weakness and selling out. Chinese thinking is deeply rooted in "principled stands"; once a position is defined as such, there is little room for compromise (except on "tactical" issues that do not interfere with China's principled stand).

The same may be said of a term like "civil society," with its images of society *against* the state, to explain the relationship of intellectuals, associations, and interest groups with their government. By using such a value-laden con-

---

pursued the arms race was not because they wanted to start a war, but out of fear that the United States would attack them if they were weak. To oversimplify, once the American negotiators adopted this perspective, their primary task became one of dealing with Soviet fears, with the assumption that the arms race would then take care of itself. This proved to be a largely correct assumption.

37. Tianjian Shi (*Political Participation in Beijing*), on the basis of a survey carried out in Beijing in 1988–89, concludes that interests are articulated in China but in a personalistic and individualistic way at the local level through "work unit" leaders. Although Western social scientists would not generally view these activities as "interest articulation" as they define it, the Chinese in this survey felt that their strategy of building relationships, *guanxi*, and complaining about the political system and its leaders at the local level through officially established institutions, such as complaint bureaus, letters to the editor, and so on was politically efficacious.

38. Taylor, *Philosophy and the Human Sciences*, pp. 42, 126, 35–36. Taylor is here drawing on John Searle's ideas.

cept, we distort our understanding of "the complicated, dynamic picture of state-society relations in a transitional communist country." Application of the concept of "civil society" becomes "a teleological exercise: speculating whether or not China would achieve a democratic breakthrough along an Eastern-Central European trajectory." The use of this concept ignores the fact that Chinese intellectuals have thought about the changing relationship between state and society in their own distinct ways, ways that reflect their own experiences and history.[39] Even analyses that invoke "corporatism" to describe the state-led control over associations and interest groups in China today risk ignoring the benefits that these organizations and their members receive from top-down governance, including, arguably, the ability to affect the policy-making process far more than they would if they were truly autonomous. Indeed, with both state and society in China in transition from socialism to something else, a number of models of state-society interaction are operating simultaneously. Choosing a label that both truly describes the relationship between the two and accurately reflects this complexity is difficult. As Tony Saich has pointed out, "Social scientists tend to dislike open-ended theories and seek to close down the range of options available for interpretation through a process of imposing order and logic. . . . In the field of state-society relations, we need to develop explanations that allow for the shifting complexities of the current system, and the institutional fluidity, ambiguity and messiness that operate at all levels in China and that is most pronounced at the local level."[40] How we might best understand the concept of civil society as applied to China will be explored at great length in this book, especially in Chapter 7, because of its importance to those who think about democracy.

Similarly, the usual English translations of the Chinese terms *guanxi* (relationships) and *houmen* (backdoor) convey only a limited sense of their critical importance to daily life and politics in China. In Charles Taylor's terminology, these terms' "intersubjective" meaning can only truly be known to those who must live in that society.[41] In China, "relationships" and the "backdoor" are essential to getting through life, from getting a telephone or more electrical power for one's home to obtaining permission to open a

---

39. Edward X. Gu, "Cultural Intellectuals and the Politics of the Cultural Public Space," p. 427.

40. Saich, "Negotiating the State," pp. 138–39, 141.

41. Taylor, *Philosophy and the Human Sciences*, p. 36.

business to receiving a residence or work permit or a passport to buying things controlled and distributed by the state. To understand the critical importance of developing relationships through doing favors, giving gifts, and cultivating a backdoor, one would have to experience the frustrating bureaucratic red tape that entails collecting countless stamps ("chops") on documents, standing in lines waiting for yet another approval, only to hear that it is "not convenient" to deal with the issue at the moment or, more simply, that "it can't be done."

For many Chinese, then, a sense of political efficacy is developed not through access to the institutions familiar to the inhabitants of democracies in the West, such as political parties or free elections at the national level, but through access to the right person at the local level.[42] Similarly, when the Chinese say that they support their leaders' emphasis on social stability and development instead of democratization, we must be prepared to accept the possibility that they are sincere. In a society whose people have arguably suffered more from the lack of law and order than from the lack of individual freedom, it is entirely possible that the intersubjective meanings of "law and order" and "freedom" are quite different from the meanings given these terms by those who have experienced only a stable society.[43]

Thus, when Chinese leaders, intellectuals, and ordinary citizens try to put into words their concerns about the potential consequences of implementing a Western-style liberal democracy in China and their rejection of a Western definition of democracy and human rights in favor of their own, we have no real way of understanding the deep chords of emotion behind their words. We have not lived in a society in which an ineffectual and oppressive government, operating under the label of democracy, gave democracy a bad

---

42. Tianjian Shi, *Political Participation in Beijing*.

43. In a survey of ten universities in Beijing during 1998–99, 28.3 percent chose "promote economic development" as the first priority, and 25.4 percent chose "maintain stability." By contrast, only 1.1 percent chose "defend freedom of speech" as the first priority (Wong Koonkwai, "The Environmental Awareness of University Students in Beijing, China," table 7). Similarly, in a survey of 586 respondents conducted by the Institute of Sociology of the Chinese Academy of Social Sciences in 1990, in response to the question "What are the most important criteria for whether a country is well-managed or not," 31.5 percent chose "social stability," 25 percent "a strong economy," 13 percent "a high standard of living," and only 9 percent "democracy" (Zhu Guanglei, *Da fenhua, da zhuhe Zhongguo shehui gejieceng fenxi*, p. 410). Numerous other studies give similar answers. On the question whether we can trust Chinese surveys and public opinion polls, see the Appendix.

name; in which the extreme deprivation of economic and social rights led to a revolution; or in which mass tyranny was dressed up in the garments of "democracy."

We tend to dismiss any rationale offered by Chinese leaders to justify law and order policies as pretexts for limiting individual rights and democracy, and we often view any former dissident who has abandoned criticism of the Chinese Communist regime as having been co-opted either by the regime or by materialism. But if an outsider does not understand an explanation or accept a justification as valid, "there is nowhere else the argument can go. Ultimately, a good explanation is one which makes sense of the behavior; but then to appreciate a good explanation, one has to agree on what makes good sense."[44] The problem in the West's understanding of China, and vice versa, is that we do not agree on what makes good sense.

Understanding a society's point of view and rationale for its actions is not the same as adopting its point of view, but we must at least try to understand a society's "self-description," even if it is confused and contradictory. This means getting inside an individual in another society so as to "understand his emotions, his aspirations, what he finds admirable and contemptible" and "to apply correctly the desirability characterizations which he applies in the way he applies them."[45] If, then, a Chinese describes a fellow citizen as being unpatriotic, even counterrevolutionary and a traitor to his country,[46] we need to understand what the essence of the term "patriotic" is for a Chinese person—what emotions and images a Chinese is likely to conjure up about the meaning of her country's achievements, values, and goals, as well as about its leadership, its flag, its territory, its history, and its future. It is unlikely an American uttering "That person is not a patriot" will experience the same intensity of emotion. Even if we believe the Chinese people have been brainwashed into these views, we must still accept them as their views. If we reject them and substitute our own understandings, it is because we believe that their descriptions of themselves are "wrong to the extent that they deviate from ours." The study of another culture such as China's

---

44. Taylor, *Philosophy and the Human Sciences*, p. 24.

45. Ibid., pp. 117–19.

46. The government's condemnation of the Tiananmen demonstrations in both 1975 and 1989 were couched in the vocabulary of patriotism. To the degree the government was able to convince the Chinese people that the participants were unpatriotic, it was able to gain popular support for its actions.

thereby becomes an exercise in ethnocentric prejudice.[47] Yet, if we accept the
fact that the Chinese have produced unique musical, artistic, culinary, and
medical traditions, and that even their brilliant contributions to mathemat-
ics, engineering, and science were based on strikingly different first principles,[48] it should hardly surprise us that they have also produced different legal, moral, and political traditions.

In short, Western political science is not objective; rather, it is rooted in
one aspect of Western political culture: "atomist and instrumentalist politics." As such, it sidelines even other relevant qualities of the Western political orientation, such as the importance of community.[49] Recent studies by
social psychologists also question what is universal and what is not and have
concluded that the use of categories and logic depends on culture: "People
who grow up in different cultures do not just think about different things:
they think differently."[50]

We must, then, listen carefully to how various groups within the Chinese
polity, including the Chinese Communist Party, frame their perspectives on
Western liberal democracy and understand what values *they* cherish.[51] If we
simply dismiss their arguments as the result of ignorance or, in the case of
the party-state, as rationales to hide a desire to maintain power by silencing
critics, we are missing an opportunity to understand their legitimate concerns and true beliefs that certain rights, processes, and institutions common
to Western liberal democracies may not be appropriate to China.

This is neither to suggest that China's leaders are not interested in stay-
ing in power nor to argue that they are not interested in democratization, for
many are clearly interested in both. As will be discussed in subsequent chapters of this book, they are particularly concerned with improving the legal
system and reshaping socialist institutions in a manner that advances democracy, equity, and economic development. Much like the Nationalist
Party did in Taiwan, the Chinese Communist Party is parceling out democratization by stages, geared to China's economic success and stability. In

---

47. Taylor, *Philosophy and the Human Sciences*, p. 124.

48. See the remarkable multivolume series *Science and Civilisation in China* that was initiated and overseen by Joseph Needham until his death.

49. Taylor, *Philosophy and the Human Sciences*, pp. 124, 132.

50. Goode, "How Culture Molds Habits of Thought." This article refers to the work of
Richard Nisbett and his colleagues at the University of Michigan.

51. On the importance of the "internal" (Chinese) critique, see Cohen, *Discovering History
in China*; and Said, *Orientalism*.

short, the Chinese Communist Party is interested in democratization, but not necessarily in Western liberal democracy; and its expansion of democratic institutions is shaped in part by a cost-benefit analysis of what will best serve the Party's desire to remain in power.

Having said all this, it must be pointed out that some Chinese reformers and intellectuals *are* using Western values to judge China, especially during the high tides of "love Western studies" (*re xixue*). But others who have traveled to and lived in the West and are familiar with Western scholarship have come to challenge many of the West's theories and principles concerning modernization and democratization. They dismiss claims to universality and believe they are merely "unique products of Western history and culture." As a result, they have come to doubt the utility of mainstream Western theories for China. They have turned to Western theories, such as postcolonialism and post-Marxism, in order "to find intellectual inspiration for a new path of modernization that would fit the Chinese essence (*guoqing*)."[52] It seems ironic that some Chinese "Confucianist" intellectuals use Western images and theories (especially those of Immanuel Kant) to attack Western theories and to resist Western cultural imperialism, but Chinese Confucianists have always had the habit of taking the ideas of their strongest rival and transforming them "into a vocabulary consistent with their own premises."[53]

THE BALANCE BETWEEN EQUALITY AND FREEDOM

Although the concept of equality has long been present in the Chinese language, it was seldom discussed before Marxism, a Western ideology, was introduced to China. Confucianism concentrated on unequal relations and the need for subordination and obedience of some to others.[54] Even under Chinese Communist Party rule, which has emphasized equality in both property and social relationships, egalitarianism has had rough going. In a sense, Leninism, with its emphasis on hierarchical structure and the subordination and obedience of individuals to those above them in the hierarchy, has

---

52. Suisheng Zhao, "We Are Patriots First and Democrats Second," pp. 35–36.

53. Ames, "New Confucianism," pp. 40–41. Ames refers in particular to Li Zehou and Mou Zongsan, two well-known contemporary Chinese philosophers.

54. Except for the relationship between friend and friend, Confucianism conceptualized all other relationships as unequal.

trumped the Marxist concept of equality. One of the greatest ironies of communism as practiced in China has, in fact, been the ordinary citizen's relentless search for inequality, for ways in which to be superior to others. The emphasis on equality, in short, has not fit well with either traditional Chinese culture or Leninism. Instead, the question of "Who's in charge?" has taken precedence.

Although Marxism shares with democracy a belief in the importance of equality, the methods by which equality is achieved and maintained, its extent, and its policy implications differ widely in communist and democratic polities. Marxism emphasizes distributive equality, the equality of results, whereas liberal democracy emphasizes procedural equality, particularly within the legal and political system. The Chinese people have resisted policies that have tried to graft equality onto Chinese culture, for although the Chinese cultural tradition supports certain aspects of equality, its dominant strain has been inegalitarian. China was, and is, a hierarchically oriented country that finds it difficult to accept egalitarianism. To this day, Chinese tend to treat people differently depending on whether they are above or below them in rank (and now, in wealth). Except for the idea of equality before the law (and hence, rule by law rather than rule by man), the egalitarian assumptions of democracy, as well as those of Marxism, have not found a welcoming environment in China. The inegalitarian assumptions (and results) that usually accompany individualism, freedom, and capitalism are in many respects far more compatible with Chinese political culture.

Nevertheless, until the reforms that began in 1979, China's leaders tried valiantly to make equality an operating principle of "socialist democracy" in China. In subsequent chapters, I will argue that China has, in conjunction with the economic and political reforms since 1979, introduced greater freedom—at the expense of equality; but here I concentrate on how China's choice of equality over freedom fits in with the development and practice of democratic principles elsewhere.

The two major Western democratic traditions have long been in conflict over the critical issues of freedom and equality.[55] The Anglo-American democratic tradition emphasizes freedom, whereas the French tradition emphasizes equality. The dilemma of democracy has been this: the more free-

---

55. The following is taken from my discussion of this topic in Ogden, *China's Unresolved Issues*, pp. 129–32.

dom, the less equality; and the more equality, the less freedom.[56] To varying degrees democracy has brought both greater freedom and greater equality, but in most polities a trade-off between the two occurs. Most modern democratic political systems are theoretically egalitarian in their political and legal spheres,[57] but neither in principle nor in practice are they egalitarian in social and economic terms. Freedom comes at the expense of equality: the freedom to pursue individual ends in income, education, and occupational status seems inevitably to allow some citizens to gain unequal access to resources. In turn, this enables them to influence the political system more than others. Studies have shown that when equality originates in social and economic redistributive policies within a political system, it is more likely to be because of the type of party system or the kind of party in power rather than because of the degree of democratization.[58]

As a socialist polity, the People's Republic of China favored equality over freedom until the 1980s. The Chinese Communists were not, however, alone in believing that development requires equality and that economic equality is as necessary as political equality. Well-known Western theorists of democracy have also held such beliefs. Harold Laski, for example, believed that without economic equality, no political mechanisms would allow "the common man to realize his wishes and interests. Economic power is the parent of political power."[59] Alexis de Tocqueville, believing that equality was a necessary principle of democracy, was convinced that the state had an obligation to minimize inequalities among people. He argued that a state must divide the sources of economic gain equally among its citizens in order to maintain a democratic form of government.[60]

In practice, Western democracies have also stressed the importance of economic equality. France, influenced by the Napoleonic codes since the nineteenth century, eliminated primogeniture in favor of equal distribution of property among all the children of deceased parents. The aim of the graduated income tax in the United States and the inheritance tax in both the United States and Great Britain has likewise been to create a more equal

---

56. Sabine, "The Two Democratic Traditions," p. 451.

57. Political equality here is defined as the right to vote for the entire adult population of a certain age; legal equality is defined as equality before the law.

58. Verba et al., *Participation and Political Equality*, pp. 1, 4.

59. Laski, "Democracy," pp. 77, 80.

60. Tocqueville, as cited in Huntington and Nelson, *No Easy Choice*, pp. 65, 66.

distribution of wealth. Distributive economic equality is, then, pursued by the wealthiest of liberal democratic states.

The Chinese Communist Party leadership justified state policies to rid China of social and economic inequalities on the grounds that those who possessed greater socioeconomic power used it to exploit those who had less. Therefore, China's leaders first tried to eliminate the basis for socioeconomic exploitation by redistributing property. Then, in the 1960s they attacked many (including party members) who had parlayed their better political status into unequal access to power and used it to exploit others. In the People's Republic, concern for equality overrode concern for freedom. Thus, the *theory* of China's socialist democratic system is not much outside the mainstream of Western democratic theory after World War II in its emphasis on equality of economic benefits: "Social income must definitely be used to prevent undue disparity between man and man. . . . The good life is unattainable where there are wide economic disparities between classes."[61]

Nevertheless, how the Chinese state interferes and the degree to which the state and the one-party system represent the people's interests raise serious questions about the position of the People's Republic within the democratic tradition. The "democratic dictatorship"[62] (a term used sparingly since 1979), which proved to be far more dictatorial than democratic, was the crucial factor distancing China from the Western democratic tradition.

The values of freedom, equality, democracy, and dictatorship are, for the Chinese, values laden with connotations and intersubjective meanings different from those in the West. They are also values in conflict with one another. As surely as China's socialist transformation in the early 1950s led to greater equality but less freedom, so the economic liberalization that began in the 1980s has led to greater freedom but has virtually destroyed any notion of economic equality. The mandate to "get rich" today means that the Chinese have the freedom to be unequally rich—or poor.

Comparative development studies in the West have noted the incompatibility between an emphasis on social and economic equality and the goal

---

61. Laski, "Democracy," p. 83.

62. Democracy and dictatorship are "two sides of the same coin," in Chinese Communist parlance. In the Chinese view, China's proletarian dictatorship became undemocratic only because, although China had eliminated bourgeois influence, it had failed to eliminate feudal influence.

of economic development.[63] Chinese leaders confronted this incompatibility after the extreme egalitarianism of the Cultural Revolution had brought production to a virtual halt. As a result, they chose to favor more rapid economic development at the expense of pure egalitarianism, a concept now in disgrace in China. Nevertheless, the general economic equality among the Chinese people (within geographical regions) at the time liberalization of the economic system began in 1979, meant that the issue of dividing up the economic pie among classes had in important ways already been resolved. For countries in the developing world, this is an issue that often plagues their political system and slows down democratization.

For much of the twentieth century, the Chinese wrestled with the meaning of the term "democracy," often in ways that suggest just how foreign it is to them. In more recent times, such as during the "democracy movement" of 1978–79, the term merely replaced "revolution" (which prevailed from 1966 to 1976). One protester believed "it implied the immediate 'withering away' of party control in basic-level organizations"; others believed it had to include capitalism, or Christianity, or liberalizing reforms, or even that all three of these ingredients were necessary. Both the United States and Yugoslavia were proposed as models to emulate. "Wei Jingsheng, the leading spokesman for the democracy movement in 1978–79, defined it in terms of maximum individual freedom and non-Marxist socialism. However, for the most part, *any future democracy was conceived of as being under the leadership of the Chinese Communist Party,* even though at times this might entail some amazing contradictions."[64]

The vast body of literature on democracy, which provides an often contradictory and perplexing portrait of democracy, has hindered efforts to agree on its meaning. Understandably, young Chinese, with little exposure to the writings of democratic theorists and no experience with the practice of liberal democracy would be confused as to its meaning.[65] During the protest movement of 1989, the speeches, wall posters, and handbills of students, intellectuals, and workers indicated the wide diversity of perspectives on de-

---

63. Huntington and Nelson, *No Easy Choice,* pp. 36, 37.

64. Goodman, *Beijing Street Voices,* pp. 7, 8. Italics added.

65. The weakness of democratic theory is evident in the 1976 manifesto of a student participant, Chen Erjin (*China, Crossroad Socialism*), who believed that if China had *two* communist parties and a separation of powers, it would be democratic. The weak knowledge of theory among those in the democracy movement of 1978–79 is also discussed in Nathan, *Chinese Democracy.*

mocracy. Indeed, the conflict within the student-led movement itself indicated the inability of these informed Chinese to agree on the *process* of democracy, much less its meaning.[66] Although there was a more sophisticated understanding of democracy by 1989, opinion was still generally confused, vague, and contradictory. (For example, some of the participants in the demonstrations appeared to think that there was something "scientific" about a democratic system that, if carried out according to its exact rules, would prevent corruption and give greater status to intellectuals.)[67] The student leaders themselves were anything but democratic in their words, actions, and organization. Their organization mimicked that of the Party—understandably, since that was the only organizational style they knew. They were hierarchical in decision making, demanded obedience, and treated each other according to rank within the movement. The top leaders were dictatorial and secretive, and many of the students who participated in the protests of 1989 subsequently accused them of abuse of authority, factionalism, and corruption. Perhaps most telling, the students refused to cooperate with the workers in the 1989 demonstrations and had little interest in workers' demands for better pay and working conditions. The students had no intention of granting leadership rights to the workers, and they never adopted the idea of "one person, one vote" as a goal. Their goal was greater individual freedom for themselves, not democratization.[68]

Today, a substantial debate is taking place among China's intellectuals over the question of whether the country should follow the Anglo-American model, the French model, or some model of its own devising. The Western models are defined by some Chinese as advocating freedom or equality, freedom or democracy, negative freedom or positive freedom.[69] The Chinese apply the concept of negative freedom to the market and define it as an un-

---

66. For a compilation of the speeches, wall posters, slogans, and handbills churned out in Tiananmen Square in the spring of 1989, see Ogden et al., *China's Search for Democracy*.

67. I am indebted to one of the anonymous readers for this point.

68. During a retrospective conference on 1989 at Harvard University in June 1999, many participants in those demonstrations who were present affirmed that this was how the students (including themselves) acted. See also Carma Hinton's film "The Gate of Heavenly Peace" (Brookline, Mass.: Long Bow Group, 1997) for statements confirming these attitudes and behavior by student leaders in Tiananmen Square in 1989.

69. "Negative freedoms" are those rights not specifically denied to citizens. "Positive freedoms" are those rights actually given in written form to citizens, as in a constitution.

fettered, unregulated free market, whose participants are "free from" government regulation and therefore free to become unequally rich. Some writers used the label "conservatism" and even "ultra-conservatism" to designate those who favored this model in the 1990s. Conservatives, they argue, want "negative freedom" or the free market at the expense of "democracy" and believe that the government should do nothing to promote equality while the market economy is getting started. Conservatives lament that before the economic reforms of the 1980s China followed the French model, favoring equality over freedom. For conservatives, the term *"liberalism* or *Anglo-American liberalism,* has almost become a euphemism for antidemocratic positions. It seems as if less democracy means more freedom, less participation means more protection for the individual, and less positive freedom means more negative freedom."[70]

This debate has been clouded by a verbal haze of Western references and terminology as well as the adoption by some Chinese intellectuals of the opaque style of Western post-modernist theorizing. In any event, according to one set of Chinese intellectuals who criticize liberals, the liberals of the 1990s were wrong to favor England's Glorious Revolution of 1688 and to reject Alexis de Toqueville and negate the French Revolution in its entirety. In their view, Chinese liberals are espousing liberalism as an antidemocratic tool, all the time relying on cliché-ridden references to "Anglo-American liberalism," "representative democracy," and "direct democracy," without knowing what these terms really mean. Finally, Chinese critics of the liberals accuse them of favoring freedom of the market over fairness and justice to the Chinese people as a whole. This style of economistic liberalism has turned equality into "a sin" because equality demands intervention by the state.[71]

Many Chinese would agree with these critiques. Conversations with ordinary Chinese as well as statistical data indicate they are opposed to both "the iron rice bowl" (lifelong guaranteed employment) and "all eating out of

---

70. Yang Gan, "A Critique of Chinese Conservatism in the 1990s," pp. 45–46. Yang left China in June 1989. He was a significant figure in the introduction of major works of Western social sciences and humanities into China in the 1980s through massive translation projects, and he published articles about freedom in the leading intellectual journal *Dushu* (Reading). He has been the editor of the Social Thought Series, published by Oxford University Press (Hong Kong), since 1993.

71. Ibid., pp. 47–48, 51.

the same pot" (egalitarianism), even though they worry about the potential economic insecurity a free market may produce in their own lives.[72] On the other hand, survey data gathered in 1990 indicated a belief on the part of Chinese workers that next to inflation, the increasing economic polarization of the rich and poor was the foremost condition likely to lead to the outbreak of social conflicts.[73] By 1995–96, another survey indicated that "experts" perceived the "income gap" as a major problem, but that they believed economic growth and stability were more important in maintaining social stability than closing the income gap.[74]

What does all this mean for understanding and acceptance by Chinese reformers and intellectuals of the many values associated with democracy? In general, the Chinese appear to be interested less in this political concept than they are in issues surrounding economic growth, social stability, and corruption.[75] Although those in the liberal democratic states might well argue that a more democratic government could deal with these problems much better than China's authoritarian government, this view is not neces-

---

72. As is noted again in more detail in Chapter 5, a 1990 survey revealed strong disagreement with the statements that "the big pot" is better than polarization and "although the big pot is not good, it can guarantee a stable life" (Zhongguo shehui kexue yuan, Shehuixue yanjiusuo, Zhuanxing ketizu, *Zhongguo qingniande toushi*, pp. 177–78).

73. Zhu Guanglei, *Da fenhua, da zhuhe dangdai Zhongguo shehui gejieceng fenxi*, p. 80. This conclusion was based on the 1990 study "Statistical Data on Chinese Society."

74. The "experts" were, however, no doubt voicing the concerns of the people as they attempted to identify "major problems in the conditions of social development." In a list of ten possibilities, "the income gap" was ranked fifth, and "the interregional gap" (in wealth and development) ranked ninth. The list of ten in rank-order of severity were corruption, inflation, social order, state-owned enterprises, the income gap, social ethos, the peasants' burden, employment, interregional gaps, and politics (see Lu Jianhua et al., "1995–1996 nian shehui xingshi," p. 38). When asked to prioritize the key factors in maintaining social stability in 1995, the experts ranked "decreasing the income gap" as number seven out of fourteen items, and "diminishing the interregional developmental gap" as number nine. Combating corruption and achieving rapid but stable economic growth ranked first and second in priority; this suggests that the experts hope continued economic growth will narrow income gaps rather than exacerbate them (ibid., p. 40).

75. Discussions with Chinese students, intellectuals, government officials, and ordinary people. In a survey done in 1990, when workers were asked to identify emerging problems in political life in China (multiple answers were permitted), 60.1 percent chose party corruption; 59.0 percent social demoralization; 31 percent an unsound democratic electoral system; 24.6 percent defects in the cadre system; and only 13 percent problems with democracy and the legal system and 6.6 percent unequal opportunity (Zhu Guanglei, *Da fenhua, da zhuhe dangdai Zhongguo shehui gejieceng fenxi*, p. 80).

sarily shared by China's intellectuals and reformers, or even by ordinary Chinese people.

Finally, when Chinese intellectuals talk about democratic issues, it is usually not with the same emphases, the same concerns, or even the same terms as are used in the liberal democratic Western states. "Equality" is still primarily seen as an economic term, not as equality before the law. And economic and social rights are still viewed as more fundamental than political rights. Protesters are still seen more as a potential source of social and economic instability than as individuals appropriately asserting their right to free speech; and economic freedom, without adequate oversight by the state, is viewed as the source of much of the venality and social instability in China today. Indeed, because of residual socialist institutions and practices, China's free market capitalism is often reduced to cronyism. More will be said about these issues in the following chapters.

In short, in China as elsewhere, more freedom often entails a trade-off with something else, especially inequality and instability. People may disagree with the choices made by political elites in China on the grounds that they continually ignore the political rights of individual citizens, but they need to understand that the choices facing political leaders there are much more complicated than most of us may have thought.

2 China's Traditional Political Culture

Classical Confucianism, along with most other Chinese schools of thought, denies that the basic unit of ethical or political assessment is the individual. Instead, theorizing begins from relationships and roles within relationships. Confucian thinkers stress reciprocal responsibilities rather than correlated rights and duties.

—Stephen C. Angle and Marina Svensson

China's course in the twentieth century owes much to its past. Even today, the Chinese polity operates on assumptions that developed over the course of Chinese history. Of particular concern to the issues addressed in this book, traditional Chinese culture has had a great influence on one important component of liberal democracy: conceptions of the rights of the ruled versus those of the ruler. (Whether such a narrow definition of rights is appropriate is discussed in subsequent chapters.) This chapter on China's political culture examines traditional attitudes toward the relationship between rulers and subjects as well as the concepts that have preoccupied China's thinkers. It makes no claim that China's culture has determined Chinese behavior or attitudes toward democracy. Rather, it focuses on the cultural constraints and impulses that any explanation of China's political system must take into account. The discussion is limited to those elements of traditional Chinese values, history, and thought relevant to the book's primary focus on today's China, that is, those elements that managed to survive the many gyrations of Chinese history and the molding and reshaping of China's political culture. There is no examination of *how* Chinese cultural values were transmitted over two millennia or how they played out at the local level and in institutional structures.

What, then, of individual freedom—the right to speak out against the government and the right of the governed to participate in their own govern-

EPIGRAPH: Angle and Svensson, "Introduction," in "On Rights and Human Rights," pp. 3–4.

ance? Authoritarian thought has dominated China's political culture for thousands of years. This dominance is evident in China's political culture and perspective on liberal democratic values and its interactions with the rest of the world. In wrestling with the issue of procedural rights versus distributive rights—between civil and political rights on the one hand and support for such values as community and so-called secondary or welfare rights in the social and economic arenas on the other—both the people and the government tend to see the balance between control and freedom differently from the way liberal democrats in the West do. China's concerns that cultural openness can undermine community and that pluralism and too much individual freedom may erode law and order are genuine and common to many countries. They must not be dismissed merely as a cloak for suppression by the Chinese government.

But is China really so far behind the Western liberal democratic states on the question of individual rights? Are its assumptions and goals really so different? The proper answer is yes, it is far behind the Western states. The fight for individual rights against the power of the state is an ongoing process, however, even in the West. For example, until a generation ago, fascism persisted in Spain. And Great Britain's legendary Official Secrets Act (1911, updated in 1989) prohibits courts from determining whether a case truly involves an issue of national security (and therefore is closed to the public)—or merely presents a threat of national embarrassment. Indeed, the act prohibits any unauthorized disclosure of the government's internal activities.[1] Britain also has a law that prohibits the press from reporting on court proceedings under judicial consideration. Parliament is only now considering a Freedom of Information Act to limit such potential abuses of the state's power. And it has only been in the past thirty years that British courts have begun to favor the individual over the state when conflicts concerning individual rights arose. Great Britain's passage of the Human Rights Act in 1998, which incorporated many provisions of the European Convention on Human Rights into its domestic laws in 2000, is expected to give individuals, for the first time, an edge when conflicts with governmental policy arise. In the United States, affirmative action issues repeatedly

---

1. For example, the British government was able to interdict the newspaper serialization of Peter Wright's *Spy Catcher* in 1987, even though it had already been published in Australia and the United States. Only ministers of the crown may determine if a case involves national security (discussions with Michael Tolley, 2000–2002).

illustrate the conflicts engendered by the desire to satisfy both community rights and individual rights. In the United States as well as in Great Britain, the courts continue to hear cases involving the right of political participation, such as the right to vote and the right of political association; the regulation of campaign financing and advertising; free speech issues, such as definitions of harmful, blasphemous, and subversive acts; freedom of the press, including libel and defamation; and the boundaries of privacy and personal freedom in areas as different as abortion, euthanasia, and sexual practices. [2]

But why is individual freedom not the highest value in China? In contrast to Western political thought, freedom has been neither the dominant theme nor even one of the main themes in Chinese political thought. The craving for freedom, individual rights, and democracy is critical to Western, not Chinese, philosophy and to the creation and evolution of Western, not Chinese, governmental institutions. Although in antiquity, both Eastern and Western political thinkers thought about such matters as virtue, the virtuous ruler, and the importance of the ruler being both wise and powerful (the "Son of Heaven" for Confucius, the "philosopher-king" for Plato), on other critical matters, these thinkers took quite different routes. Unlike Plato or Aristotle, Confucius was just not interested in the "citizen," the *polis*, the relationship between private property and freedom, and many other matters important to the development of concepts of freedom and democracy in the West. [3]

The thrust of Western political thought has been to limit the government's power over the people and the tyranny of dogma. By contrast, political thought in China began at a time of efforts by China's rulers to establish firm political control. It was inspired by the search for the best form of governance in light of this central issue. China's thinkers have, for over two thousand years, been concerned primarily with getting moral individuals to rule, but once these rulers and officials are chosen, Chinese thought says lit-

---

2. Tolley, *Freedom, Rule of Law, and Democracy in the United States and Britain*. In the 2000 elections in the United States, for example, some states were reconsidering whether prisoners should have the right to vote.

3. This is not to deny that Confucius and his followers occasionally made statements about, say, individual will. For example, "Confucius said: You may carry off [a commander-in-chief from a whole army], but you cannot deprive the humblest individual of his will" (de Bary, ed., *Sources of Chinese Tradition*, 1: 31). Such statements never became the dominant tradition of Confucianism, however. For a translated and annotated version of *The Analects*, see Waley, *The Analects of Confucius*.

tle about the issue of limiting their power. Rather, the assumption is that they should have all the power they need to govern effectively.

The dominant tradition of Confucianism has focused on maintaining social order by proper governance. The bulk of Confucian thought centers on the issue of the behavior proper to those governing so as to keep heaven, earth, and man in harmony—in short, to maintain societal order and stability. The moral emperor, through his proper performance of rites and rituals (*li*) will thereby keep the world harmonious.

Confucian "revivalists" (the "new Confucianists") contend that "the Confucian insistence on the priority of socio-political relations embedding the individual may not be incompatible with the Western discourse of human rights" and that moral reciprocity among those of unequal social ranking would be a sufficient "analogue to the concept of right." According to Anthony C. Yu, however, the more compelling argument is that Confucianism is a quintessentially inegalitarian philosophy that awards rights hierarchically and unevenly, and that it focuses not on "rights" (*minquan* or *quanli*) but on "rites," the proper performance of which guarantees good rule and a peaceful, prosperous society for the benefit of the people.[4] As Zhang

---

4. Anthony C. Yu, "Enduring Change," pp. 53–54. "New Confucianism" (*xin ruxue*) scholars, such as Tu Weiming, Wm. Theodore de Bary, and Wang Gungwu, have tried to link "reciprocity" and the emphasis on the reciprocal obligations of the sovereign, subject, father, and so on with "implicit rights." For representative writings, see Wang Gungwu, "Power, Rights, and Duties in Chinese History"; de Bary, *The Liberal Tradition in China*; idem, *Asian Values and Human Rights*, pp. 158–67; and de Bary and Tu, *Confucianism and Human Rights*.

Tu Weiming is almost single-handedly responsible for the revival of Confucianism in China. When Tu went to China in the 1980s, Confucianism had more or less been thrown on the garbage heap of history, and China's intellectuals saw no value in it. But Tu's exhortations to study Confucianism again led to the revival of the Confucian discourse in China in the 1980s. Indeed, for a time in the 1980s, Confucianism was the focus of intellectual thought. With the 1990s, Confucianism became less of a "fever" and more just one of many broader academic issues involved in the new fever of national studies (*guoxue re*).

Theodore de Bary and Tu Weiming are to be applauded for their many endeavors, through conferences, books, and articles, to examine human values in Confucianism and their relevance to China's humanistic (and economic) development today. I tend, however, to side with Henry Rosemont and agree with his argument that efforts to associate Confucianism with rights-based arguments are inappropriate. Instead, we should associate Confucianism with *moral* arguments about ruler and ruled, human relations, and community. See de Bary, "Introduction," p. 9; and Rosemont, "Human Rights: A Bill of Worries," both in de Bary and Tu, *Confucianism and Human Rights*, pp. 54–66. See also de Bary, *Asian Values and Human Rights*. Here de Bary notes the difference between the ideals of Confucianism and actual prac-

Shichao, an early twentieth-century intellectual, put it, "Our state was founded on the idea that the interests of the common people are to be sacrificed for the benefit of those at the top of society." Citing Confucian scholars in order to inveigh against them, Zhang contended that in the ten years since 1905, "the idea that the inferior should sacrifice [in order to support] the superior has now been transformed into the admonition that the private be sacrificed [in order to support] the public [good]."[5] In addition, although most schools of Chinese thought address questions of privileges and powers, these are not rights as understood in modern Western thought, and the focus is not on the individual but on relationships and responsibilities.[6]

Chinese political thought sees the Great Harmony (*datong*—the concept of a utopian society, which is far more than mere "law and order") as the goal of China's rulers; but again, achieving harmony and humanitarianism requires individual responsibility rather than individual rights, and the rule of virtue rather than the rule of law. This does not mean that individual rights and laws play no significant role in traditional Chinese thought; rather, individual rights and harmony are to be advanced through reciprocal love, respect, and tolerance instead of through mutual checks and balances. In this sense, the difference between Western and Chinese political thought and tradition is not one of ends but one of means.[7]

Chinese ethics and politics, like Western ethics and politics, have confronted the critical issues of what rights or protections individuals have when those who govern abuse their power and fail to exercise virtue. They also raise the issue of how the values and desires of an individual can be reconciled with those of other individuals. In the eighteenth century, the neo-Confucian writer Dai Zhen (1723–77) addressed the latter issue in his commentaries on Mencius: "In human life, there is nothing worse than the inability to fulfill one's life. Desiring to fulfill one's life while also fulfilling the lives of others, this is humaneness. Desiring to fulfill one's life to the extent of injuring without regard [to] the lives of others, this is inhumanity."[8]

---

tice (notably, the dominance of the bureaucratic state in imperial China; pp. 9–15, 29) and the inability of the practice of rites and morality "to curb the excesses of autocratic power" (p. 15).

5. Zhang Shizhao (1881–1973), "Zijue" (Self-Awareness), *Jiayin zazhi* (The tiger magazine) (July 10, 1914), trans. in Angle and Svensson, "On Rights and Human Rights," p. 50.

6. Angle and Svensson, "Introduction," in "On Rights and Human Rights," pp. 3–4.

7. Xia Yong, "Renquan zexue san ti," pp. 53–56.

8. Anthony C. Yu, "Enduring Change," p. 61, quoting from Dai Zhen, *Mengzi ziyi shuzheng*, p. 159.

Anthony C. Yu believes this idea provides at least the theoretical basis for true egalitarianism and asks whether Confucian communitarianism could be used to develop "a Confucian understanding of human rights that attends to the irreducible worth and dignity of the life of the individual" and at the same time provide an alternative to the West's self-motivated, non-caring individualism. As Yu notes,

To affirm the individual in the sense implied by the concept of universal human rights is not necessarily to affirm individualism in the sense that one's fulfillment is privatized or defined independently of his or her communal relatedness and participation. Conversely, to affirm communitarian values is not necessarily to subscribe to the traditional values of a given community in the sense that a person's fulfillment depends on his or her participation in the community so defined.[9]

Within Confucianism, then, statements supporting individualism and individual rights can be found, but the Confucian tradition that has dominated Chinese culture and political practice has failed to develop these potentialities. The Confucian principles of reciprocal moral obligations and duties as the basis for "rights" are based on social hierarchy, with *differential* treatment of individuals depending on rank and relationship to oneself. Thus the Chinese conceive of the self within the context of a hierarchical community.[10] And, in contrast to Western ideals of progress, including the inexorable progress toward rights-based democracy, China's political thought typically focused on a golden age in the past when the Great Harmony existed. The efforts by those who have governed China to return to this golden age (and their inevitable failure) have led to a cyclical rather than a linear view of history.

In imperial China, the officials entrusted with the daily details of ruling were those judged ethically qualified to govern, based on a civil-service examination system that tested the candidates' knowledge of the Confucian classics and thus of Chinese ethics. Confucian standards of behavior emphasize acting according to one's social ranking (for lower-level officials, for example, this meant subordination, obedience, and loyalty to higher officials), as well as personal sacrifice for the common good.[11] Apart from the order such values impose, officials were also expected to act according to the prin-

---

9. Anthony C. Yu, "Enduring Change," p. 65; and idem, "Confucianism and Human Rights."

10. Anthony C. Yu, "Confucianism and Human Rights."

11. Anthony C. Yu, "Enduring Change," p. 42.

ciple of humanity (*ren*), justice, and compassion toward the people and to treat the people as the children of the country, with themselves acting as their parents.

The Chinese language captures this cultural attitude. For example, the Chinese typically portray rulers as an extension of the family hierarchy. Thus, Deng Xiaoping, China's leader from 1978 to 1997, was referred to as "Grandfather Deng" (Deng yeye), and children in Hong Kong call the chief executive, Tung Cheehua, "Grandfather Tung" (Tung yeye). One generic term for an official (such as the leader of a county, mayor of a city, or governor of a province) is *fumu guan* (parent-official), and the people are *zimin* (children-people). The people are taken care of by the officials, just as children are cared for by their parents. Soldiers are referred to as the people's children (*renmin zi de bing*) or "our little brothers." And "the state" is the family or household of the country (*guojia*).

Embedded in this family-oriented vocabulary is the continuing belief that China's rulers must *take care of* the people and rule morally. In turn, the people are expected to be loyal and obedient to their rulers because moral rulers *deserve* loyalty. If those in charge do not rule morally and justly, the people can, and should, take action. China's "authoritarian" hierarchical culture has, in short, stood in a delicate tension with an anti-authoritarian, egalitarian strain that permits leaders to control the people only when, through merit, morality, and competence, they prove deserving of respect.

Confucianism asserts that the performance of ritual and rites will keep the government moral and prevent the abuse of power and that the recruitment of officials tested through the examination system will help ensure morality. Nevertheless, Confucianism also addresses the possibility of less-than-perfect rulers, the "What if rulers become corrupt and immoral?" question. Confucianism encourages China's officials to be critical of errant rulers as a sign of higher loyalty to the ruler. In imperial times, remonstrance was institutionalized; a group of "talking officials" was charged with criticizing the government. Some of these officials had the responsibility of admonishing the emperor, and others, the censors, had as their specific purpose "to impeach corrupt or incompetent officials." Of course, a remonstrator had to confront the possibility that if a ruler or an official was unhappy with criticism, he might be fired or even executed.[12]

---

12. Schoenhals, *The Paradox of Power in a People's Republic Middle School*, pp. 59–60.

The common people are an important ingredient in this picture of power, and they are carefully socialized into the ethics that underlie this Confucian order: obedience and respect for officials, sacrifice for the common good, and within the family, which ideally patterns itself on the order of governance of the empire, obedience and honoring of elders and parents through filial piety and the subordination of women to men and younger to older brothers. But it was precisely this obeisance to "propriety" or "rites" that, according to early twentieth-century reformers, blocked the Chinese people's consciousness of "rights." "The greatest aspects of our characters are freedom and equality; these are what differentiate us from the birds and beasts. The distinctions of superior and inferior, noble and base, by contrast, have made people lose their lofty characters. The people talk about the ritual code at every turn, worship it as a divinity and dare not go beyond it."[13]

A hierarchically ordered patriarchal system of governance that maintains order and takes care of the people is, then, assumed to be assured if both governors and governed act according to Confucian values. In particular, filial piety leads to respect and obedience not just to parents and kin but also to those who hold political power.[14] Beyond the right of almost all males, regardless of class or social background, to take the imperial examinations, equality is not a central concern in this system, but it is nevertheless a part of China's overall political culture. Education provided the one clear route up the hierarchical ladder. If a poor clan could scrape together enough money to educate one of its male offspring, it, too, could rise. This sort of meritocracy, then, had egalitarian values at its roots.

Except for the "right to rebel," little is said about the rights of the people to challenge the governing system.[15] But challenge it they did. Throughout history, protests and rebellions occurred when China did not prosper; secret sects were formed that challenged local officials or even the ruling dynasty; and petitions to officials and the ruling house were common. In short, as

---

13. Anonymous, "Quanli pian" (On rights), *Zhi shuo*, no. 2 (1903); trans. in Angle and Svensson, "On Rights and Human Rights," p. 24.

14. Anthony C. Yu, "Enduring Change," p. 46.

15. Mencius, "the most liberal of early Confucian thinkers," advised China's rulers to "listen to the people"; nowhere, however, did he say that people should have the "right to revolt." Instead, he argued against the common man participating in the political process at all. If China's rulers are bad, it is up to their advisers to admonish them and, if necessary, remove them (de Bary, "Preface" and "Introduction," in idem and Tu, *Confucianism and Human Rights*, pp. x, 8).

with any authoritarian system, people rebelled when the policies of their rulers led to misery. The ideal of order was found only when policies were successful. The right to rebel was, however, an irrelevancy: people who had grievances and enough power to rebel did so; those whose power was inadequate to challenge the government found that their "right" to rebel was severely constrained.[16]

Confucianism is, then, concerned about the relationships among various categories of people as part of its overriding concern for the peaceful ordering and proper governance of society. Within this context, it looks at the question of virtue (*de*)—what it is, how to get it, how to keep it, and how to exercise it. This applies to the emperor as much as it does to the ruling scholar-officials and the common people. The examination system for entry into China's scholar-official class and the proper performance of rituals are important ingredients of this search for moral virtue in governance.

Daoism (Taoism) likewise looks at the question of virtue, and how following the proper "way," or *dao*, will lead to virtue.[17] In the *Daode jing* (The classic of the Dao), Lao Zi advised rulers on how to achieve virtue. Unlike Confucianism, Lao Zi defined virtue not in moral terms, such as "benevolence" or "righteousness," but rather as a style of ruling. A virtuous ruler is one who effectively rules the people without their knowing it. The Daoist concept of non-action (*wuwei*) actually means acting, but without *appearing* to be acting. In Daoism, then, the individual is a subject who is being

---

16. It could, of course, be argued that it was the superior force of the new central government that succeeded the fallen imperial government that determined the direction China took. But unlike revolutions in England, France, and elsewhere, the evidence does not suggest that China's people wanted to change either the form of government or the values of society.

17. It is difficult to force Chinese thought into familiar Western concepts such as idealism, realism, positivism, or Marxism, much less democracy or human rights. If we view Chinese philosophers as if they were poets or narrators rather than analysts and see the philosophical terms they use as efforts to create images, rather than in Western terms of "structures" or "concepts," we may gain a more accurate perspective on their values and intentions. Much like the Bible, Chinese philosophical texts tend to tell stories. Thus, the purpose of *The Analects* (*Lunyu*) is to present a biography of Confucius and to show how the way he lived his life might serve as a model for others. For its part, "the *Daodejing* does not purport to provide an adequate and compelling description of what *dao* or *de* might mean as an ontological explanation for the world around us; rather it seeks to . . . provide guidance on how we ought to interact with the phenomena, human and otherwise, and give us context in the world" (Ames, "New Confucianism," pp. 29, 34).

controlled and does not know it. Since he fails to realize he is controlled, it never occurs to him to demand more freedom. If a ruler fails to be virtuous, moreover, everything simply falls apart; unlike Confucianism, Taoism offers the individual no right to rebel.[18]

Buddhism, another key component of Chinese traditional thought, emphasizes inner peace and harmony. It, too, focuses on virtue, and it offers the individual an institutional means to find virtue: relinquishing the world and entering a monastery. Of course, in many periods of Chinese history monasteries exercised enormous political power through their large number of followers. This made emperors eager to gain their loyalty and could give the monasteries significant political power, but the Buddhists' exercise of political power was usually quite indirect—by agreeing to pray for the emperor and keeping the monastery's followers obedient to the emperor. In Buddhism, then, it is again virtue, not the individual and individual rights, that is the central focus.[19]

Mohism,[20] another source of traditional Chinese thought, took universal love and "identifying with one's superiors" as its major principles—hardly the stuff of democracy and individual rights. Mo Zi counseled each group in society to take orders from and be obedient to the group above it, an assumption common to Confucianists as well as, later, to Legalists. As Burton Watson comments:

Independence of thought and action, for the lower classes at least, is a rarely expressed concept in [early Chinese philosophy]. The Taoists, it is true, talk much of freedom of thought and action, but it is a freedom which ignores or transcends the social order, not one that functions effectively within it. The concept of the hierarchical social order itself, the neat pyramid of classes and functionaries topped by the Son of Heaven, was an ideal that apparently no thinker dreamed of challenging.[21]

Virtue (or morality) is, then, a central concern of early Chinese political thought on governance, a feature that distinguishes it from the central concerns of Western political thought as a whole. Of course, in the period of Communist rule, Mao Zedong was likewise obsessed with "virtue," and defined it as being "red" or "revolutionary." In the most extreme Maoist periods,

---

18. Discussions with Michael Puett, 2001.

19. Ibid.

20. Mohism was based on the writings of Mo Ti (Master Mo), who is thought to have lived during the fifth century B.C.

21. Watson, *Mo Tzu*, pp. 7–8.

to be "red" (politically correct and actively advancing revolutionary virtues) was far more important than being "expert" (knowledgeable). Mao (as well as Chiang Kai-shek—who wrote a book about it titled *China's Destiny*; 1943) reinforced the traditional Confucian, Daoist, and Buddhist idea that the most important quality for those who rule is virtue.[22] Even more recently, in 2000, President Jiang Zemin adopted "rule by virtue" (*yi de zhi guo*) as a catchphrase to indicate the need for China's rulers to be virtuous—meaning in this case incorruptible. Although the focus on "virtue" by China's thinkers and rulers throughout history may be read as relevant to the issue of democratization, the fact that virtue, rather than the role and rights of the individual in governance, was the central concern in traditional Chinese political thought reminds us that the Chinese approached political ideas from a direction different from that common in the West.

Finally, Legalism, a competing school of thought since early times, was concerned primarily with one issue: the power and preservation of the state. Legalists engaged in ongoing debates with Confucianists about the need to base government on instruments of power and law rather than on moral suasion. They focused on the art of ruling and paid little attention to private individuals except to the extent that they needed to be controlled, and even punished, if they disobeyed the elaborate system of laws established by the ruler. Charity and mercy for the common people were disdained in Legalist thought, for the people were thought by nature to be evil. The "realism" embodied in Legalism is frequently compared to Machiavelli's emphasis on power and realism for rulers. Legalism deeply influenced the system of governance of the first emperor of China, Qin Shi Huangdi.[23] Although he is remembered in part for killing Confucian scholars and burning their books, he is also remembered for institutionalizing China's bureaucracy and legal system. After the fall of the Qin, the Han dynasty revived Confucianism, which grew to accept the idea that law and punishments were essential to maintaining order.[24] Indeed, it was because of the tenants of Legalism that

---

22. Chiang Kai-shek was emphasizing traditional Confucian virtues.

23. Legalism is based on the writings of Han Fei Zi, who is thought to have been born around 280 B.C. He did not create but rather "perfected" Legalist writings, drawing in particular on *The Book of Lord Shang*. The First Emperor ascended the throne of Qin in 246 B.C. and became the first emperor of a unified China in 221 B.C. (see Watson, *Han Fei Tzu*, pp. 3–7).

24. The branch of Confucianism associated with Mencius, on the other hand, assumed that human nature was basically good. Still, China's pragmatic rulers saw the necessity for laws. The Mencian assumption is the dominant one in the Maoist period and underlies the

law in China became equated with punishment, with criminal law, and with rule by only one man, the emperor.[25]

Confucianists also came to accept the Legalist principles that good governance needs an institutional framework and that the bureaucracy should be a meritocracy, with civil servants gaining merit through self-cultivation. But although they agreed to the idea of a meritocracy, the Confucianists changed the standards for position and promotion in the bureaucracy to ones based on education in the Confucian classics. By studying the classics and internalizing their lessons, an individual could become virtuous and qualified to be a member of the ruling class. The Confucian notion that a ruler's legitimacy should be based on morality rather than law remained the dominant tradition, with profound implications for Chinese rule in the twentieth century.[26]

Beyond the major schools of thought in early China, other important aspects of traditional Chinese culture are relevant to democratization. First, in many ways, it was inclusive and even embraced pluralism in religion.[27] Altars often would (and do) contain figures or representations of major figures from more than one religion. Most sects, especially the powerful millenarian sects in imperial China, were eclectic, unabashedly borrowing elements of several religions and throwing in elements of both science and the supernatural for good measure.[28] Pluralism and tolerance for diverse viewpoints are also evident in the establishment of the "academy"—the equivalent of a "private" school in imperial China. These were founded by Confucian intellectuals for the purpose of advancing knowledge about the Confucian classics. They gave lectures to disseminate their own views on social morality and governance. Within this system of private academies, intellectuals researched and published both orthodox and heterodox ideas.[29]

---

view that one's enemies and those who behave immorally can be re-educated. This is the rationale for mass movements, class struggle, criticism–self-criticism sessions, and *laojiao*—education through labor. All these are methods for returning individuals to their basic good nature. They are viewed as alternatives to judicial punishment, including death.

25. Wang Zhenmin, "The Developing Rule of Law in China," p. 35.

26. Discussions with Michael Puett, 2001.

27. Friedman, *The Politics of Democratization*, p. 28.

28. Discussions with Michael Puett, 2001. Today's Falungong sect and the other *qigong* sects are good examples of this eclecticism.

29. Edward X. Gu, "Cultural Intellectuals and the Politics of the Cultural Public Space," p. 409. The establishment of the Culture Academy in 1984 was, according to Gu, the result of a desire on the part of its founders to go outside the existing system of university education and "open up an independent public space" where they could discuss, research, and propagate

But the dominant form of academic training occurred in the government's own schools.

The pluralism and tolerance evident in traditional Chinese culture did not, however, translate into inclusive and pluralistic social policies. Instead, China's rulers retained authoritarian rule to ensure the preservation of the Chinese moral-political order. In good times, schools of thought that challenged the imperial system might simply be ignored; in bad times they were silenced. And rather than tolerating cultural pluralism, China's policies toward non-Han (minority) peoples tended to insist on assimilating them into Han culture (or at least demanded the appearance of accepting the superiority of Chinese culture). This was often done in the name of the security and unity of China, but the need to preserve China's national "essence" or culture was paramount. Inclusivity and pluralism took a backseat.

It could be argued that China's pantheistic and pluralistic religious tradition, its vibrant market system, the autonomy of decision making at the village level, a tradition of officials defending people against unjust policies, and the people's "right to rebel" provide cultural support for the development of democracy—if only these strands had been combined in a political consciousness of democracy and a commitment to institutionalizing it.[30] In fact, however, they were not; even though these democratic inklings existed, they never became the dominant cultural substructure or political superstructure. Although intellectuals both inside and outside China have since the 1980s expended considerable energy in digging out those aspects of Confucian assumptions, virtues, and perspectives that might support the development of individual rights or democracy in China today—indeed, as long ago as the May Fourth Movement in 1919, liberal intellectuals such as Hu Shi (1891–1962) attempted something similar[31]—that is precisely the point: these were not part of the dominant tradition of China that survived into the twentieth century.

Precisely why authoritarian thought continued to win out for over 2,000 years is a subject for historians, for the opportunities to depart from the authoritarian road occurred repeatedly over the two millennia after the founding of the first unified, authoritarian Chinese state, the Qin dynasty, in 221

---

their views on Chinese traditional culture—and how to modernize it. For culture academies in imperial China, see de Bary and Tu, *Confucianism and Human Rights*.

30. Friedman, *The Politics of Democratization*, p. 28.

31. Grieder, *Hu Shih and the Chinese Renaissance*.

B.C. Minimally it occurred each time the people grasped their "right to rebel" and "cut off the mandate" (*geming*) of a ruling house that had ruled improperly, incompetently, or unethically. Yet even at these critical junctures in Chinese history, when dynasties were being overturned, if only by default, the people made a political choice deeply rooted in their culture to allow a new ruling house, a new dynasty to be installed, and return to the same authoritarian system of rule rather than to move toward more democratic rule. It was, of course, a "choice" that was ensured by the coercive means at the disposal of the new ruling house; for with few exceptions (such as the Han and the Ming Dynasties), new dynasties were founded by military figures from the preceding dynasty. Further, traditional values that emphasized control, law, and order were backed up by institutional arrangements such as *baojia* and the concept of the *hukou*—household registration.

China's scholar-officials, who might perhaps have been the most logical group to develop "political thought," did not at these critical moments in Chinese history come forth with new ideas for structuring China's institutions. Instead, they preferred to continue, under new rulers, the traditional political system, in no small part because it was a system in which they held the highest political positions. China's potential dissident leaders and thinkers benefited too much from the system of state power and patronage to want to challenge it.

Many would argue, however, that China's ruling class truly believed in China's traditional institutions and values. The concept of an "eternal China" was, in the end, developed by centuries of Chinese rule that reflected specific values and guiding principles,[32] and it was a concept supported by rulers and ruled alike. This is not to say that for over two millennia, China's political culture never changed or that thinkers who challenged the dominant political culture never appeared; rather, China's traditional values have continued to be identifiable both within and alongside of other, more contemporary values and beliefs, and they remain dominant.[33]

---

32. Chinese rule was, of course, interrupted by the Yuan (Mongol) dynasty (1260–1368) and by the Qing (Manchu) dynasty (1644–1911). But at least in the latter case, many Chinese values and ruling precepts were there from the beginning, or crept back into Manchu rule, and by the time the Manchus were overthrown, most Chinese values and organizational principles of governance had been adopted.

33. For a discussion of political culture (but not China) in this respect, see Diamond, ed., "Conclusion," in idem, ed., *Political Culture and Democracy in Developing Countries*, pp. 411–12.

Thus, the willingness to question any person in authority who does not *deserve* loyalty and respect (based on a subjective evaluation of his or her morality and/or competence) is embedded in Chinese culture and coexists together with the "respectful" side of Chinese culture. It was not, however, until the Chinese Communist Party emphasized equality and told the people to speak out (whether through class struggle, mass movements, or campaigns) against those in authority who were immoral, incompetent, or abused their power that the traditional Chinese value of respect for those in authority was repeatedly challenged. In these new scenarios, the people truly played a powerful role—even if it was orchestrated by the Party and ultimately undermined its authority.

Chinese culture is, then, rich and complex enough to provide for just about any value, any attitude, depending on the circumstances: individualism and communalism, obedience and rebellion, hierarchy and equality, passivity and competition, "leftism" and "rightism." It is tempting to go back to Lesson 1 in Chinese-language classes: "China is a big country, and there are lots of people." However trite, these statements are fundamental to understanding Chinese political thought. For example, foreigners in China during the "ten bad years" (1966–76) were told by countless individuals of their enthusiastic support for Cultural Revolution policies, particularly for the attack on elitism and authority. Yet after the death of Mao Zedong, the fall of the Gang of Four, and the rise of the "pragmatists" to power, many of those individuals were no longer greeting foreigners.[34] Instead, another group came to the fore who said they had *never* supported the Cultural Revolution. Similarly, during the Tiananmen Square demonstrations in June 1989, we first heard from the hundreds of thousands who had supported the demonstrators' causes; then, after the crackdown, we heard from the hundreds of thousands who thought the students had gone too far and threatened law and order—and the economic development of China.[35]

---

34. Or, if they did, they had changed the statement of what they valued to accord with the party line.

35. My own research in the Chinese countryside, as well as that of Robert Pastor, who was monitoring elections for the Carter Center, indicates that the peasantry basically accepted the government's view that the crackdown on Tiananmen demonstrations was necessary. From the perspective of the countryside, far away from the field of action in the cities in 1989, the students were once again (as during the Cultural Revolution) causing chaos (Ogden, "Field Research Notes," Sept. 1999; and Robert Pastor, seminar, Harvard University, John F. Kennedy School, Oct. 8, 1998).

The point is this: with such an old and sophisticated culture and such a large and populous country, there are going to be millions of people whose voices we hear when the political or cultural orthodoxy is one they espouse. Millions of other voices will take their places when new conditions prevail or when orthodoxy is redefined. This cannot be dismissed as a mere reflection of the fear of the people to speak out against the prevailing orthodoxy. Changing conditions and events elicit different cultural values from China's society and history.

"Countervalues" have become salient in Chinese society since the time of the Cultural Revolution, but they began moving to the forefront of culture before then, perhaps as long ago as the May Fourth Movement, when China's intellectuals challenged China's political system and traditional cultural values. When Mao Zedong launched the Cultural Revolution, he simply *intensified* and highlighted an existing but not dominant ethos in the twentieth century about the right to rebel against immoral leaders, however defined and redefined. Perhaps the reason so many authority figures (teachers, supervisors, party and government officials) were able to endure hours, days, even weeks and months, of criticism of shortcomings in their revolutionary virtue from their peers and subordinates is that such practices had long been culturally sanctioned, albeit not in precisely the same form. They were expected, according to cultural norms, to accept such criticism and "learn" from it. Put into the vocabulary of the Cultural Revolution, they were to be "re-educated" and returned to society the better for it.

Contemporary studies of Chinese society allow us to think about the countervalues embedded in Chinese political culture in new ways. We may infer from the emphasis on evaluation and criticism in China that, more than many polities, the Chinese are prepared for the debate and critical evaluation demanded by a functioning democracy. Mandatory participation in politics for the better part of thirty years has equipped China's citizens with organizational and analytical tools. Probably few who have ever attended a meeting of Chinese students, entrepreneurs, or even farmers—or even simply witnessed the bickering that is ubiquitous on city streets— would think otherwise. However, the use of evaluation and criticism by superiors to *control* society is the other strand within China's dynamic culture, and it frequently quashes more egalitarian, democratic urges.

Thus, traditional Chinese culture had democratic inklings, but the *dominant* elements of traditional Chinese thought, those that survive in the twenty-first century and continue to influence Chinese thinking, are concerned with order, virtue, and the governance of society. Chinese people have tended to admire successful authoritarian leaders more than successful democratic leaders, as the results from a 1988 survey of urban youth indicates. Respondents were asked to choose one favorite from the following list.[36] The results indicate what percentage chose that individual:

1. Zhou Enlai 49.7 percent[37]
2. Mao Zedong 10.9 percent
3. Deng Xiaoping 9.2 percent
4. Sun Yat-sen 6.6 percent
5. Napoleon 4.7 percent
6. Margaret Thatcher 4.2 percent[38]
7. Lenin 2.7 percent
8. Hitler 2.5 percent
9. Gorbachev 1.6 percent
10. Lincoln 1.5 percent
11. Reagan 1.1 percent
12. Churchill 0.5 percent
13. Zhao Ziyang 0.47 percent[39]
14. Stalin 0.4 percent
14. Bertrand Russell 0.4 percent
16. Chiang Kai-shek 0.39 percent
17. Khadafy 0.1 percent

---

36. Zhongguo shehui kexue yuan, Shehuixue yanjiusuo, Zhuangxing ketizu, *Zhongguo qingniande toushi*, p. 171.

37. Studies done by the *Chinese Youth Newspaper* indicate that young Chinese who have a "personal moral model" most frequently cite Zhou Enlai as their model, with Lei Feng being the second most frequently cited. Zhou Enlai was the premier of China from 1949 until his death in 1976. Lei Feng was a model citizen who performed extraordinary feats of courage and asked nothing for himself. He died when a telephone pole fell on his head. See also the survey asking whether Lei Feng's spirit of taking delight in helping others should be advocated (more than 95 percent agreed; see Sun Jiaming, *Guannian diaocha*, item 23, p. 217). But as another survey cited below indicates, this support for Lei Feng's spirit does not seem to carry over into more general support for being selfless.

38. Thatcher ranked number 6 on the list despite the anger of the Chinese people over her efforts to thwart the return of Hong Kong to Chinese sovereignty in 1997.

39. Zhao was not very popular before he was dismissed in 1989.

18. Kim Il Sung 0.1 percent
19. Bismarck 0.04 percent
20. Khomeini 0.04 percent

This list of possible choices consisted of powerful, often authoritarian figures, with a sprinkling of democratic leaders; only one was not a political leader, the philosopher and mathematician Bertrand Russell.[40] The results may have been affected by a lack of knowledge about certain individuals on the list. In addition, the cultural and political perceptions (and biases) built into the centrally administered national curriculum for politics and history ensure that youth share a common perspective of foreign leaders, if not of their own leaders.[41] For the most part, the choices on the list reinforce the point that the Chinese prefer leaders to be intelligent, competent, charismatic, and powerful.[42] Their preference is not to limit their leaders'

---

40. Russell significantly influenced many Chinese intellectuals concerning both socialism and the study of mathematical logic from the time of his visit to China in 1921; see Ogden, "The Sage in the Inkpot." Chinese intellectuals continue to this day to be fascinated by Russell and to write about him; see, e.g., Feng Chongyi, *Luosu yu Zhongguo.*

41. All societies, including Western liberal democracies, write history as they see it. Many argue that there is no such thing as an "objective fact" in history. As Voltaire once said, "What is history but lies agreed upon?" The Chinese have since imperial times carefully managed their history and written it to accord with their worldview. During the communist era, history has been repeatedly revised to accord with the new "realities." The historical narrative at the National Museum of Revolutionary History in Beijing has repeatedly shifted to reflect the historical vision preferred by the dominant leadership. Books that teach Chinese and world history also clearly present the Chinese worldview.

42. Although the list provides fuel for endless speculation, the ranking of Hitler as number 8 on the list, above such figures as Gorbachev, Churchill, and Zhao Ziyang, deserves attention. When I asked Chinese colleagues and students about this ranking, the usual reply was that the Chinese considered Hitler a strong ruler who maintained order in Germany. They were perplexed as to why Hitler wanted to exterminate the Jews (See Ross, *Escape to Shanghai*) and why this should be viewed as reflecting on Hitler's leadership capabilities. Perhaps the explanation for their relatively lower concern with German fascism and with Hitler is that the Chinese are so focused on their own former enemy, Japan. Germany seems comparatively far away.

A 1995 survey of Beijing youth and teenagers concerning German and Japanese fascists seems to modify, if not entirely contradict, this view. This survey's results indicate that Beijing youth believed both German and Japanese fascists were horrendous, although only 6.6 percent believed that German fascists were worse than Japanese fascists ("Survey of Views of Beijing Youth and Teenagers Concerning Anti-Japanese War," *Beijing qingnian bao*, Aug. 30, 1995, sect. 8).

power but to choose capable leaders and then give them all the power they need.[43]

Finally, to this day, community concerns continue to take clear precedence over concerns for individual rights. As Lee Teng-hui put it when he was president of the Nationalist Party in Taiwan, this is, in fact, the way it should be:

> Confucianism can . . . serve to correct the deficiencies of a democratic system. While the advantages of democracy are apparent, like any other system, it is not without flaws. The democratic system guarantees and emphasizes the rights of the individual. But individualism can go to extremes, even degenerating into egotism and hedonism. . . . Individual perfection develops alongside the enhanced welfare of the group. Confucian doctrine includes a sophisticated set of theories that can balance the excesses of individualism. Confucianists remind us to emphasize neither institutions nor the individual at the expense of the other.[44]

Regardless of the continuing power of traditional Chinese thought to set values and standards, especially about the importance of the community, many Chinese act in a highly individualistic manner, often with no concern for the community. One could conjecture that it is precisely because of this that the Chinese government has had to be so insistent on the collective good taking precedence over individual rights. China has had democra-

---

The respondents' view of Thatcher may be affected by a shared (with the rest of the world) perception of her as the "Iron Lady." Chinese women in particular admire female leaders who are tough. Indeed, for more than one Chinese woman, admiration for Thatcher (and even for Mao's wife, Jiang Qing, who was not on the list), was based on the fact that "she made men afraid!"

43. This conclusion is not confined to Chinese people who have lived under communist rule. For example, in a survey of Hong Kong's people, who lived under British colonial rule until 1997, support for Chinese President Jiang Zemin and Premier Zhu Rongji had by the year 2000 surpassed the support for Hong Kong's chief executive officer, Tung Chee-hua. For Jiang Zemin, 5 percent were "very satisfied" and 62 percent were "somewhat satisfied" with his performance; for Zhu Rongji, the figures were 21 percent and 56 percent; and for Tung Chee-hwa, 2 percent and 36 percent. See DeGolyer et al., *The Hong Kong Transition Project*, tables 19 and 20 (p. 13) and table 30 (p. 19). Extensive conversations with people in Hong Kong in June 2000 revealed dismay over Tung's lack of "competence," and a commonly held belief was that he was not as "intelligent" as Jiang and especially Zhu, who was credited with dealing with profoundly difficult problems as well as could be expected. Tung was seen as ineffective in dealing with even relatively simple problems (Ogden, Research Notes, based on interviews and conversations, Hong Kong, June 2000).

44. Teng-hui Lee, "Confucian Democracy," p. 18.

tic impulses but no institutional framework to channel them in an orderly fashion.

How, then, to connect traditional Chinese thought with something recognizably "democratic"? Is traditional Chinese thought neither prodemocratic nor anti-democratic, but simply "a-democratic"? Is the demise of Confucianism essential for China's transformation into a rights-oriented polity? Or must it be maintained, albeit reshaped, if China's people are to retain a sense of cultural identity as Chinese? If Confucianism can only be salvaged by identifying it with modern Western liberal democratic values, what will remain of it as an identifiable body of political thought? As Roger Ames puts it,

Any reference to Chinese "democratic" ideals introduces terrible equivocations: The promotion of seemingly individualistic values in the absence of Western notions of the individual, autonomy, independence, human rights, and so on. . . . Contemporary Chinese philosophic developments are deeply embedded within traditional Chinese methods of philosophizing. By and large, Chinese philosophers continue to be concerned with the creative appropriation of their own cultural tradition: Marxist rhetoric and liberal democratic values are largely heuristic structures through which more fundamental traditional Chinese values are revisited, reconfigured, and sometimes, revitalized.[45]

The following chapter presents some of the issues concerning democracy that preoccupied many of China's leaders and thinkers in the first half of the twentieth century. It captures some of the dilemmas Chinese intellectuals face in using a Chinese approach, embedded in Chinese culture, to discuss concepts originally generated in a non-Chinese context.

---

45. Ames, "New Confucianism," p. 37.

3 Late Imperial China and the Republican Period

There is much about modern China which is not endearing to most inhabitants of the West: its grim Puritanism, its sometimes demented political simplicity of mind. But what it was readily open for China to become in 1911 or 1919 or 1945 was not the United States of America or Sweden or Switzerland. In the end professional revolutionaries, like amateurs, make such history as they can, make revolution *faute de mieux*. In the universe of real possibilities, if not in the universe of fantasy which they have at times invoked, the Chinese revolutionaries too have to their credit towering achievements of social betterment.

—John Dunn, 1980

What is the content of the democracy, the self-determination, for which these activists struggle? What, after all, constitutes the modernity that Chinese and Japanese Marxists have sought in bourgeois-democratic and, then, Marxian socialist revolution? Is there any way of defining it so that it is not simply a description of realities based on the experiences of other peoples in other cultures? . . . In the hegemonic Western conception, modernity constitutes a form of the assertion of one's identity, but as soon as it is borrowed or imported to a non-Western setting, it appears that the path to modernity must pass through self-abnegation. Those seeking self-determination must define their democratizing quest in new terms, terms of their own, terms that transcend this dilemma.

—Germaine A. Hoston (1994)

Many inhabitants of Western liberal democratic polities who know little of China's history and culture find it incomprehensible not only that China fell to communism in 1949 but also that in the late 1980s and early 1990s the Chinese did not join the rush of other Communist Party–led states and

---

EPIGRAPHS: Dunn, *Political Obligation in Its Historical Context*, p. 227; Hoston, *The State, Identity, and the National Question in China and Japan*, p. 444.

switch to a liberal democratic system.[1] Given China's complex history and social conditions in the first half of the twentieth century, as well as the unanticipated consequences that the adoption of socialism entailed, one could hardly suggest that the vast majority of Chinese people actively chose communism in some detached, objective manner. There were no elections, no public opinion polls, no referenda. They were too bogged down in the daily struggle to stay alive in those desperate times to make a well-informed choice. Indeed, even those intellectuals and peasants who actively sided with the Communists in the civil war with the Nationalists had little idea how the Party's policies would play out after it came to power. It cannot be forgotten, however, that the peasantry's support of the Communists and Red Army was crucial to their military victory in 1949, and the peasants came to regard Mao Zedong and the Party as the heroes who had changed their lives and created the "new China."

One thing is clear: in the first half of the twentieth century, many Chinese political and intellectual leaders did seriously consider liberal democracy in both theory and practice. Arguably, that experiment failed because of the chaos created by warlordism, internal strife, and the Japanese invasion, and not because of Nationalist policies of support for bureaucratic capitalism and a landlord economy and the corruption of the leadership, or because of the liberal democratic project itself. Nevertheless, the suffering of the people as a consequence of China's conditions was critical to the backing given to the Chinese Communists and their ultimate victory in 1949. If only by default, the failure of Nationalist policies (regardless of why they failed) to stabilize China, bring peace, and improve the lives of the Chinese people led to a Communist victory, for the Red Army's superior military power rested on broad-based support from the long-suffering masses, and it was that support that determined China's political fate. The question here, then, is not why China adopted communism in 1949, but why the individuals who came to lead the Chinese Communist Party believed communism was a panacea for China's problems.

---

1. When discussing why a people, an elite, or a particular class adopt liberal democracy, we are discussing a political system, not a liberal capitalist economic system. Further, although economic liberalization often accompanies democratization, and theorists and statesmen alike often argue that economic liberalization leads to the adoption of liberal democracy, for analytical purposes it is important to keep the two separate.

The reasons for China's turn to communism were not purely domestic. Its experience with the Western liberal democracies since the nineteenth century, as well as the behavior of Western powers in the twentieth century, deeply influenced the Chinese perspective on liberal democracy. China's relationships with liberal democratic states were shaped by this history, which cast China as a victim of Western imperialism. The Chinese belief that Western values fueled social decay added yet another layer of reasons for rejecting Western liberal democracy. Winston Churchill's adage that [liberal] democracy is the worst form of government except all the other forms of government, did not accord with China's experience.

China's experience with the Western powers and its predominantly authoritarian heritage form the backdrop for a cultural and historical understanding of China's efforts to democratize.[2] The meaning of democracy in the Chinese context was an issue even before the first attempts to turn China into a democratic republic with the overthrow of China's last imperial dynasty, the Qing (Manchu) dynasty, in 1911. The Nationalist Party, whose early leaders engineered this revolution, failed to find a form of democracy relevant to China that it could implement successfully, and the Chinese Communists inherited the task of determining what democracy could mean for China.

The initial debate over democracy from 1895 to 1911 focused on the form of democratic government China should adopt: a constitutional monarchy or a republic. After the failure to establish democracy within the context of the newly established republic, the debate turned to the best *means* for establishing an operative form of democracy in China. Then, in the 1920s and thereafter, the question turned to the *meaning* of democracy in the Chinese context. The commitment of the Chinese Communists to "socialist democracy" in turn shaped the values and institutions that would develop in the People's Republic.

The debate over democracy did not, however, end with the arrival of socialist democracy. It has continued since 1949, although it has usually been framed as a debate over control versus decentralization, control versus freedom, or control versus the delegation of authority. Indeed, many of the underlying issues in discussions about "whither socialism," the opening up of China, and reforms in the economic, legal, educational, labor, and political sectors are really about democratization. The policy outcomes of decisions

---

2. This section is adapted from Ogden, *China's Unresolved Issues*, pp. 23–33.

in all these arenas in China since 1979 have largely had the effect of further-ing pluralization, liberalization, and even democratization. To discover the fate of democracy in China, we must look below the Chinese Communist leadership's public resistance to "peaceful evolution" (*heping yanbian*) toward democracy (meaning the adoption of Western liberal democratic ideas) and instead look to what the Chinese have done to change China since 1949.

THE FORM AND VALUES OF DEMOCRACY

Chinese reformers and revolutionaries at the turn of the twentieth century understood that there were preconditions for the establishment of democ-racy in China, but their conception of it was primarily theoretical. Lacking experience with forms of governance other than authoritarian ones, particu-larly at the national level, they were largely inspired by the *ideas* of democ-racy. They cared little whether China's democracy was modeled on Western practices. Nor did they adopt the Western-based ethical rationale that indi-viduals should be protected from oppression by the more powerful and that they should have rights which the state could not encroach upon. China's re-formers and revolutionaries were not committed to individualism, freedom, or equality per se, and they did not consider the exploitation of some people by others to be unethical. Nor did they accept the Jeffersonian precept that those who exercise power cannot be trusted always to act in the public inter-est. Instead, they believed that democracy had contributed to the growth of wealth and power in the West, and they hoped it would do the same for China. "Democracy" was a prescription for establishing a nationally unified and strong modern state.[3] Unaware that, when introduced into China's so-cial and cultural context, democratic political institutions and values might not function in the same way as they did in the existing democracies, or that democratic institutions could be crippled by a political culture, the Chinese were ill-prepared for the difficulties and pitfalls that awaited them.

Many Chinese were motivated by nationalism to overthrow the Qing imperial monarchy in favor of a republic: they wanted to get rid of China's non-Han rulers. The revolution seemed only marginally a protest against the domination of one group by another, much less a desire for "freedom" and "equality." Instead, the revolutionaries were angered at the inability of

---

3. One of China's leading thinkers in the late nineteenth century, Yan Fu, wrote about these ideas; see Schwartz, *In Search of Wealth and Power*.

the Manchus to transform China into a strong modern state and to defend it from the European barbarians. Although these thinkers were concerned with finding the most appropriate form of democracy for China, their aim was to install democracy in order to unify and strengthen China and thus enable China to resist foreign aggression. Their vision was strictly utilitarian.

Neither Liang Qichao (1873–1929), the reformer, nor Hu Hanmin (1879–1936) nor Sun Yat-sen (1866–1925), the revolutionaries, appears to have thought or written much about the more abstract philosophical concepts connected with the establishment of representative government.[4] For Liang Qichao, the great difference between Chinese and Western thought lay in the Western emphasis on righteousness (*yi*). In his view, righteousness focused on the self, whereas the Chinese emphasis on humaneness (*ren*) focused on concern for others. Chinese political thought assumed that being humane to others would, through reciprocity, result in humane treatment of oneself. Liang Qichao believed, however, that for the Chinese people a reliance on humane government was foolish:

Chinese people simply hope for humane government from their lord. Thus, when they run into humaneness, they are treated as infants; when they meet inhumanity, they are treated as meat on a chopping block. In all times, humane rulers are few and cruel rulers are common, and so our people, from the time thousands of years ago when our ancestors taught this doctrine, down to the present, have taken being treated like meat as heavenly scripture and earthly precept.[5]

Liang Qichao harbored serious doubts about implementing democratic practices in China. During his travels in the United States in 1903, he observed the practices of the Chinese living there and concluded that the Chinese people, even those living in a free and democratic society, were not prepared to practice democracy. How much less so would they be in China, with its social disorder and corrupt public ethos? "Freedom, constitutionalism, republicanism—this would be like wearing summer garb in winter, or furs in summer: beautiful, to be sure, but unsuitable. . . . The Chinese people must for now accept authoritarian rule; they cannot enjoy freedom."[6] Liang and other early reformers likewise opposed implementing the concept of

---

4. For a biography of Sun Yat-sen, see Sharman, *Sun Yat-sen*; for Liang Qichao, see Levenson, *Liang Ch'i-ch'ao and the Mind of Modern China*.

5. Liang Qichao, "Lun quanli sixiang" (On rights consciousness), essay from *Xin min shuo* (On the new people; 1902), trans. in Angle and Svensson, "On Rights and Human Rights," p. 18.

6. Nathan, *Chinese Democracy*, pp. 60–61.

one-man-one-vote in China. Instead, they believed the vote should be limited to the small percentage of the adult population who were literate—a belief common to many contemporary democrats in the Western democracies, although the higher literacy rates in the West meant that larger percentages of the population were enfranchised.

Unlike many of China's early reformers, Gao Yihan (1884–1968) was familiar with Western political thought. He was one of the first Chinese to advocate distributive rights, and his writings indicate that the issue of—and ultimately the preference for—distributive or welfare rights as opposed to procedural or civil rights was being debated in China by the early twentieth century. For Gao, the priority of distributive rights was clear: freedom of speech and thought depended on the existence of "life capabilities."

We have to ask whether, in order to enjoy these kinds of freedoms, people do not also need some corresponding life capabilities? [If so,] then should society not have to provide each individual with the appropriate capabilities and facilities? The first precondition for all those who want to enjoy the freedom of speech and thought is to be able to live. If not even one's life can be protected, then it is impossible for one to receive an education. And even if one's life is protected and an education received . . . still, if there are no library facilities in society and no scholars to advise one or to stimulate one's academic interests . . . , then how can one enjoy the high-sounding freedoms of speech and thought stipulated in the constitution?[7]

Sun Yat-sen, the "father" of the 1911 Revolution, had a blueprint for democracy. His 1906 "Three People's Principles" became one of the key documents for Chinese governance in the twentieth century. For Sun, democratic government is responsive to the will of the people. The popular will, however, could not be allowed to weaken effective centralized authority. Given the pressing demands China faced, the government could not permit the people to interfere with the administration of the state, as happened in Western liberal democracies. This interpretation of democratic government fit the existing conception of the role of the government in China. Whether imperial, republican, or communist, the Chinese seemed bound by their his-

---

7. Gao Yihan, "Sheng xianfa zhong de minquan wenti" (The question of people's rights in the provincial constitutions), *Xin qingnian* (New youth) 9, no. 5 (1921), pp. 5–7; trans. in Angle and Svensson, "On Rights and Human Rights," p. 62. Gao was an important member of the liberal intellectual community in the 1920s and translated the lectures that John Dewey gave in China on social and political philosophy for the liberal magazine, *Xin qingnian* (New Youth). For more on Gao, see Grieder, *Hu Shih and the Chinese Renaissance*.

tory and culture to favor a powerful elitist government at the expense of popular democratic rule. The chaos suffered when China was under less than authoritarian rule has, to this day, confirmed for many Chinese the correctness of this view.

For all his revolutionary ideas, when it came to what democracy could mean in China, Sun Yat-sen seems to have fallen back on his Confucian heritage, his overwhelming concern for strengthening China, and his perception of reality. He explicitly excluded individual freedom as an essential component of democracy. Sun interpreted the European cliché that the Chinese were like "a sheet of loose sand" to mean that they had "excessive individual freedom." Unlike the Europeans who, Sun averred, made revolution because they lacked freedom, the Chinese needed to make revolution in order to *end* excessive individual freedom and bind themselves together so that they could resist foreign oppression. He concluded by stating:

The slogan of the French Revolution was "Liberty, Equality, and Fraternity." The slogan of our revolution is "Nationalism, Democracy, and the People's Livelihood." What is the relationship between these two slogans? Our nationalism could, in my opinion, be said to be equivalent to their freedom, because to realize nationalism is precisely to fight for our nation's freedom. . . . How should we apply the word freedom today? If it were applied to the individual, we would turn into "a sheet of loose sand." *It is therefore imperative to apply the word freedom, not to the individual, but to the nation. The individual should not have too much freedom, but the nation must have complete freedom*. . . . *To achieve this goal, however, we must all sacrifice our [individual] freedom.*[8]

Indeed, many thinkers of Sun's time argued that the Chinese had not too much but too little freedom.[9] Sun Yat-sen further believed that the idea of democracy would lead to the adoption of democracy. Monarchy merely had to vanish, a "republic" be declared, and the Chinese would start practicing democracy. Democratization would, in turn, inspire social and economic changes that would undercut traditional Chinese authoritarianism. Sun therefore saw no need to prepare for a democratic republic by establishing conditions conducive to the successful practice of democracy.

---

8. Sun Yat-sen, "Minquan zhuyi" (The Principle of Democracy), lecture given in 1924, reprinted in *Sanmin zhuyi* (The Three People's Principles) (Taipei: Sanmin Press, 1996), pp. 73, 96–98, 100, 101; trans. in Angle and Svensson, "On Rights and Human Rights," pp. 66–68. Italics added.

9. Liang Zhiping, "Cong lizhi dao fazhi."

With the benefit of some ninety years of hindsight, it seems odd to observers today that China's reformers and revolutionaries would have assumed that democracy was China's for the taking. Neither individual rights nor one-man-one-vote nor equality had philosophical roots in China. For 2,000 years, China had accepted a system that emphasized the strict ordering of interpersonal relationships according to Confucian hierarchical standards, in which subordinates were required to do the bidding of their superiors.

Sun Yat-sen's third principle, the "people's livelihood," reveals Sun's approach to economic equality and (in contrast to his spurning of ideas of individual freedom) his concern for distributive rather than procedural democracy. Under the rubrics of "land nationalization" and "equalization of land rights," the people's livelihood embraced the belief that all landowners should be allowed to keep what they had, but the state should appropriate all future increases in land values. Sun targeted property holders in urban areas, in which land values were increasing rapidly, especially in the coastal ports. "Equalization of land rights" was not, therefore, aimed at equalizing landholdings or at eliminating economic classes. It was merely meant to prevent landowners from reaping huge profits from the sale of land.[10] The Nationalist government adopted this policy after (but not before) it fled to Taiwan in 1949 and expanded on Sun's general beliefs that the people's basic economic needs should be guaranteed through government policies.

But there was more to the story than this. Ironically, in spite of Sun's espousal of nationalism and his determination to throw the foreigners out—first the Manchu rulers, then the Westerners—his vision of China's future was inspired by ideas from an eclectic group of Western statesmen and writers (via Japanese translation). These ideas failed to take root in China, however, not just because of Sun's (and others') superficial understanding of them but also because they were in many respects alien to China's political culture and its notions of authority, power, and the role of the people in government. Bound by the Confucian heritage to believe that the common people had no role to play in governing unless the emperor lost his Heavenly Mandate and that officials were to be obeyed and feared, not voted in and out of office, the Chinese did not easily grasp the Western democratic notion of governance by the people.

---

10. Hu Hanmin, "The Six Principles of the People's Report," in de Bary, ed., *Sources of Chinese Tradition* 2: 104–5.

THE MEANS TO ACHIEVE DEMOCRACY

The overthrow of the imperial monarchy and the establishment of a republic led to major changes in the institutional context for democratization, but the new republican political structure failed to function successfully. By 1915, the national parliament had become a tool of the warlords, not a representative body for the Chinese people. It was devoid of political power. Constitutions were made and unmade, and the "people's rights" were ignored. Few efforts were made to propagate the ideas of democracy among the vast Chinese population, and the people remained unaware that they were supposed to consent to their government. Isolated amid a culture and society not predisposed by tradition to democratic forms, democratic political institutions collapsed. The idea of representative government was not powerful enough to cause officials or the common people to abandon their culture-bound, hierarchical patterns of thinking about power or to exercise their rights as individuals.

The New Culture Movement was a response to the perceived need to find the *means* for giving content to democratic forms. Its major proponents, notably the novelist Ba Jin (1905–), the liberals Hu Shi and Cai Yuanpei (1868–1940), and cofounder of the Chinese Communist Party Chen Duxiu (1879–1942), argued that a cultural transformation was needed to inject vitality into the institutions of democracy. Members of the movement denounced China's Confucian heritage as incompatible with individual freedom and a constitutional regime. As Chen Duxiu noted, "All our traditional ethics, laws, scholarship, rites, and customs are survivals of feudalism."[11] Chen focused on the family as the basis of Confucian absolutism. Traditional family and societal concepts needed to be destroyed before China could have a true democracy, a society in which individuals would be free to pursue their "enlightened self-interest."[12]

Moreover, China's people needed to attain a political consciousness if representative government was to survive, and this required education. From the early reformers and revolutionaries through the New Culture intellectuals and on all sides of the political spectrum, China's leading voices stressed

---

11. Chen Duxiu, "Appeal to Youth," *Xin qingnian* (New youth) 1, no. 1 (Sept. 1915): 2, in Lang, *Pa Chin and His Writings*, p. 35. On Hu Shih, see Grieder, *Hu Shih and the Chinese Renaissance*.

12. Schwartz, *Chinese Communism and the Rise of Mao*, p. 9.

the importance of education almost more than any other single component of political rights and development in China.[13] Lu Xun (1881–1936), China's literary giant of the first half of the twentieth century, alluded to the need for education to free the individual from the ties of tradition and the ignorance and submissiveness it had bred in his famous story "The Biography of Ah Q." Lu Xun made the point that the Republic of China "would never become anything more than a republic in name" until the Chinese peasantry was liberated from ignorance and submissiveness to tradition and authority.[14] Hu Shih led the attack on ignorance with his advocacy of *baihua*, or "plain language," the vernacular that in its written form replaced the classical form of Chinese writing in the 1920s. This critical step in language reform greatly facilitated the education and nurturing of an informed citizenry.

The Chinese Communist Party readily adopted the theme of the need for mass education as well as the critique of China's Confucian traditions. In addition, the nascent communist movement added an explicit concern with economic equality and democracy. Li Dazhao (1889–1927), the other co-founder of the Chinese Communist Party, emphasized the role of the intellectuals in arousing the peasants from their passivity and making them aware of their economic oppression. Until China eliminated economic inequalities, it could not be democratic. In his view, "The solution of the economic problem is the fundamental solution."[15]

A NEW MEANING OF DEMOCRACY

The Chinese Communist conception of democracy seemed to many diverse groups to offer a better solution to the problems of China. It appealed strongly, for example, to the enormous population of impoverished tenant farmers in China. Best of all, its all-encompassing ideology promised a comprehensive solution, and China, like many systems in crisis, was looking for a total solution. From the May Fourth Movement on, China tried to find a guiding ideology with a clear blueprint, not one that encouraged people to think about alternative possibilities. To the Communists, liberal democracy

---

13. See, e.g., "Foreword" to the magazine *Renquan* (Human rights), no. 1 (Aug. 1925): 1–5; trans. in Angle and Svensson, "On Rights and Human Rights," pp. 69–73.

14. Sung-k'ang Huang, *Lu Hsun and the New Culture Movement of Modern China*, p. 59.

15. Li Dazhao, "Again on Problems and Isms," Aug. 17, 1919; cited in Meisner, *Li Ta-chao and the Origins of Chinese Marxism*, p. 111.

seemed to offer a piecemeal, trial-and-error approach at a time when the crisis in China did not afford room for experimentation. The early reformers and revolutionaries of the pre-Republican period had sought a solution to China's problems in political (representative) democracy, and those in the Republican period from 1916 to the mid-1920s sought it in social-cultural democracy. In contrast, the Chinese Communists established an *economic* conception of democracy as fundamental and outlined a comprehensive organization and ideology for a form of democracy relevant to China's needs and culture.

The Chinese Communist Party was founded in 1921 with the support of advisers from the Comintern (the Soviet-run Communist International). It represented the political institutionalization of what had hitherto been a small Marxist study group of intellectuals dedicated to solving China's problems. Up to that time, China's representative political institutions had produced only political factionalism and provincial warlordism and had done little to advance the people's interests. Nevertheless, the new Chinese Communist Party still embraced democracy as the highest value, but in its vision, economic equality and political activism were essential to the achievement of democracy. Political participation by the people would raise their political and class consciousness of the institutional basis of their oppression. In the Marxist analysis, China's traditional hierarchical social structure and authoritarian attitudes had their roots in economic inequalities. Until this economic substructure was changed to eliminate inequalities, the cultural and political superstructure would remain undemocratic.

Finally, in answering the question "Why not liberal democracy?" we should keep in mind that the Chinese Communists modeled their new party on the Communist Party of the Soviet Union and adopted the Leninist ideas of "democratic centralism" and the "mass line." As Marxists, they believed democratization entailed the expansion of governing power from a small elite or class to ever-growing numbers of people, until all the people were a part of that government. As Chinese, however, they saw democratization as acceptable only if the state remained strong.

The Nationalists did not, of course, fall into the "liberal democratic" camp. Indeed, because of Sun Yat-sen's negative views on individual rights, ideological spokesmen for the Nationalists dismissed individual rights "as an outmoded and unscientific idea, as well as one that was unsuitable to Chinese conditions," whereas the Communists criticized them "for serving only the interests of the bourgeoisie."[16] Zhou Fohai (1897–1948), a member of the Chinese Communist Party from 1921 to 1924 and subsequently a leading theoretician for the Nationalists, consistently maintained the importance of restricting the rights of certain people. He argued that the theory of natural rights (rights that all people have by dint of being human) was not applicable to China and that the goal of China's ongoing revolution was not the advancement of human rights. Instead, as the 1928 "Declaration" of the Nationalists' first nationwide conference indicated, anyone who opposed the Republic, or tried to sabotage it, should not enjoy rights or freedoms. According to Zhou Fohai, "If we allow them to continue to participate in politics and act freely, they will make use of their political rights to sabotage the revolution."[17] In short, the Nationalists' and the Communists' view of who was entitled to political rights was virtually identical at this time. It could be argued in fact that throughout their lives, both Chiang Kai-shek and Mao Zedong believed that only those who loyally supported their own respective party's rule were entitled to rights and freedoms.

In the meantime, China's pre-1949 political history remained an explosive combination of China's search for solutions to its problems in Western thought, a hatred of foreigners, and the reality of civil war and continued foreign incursions into China. While intellectuals and political leaders talked in lofty terms about democratic aspirations, the power-hungry went about their daily business of exploiting both the people and the government. In 1916, with the death of the dominant warlord, Yuan Shikai, China once again became a country at war against itself. As the president of the Republic from 1912 to 1916, Yuan had at least imposed a measure of order. Thereafter the Chinese battled each other, first under the warlords and later under the banners of opposing political parties and their armies.

Chiang Kai-shek succeeded Sun Yat-sen as the Nationalist leader upon Sun's death in 1925 and became commander-in-chief of the army. In an effort to reunite China, Chiang Kai-shek, with the support of the Communist Party, led the Northern Expedition. After Chiang and his armies had defeated the contending warlords of China, however, the unity forged by the Northern Expedition came to an abrupt halt. In 1927, the Nationalists

---

16. Angle and Svensson, "On Rights and Human Rights," p. 7.

17. Zhou Fohai, "Minquan zhuyi de genju he tezhi" (The basis and particulars of the principle of democracy), *Xin shengming* 1, no. 2 (1928): 11–13; trans. in Angle and Svensson, "On Rights and Human Rights," pp. 75–76.

slaughtered the Communists, who were growing ever stronger within the "united front." Thus the end to fighting between rival warlords was immediately followed by a civil war led by the two political parties. Furthermore, Chiang Kai-shek announced that the Chinese people were not yet prepared for representative institutions and would be governed under the "tutelage" of the Nationalists until they were ready for democracy—a time that never arrived. Combined with Japanese imperialism and war, it was a lethal cocktail for the Chinese people—and it all happened under the governance of the Republic of China.

The Japanese seized the opportunity offered by China's weakness and civil wars to gain control over vast swaths of Chinese territory. When World War II ended in Japan's defeat, the Red Army was battle-hardened by many bitter years of fighting the Japanese. Further, it had been steadily building support among the peasantry by instituting, or promising, land reform, reforms the Nationalists were never willing to make.[18] The Red Army's strategy of pitching its appeal to the broad masses of Chinese peasants, combined with a military strategy of guerrilla warfare, eventually brought victory to the Communists. In 1949, they declared the People's Republic of China.

THE ADOPTION OF AN ALTERNATIVE IDEAL

In the debate over whether the Communists won or the Nationalists lost, as much evidence suggests that the Nationalists defeated themselves as that they were defeated by the Communists. Many Chinese did not, of course, actively support the Communists, but most Chinese believed the government of the Republic and the Nationalist Party's democratic tutelage, which had transmuted into martial law, had failed them. The costs of democratic tutelage proved considerable for the Chinese in the period from 1912 to 1949, especially under the conditions of war and internal chaos. In the meantime, liberalism lost out, in no small part because liberals were so at odds with each other. Further, most liberals chose to work for and with the Nationalist

---

18. Chiang Kai-shek was unwilling to make the kinds of reforms that would have strengthened China's economy and addressed social grievances, such as the massive exploitation of the Chinese peasantry. From Chiang's perspective, these reforms were politically unfeasible. His major political and financial supporters controlled the very financial and commercial institutions that he should have reformed, and landlord support in the countryside made rural land reform unattractive to Chiang.

Party or the Communist Party (and sometimes both), rather than against either. "Most of them were ready to sacrifice their belief in liberalism to the nationalist or socialist project."[19]

In important respects Chinese liberals differed from Western liberals. A Chinese liberal was someone who embodied what were, and had always been, Confucian values. Chinese liberals were well-educated literati who fulfilled their obligation to serve their rulers as advisors. They spoke "for the people rather than to them" and made no effort to found a new political party or to put forward their own political program. They thought that through their advice alone, they could change the policies and values of China's leaders. But the liberals failed in their mission, and thus liberalism, which had lasted "a decade or two at most"—itself failed.

It failed not because the liberals themselves failed to grasp an opportunity afforded them, but because they could not manufacture the opportunity they needed. Liberalism failed because China was in chaos, and liberalism requires order. It failed because in China the common values which liberalism assumes to exist did not exist, and liberalism could provide no means to bring such values into being. It failed because the lives of the Chinese were shaped by force, while liberalism requires that men should live by reason. Liberalism failed in China, in short, because Chinese life was steeped in violence and revolution, and liberalism offers no answers to the great problems of violence and revolution.[20]

As the party out of power, the Communist Party had the advantage of not having failed to fulfill its promises, and it could promise to fulfill the Three People's Principles: democracy (albeit socialist-style democracy), nationalism (unification and the ousting of foreign imperialists), and the people's livelihood (a welfare state). But who would help the Communists carry out such a program? Although the Soviet Union had repeatedly sold out the Chinese Communist Party's interests in order to advance its own objectives in China, the Party's leaders felt they had little choice. After the United States refused to aid the newly founded People's Republic of China, Stalin's offer of help seemed to be the only option. Moreover, because the Chinese

---

19. Feng Chongyi, "The Party-State, Liberalism and Social Democracy," p. 4. See Feng for an understanding of the significant role played by liberals who adopted the "third way" and supported social democracy (or democratic socialism) from the 1920s through the 1940s but chose to work with either the Nationalists or the Communists—just as they choose to work with one faction or the other of today's Party leadership.

20. Grieder, *Hu Shih and the Chinese Renaissance*, pp. 344–45.

Communists' roots lay primarily in rural areas and fighting a revolution had not prepared them to govern the country, they relied on Moscow to provide models for building a "New China"—models that worked against the implementation of liberal democratic institutions in China.

This, then, was yet another turning point in the story of China's involvement with, and abandonment of its pursuit of, liberal democracy. China's willingness to accept a powerful central state derived in part from its historical experience and understanding of the outside world. Whenever the centralized state had collapsed, China had experienced chaos. The new dawn of democracy in China in 1912 had failed to improve the lives of ordinary Chinese. Social and economic conditions had deteriorated, and war, starvation, and disease plagued the Chinese throughout the period of the Republic of China. Elsewhere, two world wars made the electorates of the European states determined to keep their governments under control, but this same history had made the Chinese willing to accept a powerful state able to defend their interests against foreign incursions. In the Chinese view, European governments had spent huge amounts on armies, thereby causing the loss of tens of millions of lives throughout the world and wasting social resources in order to achieve questionable goals of national territorial expansion. Even worse, the Western liberal democracies had for more than one hundred years taken advantage of China's weaknesses.[21] The Chinese rejected the claims of liberal democracy to universality in part because of their own suffering at the hands of Western liberal democratic states. Not the least of the travesties they had perpetrated against China was the collusion of the Western powers with Japan at the end of World War I to allow Japan to take over Germany's sphere of influence in Shandong.

Western democracy was a weapon of European colonial powers in the late nineteenth century. Viewing democracy as the highest form of civilization created by Europe, these powers felt they had the "right" to impose their vision of society

---

21. In the nineteenth century, the success of the imperialist West in forcing its way into China resulted in "unequal treaties." Under the terms of these treaties, China was forced to cede treaty ports (including the colony of Hong Kong) and to allow "extraterritoriality," by which foreigners in the treaty ports who were alleged to have committed crimes could not be tried under Chinese law. The 1997 film *The Opium War*, directed by Xie Fei, illustrates China's association of Western parliamentary democracy with harm to China. The looting and burning of some of the great repositories of imperial China (such as the Qing dynasty's Summer Palace) and the subsequent assessment of war indemnities for damages done by the Chinese Boxers to Western legations elicited Chinese outrage.

around the world. In political values as well as in geography, race, culture, and social system, it was these powers that had a "consensus" about Western superiority. But this was a consensus not shared by China then because of its suffering under imperialism and during the two world wars. It was such doubts that led many Chinese to realize the cultural and class-bound nature of western democracy.[22]

The Chinese Communists cited China's suffering at the hands of Western imperialism "as the primary reason for the rejection of the capitalist system on moral grounds." Imperialism's impact "on China's class composition made a socialist revolution inevitable, and the revolution made a rejection of capitalism logical."[23] The Chinese people saw their country as a *victim* of other countries, with the result that they were more willing to accept a strong centralized state that promised to protect China from external aggression. In short, China seemed more in need of a strong central government than of a state whose powers were strictly limited by people's rights. In any event, as of 1949, neither the Nationalist nor the Communist Party espoused a decentralized and democratic state.

The Communists believed that Western liberal democracies had fared poorly. For Lenin, World War I was proof that bourgeois democracies started wars in pursuit of their own interests. They had "connived at the eclipse of democracy itself through the concentration of political and economic power into the hands of an irresponsible elite of bankers and military men. . . . In the name of national security, basic liberties . . . had been annulled or curtailed." Lenin, who had viewed capitalism in the bourgeois democracies as "progressive" before 1900, believed it had become increasingly "reactionary" by 1916 as it became "monopoly capitalism." This in turn led to imperialism.[24] Lenin's analysis was the basis for the Chinese Communists' thinking. Much later, in discussions in the late 1980s about this period, Chinese leaders pointedly noted that Li Dazhao had blamed socially destructive Western values for the onset of World War I. In particular, the emphasis on individual freedom had come at the expense of the whole society's well-being. The war itself "cast much doubt on the authority of European civilization."[25]

---

22. Yan Sun, *The Chinese Reassessment of Socialism*, p. 233.
23. Ibid., p. 227.
24. Cited in Harding, "The Marxist-Leninist Detour," p. 162.
25. Yan Sun, *The Chinese Reassessment of Socialism*, p. 226.

Had the failure to prevent two world wars not been enough, the Chinese Communists also denounced the Western democracies for their inability to save themselves and the rest of the world from the ravages of the Great Depression. From the Chinese perspective, the failure of representative democracy to protect ordinary people from economic decline and demagogues led to the rise of Hitler. In short, the world of Western liberal democracy had much to be ashamed of.

The Chinese believe that after World War II, the Western states promoted the concepts of democracy, freedom, and human rights as "ideological weapons to undermine the socialist world or to make Eurocentric judgments on third world countries."[26] The Chinese have hardly been alone in their view. Even in Europe, the Cold War gave rise to the idea that democracy had become "an ideology of conflict and an instrument for the advancement of personal greed."[27] Indeed, in much of the developing world today, especially in Asia, there is an abiding suspicion that the U.S. policy of spreading concepts of (American) democracy and human rights—and now free trade—is really a project to extend American hegemonic power.

But the Chinese offer other, far simpler explanations for their willingness to accept communist rule. For example, a traditional Chinese belief is that if you receive even a small favor, it should be returned tenfold. Thus, because the Chinese Communist Party satisfied the needs of the peasants by giving them land and improving their lives after the Red Army's victory in 1949, the peasants continued to believe they should be loyal to the Chinese Communist Party, despite the cruelties inflicted on them thereafter.[28] Still another explanation rooted in Chinese culture is that of "mental victory." In his tale of Ah Q, Lu Xun drew attention to the psychological disposition of the Chinese to declare a mental victory, to do nothing yet feel good. Thus the Chinese Communists reasoned that since capitalism would inevitably evolve into socialism, China need not bother with capitalism, much less liberal democracy. It could skip directly to socialism and socialist democracy and thereby outstrip the West.[29]

---

26. Ibid., p. 233.

27. Erazim Kohak, "The Faces of Democracy—Looking to the Twenty-first Century," *Kettering Review*, Fall 1995, pp. 50–52, 55–63; excerpted in Myers and Parsekian, *Democracy Is a Discussion*, p. 4.

28. Discussion with Chinese students, Oct. 1997.

29. Ibid.

Finally, many revolutions are fundamentally about who owns property. In this sense, revolutions are also about fairness, that is, a fair distribution of property and, more broadly, of benefits. As Karl Marx argued, the form of state organization and policies depends on which class wins the revolution.[30] A communist revolution is one that attempts to distribute property broadly and equally across the broad masses of people (whereas a bourgeois revolution attempts to redistribute the property of a small aristocracy among the capitalist middle class.) In the case of China in 1949, over 80 percent of the broad masses were peasants.

China's choice of socialism was not . . . [an] unpopular choice. . . . No other independent political force existed in the pre-1949 period that could assume the leadership in the national struggle against colonialism and feudalism. Nor was there any other political force to mobilize the masses of the working class. The CCP's mobilization of the lower classes naturally entailed . . . adoption of socialism in the interest of the lower classes. *Had the class composition of the revolutionary forces been different, the choice of the social system might have been different.*[31]

Were we forced to reject all other considerations of why the Chinese turned away from liberal democracy and point to just one, it would be this consideration of class. Had the major force behind China's revolution in the first half of the twentieth century been entrepreneurs and the middle class, they might well have chosen a political system that favored their class in the disposition of both property and rights. But they was not the major force behind the Chinese revolution. The class that gained power, then, adopted the political system that addressed *its* needs.

A rational cost-benefit analysis reveals much about why the Chinese adopted communism in 1949. The Chinese people, accustomed to expecting the government to take care of them, viewed government from a different angle than would those who focus on defending their rights against government encroachment. Had the Republic achieved peace and security through despotic measures, the Chinese might have eventually clamored for greater democracy. But China's experience was that even the Republic's despotic measures failed to achieve peace. Inevitably, many felt disheartened by their

---

30. See Skocpol, *States and Social Revolution.*

31. Yan Sun, *The Chinese Reassessment of Socialism*, p. 227. This refers to a post-Tiananmen commentary by the historians Liu Danian and Hu Sheng, leading historians in China in the post-1949 period. Italics added.

exposure to democracy and believed a non-liberal democratic system might be better equipped both to restore order and to offer greater benefits to peasants and workers.[32]

There are, then, several explanations for why liberal democracy failed to take root in China. There are also, however, many explanations as to why those who struggled for control of China's government in the first half of the twentieth century chose communism. A nation gets its values in part through its historical experience. We must take China's leaders seriously when they say that both their own history and that of the outside world, *as they understood it*, profoundly affected their decision to adopt communism. From this perspective, China's choice was more than a matter of default. Liberal democracy had failed, indeed, had never been implemented in China. But why turn to communism?

From the perspective of the twenty-first century, we know that communism failed to deliver on many of its promises. But at the time the Chinese Communist Party was founded in 1921 and when it gained power in 1949, communism offered a vision of a better world. Chinese party leaders believed that communism had been successful in bringing a better life to the peoples of the USSR. They did not foresee its potential to be harnessed for evil ends and the problems it would have in China in overcoming ingrained inegalitarian habits.

Marxism-Leninism is a serious political philosophy, full of ideals and hopes. To say that communism is not a legitimate political philosophy is like saying that any political party or religion other than one's own is wrong. There are inherently good values encased in the *idea*, if not the execution, of communism. Indeed, it would be illiberal to suggest that another set of ideas is not as valid as liberalism itself—as if liberalism can tolerate only those who support liberalism. Arguing that communism ultimately failed to achieve the utopia it aimed for is quite different from asserting it had no right to try. As John Dunn has observed, perhaps of necessity revolutionaries tend to be utopians.

---

32. The Chinese have not been alone in considering a political system's ability to guarantee order and stability as taking precedence over all else. Even nineteenth-century democratic theorists in the West considered order as primary, and late nineteenth-century English Fabians, including Beatrice Webb and H. G. Wells, were against extending the vote to the ignorant masses. See Levin, *The Spectre of Democracy*, pp. 40, 62–63.

They may set themselves to achieve what cannot in practice . . . be brought about. But this does not license those who are not themselves revolutionaries to adopt utopian standards of assessment when considering the achievements of revolutionaries. Those who are not utopians must employ nonutopian standards, and for them the criterion of revolutionary success is not some form of social transcendence but simply doing better: a plain improvement on how matters would otherwise have been.[33]

In short, the external critique—from those outside the world of Marxism-Leninism—is not necessarily valid. Needless to say, the internal critique—the critique of Marxism-Leninism by its own standards—has its limits, but it is, arguably, a more appropriate critique.

One can conclude that the arrival of communism in China was shaped by China's historical experience and political thought. The length and breadth of China's history and the overall continuity of political thought for more than two millennia gave the Chinese people a deeply rooted political culture that was primarily authoritarian. Against a backdrop of sinocentrism, xenophobia, patriotism, nationalism, and a certain degree of self-righteousness arising from the belief that China had been, and could once again become, a moral utopia, the Chinese victors in 1949 chose the ideology of an authoritarian moral utopia.

None of the above is meant to gainsay the fact that China has since 1949, especially since 1979, adopted many of the features (including institutions and procedures) of what we call "liberal democracy" and that its authoritarian culture has evolved. Yet, as we shall see, it still lacks some of the critical ingredients that would make it a liberal democratic polity. Moreover, many features of Chinese governance are blatantly repressive and anti-democratic. Certainly China makes no claim to being a liberal democracy and even protests against the idea that it might slide into liberal democratic governance through "peaceful evolution." Like most states today, however, China wants to be viewed as "democratic," albeit with "Chinese characteristics." As the following chapters illustrate, China can fairly claim that it has made progress along this road.

---

33. Dunn, *Political Obligation in Its Historical Context*, p. 226.

4   *The Relevance of Political*
     Culture to Establishing a
     Democratic Political System

It doesn't—or shouldn't—detract from the justice of the students' cause to say
that many of them wanted something different from our kind of democracy. But if
we admit that they did want something different, we may have to think more
deeply about what we mean by freedom and democracy. Embedded in all of our
major institutions is a notion that freedom is a universal value, as desirable to all
rational people everywhere as it is in the United States. Inspected closely, the 1989
protest movement in China does not deny the universality of freedom, but it does
force middle-class Americans to think of freedom in more of an ecumenical fashion. It forces us to consider that freedom must be taken in context, that different
understandings of freedom are possible in different cultures.
                                                        —Richard Madsen

The preceding chapters examined the highly Western, ethnocentric definition of democracy, the fit of Western liberal democracy with Chinese political culture, and why, at critical junctures, China did not adopt liberal democracy. This chapter asks why a country such as China might nevertheless
gradually democratize. It also looks at the relevance of political culture to
that process and considers the following questions:

Is a democratic political culture essential to the establishment of a democratic political system, or is it a consequence of democratization?

If a democratic political culture is a prerequisite, then how democratic
does the culture have to be?

Must a society that lacks democratic themes and attitudes break with its
culture and import those themes and attitudes?

EPIGRAPH: Madsen, *China and the American Dream*, p. 18. Madsen is referring to the student
protest movement in Tiananmen Square in 1989.

How far and how fast can a political culture evolve?

Can a basically authoritarian society handle the challenges of democratization without becoming ungovernable, and if not, how much democratization can it take before collapsing?

How do capitalism, development, decentralization, and democracy relate to one another?

What kinds of problems confront latecomers to democracy?

Finally, which elements of a democratic political culture does China possess?

WHY CHOOSE DEMOCRACY?

When an individual, a ruling elite, a political party, or a particular class that controls a political system allows democratization to proceed, it tries to control the form of democracy as well as the process and the speed of its implementation. Such calculations are based on a "rational" cost-benefit analysis. Those in power assess their own self-interest and then decide how or when to democratize. Specific aspects of democratization may even promote their interests. "Elites choose democracy instrumentally because they perceive that the costs of attempting to suppress their political opponents exceed the costs of tolerating them (and engaging them in constitutionally regulated competition). Debilitating political stalemate, or the memory or danger of collective violence, may loom large in this calculation."[1]

Elites are reluctant to undertake economic or political reforms that might lead to democracy if the immediate costs of democratization are widespread, but the benefits accrue to only a small sector of the society. For example, elites would jeopardize not only their own interests but also those of the broader society, if liberalizing reforms were in the short term likely to lead to widespread unemployment, increasing disparities in wealth, or social instability, while only the intelligentsia or a small entrepreneurial class benefited. In the event, of course, political elites may be unable to control events. Political reforms and economic liberalization generate their own dynamics, and political leaders may find it impossible to prevent the unraveling of existing political culture and institutions. Once the forces of democratization start chipping away at an authoritarian regime, the process may careen out of control before new institutions and values are firmly established. This is essen-

---

1. Diamond, *Political Culture and Democracy in Developing Countries*, p. 3.

tially what happened in Russia and some of the newly independent states of the former Soviet Union.

Where do "the people" fit into the decision to initiate the process of democratization? In many, perhaps most, cases, it is the elite that chooses to allow the political, legal, and institutional changes that bring a transition to democracy. The people benefit from democratization only to the extent the elite permits it. In the case of China, the elite chose to make economic, political, and legal reforms that eroded the underpinnings of an authoritarian system and allowed the emergence of a more pluralistic and democratic system. This, in turn, led to more reforms, which have further eroded the system.

Nevertheless, just because the elite initiated the policy changes does not mean that it was able to predict the consequences of reform or that it acted in a vacuum, isolated from public opinion. Separating out cause from effect in a cyclical process is virtually impossible. China's citizens have, for example, been far from passive, and they have spurred their leaders through countless demonstrations, strikes, and general social unrest. In 1998, there were more than 5,000 reported "collective protests" (protests by more than one person).[2] Such popular protests help shape a leadership's cost-benefit analyses. As each additional reform contributes to democratization, the elite finds it increasingly difficult to withdraw the reforms without meeting serious opposition from the people.

In the following discussion, the assumption is that the Chinese government's questioning of the pace, the scale, or the type of democratization is based in part on a rational cost-benefit analysis *and* includes a genuine concern for the good of the Chinese people. If we were to assume that the government's hesitation is merely a cynical effort to thwart the democratic process and maintain itself in power, a serious discussion of democratization in China would be impossible. Like most other governments, China's almost always undertakes a cost-benefit analysis before introducing a new measure

---

2. A study of 25 of these incidents found that eight were about unpaid wages or pensions, four about corruption, and three about financial scams. Six of the demonstrations had more than 500 participants, and ten had between 100 and 500. State-owned enterprises (eleven cases) and local government offices (ten) were the most common targets. Although the source of this information is a dissident journal, other sources confirm the general nature of these findings. See Pei, "Rights and Resistance," table 1.1, pp. 25–26. Pei's source is *Beijing Spring*, no. 3 (Aug. 1998): 100–105.

of democracy. As it turns out, many of the democratizing steps introduced since reform began in 1979 have enhanced the ability of the Chinese Communist Party to remain in power. In contrast, economic liberalization, administrative decentralization, the growing integration of China into the international economy, and corruption may turn out to be the real enemies of the Party's dominance.

FROM WHERE DO IDEAS
FOR DEMOCRATIZATION COME?

Those countries that have democracy had to "choose" democracy. That is, whether a democratic political system developed through political pressures or by overthrow of a governing elite, conscious choices were made to promote democracy. Economic development, a democratic political culture, and such factors as literacy, which are assumed to be essential to democratization, will not of themselves lead to the *institutionalization* of democracy. Someone must *choose* to institutionalize democracy.[3]

But where do people get their ideas about democratization? Broadly speaking, there are two answers to this question. They come either from their own traditions or from outside those traditions. Rarely can democracy be thrust upon a society without its having embraced the idea of democracy, with the extraordinary exception of post–World War II imposition of democracy on Japan by U.S. occupation forces.[4] One is, in fact, tempted to ask where the West got its democratic culture. It was certainly not from external sources; but many aspects of then-Western culture were also quite antipathetic toward democratic development.

Of course, to frame the issue thus—as a mere question of whether ideas about democratization come from inside or outside a political culture— ignores the view that political culture does not really matter or, at least, that it matters less than such factors as stability, a strong economy, healthcare, education, and science for the successful practice of democracy. At most, political culture as a set of attitudes and practices is only a part of what

---

3. Schmitter, "Interest Systems and the Consolidation of Democracies."

4. For all but a few of the years since the American occupation, one party has been in control; and many critics charge that Japan is really governed by a cabal of corporate giants, government bureaucrats, and politicians.

supports democratization. In the absence of human development and certain social conditions, political culture may indeed matter little. For the time being, let us put aside this difficult question and instead look at the two alternative sources for ideas about democracy.

Democracy Must be Based on One's Own Political Culture

Many of those who believe that democracy has to be a native growth argue that China has, at best, the rudiments of democracy in its own culture. For this reason, only when it evolves away from its traditional culture into a democratic culture will it be able to support a democratic political system. Within China itself, this reasoning led the Communist Party to embrace a party-directed consciousness-raising among the people in order to move China away from "feudalistic" and authoritarian patterns of thought and toward socialist democracy. Apart from everything else, it virtually eliminated the serious study of Chinese history and philosophy. Moreover, since China's feudal culture was built on exploitative property relations, the Party reasoned that the basic redistribution of property after 1949 would further the creation of conditions in which the broad masses would become the ruling class. In the process, the Party established as a goal the minimal conditions of equality of economic means, which it considered the basis of socialist democracy.

Despite claims of some success in preparing the people for socialist democracy through consciousness-raising and the redistribution of property, the government continues to argue that the Chinese people are still plagued by "feudal" (a codeword for superstitious, ignorant, and submissive) thought, practices, and social relationships and are not ready for certain democratic political institutions. China, the argument runs, is not developed enough to be permitted a higher level of democratization. Because of the people's inadequate education and superstitious beliefs, they are easily duped and must be protected against making the wrong decisions. They do not understand the broader national concerns of China and cannot be trusted with a national electoral system. Social relations rooted in the family and traditional ideas of human relationships lead generally to cronyism and corruption; if the people's behavior is not strictly controlled by regulations and punitive measures, the result will be social chaos.

Although all of this may be true in part, it may also be dismissed as a rationalization for the government's unwillingness to democratize more quickly. To its credit, however, the government has sought to remedy these aspects of China's political culture by raising the level of mandatory education. The campaign for a more "civilized" society, which began in the mid-1990s, is also an attempt to educate people into greater public consciousness—to be aware of the effect of their actions on others and the importance of the "public good." The Chinese Communist Party believes that such changes will fundamentally transform China's political culture. The Party's emphasis on the importance of education and consciousness-raising in shaping a moral society indicates that, at least in these respects, the Party remains close to its own roots and even to the roots of traditional China. China's government insists that the development of democracy must be firmly rooted in Chinese culture and sensitive to its own structural and developmental conditions; following a foreign model for democracy could prove disastrous. In contrast, the adherents of China's liberalizing movements in the twentieth century, including many would-be democrats of today, argue that China must look to foreign models and values. Other would-be democrats, however, are wary of this view and believe that China need not rely on any foreign values for democratization—that democratic values are essentially universal, and that they cannot be labeled "foreign."

Let us for the moment accept the argument that a democratic political system must be based on one's own political culture and traditions, that "political forms [follow] changes in social structure,"[5] and that China's political culture and traditions, although not very democratic, are becoming more so. Simultaneously, electoral and legal reforms and administrative and economic decentralization are helping the political system evolve toward a more pluralistic and even democratic form. This, in turn, reinforces democratic dispositions within the culture. In short, a cyclical process is occurring—changes in the political culture lead to reforms of the political and legal system, which in turn push the political culture toward greater democratization. The inklings of democracy visible thus far are the result of an evolutionary, state-controlled, and gradual process, not a revolutionary upheaval. None of this is meant to suggest that the Chinese Communist Party is enamored of the idea of liberal democracy or that it would welcome an advanced form of democracy that included a true multiparty system, national elections, and

---

5. Charles Maier ("Democracy Since the French Revolution," pp. 125–27) argues that in the case of France after the French Revolution, political democracy was inevitable because society evolved democratically.

complete freedom of speech. Nonetheless, institutional and economic development, which are *themselves* helping to transform political culture, have been critical to China's advance toward a more modern and democratic political culture.

Although many Western theorists agree with the fundamental argument that a political system reflects its political culture, they are also concerned about the potential pitfalls of such reasoning. Francis Fukuyama, for example, has noted that despite the importance of political culture for the success of democratization, it is not sufficient to guarantee democracy. For example, Nazi Germany "met virtually all of the cultural preconditions usually put forward as necessary for stable democracy: it was nationally integrated, economically developed, largely Protestant, had a healthy civil society, and was no more socially inegalitarian than other countries in Western Europe."[6] It also had a high literacy rate and a deep respect for science. But, except for its Protestantism, Fukuyama here is referring more to German culture in its developmental aspects than to culture as a set of attitudes, beliefs, and rituals. Nevertheless, the case of Germany indicates that other elements in its political culture (notably, strong nationalism, a concern for racial purity, and a dominant authoritarian strain), in its economic structure (high levels of unemployment and inflation), and in the political system (the appearance of a charismatic figure in troubled times), as well as the international system (a world depression and the heavy reparations Germany was required to pay other countries after World War I) could essentially overshadow these democratic elements. Thus, democratization of the social structure and (aspects of) political culture can be *necessary* to a democracy yet not *sufficient* to sustain it.

Democracy Must Break from One's Own Political Culture

Those who believe that countries must discover democracy from outside their own traditions are persuaded that someone, be it the political elite or the people, must consciously decide to break with an authoritarian political system and adopt a democratic political system. Liberal democratic systems, like communist systems, "did not emerge out of the shadowy mists of tradition" but were instead "deliberately created by human beings at a definite point in time, on the basis of a certain theoretical understanding of man and

---

6. Fukuyama, *The End of History and the Last Man*, pp. 219–20.

of the appropriate political institutions that should govern human society."[7] Adherents of this view believe that a country need not wait until the political culture is transformed: since a democratic political culture is the *result* of a democratic political system, not the condition for it, it can be reshaped by the superstructure of democratic political institutions. "Democracy can never enter through the back door; at a certain point, it must arise out of a deliberate political decision to establish democracy."[8]

As noted in Chapter 3, this was the path of Sun Yat-sen and other revolutionaries in China: they purposefully introduced Western-style representative institutions in 1912 in the belief that they would reshape China's authoritarian political culture. After witnessing the failure of this approach, proponents of the New Culture Movement of the 1920s and 1930s acted on the belief that China's culture had to be democratized *before* introducing democratic-style institutions, but they, too, advocated introducing democratic values and models from abroad. "From Hu Shi and Chen Duxiu through Fang Lizhi, the goal of outward-looking, reformist intellectuals is to use the levers of political power to design and implement a modern culture, which will transform China into a modern state." Many of China's intellectuals, as well as the reform-minded faction within the Chinese Communist Party itself, argued for "replacing feudalism with cosmopolitan culture" in order to bring about modernization.[9] Indeed, from the 1920s to the present, many of China's reformers have believed that "Mr. Democracy" (along with "Mr. Science") will help China become more "modern." They have looked abroad to find out how to reshape its judicial and legislative institutions and gently promote foreign models of democratization. (In the mid-1980s, when the then–Party general secretary Hu Yaobang suggested that Chinese supplement their chopsticks with forks, he really had bigger goals in mind.) Even China's Ministry of Civil Affairs, the leading advocate of free elections at the local level, has stated that "the functions of law are more than a faithful confirmation of reality; law should also be *ahead of [its] time* in some respects so as to guide the development of society and social reforms. . . . The experiences of ancient times and *other countries* can also be studied and made

---

7. Ibid., p. 153.

8. Ibid., p. 220.

9. Kraus, "China's Artists Between Plan and Market," p. 179. For Hu Shi and Chen Duxiu, see Chapter 3. Fang Lizhi, a physicist, was a leading dissident before and during the demonstrations in China in the spring of 1989.

use of in legislation."[10] In other words, China cannot be locked into history. It must move beyond what it has been and look to the outside world for ideas as to how to do so—even if it must at the same time take into account China's "unique culture and traditions."[11] And, as Premier Zhu Rongji said while in Berlin in 2000, China is ready to scrap the socialist legal system and to learn from the German system of justice in order to build a society based on the rule of law.[12]

Those Chinese, whether leaders or intellectuals, who propose looking to foreign soil for ideas, institutions, or practices, risk being attacked by cultural nationalists. The more conservative wing of the Communist Party leadership believes that foreign ideas could endanger stability and threaten Chinese cultural identity. From the nineteenth century to the crackdown on Tiananmen Square demonstrators in 1989, the government has successfully appealed to the Chinese people to support the status quo by rejecting foreign ideas and those who purvey them. Allegations by the government that those propagating foreign values are tied in some way (usually financial) to foreign countries have proved to be a particularly successful strategy in turning a nationalistic population against dissidents.

Within the broader society, much has changed since the 1980s, when a "fever" for Western ideas and institutions gripped China. Anger at Western preaching to China riles a people who believe themselves every bit the equals of Westerners (if not yet as wealthy) and hits the sensitive nerve of China's fear of again being "victimized" by the West. The numbers of active supporters of Western values of democratization, in fact, diminish significantly during tense periods in Sino-American relations—a reflection, apart from everything else, of increasing nationalism in response to perceived anti-China policies. As a result, after Tiananmen in 1989, many of China's leading intellectuals moved away from Western ideas in favor of reviving and refurbishing traditional Chinese ideas. Subsequent events such as U.S. involvement in the 1996 missile crisis in the Taiwan Strait, the U.S. bombing of the

---

10. Research Group on the System of Village Self-Government in China and the China Research Society of Basic-Level Governance, *Legal System of Village Committees in China*, p. 52. Italics added.

11. Ibid., p. 7.

12. China News Digest—Global Editors, "China to Learn from German Experience: Premier," www.cnd.org, July 2, 2000. The Chinese government has invited individuals from all types of institutions, including the U.S. Supreme Court and federal courts, to visit China and discuss how it could reshape its institutions.

Chinese Embassy in Belgrade in 1999, and the U.S. spy plane incident in 2001, had similarly negative effects on Chinese interest in a Western model of political development. There is now a "fever" for traditional culture and values, in which many Chinese intellectuals hope to find support for today's values. They have, in fact, helped create a "love ourselves" fever.

Anti-Western nationalism is propelled by China's New Left intellectuals, who are concerned about the Western orientation of China's modernization and the anti-China theories common in the West. They believe that nationalism must be based on a new Chinese orientation toward modernization and the role of the Chinese state in the international system. This would require a reinterpretation of Confucianism for the modern world and would take into account the government's economic performance and its socialist values. They oppose reforms that introduce Western institutions or Western-style policies of the free market, privatization, no-government intervention, and free trade. And, in foreign policy, although they do believe China should become integrated into the international system, the New Left believes it should be done on China's terms.[13]

Like democracy, Marxism was a foreign idea and perhaps failed to take root in China in no small part for this very reason: "Intrinsic to Marxism, as well as to social Darwinism, liberalism, and other strands of West European thought imported into the East were views on humanity, nature, and society that were fundamentally alien to those nurtured in the Confucian, Daoist, and Buddhist traditions of China and Japan."[14] Marxism did not take hold

13. Zheng Yongnian, *Discovering Chinese Nationalism in China*, esp. chap. 3. Zheng points out, however, that although the New Nationalism is very popular in China because of anger at "anti-China" theories concerning "the China threat" and because of the problems attributed to Western-oriented reforms (notably, corruption, the worship of money, and disparities in wealth), nevertheless, the adoption of capitalism as the "official" economic ideology, the development of a middle class, and many other profound structural changes favor the victory of liberalism. Similarly, at the international level, the power of the New Nationalism is constrained by the growth of liberalism and globalism within Chinese intellectual and official circles. These schools of thought recognize China's interdependence, particularly its economic and strategic interdependence with the United States, and argue that a Chinese voice in the international system is essential if China is to avoid isolation by Western forces hoping to "contain" China's development (see ibid., esp. chaps. 6 and 7).

14. Hoston, *The State, Identity, and the National Question in China and Japan*, p. 403. Marxism also ignored the importance of national characteristics and national identity to China. The possibility of the nation-state ceasing to exist, for example, was incompatible with Chinese political culture in the twentieth century. This is one of the key themes in Hoston's book, as well as a common conclusion in the works of many other China scholars.

even though the Chinese Communist Party promoted it and made enormous efforts to overcome the resistance to it of people steeped in traditional Chinese culture.

If, in spite of these efforts Marxism failed, we should not be surprised if Western concepts, institutions, processes, and values associated with liberal democracy also prove difficult for Chinese culture to absorb. History indicates that Western ideologies, embedded in Western political culture, have not been easily transferred to China. That does not mean that they cannot be, only that it may take longer than we expect.[15] Attitudes that are deeply rooted in culture appear resistant to change.

Exposure to the outside world, participation in the modernization process, institutional changes, the availability of more disposable income and consumer goods, the greater privatization of life, and the impact of communication and technology on ways of thinking and the manner in which people interact with one another and with the government—all these changes are contributing to changes in Chinese culture. It was, in fact, a mere blip in history, a matter of less than twenty years, between the time in the mid-1960s when Chinese were encouraged to "cut off the tails of capitalism" and the 1980s, when they were being encouraged to "get rich." If young people can change almost over night from being filial, obedient, and reserved to being materialistic, independent-minded, self-centered, and sexually open, other aspects of culture can also change.

Political culture does not always overlap with nonpolitical culture. That is, some things will remain "Chinese" regardless of shifts in political culture. It is in food, language, medicine, attitudes toward the body and exercise, and

---

15. The case is often made that Taiwan has been able to democratize and that the People's Republic should be able to as well. Since 1988, Taiwan has made significant progress toward democratization, although serious corruption and "money politics" are endangering its democracy. Although it is not possible here to compare Taiwan to the People's Republic, it should be kept in mind that the starting points for China and Taiwan were quite different. When Taiwan began to democratize in 1988, it already had an economy that was largely decentralized and market-based, whereas the People's Republic has had to make the difficult transition from a socialist to a market economy at the same time that it has tried to carry out political reforms. And its enormous population and far different geopolitical realities make democratization more difficult. In any event, Taiwan began democratizing only a short time ago, and the argument could easily be made that until then, traditional culture helped ensure authoritarian rule in Taiwan, as it did on the mainland.

the overall importance of family[16] that we find Chinese culture. Much of China's culture is, however, far more implicitly political and relevant to creating a more democratic political culture.

DEVELOPMENT, DEMOCRACY, AND CULTURE

Political culture is not only a composite of myths, beliefs, rituals, practices, language, social relationships, and religion but also a level of institutional development. A political culture can, moreover, be modified over time through economic growth and development. If economic development positively affects the cultural environment for democratization, then the more developed China becomes, the more prepared its political culture will be to embrace democratization—although it may not necessarily do so.

On the other hand, if development undermines the very values that have held the society together, even while introducing values associated with democracy, then development may lead to fragmentation and social disorder. Because societal and national integration is critical to the successful establishment of democracy, challenges to the traditional authoritarian social order might well prove so disruptive as to make democratization impossible. The trade-offs are, in short, difficult to calibrate, and it is understandable that the Chinese government is exercising caution in moving ahead with political reform when economic reform has already challenged the cohesiveness of China's culture and society.

For Chinese elites no less than for certain Western theorists, political culture is defined not as a strictly cultural issue in the sense of religion, beliefs, language, rituals, traditions, and social relationships but also as a developmental issue. That is, aspects of development such as national integration, high literacy rates, economic development, a rich associational life (that is, the family is no longer the basis for all activities), and a fairly low level of polarization among social classes are often seen as preconditions for democracy. This conflating of culture as a set of values and culture as development makes sense because a more "modern" culture in terms of development is more likely to be compatible with, and conducive to, democratization than a traditional culture would be. A less developed, more traditional society tends

---

16. Family and family relationships play an important role in both political and nonpolitical culture.

to be more authoritarian and to embrace hierarchical institutions. Thus, although development does not guarantee democratization, a society is less likely to democratize if it does *not* develop. And, in a cyclical pattern, a traditional political culture is likely to *become* more democratic as a society develops more modern institutions.

Of course, modern political cultures can be just as authoritarian as traditional ones, but modern political cultures tend to challenge more traditional values, substituting for them a questioning of hierarchical authority, a focus on the individual even at the expense of the family, and support for values of equality, tolerance, and knowledge. Classic studies of American voting behavior, for example, have shown that the values of tolerance and equality are associated with higher levels of education and urbanization: across the span of voters, those in agrarian backwaters are less likely to adopt liberal values than those in cities.[17] Although the rural culture of one particular society may be more democratic and tolerant than the urban culture of another society, within a given society urban culture tends to be more modern, more democratic, and less authoritarian than the rural culture. Those who are isolated from the world beyond their own traditional political culture tend to remain deeply embedded within that culture. China's rapid urbanization and increasing internationalization in the past twenty years may, then, encourage a more "modern" political culture that is compatible with democratization.[18]

Nevertheless, the Confucian political cultures of East Asia, although authoritarian, centered on the family, and supportive of the values of obedience, hierarchy, and loyalty, have been quite compatible with, indeed an asset to, modernization and development. The Confucian emphasis on the impor-

---

17. Campbell et al., *The American Voter.*

18. Other research indicates, however, that neither greater education nor greater democratic experience (i.e., political participation) leads to greater political tolerance. According to one study, in fact, there is *zero* correlation in the United States between greater education and democratic experience, on the one hand, and greater political tolerance, on the other. Nevertheless, the study shows that people who basically embrace democratic principles can be cajoled into *political* tolerance. At the same time, people, even if they embrace democratic principles and are better educated, cannot be cajoled into *social* tolerance. Thus whereas people might be persuaded to accept perspectives different from their own on, say, the relationship of the state to the individual, they cannot be coaxed into "social" tolerance, for example, a more accepting view on racial integration. Indeed, if a society becomes more democratic and allows greater freedom of individual expression, animosities and intolerance often grow greater. See Marcus and Sullivan, *Political Tolerance in American Democracy.*

tance of education, hard work, and self-sacrifice for the benefit of the family are, in fact, values usually signaled out as useful to economic development. On the other hand, the Confucian emphasis on family, obedience, and hierarchy keeps political institutions and the culture more authoritarian and resistant to democratic notions of equality and individual freedom. These cultural attributes may also encourage corruption, which seriously challenges democracy, for corruption privileges the interests of those with the proper connections and family ties over the interests of the community.

The notion that certain developmental conditions are necessary for democratization resonates with the views of certain Chinese that a country cannot "skip stages" in the advance toward communism. They were persuaded that communism, and even advanced socialism, failed because China tried to "skip stages of development."[19] The emphasis of China's current leaders on preparing the Chinese people in developmental terms for further democratization, then, need not be seen as a cynical rationale for resisting democratization; rather, it is a conclusion based on bitter experience with policies that tried to push China to a stage of development and institutionalization for which it was inadequately prepared.

DEVELOPMENT, DEMOCRACY, AND DECENTRALIZATION

Why is decentralization also relevant to development and democratization? A more developed and decentralized state is more likely to witness the growth of a middle class, whose economic power allows it a remarkable degree of political independence from the government. Governments in states at a low level of development are, moreover, likely to "control a vastly greater share of the most valued economic opportunities" than those in states at higher levels of development. Development also moderates political conflict between classes because as the lower classes become richer, not only do *they*

---

19. These were stages of development defined by Marxism according to the ownership of the means of production. Thus, China's error in the Great Leap Forward of 1958 was skipping the "socialist" stage of development, and the rationalization for moving "backward" in developmental stages toward "capitalism" (called "market socialism") after 1979 was China's unpreparedness for "advanced" socialism. The argument about "skipping stages" has become even more complex in recent years, largely because of "the simultaneous pre- and post-capitalist positioning of the 'primary stage' of socialism" (Sun Yan, "Ideology and the Demise or Maintenance of Soviet-Type Regimes," p. 330).

develop a longer-term and less extreme view of politics, but also "the upper classes are less likely to regard [them] as 'vulgar, innately inferior' and hence utterly unworthy of political rights and the opportunity to share power." Finally, because development leads to increased wealth, the ruling class is less reluctant to relinquish power.[20] The assumption undergirding this view is that in political systems such as China's, many of those in the ruling class hold on to political power in part because it gives them access to the good life. When wealth and privilege can be acquired through economic means, the monopolization of political power loses some of its raison d'être.

China's government has increasingly decentralized the system of economic control of resources, capital, labor, energy, and industrial and commercial inputs and outputs. Most sectors are no longer fully integrated into a centrally planned economy, and real power and responsibility are devolving to the lowest production units. As a result, those with incomes independent from the state, such as the burgeoning middle class, and private production units (factories, companies, individuals, and so on) are beginning to assert their own interests, even sometimes against the interests of the state.

The more a government is involved in managing the various aspects of a society and economy, the more likely it will be authoritarian.[21] Some liberal democratic governments are deeply involved in managing what is in many respects a welfare state (Sweden, France, Germany, England), but the reach of the state under a communist party tends to be deeper and more comprehensive in part because it is linked to a centralized "command" economy. Thus, the dismantling of the institutions of a command economy may lead to a more favorable environment for the growth of civil society.[22] For this reason, one could argue that as the Chinese government withdraws from one area of responsibility after another (such as the economy, the provision of housing, and the assignment of jobs), authoritarianism has decreased. With fewer sectors of the society and economy under its control, the government has less reason, and less ability, to be authoritarian.

The picture in China is, however, complicated: the decentralization of economic, and even some political, power has not necessarily led to less authoritarianism or less bureaucratism. In areas in which decentralization has

---

20. Diamond, "Economic Development and Democracy Reconsidered," p. 116 (citing Seymour Martin Lipset, *Political Man: The Social Bases of Politics* [1960], p. 51), 122.

21. Harik, "Rethinking Civil Society," p. 46.

22. Rose, "Rethinking Civil Society," p. 23.

not been accompanied by privatization, power has gravitated to officials at lower levels, and authoritarian practices have not diminished. On the other hand, when decentralization to lower levels of government has been accompanied by genuinely democratic local elections, local officials and bureaucrats have been more responsive to local needs.[23]

THE HISTORICAL SEQUENCING
OF DEMOCRATIZATION: THE PROBLEM
OF LATECOMERS

The point in history at which a country attempts to develop and democratize will affect its strategy and the speed at which it can develop. A nondemocratic culture may gradually become a democratic one through deliberate policy choices, but this takes considerable time and cannot be rushed. It certainly cannot be rushed to fit the timetables set by Western liberal democratic states. In this regard, Giovanni Sartori notes the difference "between calendar time and historical time. Copying a political model is a synchronic process based on calendar time: we import today what exists today. But in terms of historical time . . . a country like Afghanistan is about where most of Europe was in the dark Middle Ages."[24] The rationale for the formation of a liberal democracy in America was quite simple: freedom of religion and no taxation without representation, with its corollary of demanding representative power for the people. Today, liberal democratic states are expected to offer much more, yet their form of government and their level of institutional development are not necessarily the most efficient and effective for undertaking these additional responsibilities. Thus, although it is arguably rather easy for a country like China to copy a democratic model that has been carefully fine-tuned and calibrated over time from another country, the fact that China lacks a liberal past—even though it is assuredly *not* in the historical time of the Middle Ages—means that, in many respects, it must begin with the same problems with which the countries of the West began when they introduced democratic systems.[25] In short, it must go through the painful step-by-step process of "getting it right."

---

23. Ogden, "Field Research Notes."
24. Sartori, "How Far Can Free Government Travel?," p. 104.
25. Ibid., pp. 104, 107.

Given the differences in political culture, in societal, economic, and political issues, and in historical context, it is all the more imperative that China not take for granted the efficacy of the institutional and procedural solutions chosen by the liberal democratic systems of the West over a period of 200 years. To engage in the "reverse engineering" of democracy is much like the reverse engineering of a computer, or an aircraft, or a business: the final results can be duplicated, but those engaged in the task are far less likely to understand *why* a particular decision was made, for perforce they cannot participate in the discussions that rejected alternative solutions and ideas. For those who copy another country's democratic system, it is just as important for them to understand why a democratic system rejected certain solutions and policies as it is to understand why they accepted others.[26]

The obstacles to democratization that arise from the gap between historical and calendar time are compounded by another fact: China is democratizing in an international economic context that demands rapid action by governments; but democratic governments tend to move more slowly than authroitarian ones. Thus, the countries of East Asia, which entered the international economic system long after the major players were firmly established, have felt compelled to act as unitary states under the centralized "industrial policies" of their governments in order to compete successfully. Centralized economic power has left their governments with greater authority over the political system as well, and this has made it more difficult for various groups, such as labor unions, to challenge policy.

The fact that latecomers to the international economic system and democracy have different characteristics need not, however, be seen as weaknesses or even as obstacles to democracy. Instead, latecomers have necessarily had to approach both the international economic system and democracy differently from states in the nineteenth century and first six decades of the twentieth century. Indeed, it may transpire that "with the passing of time, some of the old democracies might increasingly resemble the new ones in these respects."[27]

In short, there is no one answer as to the best timing, the best method, or the proper ordering of political and economic liberalization. In the capitalist, liberal-democratic West, change occurs through a process of give-and-take

---

26. Ogden, "The Chinese Communist Party."

27. Linz, "Change and Continuity in the Nature of Contemporary Democracies," p. 182, citing Veblen.

and the interaction of thousands of various forces, without tight control from the top. So far, the late modernizers of Asia have chosen an "'authoritarian' transition to democracy."[28] China's timetable for democratization has been shaped by many factors, and China clearly believes the Asian approach is more appropriate to its own needs and conditions. China's "authoritarian transition" to democracy, to the extent the government has been able to control it at all, is directed from the top, where decisions are reached through a process of consensus formation.

But, what time is China? When the same society has both nuclear weapons and primitive religions, when it has both elections and executions, what time is it? China reflects the historical heterogeneity common to many countries.[29]

Must a Democratic Political Culture Precede Democratization?

Can a democratic political culture be created after a democratic political system is institutionalized or is it a prerequisite? In this, as in so many other aspects of democratization, the correct answer is that it is a cyclical, mutually reinforcing process. The more appropriate the conditions for democratization and the greater the number of democratic institutions, the more likely that democratic values will develop; and the more democratic the political culture, the more likely that the conditions and institutions for democratization will come into existence.

It has long been asserted in Western political science that a democratic political system cannot function well, if at all, in a (mass) political culture that is not democratic,[30] just as an authoritarian system of government cannot work in a nonauthoritarian political culture.[31] The greater the compatibility between a political culture and the political system, the easier the pol-

---

28. Fukuyama, "Confucianism and Democracy," p. 23.

29. Alexander Woodside, "Lost Modernities"; the idea comes from Sebastian Conrad's essay "What Time Is Japan?"

30. Chiang Kai-shek tried, in fact, to adapt superficially democratic institutions to the authoritarian strains in Chinese political culture. The experiment was, for this reason (and many others), plagued with difficulties from the start.

31. As James Gibson ("The Political Consequences of Intolerance," pp. 338–39) points out, however, the belief that democracy can flourish only if citizens hold certain values has been seriously challenged by surveys of ordinary Americans. That is, there is increasing doubt that findings of antidemocratic tendencies in mass political culture necessarily have political implications.

ity is to govern. The more a democratic system introduced into a nondemocratic culture reshapes that culture along democratic lines, the more likely democracy will succeed. In short, a democratic political culture need not precede the introduction of a democratic political system, but if the culture is transformed into a democratic one, it has a better chance of sustaining a democratic political system. The broader point here is that cultures are not immutable: they can and do change.[32]

The Chinese themselves have debated the issue of whether political culture is part of the "superstructure" created by the economic "substructure," as Marxists would have it, or whether the political culture can be changed independently of the economic system. "In many respects, Chinese politics for the past hundred years has been about reforming culture. . . . The Tongzhi restoration, the May Fourth and New Life movements, the Yanan rectification . . . the Cultural Revolution, and Deng Xiaoping's reforms have sought to cure China's ills by *using political power to transform first culture, and then China.*"[33] In the debate over modernization (including modernization of the political system) in the 1980s, the Chinese adopted some of the key perspectives of the May Fourth and New Culture movements of the 1920s, namely, that China must modernize its culture in order to modernize China, even if this sometimes meant adopting foreign models and values.

In short, influential Chinese have repeatedly argued, first, that culture can and must be changed in order to modernize; second, that ideas about modern culture may need to be learned from the outside world; and third, that democratic values and institutions are part of, or one of the products of, modern culture. If we assume that a certain type of political culture and political institutions either must precede the creation of a democratic system or follow quickly thereafter, then we must ask whether China has those conditions already or could possibly acquire them in short order if a more democratic political system were endorsed. Finally, as is discussed in Chapter 9, even if people have attitudes conducive to a democratic political culture, they must have the capability to make a democracy work.

---

32. See the recent book by Paul R. Ehrlich, *Human Natures: Genes, Cultures and the Human Prospect*; and the article by Natalie Angier on the book, "On Human Nature and the Evolution of Culture." Erhlich discusses the importance of cultural evolution in shaping human behavior—"all the nongenetic changes that human societies and individuals undergo, from decade to decade and moment to moment, including changes in language, technology, ethics, behavior, alliances, enmities, schemes, and visions."

33. Kraus, "China's Artists Between Plan and Market," p. 179. Italics added.

Elements of a Democratic Political Culture

What, then, are the elements of a democratic political culture? The following list is admittedly an arbitrary composite of aspects of a democratic political culture frequently cited by theorists as widely visible in existing democratic cultures. The intent of the list is to provide criteria for measuring how democratic China's political culture is. Neither the merits of the countless other definitions of a democratic political culture nor the issue of *how much* of any one quality has to be present in a culture before it is adequate to sustain a democratic political culture need be debated here.

1. Individualism and independence;
2. Tolerance of different opinions and behavior;
3. Pluralistic perspectives;
4. A concern for the public good and community;
5. Equality of opportunity;
6. Equality before the law;
7. Voluntary participation by the people in governance;
8. Interpersonal trust; and
9. Cooperative decision making based on bargaining and compromise.[34]

This list does not include those *developmental* attributes usually believed important to democratization, such as high levels of literacy, education, and healthcare; an adequate per capita income; the existence of a sizable middle class; a variety of associations; science and technology; and the institutionalization of democratic processes. These are discussed in the chapters that follow.

This list also leaves out an important attribute of a democratic political culture: self-definition. The perception of the self as "democratic" is important to thinking, and even acting, democratically. An argument can be made that if, for example, people *define* themselves as socialists and accept in theory the principles of socialism, then they are, in a fundamental way, "socialists"—just as those who define themselves as Christians and accept certain basic Christian tenets are "Christians"—even though their behavior may deviate from these principles. Similarly, if people see themselves as being democratic and accept certain democratic principles, then, shortcomings in

34. See, e.g., Almond and Verba, *Civic Culture*; Harik, "Rethinking Civil Society," p. 43; and Diamond, ed., *Political Culture and Democracy in Developing Countries*, pp. 1–4.

their practice of democracy matter little. Most Chinese do not see themselves as "liberal democrats," but, then, they do not see themselves as "communists" either. In fact, unlike intellectuals, who trumpet a wide array of
self-defining labels, ordinary people in today's post–class struggle China prefer not to think of themselves in political terms.[35] Whether, and how much,
this disengagement and lack of self-definition as "democratic" limit the ability of the Chinese to develop a democratic political culture or a democratic
political system is a matter for conjecture.[36]

Based on the criteria listed above, how democratic is China's political culture now? Can it provide the basis for a liberal democratic political system?
The preceding chapters discuss those elements of traditional Chinese political culture that have shaped present-day attitudes toward democracy. Although the conclusions reached in this book do not depend on survey data,
to gain a greater understanding of Chinese political culture, the following
analysis looks at surveys carried out by the Chinese themselves. Although
the surveys may suffer from methodological flaws, they still offer insights on
Chinese attitudes and values. I have tried to select surveys that are not politically sensitive enough to warrant the state's oversight. (For more on the
validity of Chinese surveys, see the Appendix.) Minimally, the fact that the
Chinese government carries out, and permits non-official and international
polling organizations to carry out, surveys suggests the importance the government attaches to public opinion. Just because China does not have a multiparty system or a democratically elected national parliament does not mean
the leadership ignores, or can afford to be ignorant of, the attitudes of the
people.[37] In fact, the government itself is known to carry out surveys of pub-

---

35. Whether thought of as a "political" definition or not, one identity that most Chinese
choose is "patriot." Events such as the conflict with Japan over Diaoyu Island in 1996, the return of Hong Kong to Chinese sovereignty in 1997, the bombing of the Chinese Embassy in
Belgrade in 1999, and the incident with the U.S. spy plane in 2001 bring out how important
this identity is to so many Chinese. Of course, not to be "patriotic" is, from the Chinese perspective, almost the equivalent of being a traitor.

36. For a national survey (2,200 respondents) in 1988 on what a "Chinese political person"
is, see Zhang Mingshu, *Zhongguo zhengzhi ren*. This survey asked questions about the respondents' willingness to discuss politics or participate in the political system, general attitudes
toward politics, possible reasons for participating in a demonstration, sources of political
knowledge, etc.

37. For a forceful argument about the importance of Chinese public opinion in shaping
policies during the reform period, see Alan Liu, *Mass Politics in the People's Republic*.

lic opinion precisely to find out public attitudes toward itself and whether the people would take to the streets to voice their anger.[38]

Characteristic 1: Individualism and independence.   The Chinese view of individual independence is complex, and Chinese are certainly able to hold potentially contradictory views. They seem to believe obedience to superiors is essential, yet they still feel independent in making decisions about their lives. For example, respondents in a major social science research project conducted from 1991 to 1994 strongly endorsed the statement "I live in my own way, no matter what others will think of me."[39]

Another survey, taken to measure attitudinal changes on the part of the public in Chinese cities from 1993 to 1995, provides some evidence about Chinese attitudes toward authority, the public good, and individual values such as independence. This poll, done by the Lingdian (Horizon) Company (a private Chinese company) in collaboration with the international survey firm INRA, in five major Chinese cities, compared attitudes of Chinese urban students, parents, and teachers with those in 41 other countries. It concluded that Chinese parents pay attention to inculcating in their children such individualistic values as "independence," a "high regard for knowledge and learning," and "being strong."[40] Indeed, this international comparative study found that Chinese citizens lead the world in terms of identification with values such as "independence" and "emphasis on learning and knowledge." For both values, the level of identification is higher in China than in North America and Western Europe. On the other hand, the Chinese completely ignored other values associated with democratic political cultures, such as "tolerance and respect for others." And, their levels of identification with such values as "sense of responsibility," "loyalty," "having a belief," "obe-

---

38. One survey, conducted in 1988 but not released until 1994, showed a decline in respect for the Chinese Communist Party; see Zhang Mingshu, *Zhongguo zhengzhi ren.* Another, conducted in October 1994 by the Beijing Market Research Consultancy, was a survey of 2,500 people in ten cities. It was an internal *(neibu)* publication (for leaders only) and was entitled *Will the Mainland Fall into Anarchy?* Its purpose was to measure popular support for the Party; see Gilley, "Whatever You Say."

39. Few questions received such a high level of endorsement. The average for all age groups was over 80 percent in the categories of "fully agree" and "basically agree" (see Sun Jiaming, *Guannian diaocha,* question 15, p. 216).

40. Yuan Yue, "1995–1996 nian Zhongguo chengshi shehui wending yu gongzhong xintai," p. 119. The five cities were Beijing, Shanghai, Wuhan, Guangzhou, and Harbin.

dience," and "being imaginative" were the lowest among the countries surveyed.[41]

These are quite surprising results, since they suggest that the Chinese (even if they do not value being imaginative) are quite independent in their thinking and not very obedient, the opposite of what is normally assumed. Of course, not all surveys lead to such a conclusion. For example, in another survey, in response to the question "What are a person's most important qualities?" (in rank-order for fourteen characteristics), the top results were:

1. honest;
2. upright;
3. brave;
4. confident.[42]

And, when asked to "rank the most uncivilized behaviors" (out of twenty possibilities), the number-one choice was "lack of filial piety."[43] Since filial piety is usually associated with obedience, this would seem at least superficially to contradict the findings of the other survey.[44]

Characteristic 2: Tolerance of different opinions and behavior of others and *Characteristic 3: Pluralistic perspectives.* A survey of Chinese attitudes has concluded, like well-known studies of the American voter,[45] that the "less educated are less tolerant and more authoritarian." But the study has gone even further,

---

41. Ibid., p. 119.

42. Zhongguo shehui kexue yuan, Shehuixue yanjiusuo, Zhuanxing ketizu, *Zhongguo qingniande toushi,* table 2-14, p. 109. This study was done in 1988 and studied both urban and rural youth. In this study, "youth" ranged in age from 16 to 35.

43. Ibid., table 2-13, p. 108. Interestingly enough, this was followed by "criticizing people behind their backs" (rank 2), and "using work to profit oneself" (rank 3).

44. On the other hand, since the time of the two polls, the methods, and the respondents were different, comparing the results of the two does not make a lot of sense. Indeed, a poll that was not restricted to young people and was carried out in Beijing in 1996 indicated quite different results when respondents were asked to make one choice of the most important element in social life: 58.27 percent chose "respect rights and freedom," and 25.59 percent "filial piety." The other choices were "return favors" (2.92 percent) and "make lots of friends" (13.0 percent). Still, filial piety came in a strong second. See Fan Yu and Dong Min, "Guomin falü yishi diaocha," p. 8. There were 1,438 valid responses, with a sample distribution that included most work categories, and a broad distribution of age and education levels. Individuals were interviewed at their homes.

45. Campbell et al., *The American Voter.*

to conclude that the Chinese "*at each level of educational attainment*" are "less tolerant than people in other countries."[46] Such a conclusion opens itself to a myriad of possible interpretations, but certainly one interpretation is that the government's intolerance of dissent resonates with a broad cultural intolerance of difference and dissent.

Another survey of urban Chinese youth points in the same direction. For example, over 76 percent of those polled basically agreed with the following statement: "Freedom of speech does not mean allowing the publication of reactionary speech."[47] Yet the same respondents indicated greater tolerance in response to the statement, "Imported movies that are not in harmony with our country's spirit should be censored." Some 55 percent basically opposed such censorship. This does suggest (at least in 1988, before the backlash against the West created by the Western response to Tiananmen and other events) a substantial openness on the part of many Chinese youth to new ideas, even those from abroad.[48] Generally speaking, urban youth in most societies would be the group with the most progressive values. In China's case, moreover, 1988 was the year when free speech had reached the highest level since 1949; yet the results are not consistent. Another survey, this time of a different group of respondents (Beijing residents age 18 and older), suggested that by late 1995, general tolerance within this broader age group was considerable: 87.3 percent of respondents seemed tolerant of individuals with different political views and believed they should have "the same

---

46. Nathan and Shi, "Cultural Requisites for Democracy in China," pp. 112–13. Nathan and Shi, however, asked a loaded question to elicit this response: the question concerned the tolerance of the respondent for those who sympathetically speak, teach, or publish about Gang of Four. Considering the suffering imposed on the Chinese people by the policies of the Gang of Four during the Cultural Revolution, even the most tolerant individual in China would probably oppose the right of others to speak sympathetically about the Gang of Four. It is no more surprising to find intolerance for those who speak sympathetically of the Gang of Four than to find intolerance in Germany for those who speak sympathetically about Hitler.

47. Of those responding, 51.9 percent "agreed," and 24.3 percent "agreed somewhat" with the statement; the other two choices were "do not agree very much" and "disagree" (Zhongguo shehui kexue yuan, Shehuixue yanjiusuo, Zhuanxing ketizu, *Zhongguo qingniande toushi*, p. 144). "Youth" was defined as those between the ages of 16 and 35.

48. The data are as follows: 24.9 percent "opposed" censorship, and 30.7 percent "did not agree very much." The other two categories were "agree somewhat" (17.1 percent), and "agree" (25 percent) (ibid., p. 107).

legal rights and protections as anyone else," and 94.3 percent favored greater freedom for the press to expose wrongdoings.[49]

My own experience in teaching in China in 1996–97 was that even college-educated Chinese youth, inside or outside the classroom, were decidedly uncomfortable with ideas that were not supported by the Party (some of which they classified as "reactionary" ideas). Indeed, most of the students were so locked into a mindset about the "truth" on such topics as history and international relations (as defined by the Chinese Communist Party in Chinese texts) that they could almost not comprehend an alternative viewpoint, much less accept it.

But does it matter whether or not Chinese mass political culture is intolerant if this intolerance has no political implications? According to James L. Gibson, forty years of research on American political culture has shown a low level of mass political tolerance. For example, "only 6% of the American people would allow the group they most dislike to enjoy the same political rights and opportunities that the rest of the polity enjoys." Indeed, only 13.3 percent of the American people would even allow the *fourth* most disliked group to enjoy the same political rights![50] Historically, Americans accepted slavery until the second half of the nineteenth century, and the Ku Klux Klan remains highly intolerant and antidemocratic in its objectives,[51] as do many other groups and broad sectors of society. In spite of this, the American political system is considered a strong democratic system.

What conclusions can we draw about the relevance of cultural tolerance or intolerance for difference and dissent in China's mass culture to its prospects for democracy? Gibson observes from his studies of American political culture that the attitudes and opinions of individuals are formed through interacting with others. As a result, even if it is a fear of social rejection or isolation that causes most individuals to conform to broadly held views, they

---

49. Zhong et al., "Political Views from Below," table 3, p. 476. This survey used a multi-stage random sampling procedure. The authors believe that other findings in the survey contradict any clear conclusion about Chinese wanting a freer society, especially if it entailed a trade-off with a stable society.

50. Gibson's conclusions are based on a 1987 survey; see "The Political Consequences of Intolerance," pp. 338–40.

51. Friedman, *The Politics of Democratization*, p. 27. A response to his argument might be, however, that the very fact that American political culture tolerates, and even defends, the right of such organizations as the Ku Klux Klan to exist today indicates that the overall culture is democratic.

themselves may not understand the process as coercive. It is simply part of socialization. Mass political intolerance is politically relevant, then, because it helps create "a culture of political conformity" in which ordinary citizens impose constraints *on each other*. It is the intolerance of a country's ordinary citizens toward the "rights . . . of those with unpopular political views" that limits political liberty. "People learn from the political culture that intolerance is widespread, that it is acceptable, and that there are tangible risks to asserting views that the intolerant culture finds objectionable. Political intolerance can thus define the context of politics for many citizens."[52]

Is it the fear of possible sanctions for deviance, then, that causes many Chinese to be intolerant of difference in others—and to avoid "difference" in themselves? And does the fact that it is fear of sanctions not just from society *but also from the state* that makes the relevance of intolerance greater in China than in the United States?[53] Or is the more important variable China's political and cultural homogeneity, which builds on and reinforces homogeneity and hence closed-mindedness?[54] Might the perception of a diminishing likelihood of punishment by the state in China mean, then, that the level of intolerance *within the culture* would decline? And might China's greater exposure to the heterogeneity of the world through internationalization lead to greater tolerance?

Evidence for a growing tolerance by the state of a greater range of speech and actions is presented in the following chapters, but, without empirical data, the question of the impact of this on a more deeply entrenched cultural intolerance is only speculation. In the case of the United States, however,

---

52. Gibson, "The Political Consequences of Intolerance," p. 339.

53. This is not to say that Americans believe there are no significant restraints by the state on their speech and action. Gibson (ibid., 342) found that whereas "blacks are *much* more likely to perceive constraints on their freedom than are whites," an "astoundingly high" percentage "of both blacks and whites . . . feel that the government would not allow them ordinary and quite conventional means of political participation. One-quarter to two-fifths of white Americans believe that the government would prohibit them from expressing their opposition through conventional speech and assembly activities." These activities include organizing public meetings, protest marches, or demonstrations, making speeches criticizing government actions, and publishing pamphlets. To wit, 55.7 percent of black and 61.8 percent of white Americans were unwilling to participate in a demonstration, and 51.4 percent of black and 55.8 percent of white Americans were even unwilling to wear a button to work or in public which expressed an unpopular viewpoint.

54. Gibson (ibid., p. 344) speculates that homogeneity "is not conducive to political tolerance."

Gibson concludes that there is a connection between intolerance in the political culture and a lack of political freedom; in particular, people who feel that their own freedom is limited are less likely to grant freedom (in speech and actions) to their political adversaries.[55]

Characteristic 4: A concern for the public good and community. Several questions on Chinese surveys test the degree of "concern for the public good" in China. In "The Change of Values of Contemporary Chinese Youth" (with "youth" ranging from ages 16 to 35), for example, those interviewed were asked to respond to the following statement: "Personal affairs are minor, no matter how important to you. The state's affairs are big, no matter how minor they are to you." Results from the survey in 1988, when youth in urban and rural areas were treated separately, and the survey in 1990, when their responses were merged, were quite similar: some 60 to 70 percent "agreed" or "agreed somewhat" with the statement.[56]

Similar survey results were reported in response to other sayings popular in China in the late 1980s. The survey results reveal a concern for others, "the public," the community, or the collective, rather than for oneself. In the 1988 survey, 73.3 percent of urban youth agreed or agreed somewhat with the statement "The value of life lies in giving, not taking" (attitudes of rural youth were not reported); in 1990, 70.3 percent of urban and rural youth (the two groups were not disaggregated in the 1990 poll) had the same responses.[57] Disagreement with the negatively phrased statement "If one does not live for himself, he would be killed by heaven and earth" was substantial: in the 1988 poll, 59.1 percent of urban youth and 56 percent or rural youth responded "do not agree" or "not too much in agreement." In 1990, 67.6 percent of urban and rural youth disagreed.[58] In 1988, 69.5 percent and in

---

55. Ibid., p. 350.

56. To be precise, in 1988, among urban youth 30.7 percent "agreed somewhat," and 28.3 percent "agreed"; among rural youth, 28.7 percent "agreed somewhat," and 39.4 percent "agreed"; and in 1990, for both urban and rural youth, 31.6 percent "agreed somewhat" and 36 percent "agreed." The other two possible responses were "not too much in agreement" and "do not agree." See Zhongguo shehui kexue yuan, Shehuixue yanjiusuo, Zhuanxing ketizu, *Zhongguo qingniande toushi,* p. 64.

57. Ibid.

58. Ibid. This seems to be a popular question to ask. A 1994 survey also asked this question and found 40.1 percent of Beijing youth agreeing to it. The same question was asked of young workers in Xi'an in 1991, and only 8.3 percent agreed (Shi Xiuyin, "Zhongguoren shehui xinli 90 niandai jincheng," table 10, pp. 20–21).

1990, 65.7 percent of those polled indicated agreement with the statement "Selfishness is the source of all evils."[59] Close to three fourths of those surveyed in both polls responded affirmatively to "Small rivers will be dry if there is no water in big rivers."[60] The responses to two other statements, however, reveal less than a full commitment to the public good. In 1988, among urban youth only 19 percent agreed fully and 32.4 percent agreed somewhat that "one should enjoy oneself whenever possible"; in 1990, the figures were 11.3 and 29.2 percent, respectively.[61] And in 1994, only 47.1 percent of youth surveyed in Beijing and 29.3 percent of those in Guangzhou chose the response "I should help others even if I suffer loss in doing so."[62]

The 1994 poll may reflect the government's emphasis during the reform period on the individual pursuit of wealth. Indeed, at present, Chinese characterize themselves in ordinary conversations and in the media as primarily interested in making money. During the Cultural Revolution (or more precisely, the "ten bad years") from 1966 to 1976, "Serve the People" (*wei renmin fuwu*) was one of the key slogans, and those whose actions "served the people" were considered more revolutionary and politically correct than those who did not. To admit openly to pursuing individual enrichment was considered reactionary and downright dangerous. But by the time of a 1981 survey of 1,000 youth in Fujian and Anhui provinces, only 15 percent responded that they wanted to "serve the people," and by 1989, "none of the 1004 Guangzhou high school students surveyed saw this as important."[63] A 1989 survey that asked youth the same questions as a 1981 survey found that personal interests had clearly replaced a concern for national interests as the students' top priority.[64] And, in a 1991 survey conducted by the Communist

---

59. Zhongguo shehui kexue yuan, Shehuixue yanjiusuo, Zhuanxing ketizu, *Zhongguo qingniande toushi*, p. 65.

60. Ibid. The meaning of this saying is that if the larger collective (say, the nation or the province) does not have resources, the smaller units (the villages or cities) within that collective will not have resources.

61. Ibid., p. 66. Traditional Chinese cultural values do not support this saying, but this is a measurably lower positive response to values showing concern for the public good than was indicated in response to the other questions.

62. Shi Xiuyin, "Zhongguoren shehui xinli 90 niandai jincheng," table 10, pp. 20–21. This is, incidentally, a value embodied in the Lei Feng model of serving others.

63. Kwong, "Ideological Crisis Among China's Youths," pp. 252–53.

64. In 1981, 37 percent of students responding indicated that their top priority was to "have a high salary and a secure life" or to "be a well-educated person with a high social status"; this was balanced by the 36 percent who put "making our motherland rich and powerful" first.

Youth League, 47 percent of 2,000 respondents indicated it was correct to help a fellow student "only if it did not interfere with one's own work."[65]

What is behind this growing trend of being more interested in one's own material advancement than in the public good? What relevance, if any, would this have to a concern for the political liberties of themselves and others? At least four elements in the Chinese context explain this concern for personal rather than the public welfare. First, there is widespread disillusionment with the Cultural Revolution's motto of "Serve the people," which was cynically used to advance personal interests. As a consequence of the Cultural Revolution, people have lost their idealism and interest in such values as "selflessness" and "revolution." Instead, they want better living standards. Second, China's opening to the outside world exposed the Chinese people to the gap in living standards between themselves and others, even as events were thoroughly discrediting communist political ideology, which emphasized the importance of serving the country. Third, the collapse of socialist regimes in the former Soviet Union and the states of Eastern Europe suggested that the idealistic goals of socialism and a concern for the public good were not feasible. And fourth, economic reforms after 1979 indicated that abandoning socialist policies would make a better life possible. People began thinking of how they could get rich, not how they could serve the public good, as a result of these reforms.[66] The government's promotion of individual efforts to "get rich" and become the locomotive of development for the rest of the country also contributed to this attitude.

Tension between a concern for the public good and self-serving individualism is built into a democratic political culture. The issue is balance, but it is hard to achieve that balance or measure it, or even to know what "balance" between these two values would be conducive to liberal democracy.

Characteristic 5: Equality of opportunity. Thanks to Marxism and Maoism as well as Confucianism, there is a strong belief in China that everyone should have an equal opportunity to succeed. The examination system under the imperial Chinese system was philosophically rooted in the idea that the right to succeed should be open to every male (women need not apply). Ideally,

---

By 1989, 62 percent put their personal interests first, and only 21 percent favored national interests (see ibid., p. 253).

65. Ibid., p. 257.

66. Shi Xiuyin, "Zhongguoren shehui xinli 90 niandai jincheng," p. 13.

nothing but talent mattered: one's family's place in the social pecking order was immaterial to the individual's chances to succeed. In practice, only if a male was adequately funded by his family or clan would he gain the opportunity to succeed on the exams, and thereby open the door to becoming part of China's ruling class.

The Chinese Communist Party has been committed to education for all, even though it has not necessarily been able to realize this ideal for financial and other reasons. The many efforts at "affirmative action" policies for women, minorities, and those disadvantaged by poverty (the most extreme of which was carried out during the Cultural Revolution) have also made a difference. Universities in China today are full of students from remote and impoverished villages who have managed to do well on the entrance examinations. On the other hand, efforts to institutionalize equal opportunity have been hindered by such policies as "key schools" (where resources are concentrated) and, in the 1980s and 1990s, by social attitudes (and the law) that deny an education to children of rural immigrants residing in cities without an urban residency permit. (This policy is, however, undergoing change.)

The commitment to equal opportunity is also hindered by the culturally supported practice of relying on family and "connections" (*guanxi*). Although the government now has a civil service examination in place that evaluates candidates strictly on a merit basis, family and "connections" still matter. Once recruited into a government institution, moreover, Chinese youth believe their chances for advancement are hampered if they do not have relatives or *guanxi* in that work unit to smooth the way and "protect" them.[67]

This conclusion contrasts with the results of Andrew Nathan and Shi Tianjian's 1988 survey of Beijing citizens. They concluded that there was a "sense among ordinary people of *having access to* the system."[68] Their survey suggests that a sense of equal access comes from an ability to establish *guanxi* with officials through the exchange of favors, gift giving, and bribery, but my own impression is that Chinese are profoundly aware of the inequality in ac-

---

67. Many of the students I taught in 1996–97 at the Foreign Affairs College in Beijing (run by the Foreign Ministry as a college to train students for its ranks) did not want to enter the Foreign Ministry because they had no "connections" or family there to promote their career (Ogden, "Field Notes and Interviews, China, 1996–1997").

68. Nathan and Shi, "Cultural Requisites for Democracy in China," p. 111. Italics added.

cess because of highly differentiated abilities to cultivate personal relationships. Those Chinese who come from more powerful families, attend better schools, or have more wealth or goods to offer feel they can influence government and party officials in ways that favor their self-interests. In contrast, those Chinese who lack such advantages *know* that they are at a disadvantage vis-à-vis government and party officials.

China's political culture therefore represents a mixture of attitudes toward equal opportunity that range from cultural support for equal opportunity and a perception of equal access to a belief that equal opportunity and equal access are fictions. The Chinese government's commitment to nine years of compulsory education for all Chinese youth has, however, advanced the institutional framework so necessary for a change in political culture, a change that supports the idea of equal opportunity based on achievement criteria.[69]

Characteristic 6: Equality before the law. Through its judicial circles, the Chinese government is demanding reforms in the judicial system that will support a citizen's expectation of equality before the law. The key ingredient of such reform is the elimination of interference by members of the Chinese Communist Party. This has been aided in part by the Chinese press, which is increasingly taking the initiative to report cases that expose party interference in the judicial process. Such interference, however, remains a problem that, if not intractable, is at least deeply entrenched, especially at the lowest levels of the judicial system, where the competence and integrity of judicial personnel is often questionable. The hurdles to reforming the judicial system so as to institutionalize equality before the law are formidable. The difficulties in eliminating Communist Party interference is compounded by the dearth of competent and honest judicial personnel and the importance of "connections" and bribery in determining judicial decisions. Officials at the local level are resisting the reform of the legal system, and popular participation in (or at least acquiescence to) what is essentially a culture of judicial

---

69. In 1990, only 71.4 percent went on to middle schools. As the millennium neared, the Chinese Civil Education 2000 supervisory group, together with the Ministry of Education and UNESCO, was able to announce that 98.9 percent of all children were enrolled in primary school and that 87.3 percent of all primary school graduates went on to enroll in secondary school ("UN Report Says China's Illiteracy Rate Down in the 90s," *China News Digest,* Dec. 13, 1999). Again, however, these figures probably exclude the children of rural immigrants living without a *hukou* (residency) permit in the cities.

corruption likewise undermines reform efforts. Even when the courts arrive at a decision through proper procedures and "equality before the law" is the reigning principle, court orders frequently go unenforced. This reinforces the cynical belief that only power and connections, not the laws, matter. (Reform of the judicial system is discussed at length in Chapter 6.)

Characteristic 7: Voluntary participation by the people in governance. A 1995 survey of townships in five provinces and regions indicated that the overall participation rate in free elections in villages in 1995 was 82.5 percent; 84.2 percent indicated they would argue strongly if denied the right to vote, and 76.2 percent said they would be willing to be elected as representatives to people's congresses.[70]

According to a 1990 study by the University of Michigan in collaboration with Beijing University in four rural counties, in the three activities indicating voluntary political participation (activities that do not require mobilization by local cadres) and requiring individual initiative—writing letters or offering suggestions to a cadre, working with others to solve a local problem, and contacting a delegate to the township or county people's congress or a member of the village council—fully one-third had "engaged in at least one of the more demanding, initiatory behaviors of cooperative efforts, voicing, and/or contacting" within the preceding two years.[71] The study concluded that "the objectives of participatory acts extend beyond the particularistic goals of self-serving individuals that often are assumed when observing presumably rigid and tightly controlled polities."[72]

The Michigan-Beijing study also noted the remarkable resemblance between correlates of participation in China and those in more developed participatory systems. "Indeed, an innocent observer looking at these results might easily locate them in a Western democracy. Particularly striking is the influence of education and sex as determinants of participation. Residues of an historically strong patriarchal culture continue to influence mightily the political activity of ordinary citizens. By the same token, the privileges and

---

70. On the other hand, of the women polled in eleven provinces in 1990, only 17.3 percent indicated a willingness to serve as representatives to the people's congresses (Shi Xiuyin, "Zhongguoren shehui xinli 90 niandai jincheng," table 7, p. 18).

71. Jennings, "Political Participation in the Chinese Countryside," p. 364. Jennings conclusions are based on the study in which he participated: see Eldersveld et al., *Four-County Study of Chinese Local Government and Political Economy, 1990.*

72. Jennings, "Political Participation in the Chinese Countryside," p. 362.

skills associated with education are fully as operative, if not more so, as in Western societies."[73] This study of voluntary participation, as well as other research on participation in China's political system, such as voting in village elections, leads to the tentative hypothesis that the Chinese people are to a degree already acting as if they are members of an at least partially democratized political system.

Characteristic 8: Interpersonal trust. Interpersonal trust in China is low. The Chinese people are remarkably distrustful of individuals outside their own families and personal connections. Francis Fukuyama has argued that a lack of interpersonal trust accounts for the relative scarcity of corporations in Chinese communities throughout the world: Chinese enterprises rarely grow larger than family-run companies because their owners are reluctant to turn over management to anyone outside the family.[74] Fukuyama's study examined overseas Chinese communities (and included businesses in Hong Kong, Taiwan, and Singapore), but the same lack of interpersonal trust remains evident in the style of doing business in China in the past twenty years, a period in which private businesses emerged. The result is that, whereas in most countries, three to five business firms, at most, would control over 80 percent of each industry or product line, in China, it would be remarkable if the top three to five companies controlled even five percent of the market.[75] Reasons other than traditional Chinese culture for this lack of trust are, most notably, the many "struggle" campaigns and mass movements that turned friends, colleagues, and neighbors against one another.[76]

Mainland Chinese engaging in business with foreigners prefer that those foreigners be culturally Chinese (from Taiwan, Hong Kong, Singapore, the United States, or elsewhere). This no doubt stems largely from their familiarity with the expectations of Chinese culture in regard to such matters as honor and "face," as well as the (informal) enforcement of contracts.[77]

---

73. Ibid., p. 371.

74. Fukuyama, *Trust: The Social Virtues and the Creation of Prosperity.*

75. Dwight Perkins, Harvard University, New England China Seminar, Oct. 16, 2001.

76. Many other factors, such as China's weak enforcement of contract law, could also account for this lack of trust.

77. Foreigners who have lived in China for extended periods often comment that although the Chinese people are usually friendly, it is difficult to establish genuine friendships with them. No doubt this stems in part from concerns about the possible problems connected to involvement with foreigners, and xenophobia.

One survey carried out in China, however, attributed the low level of trust to traditional introvertedness and today's irregular market behavior and morality.[78]

Characteristic 9: Cooperative decision-making based on bargaining and compromise. In the economic arena, the Chinese have pursued cooperative decision-making based on consensus-formation since 1949. Whether in agricultural communes or urban factories, determining such things as work points and defining the major and minor "contradictions" required endless discussions. Decisions by the elite behind the closed doors are also made by consensus formation.[79] But, in *public* discourse at the national level, the word "compromise" is anathema, and in Chinese political culture, it connotes weakness. China's government still tends to speak in a belligerent, didactic, and moralistic manner that does not hint at compromise or concessions. China is right; other countries are wrong. China is "victorious" in its struggles against hostile forces. China has "principled stands," which other countries question at their own peril. This aversion to compromise and a belief in an absolute right and wrong, good and bad, penetrate the entire culture. The opening of China to many other values and standards of behavior since 1979 has, however, permitted gray areas to emerge, especially in the arts, literature, and film, but also to some extent in international negotiations. This, in turn, is affecting the overall political culture of China.[80]

CONCLUSION

There is little agreement on the role of culture in democratization. It may be that culture defines the possibilities and parameters but does not determine which choices are made. Cultures are composed of a diversity of often con-

---

78. Jiang Liu et al., *1995–1996 nian Zhongguo*, p. 238.

79. Lu Ning, *The Dynamics of Foreign Policy Decisionmaking.*

80. In a survey of Chinese youth (ages 16–35) that asked, "If you disagree with others, what method do you use?" and that allowed for different responses for the methods used with the elderly, superiors, experts, and public opinion, the results were fairly evenly spread over all categories (persuasion, introspection, deference [give up opinion], insistence, or put aside). The "persuade" response was, nevertheless, the largest (ranging from 26 to 51 percent), and when combined with "insistence" on one's own opinion, suggested that the Chinese are more likely to argue a point than might be expected (Zhongguo shehui kexue yuan, Shehuixue yanjiusuo, Zhuanxing ketizu, *Zhongguo qingniande toushi*, table 1-10, p. 67).

tradictory strands. But why do certain strands become dominant? In China's case it has frequently been the leadership that has chosen which cultural elements to build on, eliminate, or ignore. Yet Chinese society is itself a participant in the formation of its own culture, even if often unconsciously so. Which aspects of traditional Chinese culture are compatible with democratization and political development as opposed to, say, economic development, remains, however, a topic of heated debate among scholars and policymakers both in China and abroad.[81]

Since 1949, China's leadership has chosen specific elements out of the many possibilities offered by Chinese culture as valuable to its institutional restructuring and modernization policies: hierarchy, elitism, (Maoist) populism, submission to authority, patriarchy, secrecy, an emphasis on the collective good, and centralized control. Like the leaders of many developing societies, China's leaders have often opted to build on certain cultural traditions as the best way to modernize, even though they were simultaneously trying to promote antithetical ideas embodied in Marxism and Mao Zedong Thought.

An examination of the nine characteristics of democracy listed above indicates that China has inklings of a democratic political culture in certain respects and not in others. Of course, the same could be said of China's authoritarian political culture: it is authoritarian in some respects, but not uniformly so. In any event, we cannot simply add up China's "score" on these nine characteristics and claim that they define China's political culture as either democratic or authoritarian. Arguably, characteristics not included that would shift the balance toward authoritarian are the continuing Chinese preference for a strong government and a view of those in government as "parents" responsible for the welfare of the people. Indeed, in a 1995 international study comparing China with 40 other countries, 51 percent of the Chinese urban public supported strong government. The corresponding figure for the United States is 25 percent, for Western Europe 29 percent, and for Eastern Europe 27 percent.[82] The Chinese preference for strong govern-

---

81. Ogden, *China's Unresolved Issues*, p. 352. For a summary of some of the viewpoints concerning the importance of the cultural variable, including those of Hannah Arendt, Raymond Meyers, Thomas Metzger, and Lucian Pye, see Johnson, "What's Wrong with Chinese Studies?" pp. 920–23. See also the many books and articles on this topic by Tu Wei-ming or Lucian Pye; and Dittmer and Kim, *China's Search for National Identity*.

82. This is a survey done by the Horizon Survey Research Company as part of a worldwide survey of 41 countries conducted by INRA, an international survey research organiza-

ment may, however, be interpreted as a concern on the part of the urban population that the government more effectively handle China's collapsing social order.[83]

Although the survey findings discussed above have interesting implications, we do not yet know, in the case of either China or any other country, the threshold for each particular value that would guarantee *enough* democratic content in the culture to support democratic institutions.[84] Nor do we know what particular mix might work. Could a people exhibit a high degree of support for, say, three or four of the values and none at all for the other five or six and still have sufficient democratic content for a transition to liberal democratic institutions? Even though many countries have made the transition from authoritarian to democratic polities, these questions cannot be answered in any scientific quantitative way. But we can at least hypothesize that were there very low support within a political culture for most of these values, the transition to democracy would be far more difficult.

Today, ordinary Chinese people as well as their leaders describe their traditional culture as "feudal," meaning that it was built on hierarchical relationships. From the time of Confucius more than 2,000 years ago, those in subordinate positions were expected to be obedient to their superiors. Mainstream Chinese culture has also been deeply elitist, for it is a society in which everyone ranks him- or herself (and are ranked) as superior to some and subordinate to others. But it has also been a highly individualistic culture, in the sense that Chinese, beyond their loyalty to family, do not tend to display the type of group loyalty that is seen in some other cultures, such as Japan's; and that they seem to be interested far more in individual self-enrichment than in the collective public good.

Respect for education is important in Chinese culture. This has provided the basis for its meritocratic and egalitarian yet also hierarchical culture. Education not only opens up the possibility of democratic participation but also gives some the ability to get rich or to gain political, economic, and intellectual power—and to gaze disdainfully on the less educated as "uncivilized."

---

tion; see Yuan Yue, "1995–1996 nian Zhongguo chengshi shehui wending yu gongzhong xintai," p. 124.

83. This international comparative survey, like so many, shows that one of the major concerns of the urban population is social disorder. In 1993, social order ranked seventh on a list of eight, but by 1995 it was number one (ibid., p. 113).

84. I am indebted to Andrew J. Nathan for correspondence (July 2000) concerning this issue.

China has, in short, contradictory values in its culture that have resulted from its multiple traditions. The dominant tradition has been decidedly authoritarian; yet there are many attitudes widely present in China today that are robustly antiauthoritarian.

It is true that "all cultures are rich in conflicting political potentialities." Were China today a democratic polity, we would have pointed to elements in China's culture that provided underpinnings for democratization.[85] It is also true that "a cultural attitude considered conducive to democracy may also help buttress authoritarianism."[86] But it is precisely because democratic elements in China's culture were *not* the dominant ones that an authoritarian system remained entrenched throughout the centuries. This is not to say, however, that China cannot overcome such obstacles as its Confucian heritage might present. Thus, although it may be true "that modern liberal democracy grew out of Christian culture, it is clear that democracy emerged only after a long succession of incarnations of Christianity that were inimical to liberal tolerance and democratic contestation. All in all, the obstacles posed by Confucian culture do not seem any greater than those posed by other cultures."[87] In short, although China lacks the intellectual roots for liberal democracy that the West had in such thinkers as Hobbes, Locke, and Rousseau or Jefferson and Madison, it may look outside for those intellectual roots, or it may choose simply to adapt the institutions and practices— the final products of those intellectual roots—and not bother with adopting wholesale a foreign philosophy of democracy.

In truth, ordinary Chinese people, and even many intellectuals, are not really interested in the intellectual roots and justifications of democracy today. They just want a political system that works. For this purpose, they look to the practices of other countries for cases of institutionalized democracy that have both succeeded and failed in maintaining order, bringing prosperity, and enhancing individual rights. This is to be expected; for just as China is inclined to engage in reverse engineering of Western technology, so, too, is China likely to engage in reverse engineering of democratic prac-

---

85. "Confucianism stressed that all could be educated; Daoism focused on freedom, the Legalist school of political philosophy was making all, including the rulers, equal before the law; and Mohism was premised on egalitarianism and the yin-yang school on compromise" (Friedman, *The Politics of Democratization*, p. 27).

86. Nathan and Shi, "Cultural Requisites for Democracy in China," p. 111.

87. Fukuyama, "Confucianism and Democracy," p. 30.

tices and institutions—even if, as noted above, this could cause serious problems. Although there is a heated debate within some intellectual circles over democratization in China, many dissident intellectuals and students have not been deeply concerned about understanding the fundamentals of Western democracy. Rather, they like what they see in terms of the practice of democracy and think it would be beneficial for China. If the strongest argument China's leaders could muster against instituting democracy were precisely that it had no intellectual roots in China and that China must flow with the tide of its own traditions, this would be the best counterargument.

When the multiple traditions that already existed in China combined with the new traditions introduced by Marxism-Leninism and Maoism, both contradictions and paradoxes in China's political culture resulted. Leninism reinforced the hierarchical pattern of institutions and values common to traditional Chinese political culture, and Marxism and Maoism emphasized egalitarian values, including the right (and obligation) of people to speak out against those in the ruling class who abused their power. Yet Confucianism had likewise asserted (according to most interpretations) that the people had the right to "cut off the mandate" of a ruler who ruled improperly or ineffectively. Could this provide the perfect rationale for free elections at the national level in China?

Arguably, a complete break with China's cultural traditions and the present-day political institutions built on that culture is not necessary to produce a form of democracy that works. Instead, it would be possible to give China's existing political institutions a greater democratic content— although the process could be more difficult than beginning with a clean slate. Still, it is worth noting that the People's Republic of China has many of the institutions that provide the basis for democracies elsewhere: legislative, judicial, and executive branches of government. Although the "division of powers" among these branches has been minimal, by the mid-1990s, the National People's Congress had become less of a rubber-stamp legislative body and had begun to challenge reports and appointments made by the central government and submitted to it. Similarly, China has always had an electoral system, but it assumed an undemocratic one-seat, one-candidate form. With the electoral reforms of the 1980s and 1990s, however, elections at the local level have become remarkably democratic. The legal system has likewise undergone significant reform as it moves toward equality before the law and greater protection of the individual against the powers of the state.

In arenas such as the judicial and legislative systems, then, it is not new insti-tutions but rather new content and new procedures within those institutions that have to be implemented. Because the institutions already exist, moving toward greater democratic content need not be disruptive (see Chapter 6).

Although some have argued that "Chinese political culture today is nei-ther especially traditional nor especially totalitarian,"[88] many would chal-lenge this view. But the broader implication of this view is that political cul-ture is no excuse for not reforming China's political system to make it more democratic. And, because cultures are not immutable, they can change along with the political system. If one were to adopt the alternative perspective, namely, that a political structure cannot escape its culture, that culture locks a society into a particular political structure forever, or that cultures are fixed and do not adapt to new conditions, this would mean that any society and its political system would be locked forever into what it already is. Since this is not the case, it is possible that over time a nondemocratic culture such as China's may evolve into a democratic one. This may happen through delib-erate choice, carefully constructed government policies, or the developmental or modernization process, which, arguably, has some democratizing aspects to it. But all of this takes considerable time, and the process cannot be rushed. Certainly it cannot be rushed to fit the timetables set by Western liberal democratic states.

If one argues that "history is not destiny"[89]—that although the past shapes the future, it does not determine it—then it may be suggested that the particular past a country has—authoritarian, neo-authoritarian, com-munist, theocratic, whatever—matters little. Because cultures are always evolving, the notion that political culture is "a body of changeless values and orientations dating back to the formation of the community (or the myths about it) many centuries ago" is misleading. Frequently, these historical lega-cies and traditions can be incorporated into or coexist with contemporary beliefs.[90]

There is no need, then, for the Chinese political system to be trapped by its existing culture and history. The past, even if it shapes the future, cannot

88. Nathan and Shi, "Cultural Requisites for Democracy in China," p. 98.

89. Edward Friedman (*The Politics of Democratization*, p. 13) argues for this perspective in the case of China.

90. Diamond, "Conclusion," in idem, ed., *Political Culture and Democracy in Developing Coun-tries*, pp. 411–12.

lock in the future indefinitely. And if one adopts the viewpoint that "democratic cultures are the consequences not the causes of democratization," one can simply ignore the argument that "democracy requires an independent, individualistic, rational, and tolerant culture as a soil in which to grow."[91]

How then to explain the contradictory propositions noted above: that China's traditional political culture was deeply authoritarian, yet democratization *is* happening? Socioeconomic theory suggests that democratization can occur even if the political culture is predisposed to oppose it because of the deterministic power of such forces as capitalism, the free market, and economic development. In other words, democratization is not an isolated political process. Economic forces may force the culture and political system to accommodate new notions. Even if the Chinese people are happy with their authoritarian culture, the inexorable forces of the market and capitalism, which help create a middle class with self-interests and a demand for rule by law, may overpower the conservative cast of traditional political culture. This does not mean that China's traditional political culture is being jettisoned; rather, there is a new shape to the values and practices of China. The result is a Chinese authoritarian system trying to accommodate the tensions generated by democratizing forces.

---

91. Friedman, *The Politics of Democratization*, p. 20.

5 Individual Rights, Democracy, and a Cohesive Community

> Now that nobody believes that Leninist communism is a path to the good society, perhaps we can entertain the idea that American-style liberalism isn't for everybody either. Perhaps there are different paths to a good society.
> —Richard Madsen
>
> Buy a home and become a boss.
> —Newspaper advertisement, Shanghai

Preceding chapters have noted that the Chinese think, speak, and write in a vocabulary that differs from that used in the liberal democratic West; they define problems differently; and they have their own ideas about what is important.[1] Many traditional concepts are so embedded in the language that they condition how new concepts are understood; the Chinese word usually translated as "propaganda," for example, has positive implications of "education" rather than "distortion of the truth," as it does in English.[2] And legal

---

EPIGRAPHS: Madsen, *China and the American Dream*, p. 58; This advertisement for Yongde Homes appeared in *Xinmin wanbao*, Shanghai, May 11, 1994, p. 15; cited in Davis, "Introduction: A Revolution in Consumption," in idem, *The Consumer Revolution in Urban China*, pp. 8–9.

1. Recent pathbreaking research in social psychology indicates that culture and language may profoundly affect not only what people think about but also how they think. In particular, in comparing East Asians and European Americans, researchers have found that East Asians pay far more attention to context and relationships, think more "holistically," have a higher tolerance for contradictions, and are less linear in their thinking. Dr. Richard Nisbett heads this research project at the University of Michigan (see Goode, "How Culture Molds Habits of Thought").

2. Hong Kong's *South China Morning Post* now translates *xuanchuan* (propaganda) as "publicity." Hence, the Chinese Communist Party's Xuanchuanbu is now called the "Publicity Department." Perhaps Beijing realized the negative connotations of the word "propaganda" in English and suggested the newspaper use "publicity" instead, although it may have been the newspaper itself that simply decided it was a more appropriate translation.

concepts promoted by the West, such as "justice," are interpreted within the context of China's legal culture, itself primarily a product of China's traditional culture.[3]

Given the different mindset that pervades the culture's practices, institutions, and even language, to suggest that the Chinese necessarily think about freedom as it is thought about in the West is like suggesting that someone who has never thought about, say, Christianity, would, upon hearing about its mindset, goals, and values, immediately understand it and want to adopt it as a guiding set of principles. Similarly, it must be asked whether people can feel deprived of freedom if they have never experienced it. That is, the simple exposure to an idea does not perforce allow one to understand it, accept it, or reproduce it. The very pervasiveness of a particular cultural tradition in a given society's practices, institutions, and even language means that the members of that society will not reproduce an idea or institution, such as free speech, in the form it is found in the culture of origin. They will view it through the lens of their own culture and adapt it to meet their needs. Nor will they necessarily find a foreign idea persuasive or a foreign institution desirable. Indeed, their lack of experience with a particular institution may prevent them from understanding it. As Giovanni Satori has remarked of freedom:

How can we ascertain whether the state of "being free" is in fact appreciated by most people in most places? . . . It is pointless to enquire about preferences [of] people who have never been offered alternatives, that is, anything to compare. . . . Innumerable people cannot prefer something to something else because they have no "else" in sight; they simply live with, and encapsulated within, the human (or inhumane) condition they find. The notions of value and freedom are highly abstract, analytic concepts that are utterly unintelligible to a large majority of the world's inhabitants.[4]

In other words, education and experience shape desires and preferences, and access to information about the outside world expands people's awareness of possibilities. A lack of knowledge and experience makes it "difficult to desire what one cannot imagine as a possibility."[5] In short, people do not

---

3. "The China Rule of Law Initiative," symposium, sponsored by the Harvard Asia Law Society, May 5, 2000.

4. Sartori, "How Far Can Free Government Travel?" p. 103, quoting from his own *The Theory of Democracy Revisited* (1987), p. 272.

5. "Introduction," in Nussbaum and Sen, *The Quality of Life*, p. 5.

necessarily desire the same thing. Even if democracy is "obviously" preferable to any of the alternatives, a people will *prioritize* what is most important to them, including aspects of a democratic system, on the basis of their cultural and historical experience.

It can safely be argued that in the absence of trade-offs such as societal disorder or the end of the paternalistic state, most people want more freedom. But in China as elsewhere, more freedom has often entailed inequality and instability. As discussed in earlier chapters, the Chinese are conditioned by their own philosophy, experience, and history to be concerned about the trade-offs between greater freedom and chaos rather than the trade-offs between freedom and government control. Thus, although some intellectuals and leaders have emphasized issues of freedom and control, except during the vibrant May Fourth movement that began in 1919, this has not been a dominant theme.[6]

Today, some of China's leaders, as well as intelligentsia in universities, think tanks, the arts, the mass media, and the Chinese Academy of Social Sciences, are paying serious attention to these topics. Indeed, in the 1980s and 1990s, as China steadily became more interconnected with the rest of the world, increasing attention was devoted to the issue of the balance between freedom and control. But China's leaders, journalists, writers, academics, and dissidents do not necessarily think about freedom, rights, and democracy in the way we might expect or want them to. And just as the Chinese people incorrectly believed throughout the 1950s and 1960s that the inhabitants of Western capitalist states lived in hellish conditions of chaos, crime, violence, and poverty, it would be incorrect for us to assume that the Chinese long for Western-style democracy and individual rights. For example, a 1990 poll conducted among rural and urban Chinese youth (ages 16 to 35) that asked "What do you consider the greatest happiness for yourself?" had the following results:[7]

---

6. Chiang Kai-shek chose "order" over extinction (i.e., eradicating the Communists before confronting the Japanese) in the 1930s in a policy known as "put the country in order before fighting the invaders" (*rangwai bi xian annei*). Similarly, rural development strategy in the People's Republic was characterized by the policy of "first tackle disorder, then poverty" (*xian zhiluan, hou zhiqun*).

7. Zhongguo shehui kexue yuan, Shehuixue yanjiusuo, Zhuanxing ketizu, *Zhongguo qingniande toushi*, table 1-13, p. 68.

Category	Percentage of respondents
Successful career	43.5%
Warm family	42.3
Understanding friends	30.5
Good health	18.4
Be respected	14.8
Contribute to society	14.3
Freedom	**9.2**
Wealth	8.9
Good position and power	4.8

Clearly, the percentage of respondents who chose "freedom" pales in comparison with the combined totals of those opting for "a successful career," "a warm family," "understanding friends," "good health," and "be respected."

A 1995 collaborative survey research study carried out in Beijing by Chinese and American researchers put the choice of individual freedom and political democracy within an entirely different context, but it, too, indicated that these qualities were not as cherished as others, notably national peace and prosperity. The following is the rank-order of the responses to the question, "Which do you feel is the most important quality?" (only one choice was allowed).[8]

Category	Percentage of respondents
National peace and prosperity	56.0%
Fair administration of justice	13.0
Social equality	10.0
Individual freedom	**6.0**
Political democracy	**5.8**
Public order	4.7
Don't know	4.2

Similarly, in a 1998 empirical survey of 350 students at ten universities in Beijing, respondents were asked to prioritize the top twelve development is-

---

8. Dowd et al., "The Prospects for Democratization in the People's Republic of China" p. 371, table 1. The authors' cross-tabulation of this information with education indicates, remarkably, that the university-educated respondents have much less interest in individual freedom than do those with little or no education (p. 373, table 3).

sues for China over the next five years. The following gives the percentage, in rank-order, of those choosing each issue as the first priority:[9]

Category	Percentage of respondents
Promote economic development	28.3%
Maintain economic stability	25.4
Develop a society where ideals count more than money	15.7
Protect the environment	11.1
Maintain social order	7.4
Develop a friendlier and more humanistic society	4.3
Increase public participation in government decisions	3.4
Fight against crime	1.4
Maintain a strong national defense	1.1
Defend freedom of speech	**1.1**
Increase public participation in community decision-making	0.6
Stop inflation	0.0

As the table indicates, freedom of speech, in the context of other priorities, was once again accorded a low value.

Nevertheless, as the Chinese gains a greater knowledge of democracy through increasing contact with the outside world, we may well expect them to revise their views on democracy and individual rights. The increasing amount of resistance and protest in China may, in fact, reflect a rapid growth in "rights consciousness," which is itself contributing to the changing nature of "democratic resistance." In the 1980s, resistance was characterized by more direct and confrontational tactics, but by the late 1990s, tactics had grown increasingly indirect, such as recourse to the legal system. In other words, the Chinese now have both a more developed rights consciousness and more institutionalized democratic processes for advancing and protecting their rights.[10]

---

9. Wong Koon-kwai, "The Environmental Awareness of University Students in Beijing, China," table 7.

10. See Pei, "Rights and Resistance," pp. 20–40.

What follows is an effort to examine the progress China has made in gaining rights. As much as possible, these rights are considered as components of China's movement toward democracy, not as separate goals in and of themselves. That is, they are not viewed as "human rights" separable from the issue of the nature of the polity. Some of these rights do not, in any event, even appear in the 1948 Universal Declaration on Human Rights.

INDIVIDUAL FREEDOM

In much of the world, individual freedom—by which is usually meant an array of individual (civil) rights—has become a mantra of government, the public, and the press, of all political persuasions. Yet even within the West, there are different views of freedom and the limits that must be placed on it. Further, notions of civic responsibilities (and laws to enforce those responsibilities) are meant to assure that freedom is not abused. In applying the Western concept of individual freedom to China, however, we tend to use an absolute concept of freedom—that is, unfettered freedom—and argue that the Chinese government has no right to constrain individual freedoms in any way. In doing so, we ignore the problems faced by China and much of the developing world in governing a population that often acts irresponsibly, and even illegally, if for no other reason than that people in a society characterized by scarcity are always pushing at the limits of control in an effort to sustain and better their lives.

Freedom is, of course, not the only criterion for evaluating a society; nor is freedom the only goal of any society. To be meaningful, freedom must entail the right to choose something that is considered of value. Moreover, the minimal requirements for a good life—food, clothing, housing, education, medical care, security—must already be in place. As Nelson Mandela said, the Republic of South Africa will not be truly democratic until all its people are educated, fed, and housed.[11] Or, as Christine Korsgaard has written, "New Liberalism" objects to "Old Liberalism" because it is "a dreary form of libertarianism. If the only thing that the state can guarantee is freedom, and not a good life, there will be no grounds for guaranteeing things that seem

---

11. Nelson Mandela, speech on receiving an honorary degree, Harvard University, Sept. 18, 1998.

clearly to be part of the good and not of freedom—food, medical care, an economic minimum."[12]

In short, for freedom to have any real meaning, an individual must have the means to take "advantage of one's rights and opportunities." Freedom cannot be guaranteed "without guaranteeing its worth. . . . The poor, the jobless, the medically neglected, the unhoused, and the uneducated are not free no matter what rights they have been guaranteed by the constitution."[13] Indeed, even Francis Fukuyama would argue that only when the "social changes that accompany advanced industrialization, in particular education" have occurred can "poorer and less educated people" demand that their dignity be recognized.[14] This concern with the *capacity* for freedom is critical to understanding the issue of freedom in China.

HOW SHOULD WE THINK ABOUT
RIGHTS AND FREEDOM?

Individual civil rights do not occur within a vacuum. They are experienced and implemented within the context of the need for a community identity and for certain "secondary" rights (primarily welfare rights). Freedom is highly subjective and contextualized. The context for evaluating "freedom," especially degrees of freedom, shifts continuously. This environment is critical to the conclusions reached both by the Chinese about themselves and by those trying to understand how they might feel. How free do various sectors of the Chinese population perceive themselves to be? How much does it matter to them that they lack more individual rights? And how can we best understand what it might mean to a Chinese person to have more freedom and individual rights?

Civil (Procedural) Rights and Welfare (Distributive) Rights

Scholars of American politics recognize that civil rights and welfare rights do not necessarily develop simultaneously and, in fact, may be inversely related such that "support for one indicates opposition to the other." Thus, voting preferences during the Progressive Era of the early twentieth century

---

12. Christine M. Korsgaard, in Nussbaum and Sen, *The Quality of Life*, p. 58.
13. Ibid.
14. Fukuyama, *The End of History and the Last Man*, p. 206.

reveal that support for women's suffrage, a civil rights issue, "was disjunctive with support for welfare reforms." More broadly, the government's attempts to address the worst effects of industrial capitalism through positive welfare policies negatively affected civil rights by contracting the electorate and even encroaching on the individual's freedom to make lifestyle choices. In doing so, the United States created a "policy paradox legacy": the institutionalization of a "regulatory welfare state" in combination with "a reactive civil rights state."[15] This policy paradox also reflected "layered political development": different institutions and branches of government are likely to generate contradictory processes and results because they develop at different rates. Policy paradoxes are also created because of the many levels of government in the United States.[16]

Moreover, conflict over values and policies arises because of "multiple traditions" that are in competition with one another. In the United States, for example, values and policies do not derive from a single liberal tradition, and policies that decrease civil rights are not necessarily "cultural contradictions." Rather, they are part of "a complex heterogeneous cultural context marked by 'inconsistent combinations.' New doctrines challenging some ascriptive inequalities are embraced even while other policies . . . reaffirm and entrench those same inequalities."[17]

In short, the path toward democracy is not necessarily linear or irreversible,[18] and the level at which it is pursued within a polity depends on the policy area involved. Governments, such as Taiwan and South Korea before the late 1980s, have had liberal economic policies but authoritarian governance. Nor have welfare and civil rights policies in the United States developed at the same pace; occasionally policies have even regressed. Thus, it makes little sense to judge China by rigid criteria of political development. There is no one model.

---

15. McDonagh, "The 'Welfare Rights State' and the 'Civil Rights State,'" pp. 265, 267, 270–71.

16. Ibid., p. 268, citing Karen Orren and Stephen Skowronek, "Beyond the Iconography of Order: Notes for a 'New' Institutionalism," paper presented at the Annual Meeting of the American Political Science Association, 1991. See also Huntington, *American Politics*.

17. McDonagh, "The 'Welfare Rights State' and the 'Civil Rights State,'" pp. 267–268, citing Roger M. Smith, "Beyond Tocqueville, Myrdal and Hartz: The Multiple Traditions in America," *American Political Science Review*, Sept. 1993.

18. Huntington, *The Third Wave*.

Freedom Is Subjective and Relative

As Andrew Nathan and Shi Tianjian noted in their 1988 survey of Chinese attitudes toward government control, the data show little support for their own assumptions about, on the one hand, the "objective role" of the Chinese state (that it "exercises close control over society") and, on the other hand, "the subjective perceptions of ordinary citizens." Thus, "although the regime in China controls the daily lives of citizens more totally than was the case in the five nations [U.S., U.K., Germany, Italy, Mexico] studied by Almond and Verba [in the early 1960s], *fewer citizens are able to identify such control.*"[19] This difference in perception may result from a different definition of government. The "work unit"—which until the 1990s controlled virtually every aspect of an urban person's life—may not be viewed by the Chinese as part of the "government." Indeed, many people consider their work unit a source of "support" (55 percent) rather than an "authority" over themselves (22 percent). Even those who view the work unit as "a source of control" do not consider it a leviathan: "its full authority is rarely exercised and people find ways to disregard it."[20]

In addition, compared to the populations of West Germany, Italy, and Mexico, the Chinese in 1990 felt more politically effective and were more likely to expect equal treatment from the government.[21] Similar results are

---

19. The Chinese also perceived that the government had a lower "salience" and effect on their lives; only 9.7 percent said the government had a great effect and fully 71.8 percent said it had no effect on their lives. This puts it at the level of Mexico during its initial stages of democracy, but nowhere near the percentages for the liberal democracies. In the United States, 41 percent of those polled said the government had a great effect on their lives. The figures for the United Kingdom and Italy were 33 and 23 percent, respectively (see Nathan and Shi, "Cultural Requisites for Democracy in China," pp. 100, 104; italics added). Nathan and Shi are referring to Almond and Verba, *The Civic Culture.*

Another study done at about the same time (fall 1988 through May 1989), conducted by the Chinese Academy of Social Sciences, found similar trends. In response to the question "How much influence does the local government have over your daily life": 22.3 percent said it had a "very great" effect, 46.9 percent said "some influence, but not great" and 27.9 percent said "not very much at all," for a total of 74.8 percent for the last two categories (Zhang Mingshu, *Zhongguo zhengzhi ren,* table 2.1, p. 31).

20. Lum, *Problems of Democratization in China,* p. 70.

21. Surprisingly, in spite of the high degree of government corruption and abuse in China, "Chinese citizens in 1990 were not very different from Germans, Italians, and Mexicans at the time of *The Civic Culture* (published in 1963) surveys in their expectation of equal treatment." Sixty-five percent of the Germans polled, 57 percent of the Chinese, 53 percent of the Italians,

reflected in the 1988 survey of urban youth in China. An overwhelming majority disagreed with the statements "Reform is the business of leaders, and it is useless for ordinary people to become involved" and "Reform has nothing to do with me."[22] In other words, they felt they had a role to play in governance. Thus, we cannot assume that the Chinese perceive their government as tyrannical just because we would find a similar level of governmental control oppressive.

Nor has the definition of freedom remained the same during the five decades of communist rule. According to one study, "freedom" (*ziyou*) was associated with the right to choose one's own spouse in the 1950s, with political anarchy in the late 1960s, with thought liberalization in the 1970s, and with individual rights in the 1980s. A poll of Chinese in the early 1990s found that they associated freedom with the following rights:

Right—	*Percentage of respondents*
to choose one's own lifestyle	30.4%
to choose an occupation and to change jobs	10.9
to express personal opinions freely	3.7
to espouse one's own political beliefs	2.2
to join various social groups	0.8
to gather and parade	0.4

Overall, however, the respondents most desired a happy life and wealth.[23]

---

and 42 percent of the Mexicans expected equal treatment from the government. What is perhaps even more impressive in terms of perceptions of equal treatment is that 50.8 percent of those with no education in China expected equal treatment, compared with 30 percent in Italy and 19 percent in Mexico (Nathan and Shi, "Cultural Requisites for Democracy in China," pp. 107–9). China's comparatively high marks may well stem from the more equal treatment of women, especially compared with Italy and Mexico in the early 1960s. On the issue of political efficacy, see ibid., p. 107, question 2.

22. Over 64 percent disagreed with the first statement, and over 78 percent with the second statement (Zhongguo shehui kexue yuan, Shehuixue yanjiusuo, Zhuanxing ketizu, *Zhongguo qingniande toushi*, tables 3-7 and 3-8, p. 144). These responses may, however, say more about authoritarian attitudes (i.e., the leadership leads, we follow) than about attitudes toward participation. On the other hand, in a survey conducted in Beijing at the end of 1995, 72.3 percent agreed with the statement that "suggestions and complaints made by the public to the government are often ignored" (Zhong et al., "Political Views from Below," table 7, p. 480). Thus, the conclusion that most Chinese still feel efficacious because they get much of what they want through gift giving, banqueting, and connections might make sense.

23. Shi Xiuyin, "Zhongguoren shehui xinli 90 niandai jincheng," pp. 12–16.

In most respects, then, control and freedom are subjective. Just as important, they are also relative. For the Chinese, their sense of freedom, their sense of how many rights they enjoy, is relative to their perception of the degree of freedom and the number of rights other peoples have, especially those in societies at a comparable level of development or in other Chinese cultures; they are relative to other values, with which freedom or rights might be viewed as a trade-off; and they are relative to China's own past experience of freedom.

Freedom and rights are not, moreover, isolated political concepts, and they do not gain meaning merely in contrast to "control." Rather, freedom and rights are also cultural, social, and economic concepts, even though greater freedom and rights in any sphere are implicitly political. Instead of being viewed merely in juxtaposition to control, then, freedom and rights may be viewed as providing options and opportunities.

Chinese academics have themselves made this point. For them, the measure of democracy is the extent to which a society provides its members with ample choices in all fields and an ability to make those choices.[24] As Amartya Sen puts it, people must have "capabilities," which are in themselves "freedom," not just the means for getting freedom. And individuals lack the "capability to function" unless they have the "freedom to achieve well-being."[25] Capabilities provide the means to act freely and make meaningful choices. "When we assess inequalities across the world in being able to avoid preventable morbidity, or escapable hunger, or premature mortality, we are not merely examining differences in well-being, but also in the basic freedoms that we value and cherish."[26] In a similar vein, Larry Diamond concludes that the leaders in democratization among the developing countries are those that have been successful at developing human potential rather

---

24. Liu Jinxi, "Minzhu xin lun," pp. 83–84.

25. Sen, *Inequality Re-examined*, pp. 49, 50. In his discussion of counterfactual choice, Sen states: "One values living without malaria, desires such a life, and would have chosen it, given the choice. Being able to live as one would value, desire and choose is a contribution to one's freedom. . . . The fact that the term 'freedom' is used in the expression 'freedom from malaria' is not in itself decisive in any way, but the relation of the results to what one would have chosen . . . is a matter of direct relevance to freedom—the freedom to choose to live as one would desire" (ibid., p. 68).

26. Ibid., p. 69.

than those that use "more capital-intensive strategies that view basic health and literacy needs as 'consumption' that must be deferred."[27]

To see the "state" in a confrontational relationship with society, with state control necessarily coming at the expense of freedom or rights and against the wishes of society as a whole, is to miss their complex and interdependent relationship. As Alexander Woodside wryly puts it, Western social scientists invented the dichotomy between state and society just to annoy the people of East Asia.[28] Indeed, even associations and interest groups are seldom confrontational with the state in China (see Chapter 7). Rather, they collaborate, often to the mutual benefit of the state and the associations, on a variety of issues.

In addition, China's citizens tend to view the state as a caretaker, with responsibility for fulfilling the paternalistic role of a patriarchal state. Thus, demonstrations of unemployed workers sitting in front of governmental offices may not be protests *against* the state as much as pleas for state assistance. The increasing number of protests in China are often cited as evidence of the growing disenchantment with the Party's rule, but they could just as easily be interpreted as evidence of the Party's growing tolerance for protest, signs of increasing instability caused by economic reforms, or a trend among the Chinese people to use public protests as the best means to extract compensation for such things as unemployment, or the destruction of housing to make way for construction. In fact, people often protest in front of government offices even if the government is not at fault in hopes of gaining compensation. The state, for example, has repeatedly warned against pyramid (Ponzi) schemes and has said that the government will not reimburse investors in such schemes for their losses. This has not, however, deterred those who have incurred huge losses from protesting in the hope that the government, fearful of instability, will compensate them in order to stop the protests.[29]

The social context also affects perceptions of freedom in another way. Political culture has a substantial influence on how much freedom people yearn for. Individuals in an authoritarian political culture tend to be less

---

27. Diamond, "Economic Development and Democracy Reconsidered," p. 127.

28. Woodside, "Lost Modernities."

29. Discussions with faculty and students, Department of Politics and International Affairs, Fudan University, Sept. 1999.

tolerant of difference and, like their government, usually are not deeply concerned with the right of an individual to express difference freely. As noted in Chapter 4, comparative studies indicate that in China individuals "at each level of educational attainment" are "less tolerant than people in other countries."[30] Arguably, the government's political control of dissidence resonates with the intolerance in China's political culture. This does not make intolerance right, but it does shed light on why so many Chinese are less bothered by the government's control of dissent than we might expect—or wish.

Another piece of evidence suggesting that the Chinese people might prefer a more authoritarian form of government is their seeming predilection for a single powerful ruler. The Chinese have historically preferred rulers who are powerful, intelligent, and able to care for the people's needs,[31] or leaders who combine charisma, intelligence, and religion. Hence in recent times the ease with which the Mao cult developed and the appeal of Li Hongzhi as the leader of the Falungong religious sect.

Like any other social construct, such as democracy or morality, freedom evolves over time. It is not an eternal absolute. The present views of Western liberal democracies on morality, freedom, and political rights differ from those of fifty years ago, and even five years ago. They are constantly debated, challenged, and redefined by various segments of society. China has the right to conduct a debate on such issues, a debate deeply influenced by changes in the culture, by economic development, and by China's position within the international system.

Although there have been major setbacks,[32] the Chinese have made progress since 1949, and especially since 1979, in creating a foundation for greater democracy by increasing the number of rights. Most of the progress between 1949 and 1979 came in distributional and welfare rights and may be seen as providing a strong basis for the growth of civil and procedural rights after 1979. Progress has, however, been achieved at the cost of unfortunate

---

30. Nathan and Shi, "Cultural Requisites for Democracy in China," pp. 112–13.

31. See Chapter 2, p. 58*n*43, especially concerning the view of people in Hong Kong that Zhu Rongji is a better leader than Tung Chee-hwa.

32. Examples would include class struggle and campaigns such as the anti-rightist and anti-bourgeois liberalization campaigns, which clamped down harshly on freedom of speech and the right to demonstrate; the Great Leap Forward, which minimized the ability of the state to provide the food and healthcare so essential to freedom; and the Cultural Revolution, which undermined social stability and productive capacity—although it did contribute to the development of basic literacy and basic healthcare.

and even sometimes devastating trade-offs in other spheres. Economic liberalization and the modernization and expanded individual rights that it has spawned may have contributed to a breakdown in community cohesiveness and in law and order, as well as jeopardized the very social supports—education, healthcare, full employment, and pensions—that are important for China's becoming a fair, decent, and strong society.[33] Finally, as noted elsewhere, the mere accumulation of rights does not necessarily add up to democracy, but their existence does suggest democratic inklings in China.

Do the Chinese have more individual rights today than they did before the Chinese Communists took over in 1949? Before 1979? Before 1989? Or, more appropriately, do they *feel* as if they have more rights? China must be judged by fair and consistent standards, and part of being fair means separating ideological bias about the innate superiority of liberal democracy from the Chinese understanding of what constitutes an equitable, fair, and just society. Those blind with outrage at the mere mention of "communism" will find it difficult to appreciate what is really going on in China.

One final caveat: a well-organized and orderly society is not necessarily the same as a society without rights. Just because the government justifies some of its policies by a need for "law and order" does not necessarily mean that this rationale is a mere excuse for restricting individual rights or freedoms. Nor is China's implementation of policies to make the society well organized and orderly necessarily evidence of fewer civil rights.

DO THE CHINESE FEEL FREER THAN
THEY DID BEFORE 1949?

The changes engineered by the Chinese Communist Party since 1949 provided a critical basis for greater freedom after 1979. The vast majority of those Chinese alive in 1949 gained considerably greater rights under Communist Party rule. What for the citizens of Western liberal democratic states have been long-established conditions of life were for the Chinese greatly desired rights, rights that eluded them before the communist take-

---

33. For example, the village, town, and county leaders whom I interviewed in 1999 indicated that rural areas that had prospered during the reform period had far more money for pensions than before (Ogden, "Field Research Notes"), but another study indicates that almost half the urban labor force does not have a pension (Liu Xinghua, "Yuxian touzi yu jichu jiaoyu").

over. Regrettably, the very liberalization for which the reforms after 1949 prepared the groundwork has, since 1979, also been undercutting some of the conditions essential for those rights. Below, I consider six areas—peace and stability, education, healthcare and nutrition, women's rights, employment, and housing—in terms of the growth of rights since 1949.

1. *The right to a peaceful and secure environment, stability, and unity.*   For more than one hundred years before the communist victory in 1949, the Chinese people struggled to escape war, chaos, and famine. Many did not know whether their homes and families were safe or when they would eat again. Individual freedom was hardly a concern. The peace, security, and relative social stability maintained by China's government since 1949[34] are the basis for all other rights in China today. Chinese leaders and citizens alike agree on the importance of order. Stability remains the top priority precisely because China was so plagued by instability in its recent history. The Chinese government rarely receives the credit it deserves for maintaining stability and unity within this enormous country in the context of a civilian-controlled military, another critical building block for the development of democracy.[35]

As we have witnessed elsewhere (especially in Eastern Europe and the former Soviet Union), even as liberalization, decentralization, and the introduction of a market economy helped provide a basis for democratization, they have also brought growing criminality. In China, for example, the number of criminal cases (including murder, assault, robbery, theft, fraud, and rape) rose from 542,000 in 1985 to 2,117,000 in 1990.[36] Banditry, drug trafficking, and drug addiction, problems that had almost been eradicated in the 1950s, have returned at a shockingly high level. Between 1991 and 1995, 46,000 drug traffickers were arrested, and more than 7,300 were sentenced

---

34. With the exception of conditions verging on civil war during the Great Proletarian Cultural Revolution.

35. The Maoist dictum that "the Party will always control the gun" has been the basis for civilian control. Except during the Cultural Revolution, when civilian leaders called in the military to quell the disturbances—and then the military refused to return to its barracks—this has remained the policy since 1949. This does not mean that the military has lacked political influence. Until the post-Deng leadership, almost all of China's top leaders had formerly been high-ranking military leaders.

36. State Statistical Bureau, Statistics Division; and Chinese Research Center for the Promotion and Development of Science and Technology, *Zhongguo shehui fazhan ziliao*, p. 33.

to death or life imprisonment.[37] Women and children are being kidnapped. Social instability is therefore threatening the Chinese people's right to a safe environment, although nowhere close to the level found in pre-1949 China. Without a secure environment, all other rights may well be endangered. This is especially relevant for economic development—itself essential for generating the wealth for securing certain other rights. The government may conclude that the further expansion of civil rights in a period of social instability would jeopardize the Party's rule. A December 1995 poll of 700 Beijing residents indicates the government has reason to be concerned: only 21.7 percent of the respondents felt the government was doing a good job of "maintaining social order." On the other hand, the government still received high marks (64.3 percent) for "ensuring a strong national defense."[38] A survey of adult urban residents in 11 cities from 1995 to 1998 confirmed social order as the leading concern in 1995 and 1996, although it had fallen to rank 4 (of 8 concerns) by 1998.[39]

2. *The right to education.*   People who can neither read nor do basic math are ill equipped to take advantage of liberalizing reforms. Literacy empowers individuals and allows them to take advantage of opportunities. When a significant percentage of a country's citizens cannot read, write, count, follow written instructions, or cope with modern technology, their ability to take advantage of opportunities to modernize or to become more integrated with the global market economy diminishes. Apart from being a hindrance to economic development and an obstacle to "the freedom and well being of people in general and women in particular," an inadequate education diminishes the "pressure for social change."[40] According to Amartya Sen, the Chinese government's attention to developing human capabilities, especially education and healthcare, before 1979 was critical to China's economic development:

---

37. Pei, "Racing Against Time," p. 33.

38. Of those polled, 39.9 percent felt the government was doing a fair job of maintaining social order, and 30.8 percent thought the government was doing a fair job of defending the country (Zhong et al., "Political Views from Below," p. 479).

39. In at least one survey, unemployment replaced social order as the primary concern in 1997 and 1998; see "1998 shenghuo ganshou." The survey was conducted by the private survey company Lingdian.

40. Sen, "Beyond Liberalization," p. 26.

We must resist the common tendency now to "rubbish" what China had already done before the reforms. The spread of basic education across the country is particularly relevant in explaining the nature of Chinese economic expansion in the post-reform period. The role of *mass education* . . . [has been] crucial in the integration of the Chinese economy with the world market.[41]

In 1982, before liberalizing reforms really took hold, 96 percent of males and 85 percent of females in the 15–19 age group were literate.[42] Many individuals in this group, educated during the Cultural Revolution (1966–76), insist that they should not be called China's "lost generation." Instead, they deserve much of the credit for being the driving force for modernization in China in the 1980s and 1990s.[43]

The government failed to achieve its ambitious commitment to nine years of compulsory education throughout the country by the year 2000, but at least it is making a serious effort to universalize education. Nevertheless, research in at least one county indicates that country people view education not as providing equal opportunity but as supporting China's "tradition of inequality" and "the flight from rural life." Students in the countryside are simply not interested in being educated in technical and vocational schools, which would provide them with skills to help their rural communities. Instead, they want to attend universities so they can leave the rural areas. Thus, although schools are more accessible, they have also led to "more and new forms of inequality."[44]

My own research in China's countryside indicates, however, that education has become a necessity for those who want to do well—whether or not they stay in the countryside. Factory managers increasingly require employees to have at least a high school education, and when cutbacks occur, the less educated are the first fired—this in spite of the fact that most factory

---

41. Ibid., pp. 28–29. Italics added.

42. Ibid, p. 29.

43. Conversations with Chinese in the United States, United Kingdom, and China in the 1980s and 1990s.

44. Paine, "Making Schools Modern," pp. 205, 234–35. This is a study of Zouping County in Shandong. This confirms my own research in Chinese villages: respondents (from Jie Long Village, in the town of Huang Lou, Pudong District, Shanghai) noted the "contradictions" of economic development: although the village may provide some funds, the poorest farmers are unable to pay for compulsory education; on the other hand, the children of the vast majority of the better-off farmers are sent to university (Ogden, "Field Research Notes," Sept. 1999).

jobs require only basic literacy. Further, with most village families adhering to the one-child policy, they can afford to send their only child through high school. And, at the turn of the millennium, even China's villagers believe that if their child is not well-educated, the neighbors will look down on them. Once again in China, status has much to do with education.[45]

In interviews conducted in 1999, local leaders in Chinese villages, towns, and counties repeatedly stated that education and healthcare had benefited greatly from the growth in local budgets, the result of economic prosperity.[46] The experiences of these areas (in Jiangsu Province and in Pudong District, Shanghai) have not, however, been shared by all parts of the country. One study found, for example, elementary and secondary schools in rural areas that were so poorly funded they could not even afford to buy chalk, and classrooms in such disrepair that they were in danger of collapsing. In recent years, some twenty provinces and autonomous regions have not paid teachers on time. Hundreds of thousands of teachers, underpaid or unpaid, have deserted education for other occupations.[47] The underfunding of education has led to an unwillingness of qualified people to go into teaching, and an increasing dropout rate from both primary and middle schools.[48]

Nevertheless, China continues to do exceptionally well in educating its youth compared with other developing countries. Chapter 9 looks in greater detail at the relationship between education and the capacity to attain greater democracy and individual rights.

3. *The right to health care and adequate nutrition.*   Hungry and sick people are rarely concerned about higher sorts of rights. In China, adequate healthcare and nutrition have led to a healthy population with high life expectancy and low infant mortality rates. As a result, Chinese people are better positioned to acquire other rights.

---

45. Ogden, "Field Research Notes," Sept. 1999. These conclusions were based on interviews in a relatively poor village about one hour from Kunshan City in Jiangsu with the elected head of the villagers' committee, the secretary of the party branch in the village, and with the villagers themselves; and interviews with the economic managers, factory leaders, and elected head of the villagers' committee in Jie Long Village, in the town of Huang Lou, Pudong District, Shanghai.

46. Ibid.

47. Liu Xinghua, "Youxian touzi yu jichu jiaoyu."

48. The budget for education decreased from 3.3 percent to 2.4 percent of GDP from 1980 to 1994 (Pei, "Racing Against Time," pp. 31–32).

Chinese leaders have emphasized preventive healthcare, including inoculation against major diseases (such as smallpox, tetanus, polio, diphtheria, mumps, measles), prevention of epidemics, and sanitation, particularly the control of disease carriers such as rats, cockroaches, and flies. During the Cultural Revolution, the "barefoot doctors" program focused healthcare increasingly on serving the masses. Preventive healthcare and treatment of routine medical problems were favored at the expense of complicated and expensive medical procedures. The 3- to 6-month barefoot doctors program (albeit at the expense of education for high-level specialists) provided training comparable to that given paramedics in developed countries. Those who completed the program could give inoculations and deal with infections, minor ailments, and even bone fractures. Barefoot doctors worked at the village level, bringing healthcare to the generally neglected hinterland where more advanced clinics, not to mention fully equipped hospitals, were few and far between. By addressing minor health problems before they blossomed into major ones, they significantly advanced healthcare in China. Today's mortality rates, almost equivalent to those in Western liberal democratic states and far below those of virtually all developing countries, indicate China's remarkable success in this area. (for more on healthcare in China, see Chapter 9).

As noted above, however, healthcare in some rural areas has been negatively affected by economic liberalization,[49] and new diseases such as AIDs have recently entered China. The impact of for-profit medical care is uneven. The income of village doctors, who are no longer paid salaries, tends to depend on the sale of medicine. In some parts of China, this means they are less interested in prevention than before, and fewer medical personnel visit villages. The cooperative rural insurance program, which used to fund rural healthcare, no longer exists for many villages. Furthermore, relative to spending on other medical services (notably, those that make money for doctors), spending on preventive healthcare has declined. Nevertheless, in other parts of China, clinics are still collectively managed, village doctors provide preventive healthcare services, and many country people are reimbursed for 70 percent of their expenses. So the picture is complicated.[50] As with education, moreover, health-

---

49. Because of budget cuts for healthcare, especially in the countryside, diseases that had nearly been eradicated by the end of the 1970s, such as schistosomiasis, had by the late 1980s again become a major problem (ibid.).

50. Walder, *Zouping in Transition*, pp. 186–87; and Ogden, "Field Research Notes," Sept. 1999.

care correlates strongly with economic growth. China's village and town leaders assert that if they can develop economically, they can easily address the problems of healthcare.[51] Healthcare for urban residents remains excellent, but access to the healthcare system is often unavailable to rural migrants without urban residency cards.

4. *Women's rights.*   Women have the right to choose their own spouse, to divorce, to be educated, and to work at jobs commensurate with their skills and education. After 1949, the rights accorded Chinese women put them far in advance of women in most developing countries. Marriage and divorce laws protected women from being treated as the property of men. The empowerment of women in the workplace, facilitated by the Communist Party's commitment to educating females as well as males, allowed women to work in meaningful jobs throughout the urban economy and government, even if the proverbial glass ceiling remained in place. These rights also empowered women in the political process. Women became participants in workplace discussions that affected their livelihood. The earning power of Chinese women, which at lower and intermediate levels tends to be the same as men's, likewise gives them a greater say in domestic matters.

Despite the significant gains made by women during the Maoist period (1949–76), when Mao Zedong reminded the country that "women hold up half the sky" (although some quipped that the women's half was heavier), and both women and men were called "comrades," attitudes have retrogressed since economic reforms and marketization began. Although one poll suggests that most Chinese (92.5 percent) still believe women should be treated equally with men and that social development is closely associated with the improvement of women's status (84.6 percent), it also reveals that traditional cultural attitudes toward women persist.[52] A perusal of want ads, as well as the actual hiring practices of companies and work units today, confirms the return of traditional attitudes toward women as sex objects (only attractive women need apply for many jobs) and the tendency to place women in ornamental jobs. The secretary/mistress is increasingly common. Today's talented women are less likely to get a position commensurate with

---

51. Ogden, "Field Research Notes," Sept. 1999.

52. For example, 74.1 percent agreed that "the female should be kind, tender, benevolent, and the male should be strong and decisive" (see "Better to Marry a Good Husband Than to Do a Good Job," *Beijing qingnian bao*, Sept. 13, 1995).

their abilities than during the period of Mao Zedong's rule. And, although they continue to enjoy the right to marry freely and divorce, to work outside the home, and to be educated, a new Marriage Law had to be considered at the turn of the millennium because the old one was inadequate to protect women in the changed conditions of China.[53]

5. *The right to a job.*   The guaranteed right to a job,[54] often referred to as the "iron rice bowl," provided dignity and a sense of being an equal member in a community. There were, however, trade-offs and drawbacks to the centralized job assignment system, for individuals were not free to choose the job they wanted, and enterprises were not free to reject workers assigned to them, even if their job skills were inappropriate. Thus, state-owned enterprises suffered from underemployment (too many people with less than a full job to do), and both the state and individuals paid the costs associated with the rigidity and immobility of the centrally controlled labor market. Apart from everything else, couples often found themselves assigned, or reassigned, to work in places so far apart that they had to live separately.

As will be noted in the following section on post-1979 reforms, since economic liberalization began, individuals have slowly gained the right to choose their own job, but they are no longer guaranteed a job by the state. Greater freedom of choice has been accompanied by a risk of unemployment.

6. *The right to housing.*   Along with jobs came housing. After 1949, almost all urban residents received housing from their work unit. As with underemployment, this was a drain on the efficiency and cost-effectiveness of work units, but the Chinese government justified it in the name of a greater social good. Both the right to a job and the right to housing are being significantly challenged by more capitalistic and market-oriented economic policies that emphasize profits over social goals. The implementation of the policy of

---

53. With new wealth, especially among China's entrepreneurial class, many husbands have started to keep mistresses, with their funds flowing to them rather than to their wives and families. In some cases, women have been particularly hurt by divorce settlements, by which the mistresses are favored financially. Many women's groups pushed for criminalizing adultery, which the National People's Congress resisted. However, it did criminalize bigamy. In the first case under the new law, a man who set up his mistress in a separate household was sent to jail. See China News Digest (July 25, 2000), www.cnd.org.

54. This refers to jobs in the urban economy. In the countryside, virtually all individuals had been incorporated into an agricultural collective by the late 1950s.

privatizing housing, which began in 1998, really means the eventual loss of an urban citizen's "right" to housing, since many of the state-owned work units that had distributed these benefits are being privatized or eliminated.

To conclude, the rights discussed above, which the Chinese acquired after the Communists gained power in 1949, fall generally into Amartya Sen's category of "human capabilities." That is, they have increased the Chinese people's ability to control their lives. One need not deify Mao Zedong to applaud the success of Maoist policies in advancing basic literacy and healthcare. Even though advanced education and medicine suffered during this same period, basic education and healthcare allowed the broad masses to take advantage of opportunities offered by economic reforms. China's people thereby gained greater freedom. As India's former prime minister Jawaharlal Nehru put it, "The elimination of ignorance, of illiteracy, of remedial poverty, of preventable disease and of needless inequalities in opportunities must be seen as objectives that are valued for their own sake. *They expand our freedom to lead the lives we have reason to value.* . . . While they can and do contribute to economic growth . . . , their value does not lie only in these instrumental contributions."[55]

Most of the rights listed above were enhanced after 1949 through a combination of China's economic development and policies that led to a fairly equal distribution of benefits among the population of each locality. China's ability to provide basic welfare rights has declined with the introduction of market liberalization that has not been accompanied by a tax collection system appropriate to an increasingly privatized economy. Greater emphasis on individual rights, including the right to private property and to "get rich," has come at the expense of much of the social and economic equality that the state had earlier tried to guarantee. This is by no means a problem unique to China—almost every post-communist society has experienced similar problems (and usually in more extreme form). Nor is it an argument against the accumulation of rights, for in spite of the polarization of wealth and a diminution of the welfare state, the society as a whole has so far benefited enormously in terms of both rights and economic development. In turn, economic development has brought with it institutional and cultural change, which has led in a cyclical process to political reforms and hence even greater institutional and cultural change.

---

55. Cited in Sen, "Beyond Liberalization," p. 2. Italics added.

DO THE CHINESE FEEL FREER THAN
THEY DID IN 1979?

Do the Chinese feel freer today than they did before 1979, when economic liberalization began, or even freer than before 1992, when Deng Xiaoping made his "Southern tour" and encouraged the continuation of economic and political reforms stalled by the conservative backlash and repression following the crackdown on Tiananmen demonstrators in 1989? When China's government moved beyond providing human capabilities and opened China to the outside world and economic liberalization, it introduced a number of new rights. To reiterate a point made above, economic liberalization is not the same as democratization, but policies resulting from liberalization have led to both improved material conditions and increased options, opportunities, and rights. Indeed, it has led to more genuine choices and greater freedom than mere political democratization would have. In short, democratization is more than a political process. It also involves social, cultural, and economic changes. China's traditional authoritarian political culture has not been jettisoned; rather, the institutional reforms have built on it and reshaped it. China's political culture is struggling to accommodate the new relationship between the individual and the state and the new expectations that have arisen in the wake of these changes.

Although there have been setbacks since 1979, in general the people's rights have blossomed significantly. In this section, I examine the burgeoning of rights in the areas of free speech and access to information, privacy, consumer goods, consumer protections, choice of work and domicile, and personal lifestyle options, as well as several miscellaneous freedoms. (Chapter 6 is devoted to the institutionalization of democracy through elections and changes in the law and in the National People's Congress, and Chapter 7 to the development of civil society through the growth of associational pluralism.) Like the right to have an education and medical care, some of the rights discussed below are important because they provide the means, the capabilities, by which individuals can acquire more control over their lives; they give real meaning to other rights. Others enhance procedural rights, such as free speech. Many of these rights—privacy, for example—do both. All contribute to a stronger foundation for democratization.

1. *Free speech and access to information.*[56]   China escaped the heavily bureaucratized form of censorship practiced in the former Soviet Union and Eastern Europe, where manuals specified precisely which types of phrases and thought were to be censored. In China, however, editors, local officials, and even writers took responsibility for analyzing the Chinese Communist Party's statements on cultural policy and figuring out which way the wind was blowing for themselves. Each cultural and propaganda unit, rather than a central office in Beijing, watched the media within its bailiwick.[57] This, of course, led to many meetings between editors and the party committee within the unit.

China has, then, always had censorship, but the party-state has usually been less directly active in this area than was the case in the former Soviet Union. (This is not to say that the Stalinist media structure did not influence Chinese journalism for the worse.)[58] This less institutionalized system has had a downside, however. In the absence of clear laws and regulations, censorship in China has been remarkably arbitrary and pernicious. Editors, radio and television program directors, and managers of museums and theaters who do not exercise "correct" control over the contents of publications, broadcasts, exhibits, and performances may be demoted, replaced, fired, or disciplined. But this situation may be changing. In an internal document issued in 2000, Beijing reportedly set guidelines that clarify the limits: penal action may result if publications, broadcasts, or performances question the leadership of the Chinese Communist Party, contradict key party and state policies, reveal military or other state secrets, threaten social stability, disregard government policies on ethnic minorities, or contain pornography. Publishing houses or other media that fail to observe these new guidelines may have their editorial committees restructured, receive warnings, be suspended, or even be shut down.[59] The guidelines sound formidable, but they seem to have been issued more to provide a legal framework in case the state

---

56. For the right of free speech in the context of the relationship of intellectuals to the state, see Chapter 8.

57. Kraus, "China's Artists Between Plan and Market," pp. 175–76.

58. Whereas previous reforms of the media took the former Soviet Union's concepts and organization as their model, reforms in the 1990s moved the media away from their role as spokesmen for the Party (Chu, "Continuity and Change in China's Media Reform," pp. 6, 13–14).

59. "Beijing Cracks Down on 'Politically Incorrect' Publishers," *China News Digest* (www.cnd.org), July 18, 2000, based on a Reuters report.

decides to censor the media, rather than because the government is planning to do so. Certainly there is little evidence of an effort to crackdown on pornography.

It is important not to misinterpret press censorship. For example, the Chinese government issued new regulations in early 1996 on the sale of economic information to bankers and traders stipulating that all economic news from foreign news agencies had to be channeled through an official distributor of news (the New China News Agency or the Ministry of Post and Telecommunications). But these regulations had as much if not more to do with the government's efforts to collect money from foreign news agencies than with news censorship. The government also has a genuine interest in prohibiting the spread of unsubstantiated rumors, which had several times rocked the Chinese stock market, such as periodic reports of Deng Xiaoping's death long before the event.

Another example is the creation of the Ministry of Information Industries, whose mission is to centralize supervision of the Internet and the spread of information. Its primary purpose, however, is to collect revenues from the use of the Internet, *not* to monitor e-mail accounts and other messages and content of the Web. (Although the ministry can prevent an account from being issued to a suspected "bad element," once an individual has an account, it is not easy to monitor.)[60]

In any case, for the past few years, the Chinese government has not only permitted but also encouraged the spread of the Internet. Virtually anyone with a phone and modem can sign up, despite occasional efforts by the government to restrict unlimited access.[61] In 1999, Bill Gates announced an agreement between Microsoft and the State Economic and Trade Commission to link over forty governmental ministries to the Internet.[62] By 2000,

---

60. Lynch, *After the Propaganda State*, p. 109.

61. Alter, "Society: Communism Is Dead, Crony Capitalism Lives," p. 30.

62. "Lexis-Nexis Country Report, 1999: China" (web.lexis-nexis.com). One survey found that substantially more Beijing middle-school students know about Bill Gates (71.7 percent) than about China's leader in computers, Wang Xuan (33.5 percent). Wang Xuan invented a way to code Chinese characters, a critical breakthrough for giving Chinese access to computers. The survey also found that 81.1 percent of middle-school students in Beijing had computer experience, and 47.7 percent had computers or learn computer skills at home ("Beijing Middle School Students in an Age of Computers: Investigative Report on Awareness of Science and Technology Among Beijing Middle School Students," *Zhongguo qingnian bao*, Nov. 9, 1996, p. 4).

the government had invested U.S.$50 billion in information technology. A new fiber-optic grid in China is facilitating the installation of new telephone line connections at an extraordinary rate. In 1990, China did not have even one phone per 100 people. By 2000, it had 125 million, or roughly one for every ten people, with 2 million new lines being installed each month. Mobile phone usage mushroomed, from 5 million in 1995 to 57 million in 2000; and the number of Internet users grew at an exponential rate, from some 50,000 in 1995 to 22 million by 2001. It is estimated that China will have 120 million Internet users by 2004. Accessibility for even larger numbers of Chinese is being enhanced by the rapid growth of Chinese-language sites, as well as by innovation. Wireless Application Protocol (WAP) technology will allow 70 million cellular phone users to access the Internet, and an additional 100 million may in the near future be able to log on through cable television.[63] Internet cafes are wildly popular in China's cities, and the government has committed itself to supplying secondary schools with computers.[64]

The Chinese have gained the right to communicate across international boundaries through mail, telephone, fax, and computers. The Internet exposes Chinese to a far wider variety of opinions and information than is permitted in the mass media, such as reports on the government's crackdown on the Tiananmen Square protestors on June 4, 1989, and the poor treatment of individuals with AIDS. Locally produced websites and "chat rooms" exercise continuous self-censorship, however, to avoid being shut down. Still, by Chinese standards, this is exciting fare. In 1999, the privately owned *Sina.com* caused a stir when it displayed China's first on-line birth on its web site.[65]

The *People's Daily* (*Renmin ribao*), the mouthpiece of the government and party, has had its own website and chat room since the bombing of the Chinese Embassy in Belgrade in May 1999. Although a "chat room mama" weeds out comments considered too critical of the Party within minutes of their

---

63. Hachigian, "China's Cyber-Strategy," p. 119; "Internet Users Rise to 13 Million in China: Survey," *China News Digest* (www.cnd.org), July 2, 2000 (information for the CND article was provided by Beijing Mainland Information Institute, based on a survey of 8,000 people in 33 cities); and "Wired China: The Flies Swarm In," *The Economist*, July 22, 2000, p. 24.

64. Elisabeth Rosenthal, "China: Web Users on Rise," *New York Times*, Jan. 20, 2000, p. A6.

65. Elisabeth Rosenthal, "Web Sites Bloom in China, and Are Weeded," *New York Times*, Dec. 23, 1999, pp. 1, 10.

appearance, the editor has allowed remarks such as "We Chinese people don't like our government" and "The Communist Party doesn't let Chinese people read newspapers from overseas" to remain. The government worries less about news on websites than it does about comments made in chat rooms. Nevertheless, it keeps chat rooms open to act as a release valve for citizens' anger and as a window on popular opinion for officials.[66] The *People's Daily* chat room has become so popular, in fact, that by 2000 specialized sections had developed within it. One site is devoted to contemporary affairs, and the participants in the *Strong Country Forum* (*Qiangguo luntan*) talk about such matters as village elections. Among those responding to questions in these rooms have been elected village committee leaders and academics from the Chinese Academy of Social Sciences, officials from the Ministry of Civil Affairs, and foreign experts and diplomats, who answered questions for many hours.[67]

All this hardly amounts to uncensored news and opinions. The government would, if it could, control the Internet and e-mail accounts much more tightly, as it tried to do in the wake of the Falungong public demonstrations in 1999. The Party's Propaganda Department has also prohibited Chinese commercial websites from publishing news unless it has already been published by the state's news media. Much of the time, the government blocks international news outlet websites, such as the BBC's and CNN's, as well as the websites of human rights' organizations. Yet for whatever reason (including incompetence), it does not block every controversial site, such as that of a London-based site advocating Tibetan independence. It is, of course, possible to get around such blocks through proxy servers abroad[68] and through organizations and correspondents using e-mail attachments. With the Chinese sending more than 20 million e-mail messages each day, and some 4 billion webpages and 4 million individual websites worldwide, monitoring the Internet is exceedingly difficult.[69]

Today China is inundated with information not only from the Internet, Reuters, and Dow Jones but also from the Hong Kong–based Star televi-

---

66. Ibid.

67. Rudolf Wagner, discussion, May 24, 2000. Wagner insists, however, that the controls on what appears in these chat rooms are very tight. That may be, but the Chinese have made phrasing their points in such a way as not to incur censorship into an art form.

68. "Wired China: The Flies Swarm In," *The Economist*, July 22, 2000, pp. 24–25.

69. Hachigian, "China's Cyber-Strategy," p. 128.

sion,[70] which is accessible via satellite dishes in major cities throughout the country. Nor is information limited to what is accessible within the country. More and more Chinese are traveling abroad to conduct business, to study, or to participate in international conferences, international scholarly exchanges, international film and writers' festivals, and international musical competitions. At home, they can send and receive faxes and make telephone calls to virtually any country in the world. The Chinese government is increasingly unable to prevent the massive flood of information from all these sources, much less control its impact on individuals. This expansion of access resulted from incremental decisions motivated in part by a belief that the benefits of greater liberalization, such as greater freedom of speech, outweighed the possible costs. One of those costs may well be the sense of Chinese identity, a serious concern of the party-state and of many China's intellectuals.

Defining "the right of free speech" in the narrow sense of the right to criticize the top Chinese Communist Party leaders directly in the press is to miss the liberalization that is going on. Before 1979, for example, Chinese hesitated to discuss politics critically even with friends and colleagues. Since the early 1990s, they have been far more willing to engage in discussion of politics with family, friends, and colleagues and to tolerate different views.[71] It would, moreover, be incorrect to assume that a large number of Chinese want to use the Internet and e-mail to express dissident political views or to organize to bring down the government. In fact, the Chinese, like people everywhere, use the Internet largely for business and commercial purposes (such as marketing), entertainment (playing games and following American basketball are great favorites), information (on science and technology, GRE tests, applications for a visa to study abroad), and social purposes (chatting with friends and finding new ones).

Thus, in spite of the training of cyber-police, the growing number of monitoring units, and occasional crackdowns on the Internet, the Chinese Communist Party appears convinced that the Worldwide Web can do

---

70. Star television is part of the Robert Murdoch mass media empire.

71. Of the 700 Beijing respondents (from both urban districts and periurban county towns in Beijing Municipality) to a December 1995 survey, 40 percent stated that they "often" engage in political discussions; another 50 percent did so "occasionally." The demographic characteristics (education, age, residency in rural or urban area, and income) of those who were interested in political discussions were similar to those in other countries (Zhong et al., "Political Views from Below," pp. 475–76).

much to enhance its popularity by helping China modernize its science and technology, widen its business opportunities, allow it access to market information, and improve its administrative capabilities. Indeed, in 1998, the government launched an initiative to get 80 percent of all government agencies, from the national to the local level, on line by 2000. Today, almost 10 percent of all Chinese sites are those of government departments. Even the Party-controlled media promote the Internet, and officials insist on the importance of the "knowledge economy," in which the Internet plays a vital role. The Ministry of Information Industries has even required the state-owned China Telecom to lower its access charges so more people can get connected.[72]

In addition, before China's "open door" brought the world to China, and the mass production and sale of television sets led to a demand for better programming, the only available ideas about politics, lifestyles, fashion, or even food were those offered by the Chinese media. State-controlled publications and programs were didactic and, at best, bereft of new ideas. Now China's media are swamped with ideas from sources other than the party-state. Indeed, the voice of the party-state is being drowned out by a plethora of alternatives. What Geremie Barme calls "a wave of national graphomania" has resulted from political relaxation and commercialization. In Barme's view, China is once again "one of the greatest writing and publishing nations on the planet."[73] This does not, of course, mean that the media and the Web are tools only for liberals and dissidents. The state also musters them for its own purposes.

China now has offbeat publications, such as Shanghai's *Xinmin Evening News*,[74] *Beijing Evening News*, and *Southern Weekend* (published by the Party in Guangdong Province) that present the world in nonideological terms (such as stories discussing the personal life of American presidents); and domestically produced movies that challenge earlier boundaries, such as *Red River Valley*, *Kong Fansen*, and *Red Cherry*. Cinema is the most rigorously censored domain in the cultural arena and is, as a result of rising costs, underfunding,

---

72. Hachigian, "China's Cyber-Strategy," pp. 118–26.

73. Barme, *In the Red*, p. x.

74. As of 1997, *Xinmin* had the second-largest circulation, after the *People's Daily*, as well as US$72 million in advertising revenues—half the total market share. However, the paper is facing potential drops in circulation as evening television increasingly takes readers away from the evening dailies (Leu Siew Ying [Agence France Presse], "China Media," Aug. 28, 1997, from web.lexis-nexis.com).

and censorship losing viewers to television.[75] Television programming has flourished with a host of new programs. Viewers have been able to opt for dramas such as *Yearnings*,[76] *Great Turning Point*, *The Heavens Above*, *Oriental Time and Space*,[77] and *Our Dad and Mom*; programs on business and the stock market; dating game shows; imitations of foreign programs, such as MTV, the American programs *Cops* and *48 Hours* (during which television crews accompany police on their beats for exposes about crime and corruption),[78] and the Chinese version of the longest-running television soap in Great Britain, *Coronation Street*, as well as foreign-produced programs on topics and themes heretofore unexplored in China;[79] domestic programming that has live audiences[80] and even live interviews (such as Beijing's *Wednesday On-the-Spot Work*), television talk shows (such as Chinese Central Television's [CCTV] *Speak Honestly*), and call-in radio talk shows.[81]

These sorts of publications and programs are exposing the Chinese to issues that were formerly taboo and to lifestyles and genres of music and art they did not even know existed. The Chinese are now aware of more than the one set of standards and values previously offered by the party-state for judging their lives and their government. Television programming is livelier since it must appeal to viewers in order to attract advertising needed to stay in business. In short, although China's media are hardly free from all con-

---

75. The script must be approved before a film can be made, and the finished film must be approved again after it has been produced and before it can be released. Because of the lack of a censorship law, individual officials may arbitrarily approve or ban a film (Sylvia Chan, "Building a 'Socialist Culture with Chinese Characteristics'?," pp. 12–13).

76. For a commentary on this soap opera, see Rofel, "'Yearnings.'"

77. According to Wang Hui ("Contemporary Chinese Thought and the Question of Modernity," p. 33), although *Dongfang shikong* (Oriental time and space) is produced by freelance producers, it is "under strict state control and must fulfill the task of creating and promoting the state ideology."

78. Jernow, "China: The Tight Leash Loosens," p. 33.

79. The Chinese can even pick up such programs as *Baywatch* reruns on satellite dishes, an American program that features virtually naked actors on a beach and has heavy sexual overtones. One could say that the characters do not express values appropriate to socialist culture.

80. Yong and Yang, "A Mass Medium or a Master's Medium."

81. President Clinton, during a visit to China that began in late June 1998, appeared on one of Shanghai's most popular live radio programs, *Citizens and Society*, a program that boasts an audience of some 10 million people. Clinton took questions from listeners on a wide variety of topics concerning China, the United States, and Sino-American relations ("Internet Usage in China Interests US President," *China Daily*, July 1, 1998, p. 2). Close to 90 percent of all Chinese have radios.

trols, their rapid proliferation, commercialization, and "the emergence of divergent voices means the center's ability to control people's minds has vanished."[82] Although the Chinese Communist Party and even the "conservative" forces of militant nationalism can also use the media for their own purposes, they must now battle with the ideas and values set in motion by market forces to get the attention of China's citizenry.

What are some of the new ideas—indeed, the new ways of thinking—that have resulted from the liberalization of China's press, radio, television, and publishing industry? CCTV's *Speak Honestly*, which airs for 40 minutes every Sunday, features both the presentation of opinions by guests without debate, as well as debates in which two guests engage in what often becomes a heated discussion of an issue. Among the topics featured on the show, which began in 1995, have been fake products and consumer protection, pending legal disputes, environmental protection issues, and excessive advertising in the media.[83] CCTV's on-air newsmagazine, *Focus Interview* (*Jiaodian fangtan*), first broadcast in 1994, also has a live-interview format. A daily prime-time program following the evening news, it concentrates on investigative reporting of local officials suspected of wrongdoing.[84] Such programs have led to a profound change in the tactics of those seeking redress in China. For example, villagers, disgruntled and angry because of persistent problems and frustrated with the unwillingness of local officials to respond, now try to get the attention of the media as the first step in resolving problems.[85]

In this respect, talkshows, as well as investigative and hotline programs are contributing to the development of a civil society. The press is becoming an investigative branch of society and frequently influences policy and the judicial system. Just as important, these programs serve as a social safety valve, allowing the public to vent their anger and concerns with the system and with the reforms within the context of what is still a party-controlled

---

82. Barnathan et al., "China: Is Prosperity Creating a Freer Society?" pp. 98–99.

83. Zhang Weiguo, "Tuokuoxiu zai Zhongguo," p. 2.

84. CNN, "Reform in China Means New Role for the Media," Oct. 17, 1999, on web.lexis-nexis.com; based on interviews with the producer of the program, Yang Dongping. One week after five (alleged) members of the Falungong set themselves on fire in Tiananmen Square on January 23, 2001, *Focus* broadcast a horrifying 20-second police video of the event (Erik Eckholm, "To Fight Sect, China Publicizes a Public Burning," *New York Times*, Jan. 31, 2001, pp. A1, A4).

85. Ogden, "Field Research Notes," Sept. 1999.

system. *Focus* is particularly successful in performing this function, serving "as a nightly ritual of national catharsis, an officially-sanctioned and carefully-managed symbolic forum through which the people come to terms with China's epochal transformations and its profound contradictions and horrendous maladies." Many perceive such programs as "the last resort for obtaining social justice within the framework of established political institutions." [86]

A 1997 poll on how Beijingers view television discussion and commentary programs on such topics as exposing social evils and exercising media supervision, as well as deep analysis on the latest important events, indicated they thought that they were "very important" (46.5 percent) or "relatively important" (34.4 percent) Respondents believed television news commentators had an obligation to expose social evils and criticize current problems, and that they should report the facts objectively and fairly. *Oriental Time and Space* and *Focus* are television news commentary programs that have been cloned by dozens of other programs, although not necessarily as well. [87]

Of course, there are still strict limits on the media. For example, the media cannot report without authorization on demonstrations or on peasants and workers who are petitioning the government; media clampdowns occur unexpectedly because of international events, new struggles for succession, Tibet, Taiwan, Tiananmen, or the formation of a new political party or trade union; and the media are rarely permitted to report on the abuse of power above the county level until the party-state has made a decision to target someone. "Flies and dead tigers (those already shot down by the state) are the media's main targets." [88]

---

86. Yuezhi Zhao. "Underdogs, Lapdogs, Watchdogs, and Other Breeds," p. 20.

87. Yu Guoming, "Beijing guan zong kai dianshi pinglun" (How Beijingers view TV discussion and Commentary programs), *Zhongguo qingnian bao*, Dec. 5, 1997, p. 8. The 1,400 respondents chosen were from 30 neighborhood committees and 10 village committees. There were 1,308 valid responses.

88. Yuezhi Zhao, "Underdogs, Lapdogs, Watchdogs, and Other Breeds," p. 22. Dai Qing, one of China's best-known dissident journalists, was jailed for ten months in 1989 for her opposition, voiced in articles and books, to the Three Gorges dam project. She finds the domestic media reluctant to publish her writings (Bay Fang, "Colourful Crusaders . . . ," *Far Eastern Economic Review*, May 7, 1998, p. 13). Nevertheless, Dai Qing, with her strong family ties to the top leaders, enjoys a protected existence and is allowed to criticize the leaders and their policies in ways others may not. She frequently travels abroad to deliver lectures criticizing the Chinese Communist Party's policies, but she usually balances her criticisms with vitriolic denunciations of leading dissidents and intellectuals.

The limits imposed by the party-state are, however, expanding steadily and are becoming more predictable. At the same time, new bullies have arisen to limit press freedom: businesses, especially ones under investigation for illegal behavior, are increasingly threatening the press with the withdrawal of advertising funds, and even with violence against investigative reporters.[89] Capitalism and market reform have, in short, unleashed forces that endanger liberalization of the press. As a result, a large swath of Chinese society, especially those who are better-educated, do not necessarily find the news credible. Although this is not uncommon to societies that have a growing diversity of news sources from which to choose, the lack of credibility has as much to do with distrust of journalists who write sensationalist stories or take bribes to write good stories about products and companies as it does with distrust of politically related stories.[90]

Radio and television hotline programs, which are aired live, are broadcast throughout China. In 1992, the government established the first specialized call-in station in China, Shanghai's Oriental Radio Station. Guangdong's Zhujiang Economic Radio Station ("economic" meaning "designed exclusively to make money") has a program called *Social Hot Topics*, which airs from 7:30 to 8:30 A.M., Monday through Saturday. Forty-four percent of all adults in Guangzhou listen to at least part of the program each day! Today, almost all the major stations have "open phonelines." (Stations in Guangdong maintain open lines for their listeners for a third of each broadcasting day.) Anyone with access to a telephone—and public telephones are ubiquitous in China's cities—may call and ask a question or voice an opinion.[91]

Before 1992, political pressures assured that sensitive topics were seldom raised, but few subjects are taboo today. Topics have included such touchy areas as the denial of benefits to urban workers without a residential permit, workplace discrimination against non-party members, deluxe housing projects for the rich, the damage to roads caused by heavy military vehicles,

---

89. Yuezhi Zhao, "Underdogs, Lapdogs, Watchdogs, and Other Breeds," p. 23.

90. A 1997 survey of readers by *China Youth Daily*, the Social Survey Center, and *Hope Monthly* found that only 32.1 percent of those with a college education saw news as credible, whereas 75.0 percent of those with an elementary education did. See Wan Xingya, "Xinwen de kexinxing shou dao tiaozhao: meiti dui qingshaonian de yingxiang diaocha zhi er" (The credibility of news is challenged: a survey of the effects of media on youngsters), *Zhongguo qingnian bao*, May 24, 1997, p. 8.

91. Lynch, *After the Propaganda State*, pp. 101–2.

problems with garbage pickup, and road congestion.[92] Listeners to radio call-in programs have heard blistering critiques of official corruption, police brutality,[93] and the failure of government policies on everything from "fake" products, minibus drivers in Beijing, and trade policy to healthcare and unemployment. Some of these shows have provided listeners with the opportunity to grill officials. Shanghai's mayor and vice-mayor, for example, have answered questions on air. Not all discussions are political, however. Divorce and sex remain the most popular topics on these programs.[94]

This is not to say that local governments have not issued guidelines for live call-in radio programs or that all callers' viewpoints or questions will be aired. These guidelines, however, are similar in most respects to concern found worldwide to prescreen callers' comments for acceptable content and relevance and to use time-delay technology to bleep obscenities or cut off objectionable callers. For example, the Guangdong provincial government's guidelines for controlling live call-in radio programs focused on five areas: [95]

1. Limits on the total number of such programs.
2. Selection of suitable topics (for example, urban construction, children's schooling, medical care, public safety) and avoidance of sensitive topics, such as political issues and sex. (*All* these issues are, in spite of the guidelines, discussed on many call-in programs. A program entitled *Hotline for Uniting Lonely Hearts*, produced by Guangdong People's Broadcasting Station, "invites listeners to share their intimate personal problems with the host and with each other." Even such extraordinarily sensitive issues as incest have been discussed on it.)[96]
3. The qualifications of talk show hosts (good political thought and sense of organizational discipline; sensitivity to news; and the ability to think on their feet and respond appropriately to unexpected questions).[97]

---

92. In one week in July 1993, the U.S. Foreign Broadcast Information Service picked up and translated programs on these topics, among many others (ibid., p. 102).

93. Barnathan et al, "China: Is Prosperity Creating a Freer Society?" p. 98.

94. Jernow, "China: The Tight Leash Loosens," p. 33.

95. Jiang Liu et al., *1995–1996 nian Zhongguo shehui xingshi fenxi yu yuce*, p. 303.

96. Sylvia Chan, "Building a 'Socialist Culture with Chinese Characteristics'?," p. 12.

97. In theory, hosts should be party members (*Ming Bao* [Hong Kong], "Communist Party Reportedly Strengthening Control Over Media," Jan. 11, 1996, from BBC, Jan. 17, 1996, web.lexis-nexis.com).

4. Ratification prior to showtime of the topic and factual content by the program supervisor, the chief supervisor, and director; screening of phonecalls during the show by the editor and supervisor.

5. Special handling for "sensitive days" (presumably those days on which sensitive political events are on deck) by arranging for calls from reliable listeners on topics that need to be guided; compressing the total program time (to lessen the amount of time spent on sensitive topics); and airing prerecorded segments rather than accepting new callers (clearly an area of limited freedom of speech).

All these venues make for far better coverage of social and economic news in print and broadcast media. Proposed changes to the marriage law, for example, were so heatedly debated in the newspapers and on radio beginning in 1998 that the National People's Congress was unable to come up with a bill it could pass for two years. Serious investigative reporting of corruption among officials, judicial personnel, and police often makes the front page of newspapers and is aired on television during prime time.

In response to competition from commercialized and popular provincial television programs, the state-run CCTV has had to develop more entertaining and exciting programs. (Some local television stations even refuse to relay CCTV programs.) Much of CCTV's programming today is the work of "independent" producers, or even joint ventures and overseas companies.[98] Some of these efforts have met with success. One popular program with an audience of 100 million is entitled *Law and Society*. According to the program's host, Xiao Xiaolin, viewers send her some 80 letters daily, most of them urging her "to expose corrupt law-enforcement officials." *Law and Society* investigations have led to punishment of corrupt officials. It is rare, however, for media investigations to cover corruption at the highest levels without the permission of the official New China News Agency. Nevertheless, such programs are bringing greater transparency even to the highest levels of government. And, although the footage may be edited prior to broadcast, CCTV is now allowed to film debates by the Standing Committee of the National People's Congress over new laws during select internal sessions.[99]

---

98. Zhang Weiguo, "Dianshi wu zhongyang," p. 2.

99. State television broadcast ten live sessions of the National People's Congress in March 1998. It even carried live a news conference during which a Western reporter asked Premier Zhu Rongji to comment on the crackdown on Tiananmen protestors. And it broadcast live

In addition, some court trials are broadcast live; "bad news," such as floods and high pollution levels (which used to be considered secret), or bombings and mass murders, is published; and the media debate what the government should do to address these problems.[100]

To paint the picture in quantitative terms, in 1970 some 5,000 new books were published. By 1990, the annual total was close to 90,000, and by 1996, close to 113,000. In 1970, there were 42 newspapers. By 1990, the number had grown to 1,444, and by 1997, to 2,163—an increase of over 5,000 percent in 25 years. Similarly, in 1970, virtually no journals were published. By 1990, there were over 6,000 *registered* journals and magazines; and by 1995 there were 8,135. There is, in addition, a large number of nonregistered magazines and illegal publications. By 1997, there were 564 publishing houses.[101] From 1990 to 1995, the number of radio stations increased from 635 to 1,210, and the number of television stations from 509 to 980. By 1995 some 54,000 ground satellite stations gave close to 90 percent of the population access to television.[102] By 1999, 750 cable television stations served an estimated 100 million customers. The government-planned National Cable Company will form a countrywide network, which will provide services such as the Internet and telecommunications connections.[103] In fact, print and electronic media are so prolific and diverse that much of their activity goes unmonitored, especially the contents of newspapers, magazines, and books. Were the state able to control them, perhaps it would, for starters, remove pornographic literature from the streets.

By the 1990s, market-oriented reforms had led the government to cut subsidies to the media. This meant that even state-controlled journals, newspapers, and publishing houses had to make money or be shut down. This in turn required the media to pay more attention to satisfying the public in order to sell advertising and subscriptions. In spite of a tendency toward sensationalism, the result has been improved quality and an increased

---

President Clinton's news conference via CCTV throughout China ("Clinton in China: The Media," *New York Times*, June 28, 1998, document 137 of 299; on web.lexis-nexis.com/univers).

100. "In the Chinese Press," *China Daily*, Sept. 17, 1998, p. 4.

101. These figures are a composite from "Human Rights Conditions: Great Success, but Lots of Problems" (chap. 17) in Weng Jieming et al., *Zhongguo fazhan baogao shu: 1996–1997 nian*, pp. 325–26; State Council Information Office, "The Progress of Human Rights in China," pp. 11–12; and Shaoguang Wang, "The Politics of Private Time," charts on pp. 162–63.

102. State Council Information Office, "The Progress of Human Rights in China," pp. 11–12.

103. "Lexis-Nexis Country Report, 1999: China," web.lexis-nexis.com/univers.

quantity of output that has allowed people to choose the types of news, programs, and perspectives they wish to hear, see, or read.

In the early 1990s, only one-third of China's newspapers were profitable. Most of these fell into four categories: evening, business, and leisure-oriented newspapers, and newspaper digests. Opposed to these were publications in five broad categories that lost money: institutional, general national, mass socially-oriented, enterprise, and military newspapers. The Chinese Communist Party decided that, as of 1994, it would subsidize only two national newspapers, *The People's Daily* and *Economic Daily*, and only one national magazine, *Seeking Truth* (*Qiu shi*). If this trend continues, many newspapers and magazines whose primary function is propagandistic or educational may be shut down.[104] In fact, in 2000, the government announced that, to prepare China for admission to the World Trade Organization and to become more competitive internationally, it was attempting to establish provincial and national "brand-name" newspapers and journals in China. Progress toward this goal required that the government end its role in the management and publication of newspapers and journals, that shoddy publications be closed, that mergers be used to create better and more profitable ventures, and that newspapers and journals specialize for targeted readerships.[105] With the end of government subsidies to the print media and the decrease in censorship, publishing has burgeoned. Now that they no longer have to compete with a state-financed press, township and village enterprises in the countryside, and even private entrepreneurs, have set up thousands of printing facilities during the past ten to fifteen years in expectation of substantial profits.[106]

With the arrival of market-driven media, consumers' preferences (as measured by regular surveys of readers, listeners, and viewers), rather than government regulations or ideological values, are shaping programming and publishing decisions.[107] Writers discuss teenage pregnancies, infidelity, relationship problems, and the joys of promiscuity. Newspapers print stories

---

104. Paul Lee, "Mass Communication and National Development in China," p. 25.

105. *People's Daily* (web site), "Party Paper Views Changes in Media," Feb. 3, 2000, from BBC, on www.lexis-nexis.com.

106. Shaoguang Wang, "The Politics of Private Time," pp. 170–71.

107. See, e.g., *The Chinese Journalism Yearbook* (*Zhongguo xinwen nianjian*), which is published annually by the Chinese Social Science Publishing House in Beijing. This yearbook publishes such information as the percentage of people who listen to specific radio programs, how often they listen, whether they want news, entertainment, or knowledge, and so on.

about sexual habits.[108] And letters to newspaper editors complain about corrupt officials, the levying of illegal taxes, and the sale of damaged seeds and other defective products.

Like consumers of mass media everywhere, Chinese readers and viewers do not necessarily opt for the most informative or the highest quality stories but for the most entertaining. Books and short stories reflect the readers' shifting preferences: "detective stories in 1980, traditional knight errant fiction between 1981 and 1983, modern knight errant fiction between 1984 and 1985, triangular love stories in 1986, pornographic stories after 1987." In parallel development with these changes in readers' tastes,

the content of *illegal* publications has gone from martial arts to murder, from pornography to obscenity, from feudal superstitions to directly attacking the Chinese Communist Party and the socialist system. The government has tried to discourage publishing houses from printing "unhealthy" and "harmful" material at every turn, but all its attempts have stopped short of achieving this goal. In the late 1980s, in the face of growing competition from hundreds of newly founded pulp magazines, even serious literary journals became more or less corrupted by profit considerations. To respond to "market signals," many of them were forced to cater to readers' tastes for supernatural martial arts, romance, fashion, violence, crime, intrigue, and above all, sex.[109]

The government is not pleased with this situation, but its efforts to restrict the publication of such materials have actually stimulated public interest and a demand for still more of the forbidden fruit. For example, the Party's Propaganda Department ordered the publishers of Zhou Weihui's stunningly popular novel *Shanghai Baby* (*Shanghai baobei*) to destroy the page proofs because of the book's graphic descriptions of sex and its discussion of such taboo topics as female masturbation and homosexuality. The book continues to circulate in several pirated editions, however, and no one is suggesting that Zhou Weihui be muzzled or sent to a labor camp. Far from it. Even as the propaganda machine was pulling her novel off the racks, film crews were documenting her career and dramatizing some of her work for a video disk to be circulated with her next book.[110]

---

108. For example, the *Beijing Youth Daily* publishes surveys on such topics as the percentage of Chinese people who make love each day. See "One Day in the Life of People Worldwide," *Beijing qingnian bao*, Sept. 6, 1995, section 8.

109. Shaoguang Wang, "The Politics of Private Time," pp. 170–71. Italics added.

110. Craig S. Smith, "Sex, Lust, Drugs: Her Novel's Too Much for China," *New York Times*, May 11, 2000, A4.

Thus far, efforts to restrict publication of such books and publications have resulted in price hikes for those titles in demand, the smuggling of significant amounts of pornographic materials into China from abroad, violation of copyright in publishing the works of popular Hong Kong and Taiwanese fiction writers, and underground printing and distribution. Some of these operations are actually backed by state publishers; others are controlled by organized "triad societies" (crime syndicates) that utilize their "connections" with highly placed individuals to avoid being shut down. Pornography, an industry that did not even exist in 1979, has invaded China through audio and video cassette production.[111] Even Falungong, the organization that the government declared illegal in 1999, still manages to print and distribute materials (or smuggle them in).

Academic bookstores, specializing in books in the humanities and social sciences, have sprung up in major cities, including Beijing, Shanghai, and Shenzhen. They carry many foreign titles, a significant percentage of which are translated into Chinese. A network of private, so-called second-class book and magazine dealers is also developing rapidly. The size of this Beijing-centered market is said to rival that of its state-run counterpart. Private bookstores and bookstalls buy from these dealers because of their high discounts and market-oriented approach. Although the contents of some of these books are pornographic or violent, these dealers also publish "progressive" books, some of which have been banned or published overseas, such as the memoir of Mao Zedong's private life by his doctor.[112] It has been suggested that this book market may be the precursor of an unofficial press in China. One thing is certain: it is destroying the official monopoly over the cultural market.[113]

Of course, the flourishing of literature, films, video cassettes, and magazines of which the regime disapproves, and even bans, is not the same as freedom of the press. And many Chinese are still dissatisfied with the lack of variety, if not the lack of freedom, of the mass media.[114] Pleas are often made

---

111. Sylvia Chan, "Building a 'Socialist Culture with Chinese Characteristics'?," pp. 15–17.

112. Li Zhisui, *The Private Life of Chairman Mao*. It was also illegally translated into Chinese and published and distributed in China.

113. Sun Peiwu, "Dalu zhengzhi zixia ershangde tiaozhang jixiang."

114. Although the following survey was done in 1991, a low point in the opening of the mass media because of the repression that followed the crackdown on Tiananmen, at least it indicates the level of urban satisfaction (well distributed according to age, gender, educational level, and occupation) with the media before it really took off again. In response to the state-

for the press to be given greater freedom to cover all the news.[115] Still, the increasing scope of topics and approaches in the mass media does indicate that overall, the state makes less of an effort to control, or is at least less successful at controlling, the cultural sphere than it was before 1979, when the only themes explored in popular culture were those approved by the Party. Many newspapers, for example, now have "weekend editions," which sometimes verge on the vulgar and the pornographic. Newspapers and tabloids insist on the necessity of appealing to popular interests in order to sell papers—all in the name of heeding the Party's call to "march toward the market." Even the *People's Daily*, an official state organ, has been told to watch the bottom line and now offers lifestyle supplements in an effort to boost appeal and sales. Its tabloid, *Global News Digest*, chronicles the romantic, turgid, and turbulent lives of singers and movie stars.[116] The overall effect of competition from these new publications has been to force China's largest newspapers to loosen up. Perhaps of greater importance, they have shifted the focus of the public from political affairs to social and economic affairs[117] and, most of all, to entertainment. Finally, overseas competition, when it has not led merely to cheap knockoffs and duplication of imported tapes, books, CDs, videos, and films, has spurred Chinese popular culture to become more creative, interesting, and attuned to commercial rather than ideological concerns.

---

ment "I can't buy the books I want to buy," 15.4 percent strongly agreed and 36.0 percent agreed, meaning that 51.4 percent were disappointed with availability. Whether this was due to unavailability because of inadequate stocks or because of censorship was not stated. In response, however, to the statement, "Those books I don't want to buy are always available," 21.2 percent strongly agreed, and 36.6 percent agreed. This implies that 57.8 percent were unhappy about the selection. In response to the statement "TV programs are meaningless," 14.4 percent strongly agreed, and 36.7 percent agreed, meaning that again some 51 percent of the population was dissatisfied with the offerings. Still, even here there is no indication what the source of the problem is. In response to the statement "I can't find a few good movies to see in one year," 18.1 percent strongly agreed, and 37.8 percent agreed; 55.9 percent were thus disappointed with the offerings. Similar rates of response came in answer to questions whether there were enough art exhibitions and whether the respondent could engage in a hobby of his or her choice (see State Statistical Bureau, Statistics Division; and Chinese Research Center for the Promotion and Development of Science and Technology, *Zhongguo shehui fazhan ziliao*).

115. Ma Licheng, "Xinwen jiedu bu xing 'zi'" (Supervision by the news media is not "capitalism"), *Fangfa*, no. 78 (Mar. 1998): 6.

116. Jernow, "China: The Tight Leash Loosens," p. 32.

117. Zha, "China's Popular Culture in the 1990s," pp. 128–31.

The same reforms that have made artists, film directors, and everyone else in the culture industry cater to the marketplace and chase after foreign funds have nevertheless had a salutary effect on those used to force-feeding official ideology, regardless of how dull or irrelevant. Now that people can choose *not* to read official newspapers or officially approved books, magazines, and films, China's leaders in the official cultural sphere must hustle to maintain their audience. Subscription rates for official newspapers fell steadily in the 1990s. By 1994, the readership of the *People's Daily* in Shanghai had plummeted to a mere 1.2 percent of those surveyed;[118] and in Guangzhou, the readership of *Southern Daily* (*Nanfang ribao*) and *Guangzhou Daily* (*Guangzhou ribao*—the official publications of the Guangdong Provincial Party Committee and the Guangzhou Municipal Party Committee, respectively, and formerly the two major papers in Guangzhou) had fallen to under 10 percent of those surveyed.[119] At the same time, *Southern Weekend* (*Nanfang zhoumo*), a 1982 entertainment spinoff of *Southern Daily*, became known as a paper with the largest number of social and political scoops.[120]

The evening newspaper *Yangcheng Evening News* (*Yangcheng wanbao*; or *City of Goats Evening News*), with a circulation in Guangdong Province of more than one million, grew to become one of China's ten largest newspapers, owing to its relatively liberal editorial policy. Apart from publishing articles that stray from the official line, it also prints articles by controversial figures.[121] Put another way, *Yangcheng Evening News*, whose circulation is second only to that of *People's Daily*, discovered "that a diet of crime, corrup-

---

118. From 1992 to 1993, circulation of *People's Daily* dropped from 2.3 to 1.65 million (Barnathan et al., "China: Is Prosperity Creating a Freer Society?" pp. 98–99).

119. Sylvia Chan, "Building a 'Socialist Culture with Chinese Characteristics,'" p. 2.

120. Scoops are often on sensitive topics, such as AIDS; see Bay Fang, "Colourful Crusaders: The Media Speak out for Social Causes," *Far Eastern Economic Review*, May 7, 1998, p. 13. Unfortunately, in recent years the government has begun to crack down on *Southern Weekend*. Some of the paper's writers and editors have been demoted, reassigned, or even fired. (Notably its editor-in chief, Jiang Yiping, was removed in 2000, and his successor was removed in May 2001.) Other newspapers, magazines, and publishing houses have also been affected by this tightening of state control (see Erik Eckholm, "China Tightens Rein on Writers and Publishers," *New York Times*, Jan. 19, 1999, p. A6; and Zhao Yuezhi, "Underdogs, Lapdogs, Watchdogs, and Other Breeds," pp. 26–30). Still, not to put too fine a point on it, removing or demoting editors and journalists is hardly commensurate with jailing them or sending them off to labor camps, the preferred methods of the pre-reform period.

121. Sylvia Chan, "Building a 'Socialist Culture with Chinese Characteristics,'" p. 9. She includes Wang Meng, the former minister of culture, and Yu Guangyuan, the economist, among these figures.

tion, sex, leisure and soft features is doing wonders for circulation—and profits." In 2000, the paper launched a morning tabloid modeled on the American paper USA Today.[122] China Culture Gazette, the official organ of the Ministry of Culture, was transformed in 1993 from the stodgy, dull, didactic voice of the Chinese Communist Party into "the coolest paper in Beijing." When the ("non-pornographic") nude photos and brash interviews in its new Cultural Weekend edition were challenged by the Ministry of Propaganda and Ministry of Culture, the chief editor (himself a hard-liner), who was responsible for censorship, reminded them of the Party's policy of "marching toward the market."[123]

In this commercializing environment, media advertising has exploded. At the end of 1978, there were only some ten to twenty advertising units in China. By the end of 1994, there were 43,000, with countless private unlicensed entities catering to smaller private and collective firms. The key administrative decision that has allowed advertising to flourish was made in 1980, when the State Council decided advertising should be under the jurisdiction not of the propaganda and educational system (xitong) but of the financial and economic system. Specifically, it fell to the State Administration of Industry and Commerce to oversee advertising. This led to the "administrative fragmentation" of "thought work" (sixiang gongzuo). In short, advertising was placed outside the reach of the propaganda system.[124]

Before liberalization of the press and advertising, state-owned enterprises and government units paid for subscriptions to official publications for their employees, and readership was close to 100 percent, simply because there were no alternatives. Now, with the bottom line ever in mind, work units have drastically reduced expenditures on such frills as subscriptions to infrequently read, party-controlled newspapers. China's official cultural establishment has tried to improve its offerings in order to be financially secure, but it continues to lose ground to unofficial popular culture. China's leaders may be wondering about the value of this growth of popular culture. For example, night after night in 1991, China's citizens put everything aside to watch the lives of the central characters unfold in the fifty-part soap opera

---

122. "Media to Promote Ethics, Culture," BBC Summary of World Broadcasts, Jan. 15, 2000, Document 5. This article is based on an interview between Mike Chinoy, CNN correspondent, and Cao Chunliang, editor, Yangcheng Evening News.

123. Zha, China Pop, pp. 105–7.

124. Lynch, After the Propaganda State, pp. 55, 57.

serial *Yearning* (*Kewang*). The series combined a convoluted, melodramatic plot with a subtle commentary on the morality of its characters' actions from the time of the Cultural Revolution through the 1980s. Old values such as self-sacrifice were celebrated at the expense of Western values of individuality. Li Ruihuan, the Politburo member assigned the job of ideological control after the crackdown on Tiananmen, publicly endorsed the series and said it showed that a program must first be entertaining if it is to succeed in conveying positive values.[125]

In short, the official response to the flowering of popular culture and the mass media, as well as to the proliferation of the channels of communication available to ordinary Chinese people, has for the most part been endorsement, not suppression. Alternatively, it could be argued that the party-state has, because of commercialization, internationalization, pluralization, the fragmentation of administrative control over the media, and the dramatic technological updating of Chinese communications simply lost control of the messages and values circulating in society except those about sensitive political matters.[126] The state, in short, may have initiated the process, but it no longer controls it. This has resulted in peculiar hybrids, with the Party's Propaganda Department owning television companies such as Hunan Satellite TV, which lists its shares on the stock market and is "obsessed with ratings and audience response."[127]

This state of affairs need not be interpreted as a "loss" for the state—or for society. Many of the same people who shouted slogans about "freedom" and "democracy" in Tiananmen Square in 1989 embraced the conservative values praised by the government in the *Yearning* series, such as denouncing "the villanized, pretentious intellectual characters."[128] Surely China's leaders must also have pondered the possibility that it is preferable for the people to be diverted through entertainment, even if it is sometimes unusually decadent, than it is for them to think about how well they are governing. As Orville Schell puts it, the Chinese Communist Party "could do worse for its

---

125. Zha, *China Pop*, pp. 25–33. The key writer for *Kewang* was Li Xiaoming.

126. Lynch (*After the Propaganda State*, p. 4) has the same opinion. Lynch—in spite of all the evidence he offers—does not, however, conclude from that evidence, as I do, that all this implies the growth of a more "liberal" public sphere.

127. Elisabeth Rosenthal, "Changsha Journal. Human Style Television: Spicy and Crowd Pleasing," *New York Times*, Oct 11, 2000, p. A3.

128. Zha, "China's Popular Culture in the 1990s," pp. 120–21.

cause than turn China into a nation of tabloid-dazed couch potatoes."[129] Entertainment as the "opiate of the masses" might create the docile population China's leaders might like.

Finally, to put China in comparative perspective, even in liberal democratic countries, it is easy to find examples of state control over the mass media—and often for the very same reasons as China exercises control. France, for example, has tried to control "cultural pollution" and sustain French national identity by controlling the content of the mass media and limiting foreign (especially American) television programming. In 1996, France banned books concerning Islamic fundamentalism on the grounds that they were a threat to the "national interest." In the same year, it also banned the sale of Dr. Claude Gubler's book, *The Great Secret*, which revealed that the late president François Mitterrand had had cancer and forced his doctor to treat it as a "state secret" from 1981 to 1992.[130] Even Great Britain is still involved in a continuing debate over whether self-censorship by the press is adequate, or whether government legislation on censorship of the press is necessary.

Within Asia, countries such as Japan and Singapore have also resisted opening up the mass media to a cultural invasion from abroad. And countries like the United States, Germany, and Singapore have tried to restrict pornography on the Internet, with Singapore adding restrictions on religious information. It is certainly the case that China does not want the Internet used for the purpose of subverting the Chinese state. Although other states may consider this ludicrously impossible, they, too, might well take measures to control or monitor the Internet if they *did* think it possible—as has been the case in all the liberal democratic countries since the attack on the World Trade Towers in New York City on September 11, 2001. Indeed, the Internet was already carefully monitored by the internal security service of every major liberal democratic country; and "information warfare," the stealing and destruction of information on computers through the use of the Internet, is a major concern for all developed states today. American companies rather arbitrarily monitor the e-mail and internet use of their employees. And in 2000, Great Britain's Parliament passed a law that gives the government wide powers to monitor encrypted e-mail traffic and other coded communications among organizations, individuals, and companies.

---

129. Orville Schell, "Maoism vs. Media in the Market," p. 42.
130. *International Herald Tribune*, Jan. 20, 1996.

Malaysia and Singapore already have such laws,[131] and the United States passed a similar law in the wake of the events of September 11, 2001. In fact, in spite of the outcry that civil rights were being stifled, public intellectuals (such as Susan Sontag), professors, and media spokespersons who described the cause of the terrorists' attack on the United States in a fashion suddenly deemed inappropriate in the context of a powerful American nationalism, found they were denounced, criticized, reprimanded, suspended, or even fired from their jobs. China's party-state is hardly unique, then, in its concern about the right of individuals and organizations to introduce ideas that are perceived to threaten either national unity, national security, or the present interpretation of the values binding the Chinese in a community or national security.

2. *Right to privacy.*   Privacy is another area in which Chinese values should not be judged by Western expectations. China's communitarian-based traditions of privacy, the citizen, and "the public" (*gong*) differ from the individual-centered values of many Western societies. Individuals cannot simply "drop out" of the community:

> In Neo-Confucian societies where the public sphere has been created by and from the state and not from the private sphere, there remain few limits to the state. . . . [The people] are always expected to behave as political participants in their communities, and the state has a right to intrude into their "private lives" in ways which the hypothesized, individualistic, capitalist-liberal democrat citizen would not accept.[132]

The ambiguity created by the lack of a clear line between the public and the private, and hence between an individual's and the state's rights, has had negative effects. Corruption, for example, is furthered if it is not clear when

---

131. The law will require anyone using the Internet "to turn over the keys to decoding e-mail messages and other data." And the British government will not have to request a court to determine the legitimacy of any search of such private data, for unlike the United States, "Britain has a tradition of unfettered and often uncontested intrusion by the authorities into citizens' privacy" (see Sarah Lyall, "British Authorities May Get Wide Powers to Decode E-Mail," *New York Times*, July 19, 2000, p. A3). Opponents of the bill believe it contravenes basic rights in the European Convention on Human Rights, including the rights to privacy, freedom of expression, and association.

132. Australian-Asian Perceptions Project, *Perceiving Citizenship*, Working Paper no. 1 (Sydney: Academy of the Social Sciences in China and the University of New South Wales, Asia-Australia Institute), 1993; cited in Frolic, "State-Led Civil Society," p. 52.

citizens may use public (state) property for private gain and when they may not—a situation not helped by fluctuations in the state's laws and regulations.[133]

The enhancement of the right to privacy in China has not evolved from new laws or policies directed specifically at protecting privacy. Rather, it has emerged from the effects of modernization and urbanization, greater leisure, economic liberalization policies, emerging property rights, and the government's decision not to enforce certain laws and policies that would restrict privacy.[134]

Economic liberalization policies have affected privacy in many ways. In particular, their impact on mobility means that 10 percent of the population (mostly individuals formerly engaged in agriculture) is on the move and no longer tied to a fixed residence. When people are freer to move into a community to live and do business where nobody knows them, this increases their privacy (and, unfortunately, opportunities for criminal activity). Of Beijing's 12 million residents, for example, 4 million are unregistered. Their whereabouts are not entirely clear, and it is difficult for the state to monitor their behavior.

The privacy arising from mobility has been enhanced further by modernization and urbanization. In the cities, the government is moving a significant percentage of the population out of enclosed courtyard housing in which people often share toilet and kitchen facilities, as well as their lives, and into high-rise apartment buildings whose tenants often do not know their neighbors. Living in self-contained apartments with their own kitchen facilities, bathrooms, and entryways, people meet only in elevators or staircases. Further, merely by becoming more modern and more urban in a market-oriented society, in which people can *buy* the services they need instead of relying on others to help them, people are finding they do not *need* community. As a result, they can more easily escape from the tendency, however unintentional, of a community to invade their privacy—to observe at close quarters the lives and attitudes of others living in the same residential unit.

---

133. Frederick Wakeman, "Corruption in China," seminar, Harvard University Asia Center, Apr. 20, 2001.

134. This would include the right to sexual freedom and sexual preference (that is, the end of the practice of punishing homosexuals or trying to change their sexual orientation) and the end of the practice of expelling students from universities for having romantic relationships.

Charles Taylor, in a discussion of "modern identity" and privacy, in contrast to "traditional identity" and the collective public enforcement of patterns and values, offers a valuable perspective for thinking about privacy as China modernizes. Taylor argues that, as people become more "modern" and more in control of their individual lives, they reject participation in collectively enforced traditional patterns (such as the subjugation of women) that have taken priority over notions of individual fulfillment. In more traditional societies, "living up to one's place is not just one's own affair; it is everyone's business." This stunning lack of privacy is a universal aspect of traditional societies.[135] It is certainly a prominent aspect of Chinese society.[136] The surveillance of neighborhoods by grannies and residential committees and the use of mass movements and criticism/self-criticism methods, which required the total involvement of everyone in one another's business, may have been communist-inspired forms, but they have deep roots in Chinese traditional culture and practices.

Shaming runs deep in Chinese culture. Before being executed, for example, criminals are paraded through the streets with placards indicating their crimes hung around their necks. To shame them further, the public may denounce them as they pass by. Public humiliation was a critical ingredient in mass campaigns, such as various anti-rightist campaigns in the 1950s and 1960s and the Cultural Revolution. Those who deviated from community standards were force-marched through a public assembly to be spat upon, denounced, and humiliated. In the workplace, coworkers would shun those bearing a bad class label or accused of having committed a political error, all in an effort to shame them through social ostracism.

Public shaming of those who deviate from social norms is common in societies that lack privacy. As Charles Taylor puts it in his discussion of the practice of "charivaris" in French villages,

---

135. Taylor, *Philosophy and the Human Sciences*, p. 260.

136. Anyone who travels to or works in China has experienced this lack of privacy. Except in today's joint-venture hotels, for example, hotel personnel feel free to enter a person's room, even without knocking. When I was a faculty member teaching in China and living in the work unit's housing, maids and administrators entered whenever they chose, from morning to night, without warning. In village elections, once the "secret" ballot is distributed, villagers prefer to sit around and discuss their choice of candidates with others. And, even when voting booths have been set up to guarantee secrecy, most villagers choose to fill out their ballot in the presence of other villagers.

shame plays an important role in societies which live by a public pattern; for whether the pattern is realized or not is always a public affair. One's life was led before everyone else, and hence shame and its avoidance played a big role in people's lives. There was no space, not just physically but psycho-socially, to withdraw into the privacy of one's own self-estimate, or the opinions of a circle based on affinity. . . . With the rise of the modern identity, this intensely public life withers. The community retreats, and the nuclear family achieves privacy. For the subject with a modern identity is looking for *fulfillment*. What this amounts to, he will discover in himself. This requires privacy. . . . And this life cannot be subject to the constant scrutiny and judgement of the whole, nor submitted to the structures of a fixed pattern, without being inhibited and stifled. . . . So the growth of the modern identity [and fulfillment] involves the *withering of community*; the villages of traditional society are among the most important examples [of communities of common life and ritual]. . . . The modern subject is bound sooner or later to find their common rhythm irksome.[137]

In China, however, a "traditional" identity was maintained even within cities, thanks to party policies that insisted on the continued community surveillance of citizens through the neighborhood and work unit and ultimately through criticism/self-criticism groups, mass campaigns, and class struggle. These practices brought the private into the public realm. And, as with traditional communities in other countries, the Chinese groups rigidly defined and enforced values and standards. In short, China's urban communities could be, and tended to be, just as traditional in this respect as rural communities. Even today, the shaming of individuals continues in work units and in schools, where there is a continual evaluation of the morality and competence of one's subordinates and superiors. Public criticism, humiliation, and shaming are still used in such evaluations. In China, "inferiors and superiors are allowed, even expected, to appraise each other, and . . . if the evaluation is a [strongly] negative one . . . it can be expressed publicly."[138]

Since the 1980s, however, the forces of rapid modernization have led to greater privacy by introducing mobility and anonymity, along with some phasing out of policies that shamed individuals publicly. In addition, with the diminution of the party-state's mobilizing abilities, values and standards are less rigidly defined and enforced. The government has moved away from mass movements as the method for implementing policies and criticism/self-

---

137. Taylor, *Philosophy and the Human Sciences*, p. 261. Italics added.

138. Schoenhals, *The Paradox of Power in a People's Republic Middle School*, p. 32; see also pp. 87–93.

criticism sessions as the way to control deviance. As a result, the party-state does not force people to interact, to come to know one another's every little foible as much as it used to do.

Privacy has also been advanced by leisure activities. The Chinese now have greater freedom to choose what to do in their spare time and more free time to pursue their own interests. And they may engage in leisure activities or recreation in private if they wish. In 1980, the average amount of free time per urban adult per day was 2 hours 21 minutes; by 1991, this had doubled, to 4 hours 48 minutes.[139] The amount of leisure time was increased by at least another 4 hours per week with the government's 1995 decision to move from the five-and-one-half-day to the five-day work week. In major cities, the majority of citizens now have two-day weekends, and a significant percentage takes advantage of this free time to enjoy themselves.[140] Finally, the rapid spread among a growing middle class of time-saving consumer goods, such as washing machines, microwave ovens, and refrigerators (eliminating the need for daily shopping) has greatly augmented the amount of leisure time available.

The new characteristics of leisure in China today—depoliticization, privatization, Westernization, and commercialization—would be less significant for democratization were they not accompanied by meaningful choices. At least for the urban middle class, choices have expanded dramatically. Apart from the chance to exercise at athletic clubs and the many opportunities provided by the sprouting of athletic associations (for activities such as fishing, mountain climbing, and biking), people may go to dance halls, karaoke bars, and cafes. Wealthier Chinese can play golf and go to bowling alleys. Domestic tourism is also booming, and several million Chinese now can afford to travel abroad each year.[141] In 1999, foreign travel had increased by more than 50 percent, with some 2.88 million Chinese venturing overseas (including to Taiwan), and an additional 1.32 million traveling either to

---

139. Wang Shaoguang, "The Politics of Private Time," table on p. 158.

140. One survey indicates that 71.9 percent of Beijing residents and 66 percent of Shanghai citizens enjoy a two-day weekend. Shopping and visiting parks and scenic spots are among the favorite leisure activities ("How Beijing People Spend their Two-Day Weekends," *Beijing qingnian bao*, Sept. 27, 1995, section 8).

141. As long as they have sufficient hard currency, mainland Chinese may now travel virtually anywhere in the world. And a growing number are able to afford to send their children abroad for summer camps, where they study foreign languages.

Hong Kong or Macao.[142] The resources of most Chinese, however, are inadequate for many of these new pastimes. The bulk of their new leisure time is spent at home, and watching television is the major leisure activity. Given the blossoming of television programming over the last twenty years, this, too, has become a far more rewarding leisure activity than it was in the past.[143]

Thus, in China today, people are far freer to spend their time as they please and out of the public view. This newly gained leisure time and privacy are key ingredients in the exercise of individual rights. Yet some Chinese are already wondering if the trade-off between community on the one hand and individual fulfillment and privacy on the other hand has been worth it. A carefully calibrated calculation of exactly how much additional freedom would cause "community" to be at risk of unraveling is, however, not possible.

3. *Right to choice of consumer goods.* Citizens who lack money to buy consumer goods or, even if they do have funds, lack access to consumer goods, do not really have the right to make choices. For many of the world's peoples, once they have satisfied the basic needs of health, food, shelter, clothing, security, and stability, the first "right" they want is a choice of affordable consumer goods. Psychologically, people who can choose from a variety of goods in plentiful supply feel "less dependent on the state for their material welfare."[144] Without choices, the *right* to choose is meaningless, as Russia's citizens learned after the collapse of the Soviet Union.

Data in the United Nations' Development Program's annual *Human Development Report* indicate a strong (though not perfect) correlation between growth in per capita income and "human development," which in turn is so important to democratization. Thus China's strong economic growth in the past twenty years has given the vast majority of its people the income necessary for greater freedom of choice and the opportunity to improve their lives through consumption. Whereas the average annual growth rate in sales of

---

142. Figures are from China's Ministry of Public Security and published in *The China Daily* (Feb. 4, 2000), in *China News Digest* (Feb. 6, 2000), at www.cnd.org. In a 1996 survey of middle school students, 72.4 percent said they wanted to study abroad, and only 6.7 percent said they did *not* ("Beijing Middle School Students in an Age of Computers," p. 4).

143. Shaoguang Wang, "The Politics of Private Time," pp. 165–68.

144. Davis, "Introduction: Urban China," in idem et al., *Urban Spaces in Contemporary China*, p. 18.

consumer goods was a mere 6.2 percent between 1952 and 1978, by 1995 it had increased by 19.5 percent. As China becomes a buyer's market, the most commonly stated quip is "The consumer is God."[145] For many urban Chinese, consumption patterns have moved beyond basic necessities to include the products of what some might call "the good life." Apart from such durables as washing machines, refrigerators, televisions, and microwaves, considerable sums are being spent on such things as travel, leisure activities, CDs, videos, cameras, toys, brides and weddings, greeting cards, karaoke, disco, dance halls, and bowling.[146] And people now eat out far more than at any time in the past, thanks to more disposable income and the proliferation of restaurants and food stands. Chinese take-out, or as they say in China, "take-out," is increasingly common. People derive enormous satisfaction from telling others that they ate unusual or expensive food, like snake, turtle, bear's paw, bird's nest soup—or in Guangdong, monkey's brains.

4. *Right to consumer protection.* The area of consumer rights illustrates the paradoxical demands of a democratizing authoritarian state: citizens may want the state to give them more freedom, but at the same time they want the state to protect them from other citizens who abuse their newfound freedom. This is one area in which citizens demand that the state, even an "authoritarian" one, exercise more control, not less.

Like sexual rights, the right to clean air, and the right to sunshine, consumer protection is considered a "luxury" right in post-industrial societies. China was one of the first nonindustrialized countries to establish institutions and enact policies and administrative rules to protect consumers against fraudulent products. These regulations resulted in part from pressures by an international community angry at copyright and trademark violations by Chinese enterprises, but ordinary citizens, entrepreneurs, and organized consumer groups within China have also pressured the government to take strong measures against producers of substandard goods. Exploding beer bottles and falsely labeled medicines have caused serious injury and even death; falsely advertised chemical fertilizers have caused significant financial and property losses; and buildings and bridges have collapsed because of shoddy construction materials. Cheap and falsely labeled imitations of well-

---

145. Ho Suk-ching, "The Emergence of Consumer Power in China," p. 16.

146. For articles on some of these aspects of consumer behavior, see Davis, *The Consumer Revolution in Urban China.*

known liquors,[147] watches, designer products, hair tonics, tapes, and CDs result in consumers' paying high prices for cheap substitutes. Some Chinese
insist that well over half the products in China are fakes, and that it would
be nothing short of a miracle if a Chinese person had been cheated only once
in her life. Even Chinese entrepreneurs and enterprises are concerned about
protecting their products and copyrights from violation by producers of
fakes.

Consumer protection is an example of a right that benefits when the government asserts more power over its citizens in order to ensure their safety
and protection. As noted in earlier chapters, the Chinese throughout history
have believed that the government should be paternalistic. Before 1979, when
the state owned and ran all enterprises, it controlled all products and bore a
responsibility for their safety and reliability. In today's freewheeling economy, however, the state needs to protect citizens against the machinations of
private entrepreneurs and non-state-run enterprises, not to mention the
shoddy products of state-run enterprises.

Consumer anger over fake and dangerous products and demands for the
state to do more have in recent years led to the creation of a number of government agencies to protect consumers' rights. Among these are the Anti-
Fake Bureau, the Bureau of Standard Measurement, the Business and Trade
Administration, and the Bureau of Inspection of Imported and Exported
Goods. The National People's Congress also passed the Law to Protect
Consumers' Rights. A raft of inspectors and administrators is cracking down
on copyright and trademark violators and imposing serious penalties, including execution. Thousands of products now bear a state-controlled holo-
graphic seal of authenticity.

In addition, in 1984, the government established the China Consumers'
Association, which is under the General Bureau of the State Administrative
Bureau for Industry and Commerce. By the end of 1994, there were 2,580 local consumer protection agencies established above the county level. If all
such agencies from the provincial down to the village and (urban) street lev-

---

147. Worse than claiming to be a famous brand, some falsely labeled liquor has been lethal.
In one incident, several dozen people died from drinking a liquor made of industrial alcohol
and water. Thousands of others have become seriously ill after drinking industrial alcohol or
simply chemicals and water bottled and labeled as liquor. The sale of liquor has proved extremely difficult to control. Many are tempted to make a quick yuan by selling fake liquor.
Literally thousands of home distilleries have sprung up since reforms began in 1979.

els were counted, there would be more than 45,000.[148] The government has designated March 15 as consumers' rights protection day. On this day, activities are organized to inform consumers about their rights in the media and on wall posters, and consumers are urged to complain about fake or shoddy products. In the new market economy, retail stores pay attention to consumer complaints. In short, the government has combined forces with interest groups, consumers, and retailers to enhance consumer protection. Advancing the people's right to consumer protection has, then, led to cooperation between the state and society, not a we-they confrontation.

In spite of these efforts to improve consumer rights, the results of a 1994 study conducted by the China Consumers' Association indicated that when consumers' rights were violated, a bare 13 percent would register complaints with a consumers' association. So China's consumers now have the institutional framework to assert their rights, but for a variety of reasons do not do so. Although in 1996, consumer associations throughout China reported received a total of 500,000 complaints, this was considered a small fraction of the cases in which consumers would have had the right to complain.[149] Nevertheless, the fact that the government was concerned enough about the abuse of consumer rights to establish the necessary organizations for their protection, and even to conduct this study, provides additional evidence that, at least in this area, the government is working to advance the rights of its citizens. Except for products and services provided by the remaining state-owned enterprises, however, these rights are not in most cases at the expense of the state's rights.

5. *Right to choose one's work and change one's domicile.* The right to choose one's own job rather than accepting a state-assigned job, and the right to change jobs, are closely connected to the demands of a modern market economy for a free flow of workers and capital. Since economic liberalization began in 1979, urban workers have been free to change jobs and establish their own residence, and farmers may leave the countryside and seek out new

---

148. Ho Suk-ching, "The Emergence of Consumer Power in China," p. 17.

149. Some of the other findings of the study were: 44 percent did not know they were eligible for compensation "for physical and financial damages as a result of using the goods and services," and 35 percent were unaware of their "right to be accurately informed about the products and services they bought and used" (ibid., pp. 18–19). It may turn out that the Chinese differ little from citizens of other countries in how they respond to problems with consumer goods.

opportunities in towns and cities. Unlike the "iron rice bowl" of the pre-liberalization period, workers are not guaranteed lifetime employment, but neither are they tied for life to one work unit. Workers now sign contracts. For the talented and the entrepreneurial, the right to choose where to work has fulfilled long-cherished hopes to improve their living standards. This right gained even more meaning beginning in the 1990s, in part because of the major business and building boom in cities that provides jobs for rural migrants and in part because starting one's own business is now an option.

The right to choose one's work was welcomed by many Chinese. In a poll in 1990, only 19.5 percent agreed with the statement "[Eating out of] the big pot [equality] is better than polarization," and 74.6 percent disagreed.[150] The vast majority also disagreed with the statement "Although [eating out of] the big pot is not good, it can guarantee a stable life."[151] At the time of this poll, China's strong economic growth had generated a considerable number of new jobs. With the slowdown in economic development and the massive unemployment that followed privatization of state-owned enterprises during the 1990s, however, polls reflected nostalgia for a greater equality of income and revealed concern about the polarization of wealth. Indeed, in a survey conducted in Beijing in late 1995, 93.4 percent of respondents agreed with the statement "The gap between rich and poor is getting too big."[152] A 1997 national survey of 2,430 urban families in 53 cities found 80.6 percent of the respondents dissatisfied with the gap between the rich and the poor.[153] And a poll in late 1999 that asked 2,800 families in more than 60 cities to list those issues with which they were most concerned, fully 80 percent listed the increasing disparities in wealth.[154] As Larry Diamond has stated, a "minimally

---

150. The figures were: agree, 6.0 percent; some agreement, 13.5 percent; don't agree very much, 29.4 percent; and disagree, 45.2 percent (Zhongguo shehui kexue yuan, Shehuixue yanjiusuo, Zhuanxing ketizu, *Zhongguo qingniande toushi*, p. 177).

151. Ibid., p. 178.

152. Zhong et al., "Political Views from Below," table 7, p. 480.

153. Sun Li, "1997 nian woguo chengzhen zhumin shehui jiben xintai diaocha fenxi," p. 151.

154. This survey was conducted jointly by the State Commission for Restructuring the Economy and the Chinese Academy of Social Science. The respondents also indicated concern about setbacks to "socialist culture," unemployment, shoddy goods, the decline of law and order and social welfare, and inadequate environmental protection. Respondents voiced satisfaction with the low inflation rate, the gradual recovery of economic growth, and China's international stature ("Survey Indicates Dismay About Falling Socialist Values," *China News Digest*, Jan. 4, 2000, item 3. www.cnd.org). See also a 1994 survey, in which fully 92.9 percent of the 1,443 respondents were concerned with an excessively large income gap (Social Psycho-

adequate" standard of living is essential for democratization. If, however, economic development leads to a significant imbalance in the distribution of benefits, "it may do little to promote democracy or may even generate stresses and contradictions that are hostile to democracy."[155] Nevertheless, in spite of the growing polarization of wealth, a 1999 Gallup Poll indicated that Chinese of all ages in all parts of the country felt their lives had improved in the preceding five years.[156]

In addition to reforms that have affected the labor market, reforms that permit individuals to buy property mean the successful are no longer dependent for housing on work units. Now workers are often able to purchase the work-unit apartments they have lived in. By the end of 1994, 30.5 percent of urban households had acquired ownership rights in one form or another. In short, what was a "welfare good" provided by the state has been privatized and commodified. As an advertisement for Yongde Homes put it, "Buy a home and become a boss."[157]

The state did not decide to relinquish certain controls over its citizens' lives, such as the assignment of jobs and housing, in order to advance democracy. Instead, it was the result of the series of governmental decisions to put efficiency of production and profits ahead of the socialist goal of full employment. The rapid growth of the economy has not compensated for the loss of tens of millions of jobs due to the downsizing of state-run enterprises. The work week was reduced from 48 hours to 40 primarily to keep more people employed, but it has also improved the quality of life by allowing additional leisure time for the employed.

The overall effect of the diminution of the state's control over jobs and housing is a heightened sense of freedom to make important life choices. Nevertheless, under China's still tightly controlled household registration

---

logical Attitude Research Project Team, "Zhuanxin shiqi de Shanghai shimin shehui xintai diaocha," p. 82). These polls reflect a dramatic change in popular attitudes since 1988 and 1990.

155. Diamond, "Economic Development and Democracy Reconsidered," p. 126.

156. The respondents were also confident that their lives would improve during the next five years. The findings are from the Gallup Organization's Third Survey of Consumer Attitudes and Lifestyles in the PRC, conducted in 1999; see Palmer, "What the Chinese Want," p. 232. I am assuming that this poll refers only to material improvement.

157. The advertisement appeared in *Xinmin wanbao*, Shanghai, May 11, 1994, p. 15; cited in Davis, "Introduction: A Revolution in Consumption," in idem, *The Consumer Revolution in Urban China*, pp. 8–9. For more on housing ownership, see David Fraser's article in *The Consumer Revolution in Urban China*.

(*hukou*) system, it is extremely difficult to change from a rural to an urban residence, except in China's smaller cities and towns. The trade-off for rural workers is that with the right to move to the cities has come the possibility of having no home—and no job—at all. Tens of millions of migrant peasant workers have inundated the cities, and although many find jobs and a place to sleep, countless others do not. They frequently resort to crime, clog the transportation system, and ignore the family planning program because they lack an officially registered household. They are a major source of instability in the cities and are deeply resented and distrusted by longtime city residents, who regard them as latent criminals. Urban residents often pressure the city government to destroy their shanty towns and to round them up and send them back to the countryside.

When discussing individual rights in China, then, it is important to specify *whose rights* we are discussing: the rights of the still employed or the rights of the unemployed? The rights of privileged urbanites to keep others from sharing in their lifestyle or the rights of vast numbers of country people to move and work where they choose while receiving the same educational, housing, and healthcare benefits as those who have urban household registrations? So far, the rights of the gainfully employed and of officially registered urban residents have received far more respect because their power to influence the government's policy far exceeds the power of the migrants.

6. *The right to personal style.*   For those living in countries where the right to such matters of personal style as clothing, hairstyle, makeup, music, entertainment, and recreation has never been contested, classifying personal style as a "right" might seem incomprehensible. Having suffered through the stifling conformity of the Cultural Revolution when one style fit all, however, the Chinese have embraced this right with an enthusiasm that might in other countries have been reserved for the freedoms of religion and speech. Chinese people now dress according to personal taste and listen to whatever music they like. Disco, hip hop, rap, and punk bands are wildly popular in China, even if the lyrics are a subdued Chinese style that avoids expletives and emphasizes traditional values (like love of family) instead of sex and violence.[158] The government does not ban Hong Kong and Taiwan stars, whose performances are sold out to "screaming worshipping fans"; nor does

---

158. Peter Hessler, "The Rap of Khan," *Boston Globe*, May 7, 2001, pp. B7, B9. This article was about rap in Mongolia, but China has rap as well.

it ban rock star Cui Jian from singing lyrics that express disillusionment and alienation. Ironically, the commercialization of China's rock music has made it as "politically" safe as any other category in music stores, even when its content is politically radical.[159] The right to express personal style has been given substance by the broad range of consumer products provided by a rapidly growing economy.

It is difficult to measure the impact of the right to personal choice on the overall process of democratization, but arguably once individuals start making independent decisions about their lives on a daily basis, rather than simply taking orders from the party-state, they will be more prepared to think independently about other issues. It is this change of mindset that is critical to democratization. In the meantime, the Chinese right to personal style makes people feel freer than they did in the past.

7. Miscellaneous rights.   Other rights emanating from economic liberalization are meaningful and satisfying to a significant swath of the population:

the right to "get rich"[160]
the right to inherit money and property
the right to buy and sell stock
the right to acquire hard currency.

In developing societies such as China, what is most wanted and needed tends to shape the notion of which "rights" are most valuable. One American researcher, who at every opportunity pressed the local people in various villages to talk about their most cherished right, assumed they would mention free speech. She was stunned to find that they uniformly said "roads." Without roads, country people cannot get their products to market in an efficient and timely matter. Without the "right" to roads, in their view, they had no

---

159. Zha, "China's Popular Culture in the 1990s," pp. 133–35.

160. A Gallup poll conducted in 1994 and 1997 among both rural and urban Chinese consumers asked about their attitudes toward life. Only one choice was allowed. Of the six choices available, the most commonly chosen response in both years was "Work hard to become rich" (68 percent in 1994, 56 percent in 1997). See "Gailuopu yanzhong de Zhongguo" (China in the eyes of Gallop), *Zhongguo qingnian bao*, Nov. 21, 1997, p. 8. The other choices were: Live in my own way, without thinking about fame and wealth; study hard to become famous; spend every day carelessly; resist evil and live an upright life; be totally selfless for the good of society.

opportunity to develop economically and thereby increase their wealth and well-being.[161] And an increase in wealth enhances their ability to attain basic "human capabilities."

CONCLUSIONS: CHINA'S GRADUAL
EXPANSION OF RIGHTS AND DEMOCRACY

If the Chinese had been given the choice between the rights mentioned above (all attained within the context of one-party control, order, stability, and development) and freedom of speech as defined in the West (that is, the right to challenge one-party rule and to criticize leaders publicly), would a majority of the Chinese population have chosen free speech? For the more than 70 percent of the population that lives in the countryside, the answer is probably no. Some surveys have been conducted in cities, but without the original data and more knowledge of how the surveys were conducted, the results must be accepted with care. (See the Appendix for a discussion of validity of surveys.) For example, in a survey of urban youth conducted in 1988, respondents were asked to rank eight criteria for "evaluating whether a country is well-managed." The results were as follows:

1 = social stability and justice
2 = high standard of living
3 = its national power
4 = high international status
5 = *full protection of freedom and individual rights*
6 = have a sort of concept of universal harmony
7 = a low polarization of wealth
8 = the development of society's wealth and power.[162]

In a 1990 survey of both rural and urban youth, respondents were asked to answer the question "What is the most important standard for judging whether a state is doing well or not?" Again social and economic stability ranked high.

---

161. Ann Thurston, at a New England China Seminar, Harvard University, winter 1999. The same observation about the need for roads has been made countless times by those involved in formulating policies for rural development in underdeveloped societies.

162. Zhongguo shehui kexue yuan, Shehuixue yanjiusuo, Zhuanxing ketizu, *Zhongguo qingniande toushi*, table 3-1, p. 140.

1 = social stability
2 = strong economy
3 = high standard of living
4 = widespread, commonly held beliefs
5 = *high degree of democracy*
6 = high international status
7 = low polarization of wealth
8 = development of (national) wealth and power.[163]

And, in a 1995 survey of Beijing residents over age 18 (chosen by random sampling), done by Western-trained Chinese social scientists, 94.8 percent of the respondents agreed with the statement "I would rather live in an orderly society than in a freer society which is prone to disruptions." In this same survey, respondents indicated a very high level of tolerance for individuals with different political beliefs (89.3 percent) and showed strong support for a freer press (94.3 percent).[164] This would seem to support the conclusion that even many Chinese who would welcome greater freedom of speech would choose stability over freedom if required to make a choice.

As far as we know, only among a small percentage of an already small segment of society—well-educated, urban intellectuals—does an interest in freedom of speech (that is, freedom of speech for the purpose of challenging the Party's legitimacy and policies) take precedence over other rights. The fact that economic liberalization and the introduction of enhanced rights were more successful than in the former Soviet Union, which introduced free speech simultaneously with economic liberalization, may also be because the rights the Chinese people have gained have been broadly distributed, whereas those rights they have not yet gained would affect a more narrow, albeit critical, spectrum of the population. As Yan Sun puts it in her discussion of Russia, "Has the freedom of a few politicians to engage in open power rivalry and of a few intellectuals to engage in open discussions really signified the end of alienation and the restoration of human integrity in post-Communist Russia? . . . Or will China have the last laugh because its transition to a politically more open society will be more solid and less painful in the long run?"[165] Put another way, the greater freedom of speech enjoyed by Russians has not been

---

163. Ibid., table 3-3, p. 141.
164. Zhong et al., "Political Views from Below," table 3, p. 476.
165. Yan Sun, *The Chinese Reassessment of Socialism*, p. 269.

as beneficial to the broad masses of Russian people as have the many substantive rights the Chinese have acquired since 1979. Similarly, the freedom that the people of India have as a result of democratic institutions and the right to free speech is, because of the prolonged and widespread malnutrition and inadequate education, healthcare, and development there, not the equal of the freedom the Chinese have. (For more on this point, see Chapter 9.)

This chapter focuses on the *growth* of rights. It makes no claim that China has reached a final goal of an absolute guarantee of individual rights, nor that the state's decision to relinquish certain powers, such as the assignment of jobs, was intended to advance democracy. The result has, however, been an increasing number of rights for China's people. The government has on occasion suddenly withdrawn or curtailed some of the rights discussed above, notably the crackdown on demonstrators in 1989, and the arrests of the organizers of a fledgling political party in 1998 and 1999 and of activists within the Falungong sect since it began publicly demonstrating against the government in 1999. Further, certain substantive rights such as education and healthcare have experienced considerable setbacks in the poorer parts of China as a result of liberalization. Nevertheless, in general there has been substantial progress.

The Chinese have by no means acquired an absolute right to free speech, but the trend in China in the past twenty years has been toward greater overall procedural and substantive rights. These include greater freedom to influence the political system and leadership through the electoral system and the National People's Congress; greater rights to choose one's lifestyle, job, and domicile; greater privacy; and expanding parameters for free speech in the mass media, the arts, and culture generally.[166] On the other hand, economic liberalization and modernization have undercut Mao Zedong Thought and the Chinese Communist Party's values such as equality in the distribution of material welfare. One consequence of the resulting ideological vacuum is a growing tendency to return to traditional Chinese values, some of which the Party labels "feudal." Particularly in the countryside, the restoration of Confucianism and traditional values is antidemocratic in tone and implication. The re-emergence of superstitious religious practices that permit religious leaders to control their followers' behavior and extract money from them has laid the basis for the revival of patriarchal attitudes and practices. It has also provided part of the framework for the re-

---

166. Shi Xiuyin, "Zhongguoren shehui xinli 90 niandai jincheng."

emergence of corruption and oppression by the "black societies" that pervaded the basis of China's authoritarian, elitist, and oppressive society before 1949 (see Chapters 6 and 7).

Another side effect of the economic reforms has been the re-emergence of the traditional cultural emphasis on the subordinate role of women and the return of exploitative practices that were largely eradicated or at least ameliorated from 1949 to 1979: prostitution, preferential hiring of men, and violence against women. Since elimination of the women's "quota" in provincial and national people's congresses, women's representation in legislative assemblies has declined markedly.

In short, the introduction of liberalizing reforms, including, as we shall see, democratic elections, has had some rather undemocratic effects, but the responsibility for the negative effects as often as not can be attributed to Chinese culture, as well as economic, social, and demographic conditions, rather than primarily to party leaders and communist ideology. This should make us hesitate before insisting that any democratic reform is an unqualified good; sometimes the effects may differ from those we would anticipate because of conditions in China. Further, as noted above, in almost all polities there is a trade-off between equality and freedom, with freedom coming at the expense of equality. It is hardly surprising that economic liberalization, which has given the Chinese an enormous amount of economic freedom, has come at the cost of economic equality.

Freedom and rights are not, then, just isolated political concepts, and they do not gain meaning merely in contradistinction to "control." Rather, as noted above, freedom and rights are also cultural, social, and economic concepts, even though greater rights in any sphere are implicitly political. Instead of being viewed merely in juxtaposition with control, freedom and rights may be seen as providing more options and greater opportunities.

Most of China's reformers appear committed to a steady expansion of individual rights. Nevertheless, they are still unwilling to relinquish their power to limit or even withdraw those rights if they believe they are being used to overthrow the Party's rule, destabilize China, or inhibit economic growth. Viewed from the perspective of leaders who are products of Chinese culture and who govern a people in whom these same values are deeply embedded, the paternalism, clientelism, corporatism, and authoritarianism that characterize Chinese governance make more sense.[167] In a rapidly developing

---

167. On clientelism and corporatism, see Chapter 7.

country, which threatens to collapse into chaos if a delicate balance between freedom and control is not maintained, the gradual and sometimes hesitant approach to political liberalization is more understandable. China is not ready for a "velvet revolution," and the costs of any other type of revolution could be intolerable to the Chinese people.

Analysts must be honest about China. There are individuals and groups who would like to overthrow the Party's rule but who do not offer a positive alternative, and there are dangerous and subversive elements who threaten to destabilize Chinese society but have not the slightest interest in promoting democracy. Just because the government's methods for dealing with them are not as refined as those found in the liberal democratic countries—indeed, the state is often crude and even cruel in its response—does not mean it lacks a legitimate reason for concern.

There are also countless Chinese who find fault with the regime, but their faultfinding differs little from that common in more liberal polities. Just because people complain and criticize their government and want it to reform does not mean they want it to be overthrown. Thus far, there is no evidence that the majority of Chinese would welcome such a change, any more than would their leaders. They nevertheless are delighted, when no concomitant costs are involved, with their new rights and are gently pushing for more.

6 The Institutionalization of Procedural Democracy

> There are many conspicuous issues of justice and injustice involved in the political choice of social institutions all over the world, and it is not easy to accept the definition of a political conception of justice that rules most of them out of court on grounds of ideological remoteness from constitutional democracies.
>
> —Amartya Sen

> The concept of the rule of law originated in the West. It is not a product of Chinese culture. There is scarcely [any] foundation for this concept in Chinese legal traditions. Law has traditionally been equated with the concept of punishment and only referred to criminal law. For thousands of years, China was under this rule of punishment, or rule of criminal law. More accurately, this rule was the rule of only one man, namely the emperor.
>
> —Wang Zhenmin

This chapter focuses on the institutionalization of democracy through legislative and legal reforms and through the growth of electoral rights and procedural democracy in work units, villages, and urban districts. Procedural and civil rights are of particular interest to those advocating greater democracy in China. The right of individuals to participate in the choice of their institutional, work unit, village, or urban district leaders through surveys, discussions, and especially through elections is an important step toward democratization in China. In this arena, there is a strong sense of forward momentum in China today, as well as a growing sense that the countryside is ahead of the cities in electoral rights.

EPIGRAPHS: Sen, *Inequality Re-examined*, p. 79; Wang Zhenmin, "The Developing Rule of Law in China," p. 35.

VILLAGE ELECTIONS AND SELF-GOVERNANCE

The Government's Reasons for Institutionalizing Elections

By the early 1980s, peasants in many of China's villages had forced the government to terminate the collective system of communes and brigades as the basic levels of rural administration and to redistribute land. Once the communes were officially disbanded in 1984 and no longer served as the basis for production and governance, the state found it increasingly difficult to administer the countryside, especially in the areas of tax collection, social welfare, land redistribution, and birth control.[1] When the "household responsibility system" was instituted to replace the collective form of production, peasants began to ignore government regulations on family size, assaulted tax collectors, and refused to hand over government-set quotas of grain to state depots.[2] Violence became commonplace as authority relationships based on the collective and local control by the Communist Party collapsed. Relationships between cadres and the local people grew increasingly tense, and economic reforms generated considerable financial and social instability.

The very existence of the Chinese Communist Party was threatened by its inability to recruit new members and the refusal of party members to engage in organizational instead of entrepreneurial activities. In some villages, the three mainstays for organizing the inhabitants of rural areas—the Communist Youth League, the All-China Women's Federation, and the People's Militia—disappeared. Some villages would "fake these organizations as needed, pasting up false membership lists whenever an inspection team [swept] down from a high level."[3]

Solving the problems of governance in rural areas quickly became a concern not only in village discussions but even in the media. Newspaper articles about rural areas noted the prevalence of illegal gambling, "murder, beatings, robbery, and abduction and sale of women and children" and the organization and activities of illegal parties (such as the Black Shirt Party

---

1. Li Gang, "Deng hou Zhongguode keneng qianjing." Land distribution is an ongoing process because some people migrate to cities, others, including soldiers, return after a long absence, and the number of family members increases or decreases over time.

2. Mufson, "A New Day in China?," p. 155.

3. X. Drew Liu, "A Harbinger of Democracy," pp. 51–54.

周庄镇全旺村第七届村民委员会
选举大会

The incumbent chair of the Quanwang Villagers' Committee makes a campaign re-election speech before the assembled villagers, who will vote as soon as all the speeches have been made. Quanwang Village is located within the jurisdiction of Kunshan County and the highly prosperous tourist town of Zhouzhuang, about an hour's drive from Shanghai. Because Jimmy Carter was there to "monitor" the election, all the stops were pulled out. Most elections are not held on playing fields decorated with potted plants, not to mention a viewing platform for the Chinese and American dignitaries and the press that would have done any racetrack proud. (All photographs taken by the author in September 2001.)

and the Ax Head Party) and "black societies" (*hei shehui*). Village democracy would then be proposed as the antidote to this rising tide of lawlessness and chaos and to the collapse of administrative and financial order. To address this leadership vacuum and social instability, as well as to prevent government officials from taking away their newly won economic rights, peasants in a number of villages spontaneously initiated village elections. Idealism about "democratization" was not the major motivation for elections.[4] Economic reforms had already given the peasants a greater voice in production and marketing decisions and led them to demand changes in the political system to protect those new economic rights and stabilize the countryside.

Nor was democratization the government's major motivation when it

---

4. Ibid.; and Kelliher, "The Chinese Debate over Village Self-Government," pp. 65–67.

When the candidate asked if there were any questions, an elderly villager stood up, and a titter went through the crowd. He reminded the incumbent chair that at the last election he had promised to rebuild the senior citizens' home, an elementary school, and a public bathhouse that would be demolished when a road was built through the village, but that he had not fulfilled his promise. The villager received a huge round of applause from the more than 850 villagers assembled to vote.

decided to institutionalize village elections. As with most other policies to implement greater democracy in China, the leadership closely analyzed the costs and benefits of enfranchising the people. China's leaders seem to have concluded that, on balance, greater village autonomy would further the party-state's interests better than continuing a system of centrally directed government. Beijing may have theorized that village democracy would improve political order, but the government is reluctant to make institutional changes or pass laws before it knows the likely outcome. What really tipped the scale in favor of village elections was the obvious success of these unauthorized elections in bringing better leadership to rural areas.

Faced with difficulties in controlling the rural population, then, the government could have chosen to revert to coercion or mass campaigns and class struggle, the familiar tools of the Maoist period. Instead, in the context of economic liberalization and with an administrative system in collapse, it decided to try village elections. Those elected to villagers' committees would

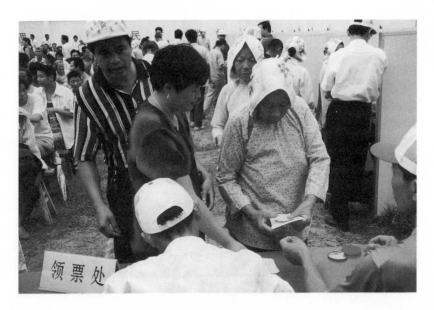

Villagers presented their registration paper to the officials in order to receive their ballots. Those villagers who were not registered could not vote.

then take over many administrative tasks—tasks that town and township officials were happy to relinquish, because their performance in these areas did little to advance their careers—maintaining irrigation canals, repairing bridges, mediating disputes, and operating schools and health centers, as well as making sensitive local decisions such as allocating land for housing construction and reallocating farmland among families. Town and township officials also welcomed the opportunity to divest themselves of the responsibility for implementing unpopular centrally mandated government policies, notably, the population control policy, tax collection, and grain procurement, yet many strongly opposed village elections.[5]

Villagers' committees were also made responsible for providing food, clothing, medical care, housing, and burial expenses for the childless and infirm elderly, helping the poor, supporting the army, and giving preferential treatment to families of those who fought in the revolution, as well as for

---

5. Gamer and Shou, "Township Elections and the Transformation of Local Power Structures," pp. 55, 59.

The villagers were then checked off the official registration list.

preventing gambling and "superstitious activities."[6] Before they gained the legitimacy conferred by elections, town and village cadres tended to rely on coercion, trickery, threats, and violence to fulfill state demands and to force villagers to acquiesce in policies they abhorred.[7] Indeed, this remains a good description of the (alleged) behavior of town and township cadres, who are not elected and therefore lack legitimacy in the eyes of country people.

In short, reformers within China's leadership believe that instead of

---

6. Research Group on the System of Village Self-Government in China and the China Research Society of Basic-Level Governance, *Legal System of Village Committees in China*, pp. 70–71. While interviewing in China in September 1999, I heard many examples of the responsibilities of village leaders. In a village in Kunshan County, Jiangsu, which I will call "Su" Village, the elected head of the village committee discussed the problems he faced in getting residents to take care of their parents. He first encourages the villagers to heed traditional Chinese morality; if all else fails, he has the offenders taken to court.

7. Kelliher, "The Chinese Debate over Village Self-Government," pp. 70–71. My own interviews in China in September 1999 indicated, however, that, at least in Pudong District of Shanghai Municipality and in Kunshan County in Jiangsu, peasants did not resist birth control policies, since they had long ago recognized the need for population control because of limited land.

Villagers lined up to vote in one of the cubicles.

undermining the state's control, greater self-government at the village level will enhance its power and advance its goals. Those elected need not be party members; they just have to be individuals who will effectively implement the Party's policies.

For these reasons, in 1987 the government promulgated the Organic Law of Villagers' Committees, the Organic Law of the Local People's Congresses and Local People's Governments, and the Election Law of the National People's Congress and Local People's Congresses. The Organic Law of Villagers' Committees established the following principles:

1. Direct election by villagers of villagers' committees;
2. More candidates than the number of offices;
3. Secret ballots;
4. Majority vote;
5. Elections every three years;
6. Public counting of ballots;
7. The right of candidates to campaign.[8]

---

8. China Rural Villagers Self-Government Research Group and China Research Society of Basic-Level Government, *Study on the Election of Villagers Committees in Rural China*, pp. 51, 52, 57.

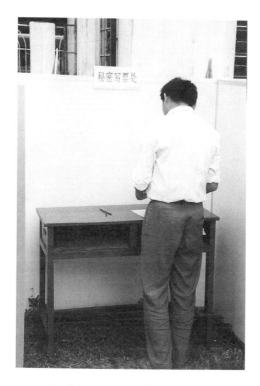

A villager voting "secretly" in a cubicle.

The right to vote every three years for leaders of villages, where most day-to-day decisions affecting the inhabitants' lives are made, has greatly expanded meaningful political participation. China's 800 million villagers may register their approval or disapproval of local leaders through the elected villagers' committees and representative assemblies, which have the power to discuss and decide such things as local birth quotas, financial expenditures, construction, and production, engineering, and public welfare facilities.[9] In spite of problems in properly implementing elections in many villages, this is

---

9. The government instituted the "representative assemblies" because in certain rural areas villagers are spread out over a large area, and realistically many would not be able to attend most of the village assemblies. There is one representative for every ten to fifteen households. The assemblies monitor the villagers' committees and participate in the committees' key decisions, thereby giving voice to the villagers' priorities and concerns (Research Group on the System of Village Self-Government in China and the China Research Society of Basic-Level Governance, *Legal System of Villagers Committees in China*, pp. 50, 61–62).

代写处

Officials sit in a cubicle to help the illiterate vote. Because of the many elderly people in this village, this service was important. The second official was there to check the other official's accuracy. Some localities require at least one of these officials be from outside the village. Presumably an outsider will have no vested interest in the election outcome.

a significant advance for democratic participation and self-rule in China's vast countryside.

The Electoral Process

Do the "best" candidates win seats on China's villagers' committees? And who are the best candidates in the eyes of voters whose needs, attitudes, and values are shaped by the local power structure, traditional Chinese rural values, local conditions, and the economic and social structure? This section sets out to answer these questions by examining electoral reforms, the results they seem to produce, and the villagers' perceptions of those results. It looks at the various factors that may hinder the best candidates and why this may or may not be perceived as unacceptable to the local electorate.

The villagers then cast their ballots in the celebratory bright red ballot boxes at the front of the field. Each villager casts two ballots, of different colors, one for the head of the villagers' committee, and one for the members of the committee.

Electoral rights have steadily been refined and made more meaningful since they were first institutionalized in 1987, most recently in November 1998. From the beginning, in the original 1987 Organic Law of Villagers' Committees, the role of the village *party* committee (whose members are chosen by Communist Party authorities at both the township and the village levels) was supposed to be limited to screening candidates selected by the villagers to assure they were qualified and, of course, not "antiparty." Because the Party retains power at the township level and above, however, its power at the village level has remained significant. This does not necessarily mean that those village elections in which the village, town, or even county party committee still controls the nomination process are a sham, for how the Communist Party chooses to wield its power varies widely from place to

Villagers voted by the *zu* in which they reside. They have been organized by these same "teams" or "small groups" since the first stage of collectivization in the early 1950s. These villagers had assembled on a blistering hot morning in September 2001 before 8 A.M. and had patiently waited for President Carter's delegation to arrive before beginning the proceedings. Normally, villagers would come to hear the candidates speak (now required), vote, and then go to work; they would reassemble several hours later to learn the outcome of the elections.

place in China. Inland agricultural regions, where the Party continues to interfere, lag in institutionalizing truly competitive elections. Meanwhile, villages in coastal provinces (especially Fujian) have taken the initiative in improving the electoral process by mandating changes in their local electoral laws. Examples of these innovations include:

1. Village elections may no longer be delayed by a superior body.
2. Voter eligibility has been clarified.
3. Voters must register at least 25 days before an election. The names of all those who have registered are then publicly posted, and individuals may be challenged and deleted from the registry.
4. Efforts are being made to eliminate the practice of voting through proxies, such as one's husband.
5. The minimum number of persons needed to nominate a candidate has been reduced from five to one. A person may also nominate her- or himself.

Through sun and rain, the villagers remained patiently seated for over four hours.

6. Only a non-resident may serve as a scribe for the illiterate.

7. Candidates are increasingly being required to give speeches, outline their platforms, and participate in a villagers' assembly during which they may be questioned about their ideas and promises.

8. A "primary" must be conducted to determine the final candidates on the ballot when there are too many candidates running.

9. Incumbent members of villagers' committee must submit a report on the village's finances and work completed.

10. Procedures for recalling unacceptable village leaders and selecting (or even electing) the village election committee have been discussed and even adopted in more advanced villages.

11. Efforts are also being made to eliminate the custom of circulating ballot boxes, except as necessary to allow the handicapped, sick, and elderly to vote. When a box is moved, three people must accompany it at all times. Polling stations have been introduced to eliminate the need for some villagers to travel long distances in order to vote.[10]

---

10. Carter Center, "The Carter Center Report on Chinese Elections." This report was based on an on-site visit to China in August 2000, as well as videos of elections in other villages, and data collected by the Ministry of Civil Affairs in Beijing.

While the villagers waited, the election officials
sorted the two types of ballots.

The right to *nominate* candidates is, of course, critical for truly democratic elections. Without that right, voters may face a choice of voting for the least objectionable person. In this respect, China has made remarkable efforts to ensure truly democratic elections. Before 1998, village groups, families, or even individuals could nominate candidates, but the nominees had to be approved by the village (and even the town) party committee. Villagers often saw the process as one in which a higher authority made the decision, and they just circled the names on the ballot.[11] Furthermore, "party interference can crush all meaning out of the elections and turn the process into a sham in some locations . . . ; [but] it is equally true that a supportive party leadership at the county and provincial levels can restrain township and village

---

11. Xiang Jiquan, "Zhongguo cunmin de gonggong canyu," p. 43. The three villages Jiang studied are in Henan, Shandong, and Gansu provinces.

They then stacked and recounted all the valid
ballots and noted how many were invalid.

officials who might otherwise skew the election results their way."[12] In 1998,
in an effort to combat party interference, the Ministry of Civil Affairs
promulgated a law that prohibits Chinese Communist Party involvement in
the nominating process. Every candidate on a village ballot is now supposed
to be a write-in candidate: in *haixuan* elections ("sea elections"), villagers are
issued a blank ballot and write in a name for each position on the villagers'
committee. Then a run-off ballot is prepared with the names of the top candidates (with one more candidate than the *total* number of positions—
although there are now efforts to make sure that there is more than one candidate for *each* position). Even if a candidate is "antiparty," the Party has

12. Tyrene White, "Village Elections," p. 266.

Officials then called out the votes to a recorder at a blackboard, who used the traditional method of keeping track of a count by using the five strokes in the character *zheng*.

been told not to intervene—although no known test case of such a candidate has yet occurred.[13]

Electoral procedures in most of China's villages are not, however, so advanced that the villages have freed themselves from the Party's control. In spite of the 1998 law, many villages rely on the local party committee to nominate candidates, or at least to screen out objectionable candidates or winnow down a large field of candidates nominated by the villagers.[14] Still,

---

13. Another form of village election permitted by the 1998 law is for the top two votegetters to be the candidates for the head of the village committee; the next four become nominees for members of the village committee. This means that one of the top two votegetters will not win election to any post. Two ballots in different colors are printed up, one for the head of the village committee and one for the three seats on the village committee. The voters circle their choices. There is also a place on both ballots to write in "other" candidates. Illiterate villagers may ask someone whom they trust, including an election official, to write in or circle a name (Ogden, "Field Research Notes," Sept. 1999; interviews took place in "villages" in Shanghai's Pudong District, with the party secretary and the deputy director of the town of Tang Zhen, and with the elected head of the village committee of Jie Long Village, in the town of Huang Lou, in Pudong District).

14. X. Drew Liu, "A Harbinger of Democracy," pp. 55, 62, 71.

When the election was finally over, the villagers left for a late lunch. Behind the wall of the now-empty playing field are the spacious new houses of some of these many well-to-do villagers. Most of these villagers no longer till the fields but instead work in the profitable tourist trade or in village factories. As in so many villages close to major commercial centers, development has meant a great many buildings and paving over of agricultural land.

now that experiments with truly democratic elections have been successful in some parts of China, the government is pushing all villages to implement the 1998 electoral law.

Even if local party leaders do not directly interfere in the nomination process, they may still not have relinquished all influence and control. For example, in one village in Pudong District in Shanghai Municipality, each of the village's thirteen "small groups" (*xiaodui*), each of which is led by a party member, held discussions about "potential" candidates for the elections. Although the discussions did not result in a formal nomination, they focused on who was "qualified" to be a candidate and heavily influenced the villagers' write-in choices. The discussions are all the more significant because candidates usually do not campaign.[15] They are, however, under increasing pres-

---

15. Discussion with the elected head of the village committee in Jie Long Village, in the town of Huang Lou, Pudong District, Shanghai. However, in Su Village in Kunshan County, villagers said they used to discuss the candidates but no longer did so (Ogden, "Field Research

sure to present their political platform publicly, usually in a speech to the assembled voters just before they cast their ballots. Villagers are allowed to
question the candidates, and they occasionally do so—although this pro-
duces a degree of discomfort among the villagers.[16] In some rather enterpris-
ing villages, recordings of the earlier campaign speeches of the incumbent
nominees are played before they speak![17] Discussions within "small groups"
no doubt help prevent too many individuals from being named on the "primary" ballot, which could be a serious problem in the new *haixuan* form of
nomination. Some villages no larger than a few thousand people have nominated dozens, even hundreds, of candidates. This made it virtually impossible for any one candidate to win a majority of the votes on the subsequent
ballot, and a run-off election was usually required. Nevertheless, since
the ballot for the "primary" is secret, villagers are free to make their own
choice.

Villages that are trying to implement the new electoral law have encountered problems just as daunting as party interference. The frequent lack of
printed, standardized ballots, for example, and the resulting variety of ballots
used have interfered with implementation of the secret ballot and led to confusion in counting the vote.[18] Gansu province has stipulated that "in places
where the secret ballot is difficult to implement, voting by a show of hands
can be used with the consent of the majority of villagers." In Chongqing City,
the regulations permit other forms of voting if implementing the secret ballot is difficult. One method is to give the villagers beans and have them
"place the beans into the bowl of the candidates of their choice."[19] In some
villages, a representative of the village "small group" distributes the ballots to
the members of the group, tells them what name(s) to circle (or does it for

---

Notes," Sept. 1999). The only restriction in local campaigns are no false promises and no personal attacks (Tony Saich, Harvard University, New England China Seminar, Feb. 9, 2000).

16. For example, at the election I witnessed in Quanwang Village in Zhouzhuang Town,
Kunshan County, Jiangsu, an elderly man stood up and asked the incumbent why he had not
carried through on promises made during a previous election campaign (see the photograph
on p. 185).

17. Jimmy and Rosalyn Carter, conversation, Sept. 2001.

18. China Rural Villagers Self-Government Research Group and China Research Society
of Basic-Level Government, *Study on the Election of Villagers Committees in Rural China*, pp. 9, 58,
referring to problems in Shandong province.

19. Ibid., p. 57.

them), has the villagers put their ballots in a box, and personally (and without supervision) returns the box to the village office.[20]

Illiteracy can also pose a serious problem, as those who have monitored elections in developing countries know.[21] The illiteracy rate in China's countryside still hovers between 12 and 15 percent (it is disproportionately higher in poorer villages), which means that a significant percentage of the electorate is unable to nominate candidates on the write-in ballots or identify candidates' names on the voting lists. Some villages have tried to solve this problem by hiring people to fill in the ballots for illiterate voters.[22] Although this necessarily violates the principle of secret ballots, it ensures the right to vote to what may be a significant percentage of a village. In a village election I witnessed in September 2001, the election committee provided two individuals in each voting booth for the illiterate. This was done to ensure that the person recording the illiterate voter's choice recorded it correctly.[23] (In 1999, in the first [but constitutionally illegal] election of township officials

---

20. Ogden, "Field Research Notes," Sept. 1999.

21. The author was an international monitor for the 1994 national elections in El Salvador. Illiteracy was the single greatest obstacle to a fair election at the voting polls. In the city of San Salvador, as many as 10,000 voters were assigned to one polling location. Lines to vote were arranged alphabetically, but voters who could not read often stood in the wrong line. After waiting for as much as one hour to get to the head of the line, they would find out that their names were not on the list because they had stood in the wrong line. Because candidates ran as members of political parties, which were identified by logos, voters could easily determine which party (if not which candidate) they were voting for. In China, however, candidates run as individuals, not as members of a party.

22. The Carter Center has suggested to the Ministry of Civil Affairs that this could be remedied by requiring that scribes for illiterate and handicapped voters should come from a village other than the one in which the election is being held (Carter Center, "The Carter Center Report on Chinese Elections," p. 25).

23. Out of approximately 850 voters in the village of Quanwang, an unusually large number appeared to be over 70 years old. Most of them voted in the booths that had people to record the votes of the illiterate. Quanwang Village was awarded the title of "The Model Villager Autonomy Village" in 2000; and the Jiangsu Patriotic Health Campaign Committee named it "The Most Sanitary Village at the Provincial Level." Its primary source of income is tourism, industries, services, and aquatic culture. Many of Quanwang's villagers live in houses that resemble two-story American suburban homes. In short, this was hardly a typical village. The presence, moreover, of former President Jimmy Carter and the Carter Center delegation (including myself) hardly made this a typical election.

held in China, election officials put photographs beside the candidates' names so that illiterate peasants could recognize them.)[24]

Finally, China's villagers do not necessarily understand the democratic process in the same way someone long-immersed in democratic institutions might. Voting by proxy, marking ballots in groups rather than in the privacy of a voting booth even when one is available, sending representatives around the village to pick up ballots, and deciding how to vote through discussions with other villagers at the voting station are still widespread practices. They are good examples of how community-oriented values and the lack of a sense of privacy in the countryside shape elections in ways that make China's experience of democracy different from that of the generally more urban citizens of liberal democratic states.[25] We would be incorrect to assume that the Chinese are necessarily distressed by such practices.

The Chinese government appears committed to fair and honest elections at the local level. The Ministry of Civil Affairs, which began work on the Organic Law of Villagers' Committees in 1984, revised the law forty times before it was finally approved by the National People's Congress in 1987; it continues to revise it. But implementation has not been as easy as those accustomed to elections might think. Improving the understanding of democracy and the relevant electoral laws by basic-level rural officials and villagers is critical to the success of democratic elections. Recognizing that in the first round of village elections some local officials "regarded elections as a show" and believed that the election results "would eventually be determined . . . by superior authorities," the ministry launched a legal education drive that included the study of the Organic Law of Villagers' Committees.[26] Nevertheless, one of the major complaints about the elections remains that there is

---

24. This election was held in Buyun, a town of about 16,000 in a remote part of Sichuan province (Michael Laris and John Pomfret, "Chinese Quietly Test Democratic Waters," *Washington Post*, Jan. 27, 1999, p. A16). Apparently the Party will have more of a role in selecting the final candidates in the town's elections in late 2001.

25. Ogden, "Field Research Notes," Sept. 1999; Elizabeth Perry and Merle Goldman, observation of elections in China, discussion, Jan. 1999; Robert Pastor, monitoring of elections for Carter Center, discussion at Kennedy School of Public Affairs, Harvard University, Oct. 8, 1998; Anne Thurston, observation of elections in China, 1998.

26. Research Group on the System of Village Self-Government in China and the China Research Society of Basic-Level Governance, *Legal System of Village Committees in China*, p. 51; and China Rural Villagers Self-Government Research Group and China Research Society of Basic-Level Government, *Study on the Election of Villagers Committees in Rural China*, p. 12.

insufficient training of election organizers and insufficient education of villagers about the electoral process. The latter complaint is not entirely justified, since the tendency of villagers to lodge large numbers of complaints with higher authorities when elections go awry suggests a rather high level of "democratic consciousness."[27]

The inadequate training of election officials and corruption of the electoral process are suggested by such practices as voting by the dead and children[28] (practices not unknown in the United States). In an effort to tackle such problems, the Ministry of Civil Affairs asked the Ford Foundation (which has offices in Beijing) to train local officials and to give advice on ensuring secrecy, honesty, and fairness. The government's pride in its progress was indicated when President Jiang Zemin invited former President Jimmy Carter to send observers from the Carter Center to monitor China's March 1997 elections. Since that time, the Carter Center has continued to send teams to observe China's local elections and continues to consult with the Ministry of Civil Affairs on the best way to improve the elections. To this end, the Republican Institute, the Asia Foundation, and the European Union are collaborating with the Chinese government on various projects to promote self-governance and greater transparency at the village level. The Carter Center, in collaboration with the Ministry of Civil Affairs, has set up a Village Election Data-Gathering System, which is used to report election data. The data are gathered in the Ministry of Civil Affairs office in Beijing.[29] Just as significant, in 2001, the ministry and the Carter Center jointly sponsored a conference in Beijing on local elections and self-governance. It was attended by 170 provincial, county, and party officials, as well as researchers who study these issues. The participants openly discussed not only how to improve the electoral system and local self-governance but also how to take the next step and institutionalize elections at the township level—a step considered essential to the betterment of village self-governance. The point was repeatedly made that since the township is the lowest level in the government hierarchy and the level of government that dispenses or withholds resources for village projects, it is essential that township officials be

---

27. Gadsden, "Grassroots Elections, Grassroots Challenges," pp. 44–45.

28. Letter from Yang Lihu (People's Armament Department, Jinquan, Gansu), "Xuanju weifa shi weidade weifa" (Illegal voting is the biggest illegal act), *Renmin ribao*, Sept. 8, 1998, p. 11.

29. Carter Center, "The Carter Center Report on Chinese Elections," p. 6.

held accountable for their actions. The fact that discussions of township elections are occurring is no guarantee that they will be implemented soon, but they are an important first step.[30]

Transparency

Further efforts were made to advance democracy and get the best candidates into office in November 1998, when the National People's Congress passed a new law requiring that all financial and administrative records of villages (but not townships) be open to inspection by villagers. Members of villagers' committee and their wives were also required to make their income and the sources of that income public. Not surprisingly, village officials who have questionable sources of income, are using village funds to benefit either themselves or their families, or are making a profit from enterprises funded by the villagers are resisting implementation of these regulations. In villages with open books, the greater transparency has lead to greater legitimacy for village officials. Indeed, I found a dramatic contrast between the attitudes of villagers toward local officials in the poorer and more backward area of Kunshan County, where officials said it would take up to a year to "prepare" their books for inspection, and the attitudes of villagers in Tang Zhen, Pudong District, where account books are available for examination. Just about everything concerning local government in the latter, including plans for the next several years, are posted on the walls of village offices. In contrast, Kunshan County villagers had less trust in their local elected officials, who clearly had things in their accounts they wanted to hide.[31]

"Surgery of numbers" is still a common practice among village leaders. The data presented by officials vary according to the person asking to see the books: one set of accounts for villagers asked to pay taxes and fees, another set for the media, and still another for reporting village income to higher levels. Many village officials are said to keep "three different sets of statistics—

---

30. Discussions at the International Symposium on Villager Self-Government, Beijing, Sept. 2–5, 2001.

31. The villages that displayed their records and had opened their books to villagers were under the jurisdiction of a "model" town, Tang Zhen, in Pudong District, Shanghai Municipality; these villages cannot be considered typical. The fact that it was a model does not, however, mean it is uniquely well developed in self-government; for in spite of its rapid economic development, the areas in and around Shanghai have lagged behind the national norm for advancement in local self-government (Ogden, "Field Research Notes," Sept. 1999).

one for reporting good news, one for complaining about bad conditions, and another for a reality check." Especially now that "model" villages are receiving economic rewards for "reaching the standard" (*dabiao*), village leaders are tempted to inflate statistics to indicate stronger economic growth.[32]

The Results of the Electoral Reforms

Electoral reforms have spawned a tendency for the village party leader to divide control over the local economy with the head of the villagers' committee. The party leader controls local industry, and the elected village head is in charge of land division, agriculture, fees, and taxation—a marriage made in heaven. On the other hand, since the village party leader is often fairly wealthy and controls the leading village industry, he will frequently campaign to become village head as well. In addition, nonparty candidates elected to the villagers' committee tend to be recruited to the village party committee. Members of the two committees "share the same trousers, like a husband and wife."[33]

Alternatively, the individual who heads the villagers' committee may either already be the village party branch secretary (or vice-secretary) or assume that role after winning election. The lack of an arm's-length relationship between the two leading village positions has nevertheless been viewed positively by those favoring elections: "concurrent office-holding may lead to popular control over the local Party. Today, if a party branch secretary wants to . . . head the villagers' committee, then he or she must submit to an election."[34] Thus, far from abdicating control over daily administrative affairs, the Chinese Communist Party is well represented on villagers' committees; however, the village representative who is elected *before* gaining mem-

---

32. Xiaobo Lu, *Cadres and Corruption*, pp. 169–71. Cadres receive financial rewards, for example, if their village "reaches the standard" of nine years of schooling for every child, pays its grain quota, or adheres to family-planning regulations. Officials in some areas are, in fact, financially rewarded for every abortion they are able to get (Xiaobo Lu, "Taxation Without Representation in China," New England China Seminar, Harvard University, Apr. 16, 2001).

33. Observation of a Su villager in Kunshan County. The secretary of this particular village party committee had started his own (private) factory and was too busy to run for village head (Ogden, "Field Research Notes," Sept. 1999; and conversation with Susan V. Lawrence, Nov. 19, 1997).

34. Kelliher, "The Chinese Debate over Village Self-government," pp. 84–85.

bership in the Party is less likely to act as an extension of the Party and more likely to be a representative of local interests.

At the same time, the initial steps toward the democratization of village party governance are being taken. This is extremely important because in most villages, the party branch is at least as important as the villagers' committee—if not far more so—in governing the village. By the mid-1990s, several provinces in China had adopted the "two-ballot system" (*liangpiaozhi*) for determining village party secretaries. This system, which arose because of one Shanxi village's anger with the abuses of the village party branch secretary, allows villagers who are not party members to participate in nominating candidates for this position. Representatives from each family attend an all-village assembly. There, each representative casts a secret vote on a blank piece of paper (or one listing all members of the village party branch) for one person to be chosen as the nominee by the township party committee. Although the Party insists that this is not a "primary" but a "vote of confidence" by the villagers, the Party is supposed to be bound to nominate as the official candidate whoever received the most votes on this first ballot. This system allows villagers to screen out candidates they do not trust and the Party to have final control in the second ballot, which is limited to village party members.[35] Villagers are indirectly but decisively affecting the choice of village party chief in another way: a party chief who loses the election for chair of the villagers' committee may be seen as "not good enough to continue as the party chief."[36]

Other factors may inhibit the most qualified candidate from either running for or winning election to the villagers' committee. For example, in the countryside, the township is the lowest level of government with salaried officials. Technically, elected village officials are not "government" officials, and the central government does not pay their salaries. Thus, monetary compensation for their work may be quite low in the poorer villages and nonexistent in the poorest villages. Even so, individuals still run for elections because an official position allows them to make decisions beneficial to themselves and their relatives. A village official has extensive power, which can be used to

---

35. At least 80 percent of adult villagers or their family representatives must vote on the first ballot, and at least 80 percent of all village Party members must cast votes on the second ballot for the election to be valid (Li Lianjiang, "The Two-Ballot System in Shanxi Province," pp. 103–7).

36. Benewick et al., "Self-Governance and Community," p. 5.

gain far more than a mere government salary. Still, many villagers refuse to run for election because they are required to make decisions that generate hostility toward themselves, and in a small village it is difficult to escape face-to-face encounters with this anger.[37] Cadres who carry out unpopular policies or offend villagers have been beaten and even murdered. In one village, the village office was dynamited. "Villagers have poisoned their cadres' water buffalo, trampled their poultry, hacked down their crops, burned their houses, and sprinkled broken glass in their rice paddies."[38]

These sorts of problems do not encourage good candidates to run for elections. Even if strong candidates are willing to run, the "best" candidate may lose because he or she is reluctant to campaign vigorously against an incumbent for fear that a winning incumbent may seek revenge, an option rooted in Chinese culture. There are also stories about party cadres whose failure to win re-election has led them to punish the villagers responsible. In 1996, one village party branch secretary who failed to be re-elected set a fire that severely damaged both his own and adjacent villages.[39]

Cultural factors such as the chance of a "loss of face" may also inhibit the best individuals from running for village office. Although Westerners might also consider the potential humiliation of losing, the Chinese concern is unusually high and arguably accounts for the biggest difference between Chinese and American elections. For the foreseeable future, "face" will probably continue to be critical to decisions about running for elected office, whether in villages or elsewhere.[40]

Nevertheless, the institutionalization of elections since the 1987 Organic Law went into effect has guaranteed villagers a voice in deciding who will determine economic policies, and given them the right to remove from office anyone who disappoints them. The secret ballot and the right to vote for village officials has thus far not disempowered the Chinese Communist Party, but that is not the point of China's elections—and cannot become the objective unless a true multiparty system is approved. For the time being, even

---

37. Ogden, "Field Research Notes," Sept. 1999.

38. Tianjian Shi, *Political Participation in Beijing*, pp. 53–54; and Kelliher, "The Chinese Debate over Village Self-government," p. 72.

39. Sun Peiwu, "Dalu zhengzhi zixia ershangde tiaozhang jixiang."

40. The potential loss of face involved in losing an election is not confined to village elections. It also characterizes election to such positions as university department chairmanships (conversation with a colleague from Beijing University, July 1998).

candidates who belong to the Communist Party run not as party members but as individuals. Candidates who are not party members are likewise running as independents.

In any event, since everyone tends to know the other residents of the village, a party label is not so necessary for identification. Candidates' "platforms" consist of their character, abilities, and promises, and the issue of party membership may not be relevant. In theory, before the April 1998 electoral law that prohibited the Party's involvement in the nomination process, all candidates running for villagers' committees had to be approved by the Communist Party. As long as they were competent and did not openly attack the policies of either the government or the Party itself, however, they were usually approved. As of 2001, more than 40 percent of the members and the heads of village' committees were not members of the Party at the time of their election.[41]

The election and re-election of incumbent Communist Party members as village leaders need not be seen as a sign of the weakness of the democratic process. What villagers want from a village leader is competence, honesty, an ability to make the village economy grow, and an ability to defend village interests against pressures from above. It is quite possible that villagers will see a member of the Party as the person most likely to meet these needs, sometimes precisely because he or she is a party member. In villages in which powerful clans bully the weak, moreover, a party that is both strong and uncorrupted "would be a welcome improvement, especially if it could eliminate clan violence and break up criminal gangs."[42] But of course, most clans can field a fair number of party members, who will no doubt attend to the interests of their own clan first. In some villages, in fact, it is not that the formal organization of the Party has been replaced by clans, but rather that they reinforce and penetrate each other.[43]

---

41. Discussions at the International Symposium on Villager Self-Government, Beijing, Sept. 2–5, 2001.

42. Tyrene White, "Village Elections," pp. 266–67.

43. Xiaobo Lu, *Cadres and Corruption*, pp. 184–85. A report by the Party's Organization Department in May 2001 indicated, however, that violent and larger confrontations between villagers and officials were on the increase. Why? Although the report pointed to stagnating incomes and illegal fees, it also suggested that the election system itself, *by creating "rival centers of power in many villages*," has pitted elected village heads against village party leaders. "Thanks to the party's jealously monopoly of power, the only other forces now capable of exerting their

The institutionalization of village elections has not gone uncontested. Indeed, many township officials responsible for instituting elections in villages believe that elections will undercut compliance with the policies of the central party-state. They argue that villagers, who resent having to comply with state policies on birth control, tax collection, and grain procurement, prefer to elect those who will be ineffective or easily bribed into not performing their duties.[44] The implication of this argument is that most villagers assume they can be "free-riders" and not pay for the "collective goods" of population control, taxes for necessary social services, and so on. This argument is less persuasive than the argument of those who support elections, because the rational choice for villagers would be to choose someone who is fair to *all* the villagers and who would ignore bribes; for once an official is willing to accept bribes, it means that all other villagers will probably have to submit bribes, perhaps higher ones, to get the official to address their concerns—especially when resources are finite. Further, cadres who are ineffective in carrying out unpopular policies will no doubt be equally ineffective in carrying out policies *popular* with villagers, so it would be rational for villagers to elect effective officials.

Nevertheless, in the view of opponents to elections—largely town, township, and county officials—villagers are hostile to the state's demands and use democracy as a weapon to get revenge. They are "too vengeful, self-serving, feudal, superstitious, faction-ridden, and gullible to vote. . . . They are materialistic and short-sighted, so they vote against the common good." Opponents of elections have worked hard to prevent their being implemented. Their preferred methods of resistance are to go through all the motions of implementing the election law without really doing so or to attempt to subvert local self-government once it is in place.[45]

The supreme irony of first introducing elections in the countryside, where "feudal" thought is more entrenched, cannot be overlooked. But, the reformers within the Ministry of Civil Affairs believed the issues in the countryside were more pressing, and the potential positive outcomes of elec-

---

interests collectively are generally undesirable: criminal gangs, clans and the self-interested rich" (*Economist*, June 30, 2001, p. 22; italics added).

44. Kelliher, "The Chinese Debate over Village Self-government," p. 79.

45. Kelliher (ibid., pp. 79–81) notes that numerous surveys corroborate these findings about the attitudes of local cadres. See also Xu Wang, "Xiangchun Zhongguo de jichen minzhi," pp. 150–53; and Gadsden, "Grassroots Elections, Grassroots Challenges," pp. 43–44.

tions (for the continuation of the Party's rule and economic development) far greater, than they would be in the cities. In terms of attitudes and behavior, it is difficult to differentiate township and county officials from the villagers whom they criticize. Although the town, township, and county officials' negative views of villagers may well be valid, their primary motive for resisting elections and autonomous self-government for villages is arguably their fear of losing power over the villages. The Ministry of Civil Affairs and its lower-level branches have steadfastly worked to overcome such resistance. But the town, township, and county officials who oversee village elections are *not* subject to the electoral process. Instead, other unelected authorities determine their "careers, incomes, and bonuses." They all too often find themselves "at cross-purposes with village cadres who live in intimate contact with their electorate and are subject, to some degree, to public accountability." As a result, they are inclined to oppose the institutionalization of village elections, or failing this, to manipulate the electoral process so as to ensure that the elected local leaders will be compliant with their wishes.[46]

Clans and Black Societies (hei shehui)

The residual effects of traditional, "feudal" culture,[47] a low level of development, and long-entrenched socialist institutions and practices give weight to the Chinese leaders' argument that China is not ready for the introduction of a liberal democratic system. "Feudal" characteristics are strong in rural China because educational levels are relatively low and because power is often based on underground societies and family ties writ large in the form of clans. These do indeed undercut efforts to democratize China, or at least they make the process messy.

How did underground societies regain power in China after elections were introduced in the 1980s? After 1949, the Red Army demobilized lower-ranking officers, who were then assigned as government officials and party secretaries to villages throughout China. These officers had been in the Red Army for a sufficient amount of time to be fully indoctrinated into the Party's values. Even if they were assigned to their home village, given their

---

46. Tyrene White, "Village Elections," p. 267.

47. In particular, the Chinese label attitudes of submissiveness to authority, patriarchy, nepotism, and gift-giving, bribery, and entertaining for the purpose of developing "relationships" as "feudalism."

relatively high level of political consciousness, they would probably not join (or rejoin) a "black society" or a religious society in the village. These government officials and party secretaries were made responsible for eliminating religion, the black societies, and clan organizations as sources of power within the villages. In general, they were quite successful. Over time, however, some local party leaders became corrupt—but most dared not stray too far from party morality; for under Mao Zedong's leadership, party discipline was severe. Local leaders were afraid of being caught in a party rectification campaign that would destroy their political career and curtail their privileges.[48]

All this changed as economic liberalization gained momentum in the early 1980s and undercut the Party's position as disciplinarian and role model in the villages. Since the introduction of elections in 1987, local village leaders, who were often the local party leaders as well, have worried less about being disciplined by the Party. Now they are *elected*, and their responsibility is to the people who elected them, not to the Party. As is the case in Western liberal democracies, nothing prohibits the electorates from re-electing corrupt village leaders. Furthermore, if the village leader is simultaneously the leader of the dominant village clan, or the leader of a black society or religious group, villagers may find themselves subjected to pressures, including bribes, to re-elect him, even if he is corrupt or incompetent. Villagers tend to vote for fellow members of their clan, regardless of competence. If the dominant clan is also wealthy, it may even buy the votes of nonmembers to ensure victory. As a result, elected leaders in some villages are the heads of the largest and/or most powerful clan organization. They are not necessarily the most qualified leaders. Why, then, do township leaders, who still participate in selecting those candidates to be put on the ballots in many villages, not choose individuals who are not corrupt? Because the black societies also bribe the township leaders.

Black societies often use religious superstition, bribes, and other illegal dealings (for example, granting illegal licenses, smuggling, gambling, and prostitution) to gain the villagers' allegiance and thereby gain power over the local economy and political system. In some localities, the village *party* branch has lost almost all power as a countervailing force because it, too, is controlled by

---

48. This discussion of black societies and clans is based on discussions and correspondence with colleagues from the Department of Politics, Fudan University, Jan. 1998 through Sept. 1999

heads of black societies, clan leaders, religious leaders, and/or economic leaders. These roles are often wrapped up in one person in a single village.[49]

In some localities, only the black societies are able to maintain order. Sometimes they are even *hired* by aggrieved villagers, because the government is unable or unwilling to find and punish criminals who are extorting money or involved in other illegal activities.[50] And if a clan or black society uses illegal, even criminal, means to gain control or to punish those outside the group, say, for not repaying a debt, it may also bribe the local police not to investigate the case. As one traditional saying popular in China today puts it, "Fish cannot survive in clean water"[51]—another way of saying the system does not work without corruption.

Beijing did not anticipate that elections would lead to the re-emergence of local black societies and of clan leaders who had been driven out of power in the post-1949 period or to the flowering of corruption (including the purchasing of votes). But it is a difficult problem to tackle because *so many* local leaders are heads of black societies, clans, and/or religious organizations.[52] If the frequency and vehemence of villagers' protests against interference in the electoral process by town and township cadres is any measure, however, interference by clans seems insignificant by comparison.[53] National leaders faced a dilemma: restore the control of local party branches, which had themselves grown corrupt and incompetent, over villages, or continue with elections, which have allowed the "feudal" aspects of Chinese culture to re-emerge. China's leaders have so far opted to keep elections and to strengthen the electoral system. In doing so, they hope the villagers will realize that it is their own elected village leaders, not the central leadership or the Party, who are responsible for corruption at the local level.

---

49. My own field research in China in 1999 did not confirm these findings, but I visited only a few villages, towns, and counties, compared to my Chinese colleagues. If nothing else, this confirms the dangers of generalizing about anything in such an enormous and complex country as China!

50. Some Chinese believe the August 1998 murder in rural China of a woman from Taiwan was the work of a "black society." Together with her husband, she was involved in business dealings in which, according to reports, they had not repaid debts to one of the society's members.

51. The title of a forthcoming book by Wu Jieh-ming.

52. When I asked about black societies during my visits to villages in China, I was told that there were none, at least not in the villages I visited (Ogden, "Field Research Notes," Sept. 1999). I could not verify whether this was true.

53. Gadsden, "Grassroots Elections, Grassroots Challenges," p. 45.

Villagers' Assessment of Impact of Elections

The reformers believe that village elections will generate better local leaders and that greater local self-government will help China develop more rapidly, diminish local resistance to government policies, and control official corruption at the local level. Villagers in many parts of China are, however, still distressed by the arbitrary imposition of fees and fines and the corruption of local officials.[54] They also accuse village officials of favoring their own families and friends by, among other things, allocating the best land to them, permitting them to build houses in the best locations, allowing them to give birth to more than one child, and not collecting adequate taxes from them while levying illegal fees and fines on other villagers.[55]

Every village has different problems. For example, although the residents of Su Village did not think their local officials very competent, they insisted there was too little at stake in their poor village to offer a bribe to officials! Land was allocated by writing the number of each parcel on a piece of paper and then rolling it into a small wad. Each villager then drew one out of a bowl. Furthermore, because both the population control policy and the grain quotas were determined by the government, not village officials, villagers seemed to think their leaders were simply following orders. In any event, once the village's books and accounts are "prepared" for public perusal, corruption and bribery will face other hurdles.[56]

The Ministry of Civil Affairs believes that elections of villagers' committees and village self-government can help resolve such issues, whereas the use of coercive measures to implement policies could exacerbate social instability.[57] A former villager from an impoverished village in Shaanxi province averred, however, that township officials still use violence and force to implement state policies. For example, although one member of each villagers'

---

54. In Su Village in Kunshan County where I interviewed both leaders and ordinary villagers, peasant families complained about the annual collection of a tax of 100 RMB per adult to build a road. So far there was no sign of road construction, and the village leadership refused to say when the taxes would come to an end. The village committee also collects taxes for irrigation pumps and other services.

55. China Rural Villagers Self-Government Research Group and China Research Society of Basic-Level Government, *Study on the Election of Villagers Committees in Rural China*, p. 13.

56. Ogden, "Field Research Notes," Sept. 1999.

57. China Rural Villagers Self-Government Research Group and China Research Society of Basic-Level Government, *Study on the Election of Villagers Committees in Rural China*, p. 13.

committee (usually a woman) is responsible for implementing the state's population control policies, it is often township officials who enforce the policy. They will do such things as arrive unannounced in the village in the middle of the night and give a woman a (forced) abortion themselves or drag her to the local clinic or hospital to have it done. If villagers have not paid their taxes, the township cadres will suddenly take part of their harvest. This is precisely the type of coercion that the government hopes will be curbed through institutionalized elections and self-government; but since township officials lack a personal relationship with most villagers, it is easier for them than for the elected village official to impose state policies.[58] A villager from Jiangsu commented that the reason town officials intervened so frequently in village affairs was that there were too many town officials with nothing to do.[59]

Villagers do not, however, necessarily care about corruption, as long as they ultimately benefit. Village officials with extensive family and personal ties with officials at higher levels (or even with factory managers) may, for example, be viewed as better positioned to protect their fellow villagers from pressures from above or get them jobs in township enterprises.[60] Villagers tend to think township officials are more corrupt than village leaders, largely because they have more to offer in exchange for bribes. Villagers also consider township officials the "heavies" in government. They are the ones who have tended to oversee the nominations of village elections, make demands on the villagers to fulfill state policies, and penalize them for their failings.[61]

---

58. Discussions with a former Shaanxi villager (Ogden, "Field Research Notes," Sept. 1999).

59. Ogden, "Field Research Notes," Sept. 1999. A 1999 study carried out by the Institute for Rural Development (the Chinese Academy of Social Sciences) found that among township cadres surveyed, 9.1 percent believed it was fair and reasonable to arrest the *parents* of a child who violates the family planning regulation (Wang Binglu, "Yingxiang xiangzhen ganbu falü yishi xingchengde zhuyao yinsu").

60. Tyrene White, "Village Elections," p. 266.

61. A survey conducted in 1990 asked villagers their view of township government. In response to the question "Is grassroots democracy appropriate for [this] economically less developed region [of Ningxia]?" 22 percent said yes, 52.9 percent said no. In response to the question "Who in the countryside needs to improve their consciousness of legality?" 50.7 percent said the peasants; 20.9 percent said township cadres; 19.4 percent said party members; and 8.1 percent named village cadres. In response to the question "When communicating with township authorities, whom do the peasants usually contact?" 31.7 percent replied "cadres in villages"; 14.8 percent bypassed township cadres and went directly to the superiors in the county; only 14.1 percent chose "township representatives." In response to the question "What must be established for direct, democratic supervision by the people [of township government]

Within the new framework generated by economic reforms, China's rulers are also compelled to satisfy popular demands for modernization in order to maintain legitimacy. Villagers seem, in fact, far more interested in economic reform than in democratization,[62] and some villagers—including some elected village leaders—think that elections make little difference. The members of Su Village in Jiangsu province, for example, insisted that it was not democratic elections and self-government but roads and factories that would bring prosperity. Their village was poor, they said, because it had no roads and only one factory. They did not think they would get more factories without building roads, and they believed village elections had done nothing to alleviate the situation. In short, they saw no connection between elections and economic prosperity. In some villages, this is no doubt because they have re-elected the same officials they had before village elections were institutionalized. [63]

In an even poorer village in Shaanxi province, ordinary villagers likewise thought elections mattered little, and they knew very little about politics. They did think that the economic reforms had made a difference, but they felt that roads and factories were even more important.[64] They lacked a

---

to be effective," 58 percent chose "a system in which people's opinions are effectively taken into consideration for evaluation of cadres" (but they did not say that required elections), and 35.5 percent chose "the election and dismissal of cadres by the people." In response to the question "Do peasants dare to criticize township government?" 65.8 percent said yes, and 8.2 percent said no. This survey, done in Ningxia Autonomous Region, was conducted in May 1990, before China's second round of liberalization (in 1992). The respondents were 500 ordinary villagers, and 500 cadres, of whom 250 were township cadres and 250 village cadres. See Li Kang, "Zhengtong renhe zhi yu jichen shequ."

62. Urban dwellers hold similar views. In an October 1994 survey of 2,500 people in ten cities, 54 percent of the respondents "agreed with the party's oft-repeated line that economic development, not greater democracy, is the most pressing national need" (Gilley, "Whatever You Say," p. 36).

63. I asked villagers and (separately) their elected village officials about the importance of elections. They usually responded that it was economic reforms, not elections, that had made a difference. In Su Village in Kunshan County, the elected head of the villagers' committee said there was absolutely no difference in how the village was run before and after the elections. Since the time of the 1911 Revolution, *it has always been the smart and powerful people who controlled this village*, regardless of changes from the Nationalists to the Communists, from pre–Cultural Revolution to post–Cultural Revolution, and from pre-reform to post-reform (Ogden, "Field Research Notes," Sept. 1999).

64. The trip sponsored by the Carter Center to Zhujiaqiao Village in Rongchang County, Chongqing Municipality, Sichuan, in January 1999, also lends support to the view that villagers see roads as far more important than almost anything else. Of the four questions posed by

"consciousness," however, that "democracy" was a way to gain roads, facto-ries, or economic prosperity. And they certainly did not see elections as a step toward the right to free speech.[65] Elections also seemed relatively unim-portant to villagers in a remarkably prosperous village in Pudong District,[66] at least in the sense that there has been almost no change in officeholders since the first set of elections.[67] Other researchers have also found that the more prosperous villages are not necessarily the most advanced in promoting elections and self-government.

One of the more compelling interpretations of these examples is that as long as the economy and the village generally are doing well, villagers pay lit-tle attention to elections. If they are doing poorly in spite of elections, villag-ers will think elections, and hence leadership, irrelevant. In short, there is lit-tle evidence that the institutionalization of village elections has inspired villagers to seek more democratization.

Villagers' attitudes toward elections also suggest that if control over in-come-generating activities remains in the hands of the village *party secretary*, village elections matter less. In villages with income-generating enterprises, real power resides with those who control them. In villages where agriculture is the primary source of income, and opportunities for migration and em-ployment in town and village enterprises are limited, however, the villagers' committee is far more likely to have significant power. Furthermore, because the inhabitants of such villages are more affected by the outcome of elections, they are more likely to have truly competitive elections.[68] In short, Chinese villagers' attitudes toward elections and democratization are shaped by far more complex forces than the desire to have the right to vote for their leaders.

China's reform leadership, well-represented in the Ministry of Civil Af-fairs, does think there is a connection between elections, good leadership,

---

villagers to candidates after they gave speeches, the first and third were about building roads to the village (Carter Center, *The Carter Center Report on Chinese Elections*, p. 6).

65. Discussion with a former villager from Shaanxi (Ogden, "Field Research Notes," Sept. 1999).

66. The village has 30 factories and enterprises and an annual village revenue of 13,000 RMB (US$1,625) per capita.

67. Discussion with the elected head of the villagers' committee in Jie Long Village, lo-cated in the town of Huang Lou, in Pudong District (Ogden, "Field Research Notes," Sept. 1999).

68. Oi and Rozelle, "Elections and Power," p. 531.

and economic prosperity. Today, it is less concerned with *control* over the economy and more focused on local self-government and the decentralization of power as the best way to develop China. The reform leadership does not appear to see the growth of procedural democracy at the village level as threatening. This ministry is, however, one of the weakest in the central government, and its regulations are more easily ignored than those of other ministries and agencies.

Ironically, Communist Party officials in many localities are interfering less in the electoral system simply because they have lost interest in their role of political guidance. They, along with many of the better-educated and potential village leaders, are too busy being entrepreneurs and making money. Furthermore, many officials who are getting rich by manipulating a corrupt system of governance are not interested in promoting democratization.[69] But others believe they can advance their self-interests by being elected as a village official.[70] So electoral reform that would lead to the "best candidates" winning is not on the agenda of many of the individuals who could most effectively promote it at the local level.

Perhaps just as unfortunate, villagers are themselves losing interest in elections in some localities because there are too many of them, for villagers are also expected to participate in the election of town and township deputies to people's congresses. There are about 48,000 people's congresses at this level in China, but they are still largely rubber-stamp legislatures that meet only a few days each year and lack any real authority. Villagers feel these deputies do nothing to serve their interests and that participation in these elections is a waste of their time. Furthermore, if the candidate for a deputy's seat receives less than 50 percent plus one of the total votes cast, the election must be rerun. The result is that many villagers will not vote in elections of town and township officials unless they are paid to vote. Finally, the more than 100 million villagers who are on the move usually lose their right to vote in their new locality, even though they could if they had a letter from their own village giving them permission. In any event, the new suburban towns created by massive migration usually do not encourage migrants to

---

69. Interview with former official of Kunshan County (Ogden, "Field Research Notes," Sept. 1999).

70. Gamer and Shou, "Township Elections and the Transformation of Local Power Structures," pp. 67–68.

vote because these newcomers outnumber native residents, whose interests are often in conflict with theirs.[71]

Political Participation and Sense of Efficacy

How often do the Chinese use the electoral system and other channels available to them to express their concerns and interests? And how effective do they feel their participation is? A survey of four rural counties in China in 1990 studied various means of conveying concerns or interests. In terms of "autonomous acts of political participation" that require highly purposive and demanding actions, Chinese living in rural areas were found to "compare surprisingly well with Chinese in urban areas and with national samples in more developed countries." Rural Chinese did not do as well in "co-operative, group-based efforts to solve problems." In comparison to the citizens of most democratic countries, they tended to act in an atomistic way that favored their own individual interests. For country people anywhere, but especially in rural China where group decision-making was common for decades, this is a surprising result.[72]

Two areas in which rural Chinese did well were "voicing" (writing a representative) and "contacting" (getting in touch with a representative). When rural Chinese were concerned with addressing communal goals, such as in-

---

71. Liu Yawei, "Grassroots Participation in China," Harvard University, New England China Seminar, Dec. 3, 2001.

72. Data for this study come from Eldersveld et al., *Four-County Study of Chinese Local Government and Political Economy, 1990*. All interviews in China were conducted by students trained at Beijing University and under faculty supervision. There were five measures of participation (Jennings, "Political Participation in the Chinese Countryside," pp. 362–63):

1. "Have you attended a local party meeting recently?" (8 percent);
2. "Have you ever worked with other people, including family and relatives, to try to solve some local problem?" (12 percent);
3. "Have you ever written a letter to a cadre or offered an opinion or suggestion to a cadre?" (14 percent);
4. "Have you ever contacted a delegate to the county people's congress or township people's congress or a member of the village council?" (24 percent);
5. "Have you attended an all-village meeting recently?" (47 percent).

Although attending a party or village meeting might reflect mobilization efforts by local cadres rather than individual initiative, the other three activities certainly did require initiative. It is also significant that 14 percent wrote a letter or contacted a cadre even though such action meant "going on the record" (ibid., pp. 363–65).

frastructure needs, agriculture, and economic enterprise, they resorted to contacting and voicing more often than they did to autonomous acts or group-based efforts. This is true in spite of the fact that the educational level, which is normally associated with such activities, is far lower in China than in many other countries looked at in these cross-country comparisons.[73]

In Su Village in Jiangsu, the head of the villagers' committee said that well-educated villagers make more demands on upper-levels of government and are more inclined to criticize the government. But ordinary villagers pay little attention to government above the village level. When they are upset about something, they go, either individually or collectively, to see the head of the villagers' committee or the village party secretary. Normally, they just complain; sometimes they send a letter to the next higher level of government, the township. Because their writing skills are weak, however, some of their letters are virtually incomprehensible, leaving officials in the dark as to what they want.[74]

Complaints tend to fall into two categories. First, people complain about personal matters, such as family squabbles, which in more modern polities would not be considered the business of a public official. While I was in the office of the village's party secretary, he received a telephone call from an elderly villager upset about the care he was getting. He did not like the caretaker and wanted the party secretary to see to the matter. The secretary said that this was typical of the problems he dealt with. Villagers expect him to handle personal issues. This sort of relationship between villagers and local officials reinforces the universally held view in China that officials are the parents of the people, or *fumuguan* (parent-officials), and have an obligation to take care of them.[75]

Second, just as time-consuming are complaints arising from economic liberalization and privatization. For example, now that land is privatized, it is once again divided into small parcels. To get to one person's plot, machin-

---

73. Ibid., pp. 364–65, 370.

74. Ogden, "Field Research Notes," Sept. 1999. One study found that village committees encourage villagers to write letters and express their complaints by setting up a "reporting box" for villagers to drop their letter in and by offering rewards for good suggestions; see Xiang Jiquan, "Zhongguo cunminde gonggong canyu," p. 44.

75. Voicing of demands can be far more strident. For example, if the township has borrowed money from the villagers and not repaid it, villagers may go together and protest at township offices or block roads into the town (Ogden, discussions with village party secretary and the head of the village committee as well as villagers; "Field Research Notes," Sept. 1999).

ery must cross other peasants' parcels and may damage their crops. Similarly, boats and harvesters and other equipment that used to belong to collectives are now the property of a particular individual or household. At harvest time, everyone in the village may want to use the equipment within a short period of time. So they ask the head of the villagers' committee to decide what should be a privately resolved matter—because again, the village head is seen as a parent-official. The village head usually appeals to the villagers' sense of "morality" (*daoli*) and fairness, but often to little avail. Since neither side is completely right or completely wrong, the issues are difficult to handle. Village leaders must exercise caution because they live in the same village as the parties in the dispute. Another type of problem arising from economic liberalization is the refusal of children to care for their elderly parents. Because it is the law in China that children must provide for their parents, it is illegal for them to refuse to do so. Again, the village head will appeal to the children's sense of morality. But, in this case, if they do not comply, the children can be taken to a government office and *ordered* to provide for their parents. If they still fail to do so, they can be arrested.[76]

The 1990 survey of four counties also found that pluralism is flourishing in the Chinese countryside and that those who participate in the political system do so for more than the particularistic self-serving reasons that tend to characterize the participatory behavior of individuals in more authoritarian polities. The study noted that participation levels were influenced by individual traits (such as gender and education) and contextual matters in much the same ways as they were in more democratic societies. In fact, the study found a remarkable resemblance between "more developed participatory systems" and China.

Indeed, an innocent observer looking at these results might easily locate them in a Western democracy. Particularly striking is the influence of education and sex as determinants of participation. Residues of an historically strong patriarchal culture continue to influence mightily the political activity of ordinary citizens. By the same token, the privileges and skills associated with education are fully as operative, if not more so, as in Western societies.[77]

---

76. Ogden, discussion with the head of the village committee in Su Village, Kunshan County, Jiangsu, "Field Research Notes," Sept. 1999.

77. Jennings, "Political Participation in the Chinese Countryside," p. 362; quoted material on p. 371.

An investigation of political participation in villages in 1998 also revealed that villagers had access to and took advantage of several ways of articulating their interests. Apart from voting, these were meeting with village leaders; attending meetings (for political study, enterprise management, and village affairs); writing letters of complaints to the village leaders; filing lawsuits against village cadres (rare); and protest (both public and private, legal and illegal) against unpopular (or unreasonable) policies, such as family planning, taxes, and grain procurement. Participation in the political system may be spontaneous or mobilized, but, this study concluded, voting in village elections still tends to happen in response to mobilization. The ability to mobilize the population of a village is in proportion to its level of economic development. The more developed villages have more organizational and material resources available for mobilization. Their residents do not, however, necessarily express personal interests more freely, and the governments of such villages tend to use their resources to favor community interests over personal interests.[78]

To sum up, in spite of China's traditional culture, its relatively low developmental level, and the continuing effects of socialist institutions, practices, and attitudes, villagers nevertheless participate at a remarkably high level. The electoral and representative system in the countryside cannot be dismissed as a sham, a front for the implementation of dictatorial policies. The level of participation in elections and the habit of contacting village representatives who won the elections to express interests and concerns, either about village issues or township governance, are impressive. And, contrary to the views of sophisticated Chinese urbanites, Chinese villagers, even those with a low educational level, are quite capable of making rational and informed choices. Even if their views are still rooted in "feudalism," they have the capacity to judge who will make the most competent officials and which officials will best address their needs.

It has been argued that village elections and economic reforms are rapidly politicizing China's peasantry and that it is unwise to assume that China's peasants will play the same passive role in democratization as their counterparts in Europe and America. Chinese villagers are gaining a political consciousness, a sense of efficacy, and an independence from state authority. Greater autonomy is, in turn, becoming institutionalized through elections. Elections are also enhancing the organizational capability of the peasantry. As a result, it would be foolish to dismiss the potential power of the peasantry in

---

78. Xiang Jiquan, "Zhongguo cunminde gonggong canyu," pp. 43–47.

democratizing China or even in revolutionizing China.[79] If arbitrary taxation, corruption, and violence by township officials continue to anger China's villagers, they might well use their newfound power against the state—a possibility lessened thus far by the seeming inability of villagers to organize so they can band together with other villages. Thus far, peasant tax revolts have not been protests against the regime as such.[80] Villagers' anger has, rather, been unleashed sporadically in the form of violent street protests in towns and county seats, as well as the injury and even murder of tax collectors.[81] It would undoubtedly cause some interest in the United States if a revolution in China began with the slogan "No taxation without representation!"

Now that taxes are no longer paid by the collective but come out of an individual's pocket, China's villagers are demanding representation to protect them from excessive and arbitrary taxes and fees. Anger at burdensome taxes is also behind the demand for greater transparency: villagers want open account books so they can see what taxes are being levied, on whom, and for what. Taxation without representation—and without services provided in return—is helping to destabilize the countryside, but it is also proving to be a force for democratization.[82]

URBAN ELECTIONS: NEIGHBORHOOD RESIDENTS' AND PROPERTY-OWNERS' COMMITTEES

Because more than 70 percent of China's population still lives in the countryside, and because the impact of elections on local power structures has been far more profound in rural areas than in urban areas, most of the commentary on local elections and self-government has focused on the villages.

---

79. Zheng Yongnian, "Xiangcun minzhu he Zhongguo zhengzhi jingcheng."

80. Village leaders have, for example, increased fines, levies, and taxes in order to upgrade a village's facilities so that it can gain "model" status. In Shandong in 1991 alone, there were 619 levies to raise standards to pay the cost of inspection activities so that villages could compete for the coveted "model" status (Xiaobo Lu, *Cadres and Corruption*, p. 173).

81. Villagers who murder cadres and township cadres who murder villagers do not seem to be severely punished by the state. At most, township cadres appear merely to be transferred elsewhere (Thomas Bernstein and Xiaobo Lu, "Taxation Without Representation in China," Harvard University, New England China Seminar, Apr. 16, 2001).

82. Ibid. It would at this point be misleading, however, to portray the countryside as seething with anger at burdensome taxes; the number of townships in which peasant protests have been reported is still a tiny percentage of the total of 40,000 townships.

Nevertheless, procedural democracy has also made progress in the cities. Urban neighborhood residents' committees (*zhumin weiyuanhui*) came into existence in the early 1950s. Efforts to revitalize and improve them in the 1980s culminated in the Organic Law of Urban Residents' Committees, which went into effect on January 1, 1990. Unlike villages, however, the decision to initiate elections for urban residents' committees came from the top down, not the bottom up.

The residents' committees are administrative organs in charge of daily affairs within a defined urban neighborhood. According to a poll carried out in 127 cities, each residents' committee holds an average of ten meetings open to all residents every year.[83] A typical residential group comprises all the families in a building, usually between 40 and 60 households. Each neighborhood residents' committee includes about ten such contiguous residential groups. The committee's size depends on the numbers of residents in its territory. Most committees have three to five members, but there are committees with as many as 30 members. Committee members are supposed to be elected, but in practice the committee chair tends to recruit the members from "reliable and warmhearted retirees."[84] Alternatively, they recruit women and less educated residents because most residents do not want to serve on a committee they believe provides trivial services (delivering newspapers) or is intrusive (enforcing compliance with the birth control policy, collecting fees). By contrast, the villagers' committees make decisions seen as critical, such as how collective land will be used, the reallocation of land, and the determination of projects for modernizing the village.[85]

In addition, urban democracy also suffers from problems in the electoral system that make it less likely that good candidates will run. For example, although the government determines the final list of candidates for the committees, winning elections does not actually help them. If they are endorsed by the government, they are *supposed* to win. Losing, on the other hand, "clearly exhibits to authorities their incompetence and usually blocks their way to further promotion. In many cases, the authorities transfer them to other leadership positions . . . usually to unimportant posts."[86] Nevertheless, when elections for neighborhood committees are carried out properly, urban

---

83. State Council Information Office, "Progress in China's Human Rights Cause in 1996."
84. Shaw, *Social Control in China*, pp. 56–58.
85. Benewick et al., "Self-Governance and Community," p. 4.
86. Tianjian Shi, *Political Participation in Beijing*, p. 38.

democracy has benefited from the same basic changes in electoral procedures as in the rural areas: more than one candidate per seat, a secret ballot, and election by majority vote.

Since the government's mid-1990s decision to privatize work-unit housing, an increasing number of urban residents now own their own apartment. Many have even formed "property owners' committees," which are classified as "social" or "mass organizations" (*qunzong tuanti*) and fall under the jurisdiction of the Land Administration Bureau. Because residents are far more assertive about their property rights than they are about general political rights, property owners' committees are very active organizations.[87] Although the state maintains fairly strong control over the residents' committees, its influence on the new property-owners committees is only indirect. The new committees are, however, an important component of China's growing "corporatism." In a sense they compete with the old committees over the management of daily affairs, but they also function as a counterweight to the large and influential real estate companies that have sprung up as a result of market reforms. By allowing residents to organize and contend with these real estate companies, the state is able to reduce its own role in adjudicating neighborhood disputes. This decentralization and pluralization of power bases benefit both urban residents and the state.[88]

Nevertheless, China's cities have not witnessed as dramatic a change in local government as have China's villages. This is because cities, unlike rural villages and towns, did not lose their administrative structure with the coming of economic decentralization. Once the communal structure was abandoned in the villages, the government had to institute a new form of local government to maintain order and promote development. The villagers' committees were created to address this need and given some carrots and sticks to carry out their responsibilities. But in the cities, the overall administrative structure remained in place. Housing, tax collection, sanitation, security, population control, and other such matters were still handled by the city administration or indirectly by the city through the work unit;[89] and work units largely overlapped with the neighborhood residents' committees, making the latter's role either redundant or subordinate to the work unit.

---

87. Discussions with Chinese students and civil servants from China's cities, 1998–99.
88. Ibid.
89. Tianjian Shi, *Political Participation in Beijing*, p. 37.

This is changing because, as part of their efforts to become more efficient, work units spin off nonproductive activities, such as their welfare responsibilities and their role as the grass-roots implementers of the Party's policies. Work units are already delegating many of the more onerous aspects of these policies and administrative duties to the elected neighborhood residential committees. For example, apart from acting as mediators in neighborhood and family disputes, preventing crime, managing social welfare services, and keeping social order, the residents' committee is (like its village counterpart) now in charge of administering the birth control program and overseeing government campaigns, such as the "socialist spiritual civilization" campaign and the campaign against the Falungong that began in 1999.[90] Neighborhood residents' committees must also manage the large influx of migrants, who belong to no work unit. Moreover, the government is itself attempting to streamline its operations by, in part, requiring these committees to pick up many of its management functions.[91]

The neighborhood committees have encountered heavy weather in carrying out their assigned duties. The large number of households in a committee's jurisdiction, the many functions it is asked to perform, changes in the neighborhood population as workers move out of their work units and sublet their apartments, the ability of many residents in the new multistory buildings to conceal their activities, and their unwillingness to share information with or participate in the work of the neighborhood residents' committee—all these exacerbate the committee's difficulties. Moreover, the committee's position at the bottom of the urban administrative hierarchy, with the work unit and street offices, the district government, and the city government above it, combined with the fact that the committee's duties overlap with those of higher units means that any of these higher units can overrule its decisions. For example, a common problem in major cities is in-migration from rural areas. It is usually the neighborhood committee that must make all the arrangements for and control the migrant labor force in its area, both for security and for economic development reasons; yet when it tries to collect rent from the migrants, the committee often faces a fight with the street office for control over the space and the rent—and the street office

90. Shaw, *Social Control in China*, p. 256; and Ben Read, "Urban Residents' Committees in Beijing," seminar, Harvard University, Fairbank Center, Aug. 16, 2000.

91. Benewick et al., "Self-Governance and Community," p. 6.

usually wins.[92] Compounding the weakness of the neighborhood committee is its lack of sanctions against those residents who fail to comply with policies required by higher levels of government. To make matters worse, the committee must represent the interests of the work unit (if it overlaps with the district) rather than its own constituency.[93]

The result of all these factors is that elections for the neighborhood residents' committee matter far less than elections for villagers' committees. Indeed, the parent street office can dismiss any elected member of the neighborhood committee for incompetence, obstruction of the work of the government, corruption, or simple obstreperousness.[94] Regardless of how committee members are chosen, urban residents generally prefer the nanny-like mediation practiced by the committee to the potentially more invasive and coercive measures of the police and public security bureaus. The dispensing of justice occurs largely outside the formal judicial system. Neighborhood "mediation" and "security committees," composed of residents, operate under the local public security substation, but the grass-roots public security bureaus also become involved and usually do not bother to consult the courts or procuratorates.[95] (A survey conducted in the Beijing area indicated that 88.04 percent of the respondents preferred mediation to going to court to resolve a dispute.)[96] Thus, although many of the neighborhood elections are not truly democratic, the people in those neighborhoods are not necessarily displeased with the committees. If a committee does its job well, is not heavy-handed in its approach to residents, does not interfere

---

92. Ben Read, "Urban Residents' Committees in Beijing," seminar, Harvard University, Fairbank Center, Aug. 16, 2000. In addition to the city government, Beijing (with a population of 10 million permanent residents and more than 3 million transients) has ten district governments, 118 street offices, and 5,026 residents' committees.

93. Tianjian Shi, *Political Participation in Beijing*, p. 38.

94. Ben Read, "Urban Residents' Committees in Beijing," seminar, Harvard University, Fairbank Center, Aug. 16, 2000.

95. McCormick, *Political Reform in Post-Mao China*, pp. 113–20. Public security personnel themselves often exhibit a nanny-like approach as well. For example, juvenile delinquents are carefully watched and their families are contacted frequently to make sure they are doing well. Special efforts are made to ensure that they get jobs so that they will be less likely to commit crimes again (discussions at Cambridge University with Xi Feng, a high-level official within the National Public Security Bureau, Jan.–Feb. 1997).

96. Fan Yu and Dong Min, "Guomin falü yishi diaocha," p. 8. There were 1,438 valid responses. All respondents were over eighteen, and a variety of occupations and levels of education were represented.

too much with their lives, and keeps the neighborhood in order (including controlling migrants and their businesses), then residents care little whether it was "democratically" chosen or not. Further, if the building of "community" rather than "democratization" is the measurement, then many of the elected neighborhood committees may be judged a success, for they do help to build informal social organizations among neighbors and sponsor activities (such as morning exercises, tea parties, and dances in the evenings) that bring residents together. Committees whose members are pleasant and better educated, in areas with a stable, employed populations, seem to be more successful at building community.[97]

Economic liberalization has had some serious negative repercussions for the spread of democratic procedures in China's cities. China's government has been reluctant to allow greater democratization in the cities. It can hardly justify its reluctance by pointing to the "feudal" characteristic of urban residents, for with the exception of the increasingly large number of migrant laborers in the cities, residents are well educated and not generally superstitious. But, faced with worker unrest, which has grown steadily as tens of millions of workers have become unemployed when socialist economic policies were jettisoned in favor of capitalist ones, the state has been reluctant to augment the political power of urban residents. Workers in some money-losing state-owned enterprises are, however, demanding the right to elect their enterprise leaders in hopes of reversing the decline.[98]

Still, the role of the work unit in carrying out government welfare responsibilities and ensuring social stability and political control has changed considerably since the mid-1980s. Political and economic decentralization, with the market replacing central planning as the instrument for allocating resources, and the increasing mobility of the population have significantly undermined the power of the work unit.[99] At the level of the urban work unit and neighborhood, then, it appears that the state's control over its citizens is being eroded. This trade-off of control for freedom is, however, being accompanied by deteriorating social stability.

---

97. Ben Read, "Urban Residents' Committees in Beijing," seminar, Harvard University, Fairbank Center, Aug. 16, 2000.

98. Sun Peiwu, "Dalu zhengzhi zixia ershangde tiaozhang jixiang."

99. Dittmer and Lu, "Structural Transformation of the Chinese *Danwei*," p. 115.

Nevertheless, a survey conducted by the Chinese Academy of Social Sciences at the height of liberalization in 1988–89[100] (before social instability had reached its present heights) indicated that the urban "political person" believed ordinary people should participate more in politics. For example, 77.6 percent responded that "politics is a matter for the public" rather than "for the leadership," and 46.7 percent agreed that "politics is a good thing" rather than "a bad thing."[101] The responses to another question revealed that other goals were seen as more important than democratization, however. Asked to choose one of seven possible objectives of political reform, only 5.7 percent chose "guaranteeing citizens' freedom and rights" and only 14.5 percent "gradually establishing a democratic system." The choices that received the highest scores were "improving people's living standards" (17.1 percent) and "clean government" (36.9 percent).[102]

Others questions found a high degree of engagement with political issues: 78.3 percent talked often or occasionally about politics at work, and 86.1 percent thought demonstrations acceptable if they were "necessary" or could be of some use.[103] The means by which people preferred to express themselves were spread fairly evenly over a number of possibilities:

Method of expression	*Percentage of respondents*
report to work-unit leaders	15.1%
report to government agencies	15.1
tell people's representatives	13.6
report to radio, newspaper, and television	7.8
tell others	6.1

---

100. The survey began in the second half of 1988 and ended in May 1989, just before the crackdown on Tiananmen Square demonstrators and the retreat from liberalization. Respondents ranged from age 15 to 75 and lived in thirteen cities, including Shanghai, Guangzhou, Xi'an, Shenyang, Guanyuan, and Daqing. There was a total of 2,200 respondents, with 1,995 valid responses (Zhang Mingshu, *Zhongguo zhengzhi ren*).

101. Ibid., table 1.8, p. 22; table 1.3, p. 18; and table 2.8, p. 39.

102. Ibid., table 2.14, p. 46. The other responses were "to eliminate bureaucratism (red tape)," 9.5 percent; "to separate the party from the government," 8 percent; and "leadership succession," 1.8 percent.

103. Ibid., table 3.9, p. 63; table 4.2, p. 67; and table 5.1, p. 87. Responses to another question indicated that acceptable reasons for demonstrating were corruption in the leadership (27.8 percent), intolerable inflation (26.2 percent), and serious mistakes in state policy (18.8 percent). The banning of books, magazines, or movies was not considered a good reason for demonstrating, with only 0.5 percent choosing this response (ibid., table. 5.4, p. 94).

work with others in an
  organized manner   3.6
write to leaders   2.8
demonstrations   2.1
organize gatherings to
  discuss and report to
  concerned departments   1.8
none of the above   26.4[104]

This interest in political issues and willingness to speak out did not translate into great enthusiasm for holding office or for elections, however. Only
22.4 percent said they would like to be an elected people's representative, 33.6
percent said they would serve if elected, and 35.0 percent indicated an
unwillingness to hold public office. As with villagers, a significant number—
32.7 percent of the voters in urban districts surveyed—did not think it mattered for whom they voted (and 35.4 percent said they voted just to fulfill
their obligations as citizens), and less than half (45.1 percent) could even remember for whom they had voted at the last election, much less whether
their choice had been elected (30.5 percent remembered).[105] The lack of interest in elections and the belief that participation is ineffective may reflect a
lack of interest in democratizing China, or quite the contrary, it may be that
urban residents think that democratizing China matters, but that participation and elections (as presently conducted) are irrelevant to it. This question
remains to be investigated.

The results of one measure of democracy were less encouraging: fully 73.8
percent said that in their experience, participation in elections and other political processes had not affected local policy.[106] An individual's willingness to
participate reflects in part his or her expectations of being able to participate
effectively. In this regard, only 19.7 percent of the respondents in the Chinese

---

104. Ibid., table 5.2, p. 89. A control question, however, suggested that the situation could
alter the choice of means considerably. In response to a question about a newly built factory
in the neighborhood making a lot of noise and disturbing the neighborhood, for example, 36.7
percent chose "report to government agency" (ibid., table 5.3, p. 91).

105. Ibid., table 3.3, p. 52; and table 3.6, p. 56; table 3.9, p. 68; and table 4.2, p. 67. It may be
the case that the percentages of Chinese willing to hold elected office and those unable to remember for whom they voted for in the last election differ little from the percentages in
Western liberal democratic countries—or are even higher.

106. Ibid., table 7.2, p. 130.

Academy of Social Sciences study expected that they would in the future have the power to influence the government's decisions, and 32.9 percent said they would not.[107]

THE SELECTION OF LEADERS

Although the practice is not mandated by law, work-unit authorities often encourage surveys, discussions, or even elections in the hope of identifying competent and respected individuals with the potential to become leaders. Beginning in the 1990s, those government officials from the town to the province level (with the exception of provincial governors) being considered for promotion have had to be evaluated. Through questionnaires or interviews with the official's colleagues and subordinates, those in charge of promotions can acquire "objective" evidence for their decision. If this system is broadly implemented within China's civil service, it may also motivate China's tea-sipping bureaucrats to work harder and to be kinder to their subordinates.

As with the broadening of the rights of citizens in other areas, the state's motivation for involving workers in the selection of their leaders may not have been to promote democratization as a goal, but to use a democratic process to further the goals of economic rationalization, such as replacing the leaders of poorly managed state-owned factories or exposing and eliminating corrupt work-unit and government officials. Since the Chinese government stopped using political campaigns to check the corruption and abuses of local leaders in the late 1970s, workplace elections have become one of the preferred alternatives.[108] Whatever the motive, however, consulting and involving workers in the choice of their leaders suggests at least the inklings of a democratic process.

Surveys are more common than elections in institutions. As noted in the Appendix, all sorts of official, semi-official, commercial, and private organizations in China conduct surveys to collect data for policy and

---

107. Perhaps reflecting ambivalence about China's evolving political system, 42.1 percent replied, "It's hard to say" (*shuo buqing*; ibid., table 4.6, p. 72).

108. Tianjian Shi (*Political Participation in Beijing*, p. 39) also states that in those state-run work units in which the iron rice bowl (lifetime employment) still exists and incompetent or corrupt officials cannot be fired, elections allow them to be removed from leadership positions.

business decisions. The government organizations in charge of various *danwei*, from research institutes, universities, and factories to state-controlled television stations and shipping companies, survey employees to discover their preferences before selecting *danwei* leaders. In an era when performance and profits matter, choosing leaders respected by their colleagues is essential.

In the case of universities, the Ministry of Education almost always conducts a survey before it changes either departmental chairs or university presidents. When choosing a departmental chair, the ministry submits a list of candidates and asks the professors and staff in the department to choose one. Those who vote never see the survey results, but it is unlikely the Ministry of Education would appoint someone who has no departmental support. The ministry also surveys university employees to determine the level of satisfaction with such things as housing, salary, and workload. This is one way the higher levels of the state can check the various work units they supervise; in the process, the workers get a chance to register an opinion. Similarly, some government surveys within universities try to measure student attitudes and concerns.

How reliable are such surveys, and how much do the results affect the government's decisions? According to informants, whether the survey is anonymous or not is irrelevant. An employee who criticizes university leaders in a survey will not be punished because, at this point, the government wants people to voice their opinions through *official* channels such as government-sponsored surveys. The government sees this as a far safer outlet for grievances, anger, and criticism than such *public* outlets as street protests or "large character posters" displayed on walls, which can become rallying points for public protest. Further, the government believes that surveys provide a better understanding of what is going on at the local level—particularly when it suspects corruption or incompetence among local leaders.

In China today, survey respondents in *danwei* do not generally believe they risk punishment if they are critical of the Party or local leaders. Indeed, employees tend to see government-run surveys as a chance to express grievances and preferences. Employees believe, for example, that if enough of them express dissatisfaction with their housing, the government might respond by allocating more resources to the work unit. The government wants to know the level of discontent among workers and students as well as their concerns. The perception is that it would not punish people for their answers even if it knew their identities.[109]

There has also been a change in the values and procedures for recruiting civil servants, who can be seen as a pool of potential future leaders. During the Mao Zedong era, political consciousness and "redness" were the dominant criteria for selecting bureaucrats, and there were no measurable, objective standards for evaluating candidates. The reintroduction of a civil service examination has led to an emphasis on professionalism and expertise. The examination system *institutionalizes* a more equitable and democratic process and makes it more likely that talented people will become government civil servants and, later, officials. In turn, these officials are more likely to address administrative issues in a professional manner because they gained their position through an examination rather than through political correctness or *guanxi* (personal relationships or cronyism). The government is implementing measures to reduce unprofessional behavior, such as procedures aimed at preventing officials from taking bribes or accepting gifts or favors in exchange for performing ordinary administrative matters.[110] By no means have these efforts been completely successful, but at least the government is aware of the problem and taking steps to remedy it.

GREATER LEGAL PROTECTIONS AND RIGHTS FOR INDIVIDUALS

Most critics of China's legal system, especially human rights groups such as Asia Watch and Amnesty, focus on the system of criminal justice. In spite of their good intentions, they quite incorrectly tend to treat the system

as unreservedly violative of human rights. They fail to recognize that for all its many abusive characteristics and practices, the Chinese system is appreciably more complex than can be captured in so simple a dismissal. . . . Nor do they heed the nuanced fashion in which many Chinese who are as sincere and dedicated to human

---

109. Discussions with faculty, Department of Politics and International Affairs, Fudan University, 1998. Before the 1990s, such surveys would not necessarily have been confidential and might even have been used to ferret out dissidents.

110. For example, in 1996, in an effort to prevent officials from refusing to process passport and license applications unless they received a bribe, the government set up specific procedures and time limits for such applications.

rights as they view their own legal system and the question of what are universal human rights in a Chinese context.[111]

There also tends to be a lack of understanding of the strength of popular support in China for many actions which the international human rights community correctly sees as violations of human rights—in this case rights associated as well with the growth of democracy. Although popular support for state actions that violate human rights does not excuse the state's behavior, it does allow us to see that repression in China does not generate as much criticism as we might expect. For example, when President Clinton visited China in 1998, President Jiang Zemin stated publicly that the government arrested dissidents because they did things that were "illegal." Many Chinese did not agree that the dissidents were doing anything illegal—but they *did* think that they should be arrested. In one case, that of the dissident Wei Jingsheng, the Chinese with whom I have spoken who knew who he was[112] did not support his ideas, such as that the United States should use economic sanctions to punish China for violating human rights. Chinese intellectuals and even dissidents do not seem concerned to protect the basic principle of the "right to free speech" when they disagree with the content of that free speech. This does not mean that the Chinese are unwilling to publicly challenge the courts' inability or unwillingness to protect human rights.[113] Indeed, since the reform period began, these demands have grown

---

111. Alford, "Making a Goddess of Democracy from Loose Sand," p. 65. The efforts of China to institutionalize the rule of law and human rights are documented in Wang Zhenmin and Li Zhenghui, "The Developing Human Rights and Rule of Law in Legal Philosophy and Political Practice in China, 1978–2000." Among other developments, the authors note that conferences and courses on human rights and the rule of law (and even special law courses for China's central leaders), as well as the involvement of China in international human rights and rule of law activities have grown steadily since the "rule of law" was incorporated into the Constitution in 1992.

112. Wei Jingsheng was first arrested in 1979 for publishing anti-party items during the Democracy Wall movement of 1978–79. He was sentenced to fifteen years in jail. After he was released, he continued to make anti-regime statements and was again imprisoned. He was released for medical reasons in 1997 and expelled. In the West, he was China's best-known dissident, but in China by the 1990s even well-informed university students rarely knew who he was.

113. For example, Guangdong Province's delegates to the National People's Congress session in March 2001 attacked "China's top judge over a sub-standard legal system and lack of respect for human rights," contending that "the government's crackdown on Falun Gong was full of 'sharp contradictions,'" and demanded reforms that would ensure that judges were of higher quality ("NPC Delegates Call for Judicial Reform," *China News Digest*, Mar. 13, 2001).

steadily louder as law has gradually replaced ideology as the primary arbiter of morality.

The development of a strong legal system in China has been hindered not just by the fact that it served as a tool of the state, and that both law-making and judicial decisions were subject to intervention from the Chinese Communist Party. It was also deterred by the dominant social context of an agrarian society, in which disputes were usually mediated, and only criminal cases tended to be adjudicated by courts. The idea that the legal system should be engaged in dispute resolution, promote justice and rights, and treat all equally before the law, is a product of the reform period.[114]

Most Chinese commentators would agree that a strong legal system is essential, both to further economic development and to guarantee civil rights.[115] Initial efforts to strengthen the legal system involved an expansion of judicial personnel and writing new laws. The number of lawyers grew from 2,000 in 1979 to 100,000 in 1997. Most work in the commercial, not the criminal, sector.[116] According to the Ministry of Justice, by 2000, China had more than 60,000 law students, and 260 law schools. China had one lawyer per 11,000 people (as compared with one for every 300 people in the United States, one for every 700 in Great Britain, and one for every 6,300 in Japan).[117] In addition, the many laws and legal regulations written since 1979 have strengthened the rights of China's people against the government—and against each other.

Legal reform is openly discussed today in journals and newspaper articles, as well as within the closed circles of legal scholars and relevant officials. China's central leadership clearly wants to establish an independent judiciary. In particular, China's top leaders are determined to curb the Party's ability to influence judicial decisions and to eradicate corruption among judicial personnel. Although the reformers may *want* judicial reform, however, they do not necessarily know *how* to get it. The Judges Law provides a good example of the difficulty of knowing how to reform the judicial system. The

---

114. Wang Zhenmin, "The Developing Rule of Law in China," p. 35.

115. Liu Jinxi, "Minzhu xin lun," p. 85.

116. Alter, "Society: Communism Is Dead, Crony Capitalism Lives," p. 31.

117. In addition, there were 985,313 people's mediation committees, 10,273,940 mediators, 57,029 professional legal assistants, 35,207 township and neighborhood legal service agencies, and 119,155 legal service workers, who serve as legal consultants for 488,569 town and township enterprises (Liu Han and Li Lin, "Woguo fazhi jianshe 20 nian chengjiu yu zhanwang"). Most of these personnel are, however, carryovers from the pre-reform legal structure.

1995 Judges Law allows the people's congress at each level to elect and remove chief justices ("presidents") of the courts under its jurisdiction every five years. The president of the Supreme People's Court is, therefore, elected and may be dismissed by the National People's Congress, whereas the *judges* of the courts are *appointed* by (and may be removed by) the standing committees of the people's congress at each level. Each people's court must submit an annual report on its work to the people's congress that oversees it. In the past, the courts had no problem garnering enough votes from their supervising people's congress; but in February 2001, the City People's Congress of Shenyang in Liaoning province rejected the work report submitted by the City People's Court—an event interpreted by the Chinese as a major step away from the "rubber stamp" role of the congress.[118]

In 1998, the Standing Committee of the National People's Congress enacted a new regulation that allows the people's congresses at each level to intervene in particular cases in which they believe possible judicial corruption or wrongdoing might be involved. This was not acceptable to legal reformers who, working through the Legal Advisory Committee of the National People's Congress's Standing Committee, has tried to get this regulation withdrawn because it would interfere with the "separation of powers" between the legislative and judicial branches. With judges both appointed and removed by the congresses, undue interference of the legislature in the judicial branch occurs. Many scholars have written articles in Chinese law journals arguing that the principle of judicial independence should outweigh the principle of supervision by the congress and, therefore, that judges be given lifetime appointments.[119] Legal reformers also argued for the need for media coverage of legal proceedings in order to guarantee judicial fairness and curb judicial corruption. Their proposal was officially endorsed; and in 1998, CCTV for the first time televised a live nationwide broadcast of a courtroom hearing.[120]

---

118. Wang Zhenmin, vice dean and associate professor, Tsinghua University Law School, Beijing, correspondence, July 2001.

119. Ibid.

120. "Media Supervision of Court Controversial," *China Daily*, Nov. 10, 1998, from web.lexis-nexis.com/universe. Prior to this, regional television stations had already been covering court trials. Although not "live," they edited scenes from a courtroom trial to make it more appealing to viewers. As one commentator noted, court television is not nearly as interesting as in the United States because there is no jury, and lawyers and procurators sit passively in their assigned seat, usually only responding to the judge's questions. Without the

The reforms to date reveal that a number of the problems in the judicial system are deeply rooted in the Chinese context. Although many Chinese are studying in Western law schools and the legal community has sought the advice of Western lawyers, legal scholars, and judges, the Chinese are just not able to apply Western principles and be done with it. Instead, they must address some fundamental issues before reforms will be meaningful.

What concrete steps have the Chinese taken to bring about judicial independence?[121] First, judges are to wear black robes. Some might be amused that this was the very first step, but China's legal reformers believe that a fundamental issue is the lack of respect for judges. During the Cultural Revolution, the judicial system was virtually destroyed, and when it was resurrected after 1975, most of the judges were demobilized military personnel assigned to the courts.[122] They were rarely qualified to make decisions about legal matters and wore their military uniforms. So, to promote respect for judges and establish the concept of the judiciary as an independent branch of government, judges are to wear black robes.[123]

Second, the salaries of judges are to be increased. The goal here is to make judges less susceptible to bribes and to attract talented law school graduates who have other career options.

Third, criteria for being a judge did not previously exist. Judges and other court personnel were even ignorant of what the law actually was, a problem exacerbated by the vast number of laws and regulations "promulgated by a bewildering variety of governmental and quasi-governmental bodies," the lack of indexes thereto, contradictory rules, and the lack of a "regular system of case reporting that would allow judges to see how other courts had handled similar problems."[124] The chaotic nature of the legal system means that qualified judges and judicial personnel are even more important.

---

confrontational element of American trials, it makes for quite dull television watching. See He Weifang, "Dui dianshi zhibo tingshen guocheng de yiyi" (Some arguments against live television coverage of the court trial process), *Zhongguo lüshi* 1998, no. 9: 60–61.

121. The following information about changes to the system of judicial personnel is based primarily on discussions and correspondence with Wang Zhenmin, 2001.

122. Clarke, "Dispute Resolution in China," p. 257.

123. As Wang Zhenmin remarked, when Justice Kennedy of the U.S. Supreme Court goes to China, the Chinese do not understand why the U.S. embassy makes such a fuss about his travel arrangements. In their view, he is just a judge, a lowly position in China. Of course, even judges in Western liberal democratic countries have worn black robes, even wigs, as part of an effort to shape a respectful image of judges.

124. Clarke, "Dispute Resolution in China," pp. 258–59.

The 1995 Judges Law lays out specific qualifications for judges. Demobilized military officers will no longer be assigned to the courts. New judges must now have formal legal training so that they can make decisions based on law, not politics and their own personal views. The law requires that new judges have specialized in law at the undergraduate or graduate level or, if they did not, that they at least have "professional legal knowledge" and have worked in the judicial system for a minimum of two years. In addition, each court must establish an "examination and appraisal committee" to undertake an annual review of judges. Judges may be dismissed for a number of reasons, including an "incompetent" rating in two consecutive years.[125]

The Judges Law, as well as the Procurators Law, were further revised by the Standing Committee of the National People's Congress in June 2001. Both revised laws raise the requirements for becoming judicial personnel. The laws establish a national unified judicial examination, which must be passed by all those applying to become judges, procurators, and lawyers. Further, as of January 2002, all current lawyers, judges, and procurators who do not meet the other requirements already in effect, namely that they have a college degree, must take the exam and pass it or lose their positions. A unified judicial examination for lawyers, procurators, and judges is important in part because, at present, the education of judges is often far lower than that of lawyers who argue cases before them. Thus, they are not really competent to evaluate the cases. It is important for reaching the goal of judicial autonomy that all three parts of the judicial system have the same educational background.

In this regard, the next step being planned in China is to unify legal education itself. At present there are nine different law degrees, which means there is no unified standard of education to be tested by the judicial examination. The goal of legal reformers is to have just one basic law degree, like the J.D. degree in the United States. In addition, legal reformers are insisting that the quality of the law schools—most of which do not even have libraries—be improved. As with the increase in salaries, it is hoped that educational qualifications that demand a higher quality of judicial personnel will help combat judicial corruption and enhance judicial autonomy.

Fourth, the judicial system is to become financially independent of local governments. China's legal reformers believe financial autonomy is crucial to judicial autonomy. If judicial personnel are no longer paid by local govern-

---

125. For a discussion of the 1995 Judges Law, see Lubman, *Bird in a Cage*, pp. 254–56.

ments, the power of members of local governments to interfere in the judicial system will decline For example, one study found that party and government leaders at the county level believed that the work of town and
township cadres below them directly affected their own work. As a result,
county leaders may interfere in a township court trial in which township
cadres have been accused of illegal administrative behavior out of concern
that a court ruling against the cadres will impede their own work. Because
the party and the government control the court's personnel and finances, the
court finds it difficult to ignore their opinions. There are, for example, a
large number of violations by town and township cadres in carrying out the
family planning policy, but the court will rarely even agree to hear these
cases. In short, the understanding of many officials is that the law should not
get in the way of work that must be carried out.[126] Clearly a major change in
attitudes will have to occur before Chinese officials put the protection of legal principles above concerns about carrying out policies. Until this happens,
the legal practices and values essential for democracy are likely to remain out
of reach.

Fifth, many articles in legal journals have proposed that there be two sets
of courts, national and local. In most cases, a trial is held in the province in
which the defendant resides. This makes sense when both sides to a dispute
are from the same locality, but when one party is not, it often leads to decisions unfair to the outside party. Legal reformers believe that national courts
would lead to more justice. Local courts in China tend to protect local power
interests. Local judicial personnel usually write their own laws without consulting anyone outside the locality. These laws are prejudicial to local interests. This is in contrast to national laws, which are generally perceived to be
much fairer. In 1979, the Standing Committee of the National People's
Congress set up its own department called the Legal Affairs Commission,
which in turn created a think tank to devise the best laws for the entire
country. One division does research on foreign laws, and another sends its
staff to a wide variety of localities in different parts of China to understand
the impact of laws locally. Based on their conclusions, the Legal Affairs
Commission makes recommendations to the Standing Committee, which
decides whether to promulgate the laws. (The Standing Committee of the
National People's Congress promulgates the "less important" laws, whereas

---

126. Wang Binglu, "Yingxiang xiangzhen ganbu falü yishi xingchengde zhuyao yinsu."

the National People's Congress as a whole promulgates the "more important" laws. The Standing Committee determines which laws are more and which are less important.)

Finally, and perhaps critically for establishing a broad framework for thinking about the judicial system, in 1997, the Fifteenth National Congress of the Chinese Communist Party set the goal of establishing a comprehensive legal framework by 2010 and "explicitly incorporated the rule of law as a basic guiding principle in the Party's official document." In 1999, the Ninth National People's Congress amended the 1982 State Constitution to endorse the rule of law as a basic principle, thereby making it into a constitutional principle.[127] Together with the State Compensation Law (1994), the Judges Law (1995), the Law on Lawyers (1996), and many other legal reforms, the explicit endorsement of the rule of law has helped change the role of the law away from serving as a tool by which the state governs the people and justifies its policies and toward the role of protecting the interests of society. The accretion of legal and judicial reforms are reinforcing this underlying principle.

Although the National People's Congress is becoming increasingly independent of the Party and the government, it is engaged in a struggle with the Supreme People's Court over lawmaking powers. The Congress is constitutionally the sole maker of law, but the Supreme People's Court is challenging this in a manner reminiscent of problems Western liberal democratic system have faced in "defining the relationship of the courts and the legislature," which, as in the West, are sometimes at loggerheads. In China, one view is that the courts should interpret the law and that such interpretations should influence "similar cases in the future . . . because they articulate legal rules to meet challenging circumstances in society." Opposed to this is the notion that courts are the "faithful servants of the legislature and only 'apply' laws." Although law is now supposed to serve society, not the state, it will take time to move beyond viewing laws as a mere tool of the state—a perspective that permits "the legislative or administrative body that promulgated a rule [to] interpret it." As it stands, the judiciary may only interpret laws and rules made by other agencies, such as ministries, in order to clarify and strengthen them. It cannot change their original meaning. Indeed, it is *"these agencies' own interpretation of such rules [which] must be followed."*[128]

---

127. Wang Zhenmin, "The Developing Rule of Law in China," p. 37.
128. Lubman, *Bird in a Cage*, pp. 281–83.

So far, China lacks a body with the authority to adjudicate constitutional legal issues. The Supreme People's Court, for example, may not interpret any laws other than those promulgated by the National People's Congress and the State Council, and it does not have the right to invalidate any laws.[129]

Moreover, the Supreme Court's "judicial interpretations" are not necessarily enforceable in lower courts. The interpretations of the law made by the Standing Committee of the National People's Congress, on the other hand, are enforceable, at least on paper. But so far, compliance with those interpretations seems to be voluntary.[130] It is in large part to settle the issue of which body has power over the other that some of China's legal scholars are proposing that the National People's Congress set up a Constitutional Commission. It would meet regularly to interpret China's State Constitution—and, therefore, would play an important role in how the constitution is enforced. It would be housed in the Congress itself but would be independent. Why not turn this function over to the Supreme Court to ensure a separation of powers? Because constitutionally, the National People's Congress is the highest law-making body of the state, and therefore, only it has the institutional authority to effectively challenge a law or policy that violates the constitution.[131]

These and other issues of legal reform are regularly debated in scholarly legal journals and at conferences and meetings at which the legal community interfaces with the government. In contrast to the past, when the party-state would cut off debate about legal issues that might in any way diminish its ultimate authority, today the process by which laws and the judicial system are being reformed is relatively open and dynamic. The various participants involved in the debate may differ dramatically, and of course, the concerns of "conservatives," who tend to resist reforms, must be addressed by the reformers. But it is the state itself that has encouraged legal scholars to think about how best to reform China's laws and judicial system.

---

129. Ibid., p. 282.

130. From 1987 to 1997, the National People's Congress exercised its administrative oversight by examining 28,000 regulations kept in the State Council's records. It determined that 1,500 had problems. The State Council agreed to voluntarily alter or repealed 400 of these. See Liu Han and Li Lin, "Woguo fazhi jianshe 20 nian chengjiu yu zhanwang."

131. Wang Zhenmin, "The Evolution of the Chinese Constitution in the 20th Century." As Wang notes, it is better to have timely and regular interpretations of the constitution than it is to repeatedly amend it so that it can reflect social reality.

Lawsuits and Enforcement of Court Decisions

Before the reform period and the awakening of China's citizens to their rights, lawsuits—especially against the state—were almost unheard of. By the 1990s, however, ordinary citizens saw the judicial system as increasingly accessible and moved beyond their traditional fear of becoming involved with the judicial system. Lawsuits involving labor relations, education, protection of consumers' rights, taxation, and corruption became relatively frequent, and from 1990 to 1997, the number of economic dispute cases filed in a court of first instance increased nearly 150 percent, from 598,317 to 1,478,139. Over the same time period, the number of civil cases handled in a court of first instance rose 75 percent, from 1,849,728 to 3,242,202.[132] Clearly, lawsuits against the government or private individuals are, like the hundreds of thousands of commercial disputes adjudicated in China today, being addressed in the *courts* rather than by the Chinese Communist Party or the state bureaucracy.[133] This is one more way in which law and the judicial system are moving toward serving society rather than the state.

Polling data indicate, however, that the public's confidence in the legal system's fairness is stronger than its confidence in law *enforcement*. Law enforcement workers are seen as having a bad attitude. Moreover, citizens expect legal help to be expensive, and they are consequently reluctant to seek it.[134] Laws are meaningless without institutional support at the local level. "Governments cannot simply demand that laws be respected; individuals must first understand these [laws and] new institutions before they can be followed and meaningfully enforced."[135] A study carried out by China's Supreme Court disclosed that in 1993, almost half of the cases adjudicated by the courts were not enforced by the end of the year.[136]

There are several reasons for the lack of enforcement. First, few penalties exist if someone refuses to enforce a court order. Second, because the power

---

132. Lubman, *Bird in a Cage*, tables 6 and 7, pp. 254, 255. For all years from 1990 to 1997, about half of the civil cases were marriage or family disputes, one-third involved debts, and the rest concerned torts or housing.

133. In 1984, the courts handled only 90,000 commercial cases. By 1993, the number had increased tenfold to 900,000 (Pei, "Racing Against Time," p. 42.)

134. Yuan Yue, "1995–1996 nian Zhongguo chengshi shehui wending yu gongzhong xintai," p. 121.

135. Guthrie, *Dragon in a Three-Piece Suit*, p. 211.

136. Pei, "China's Evolution Toward Soft Authoritarianism," p. 84.

to enforce court orders comes from the bureaucratic rank of a particular judge, and because that rank is usually lower than that of the chief government executive at the same level, "courts often lack sufficient bureaucratic clout to enforce their judgments against administrative units. . . . It is simply alien to the way China functions that a lower-level official from one bureaucracy should be able to give orders to a higher-level official from another."[137] Third, law enforcement workers are often bribed not to enforce judicial decisions, such as awards of compensation for property damage, division of property from a divorce, jail time, or fines.

Finally, there are cultural reasons. In 1998, the Institute for Rural Development (part of the Chinese Academy of Social Sciences) carried out a survey among township cadres to discover why court decisions were so infrequently enforced. Most prominent among their findings was the influence of tradition, culture, and habit. Many respondents explicitly stated that when the law conflicted with their leaders' opinion, they obeyed their leaders instead of the law; when the law conflicted with a personal relationship, they sacrificed the law. Although aware of the existence of some state laws, many cadres did not care about the concrete implementation or details. They also believed that the law applied only to ordinary people, not to themselves, and so they frequently disobeyed the law, for example, by levying and collecting illegal taxes. The survey also found that 31.9 percent of the respondents thought that in order to maintain good personal relationships, it is understandable, although wrong, to favor superiors, colleagues, relatives, and individuals from their own jurisdiction (such as by levying lower fines, taxes, and so forth on them than on outsiders).[138] Problems such as these indicate that although countless laws have been passed to reform China's legal system, these laws will not be followed until deeply-rooted cultural attitudes on the overriding importance of interpersonal relationships change.

Administrative Law

After 1949, Chinese legal theory and practice drew a distinction between "law" and "administration." The purpose of "law" was to deal with what Mao Zedong called the "antagonistic contradictions" between "the people" and "the enemy." These were very serious issues that required the use of the co-

---

137. Clarke, "Dispute Resolution in China," pp. 264–65.
138. Wang Binglu, "Yingxiang xiangzhen ganbu falü yishi xingchengde zhuyao yinsu."

ercive instruments of the state. The purpose of "administration" was, on the other hand, to deal with the "non-antagonistic contradictions" *among* the people. This was out of a recognition that "not everyone who disturbs social order is an enemy." In such cases, it was deemed inappropriate to use the courts and law. As a result, a variety of "administrative" institutions and "administrative" sanctions were created to handle the non-antagonistic types of social deviance among the people[139] and to enhance social control. But over the years, these sanctions were widely abused, often being used against feisty subordinates and those known to harbor viewpoints that differed from those of the leadership but fell short of being "counterrevolutionary." Those subjected to administrative sanctions rarely had recourse to the legal system. Arguably, after 1949, individual rights were more abused by sanctions made under administrative law than under the formal law of the judicial system.

During the reform period, Maoist concepts such as "antagonistic" and "non-antagonistic contradictions" seemed inappropriate to a modernizing China and gradually lost salience. In an effort to depoliticize the legal system and make it more just, the National People's Congress has approved laws that strengthen the rights of citizens accused of wrongdoing by China's administrative organs, a major step forward in protecting individual rights. In 1990, it began by promulgating the Administrative Litigation Law, which gives both individuals and legal persons, such as organizations, the right to sue "administrative organs and their staff when their legal rights and interests are infringed upon by specific administrative actions of these organs and persons." These cases are heard in the courts. Prior to this law, a complaint against an administrative organ was usually heard by the administrative organ in question, hardly a sure course to justice. And whereas it used to be pointless to appeal administrative decisions, it has become increasingly common for those decisions to be overturned if they are challenged.[140]

---

139. Clarke, "One Step Back Permits Two Steps Forward."

140. Wang Lu, *Baishude qishi*. According to statistics provided by China, in the five years from January 1990 to December 1994, 167,882 cases involving administrative law were brought before the people's courts. The majority of these cases involved basic civil rights, including individual and property rights. "Since the implementation of the Administrative [Litigation] Law, two-thirds of the cases have ended in a change of the original decision made by the administrative organs" (State Council Information Office, "The Progress of Human Rights in China," pp. 10–11; see also the cases given in *Renmin fayuan nianjian 1992*, in which government agencies and organizations are the defendants).

Although a significant number of lawsuits had been filed against the government for wrongful exercise of administrative power before the Administrative Litigation Law, the number rose sharply after the law was passed,[141] but it is still rare to succeed in suing the state above the local level.[142]

Even after the Administrative Litigation Law went into effect, academics and legal reformers continued to insist that more needed to be done. Although the Law on Administrative Procedure improved the situation, quite a few administrative rules and regulations still aimed to regulate and restrict, rather than protect, people's rights, especially their political rights. Both society *and the state* must, legal reformers asserted, be ruled by law.[143] Law should take precedence over administrative decisions, and there remained a need to limit administrative discretion to restrict citizens' rights and interests, especially by handing out administrative penalties. These penalties could result in disciplinary measures implemented without the authority of the law and without the right to appeal to the legal system; and the penalties could also affect property rights and limit freedom of speech, demonstration, and other individual rights. For example, administrative penalties concerning the media and publications include confiscation of publications or income deemed unlawful, closure of publishers or media outlets, fines, revocations of licenses, and penal detention of the publishers, producers, and sellers of the allegedly illegal material. Only public security organs can detain people, but seemingly any administrative unit could impose fines, collect taxes, confiscate property, or revoke licenses. This needed to be clarified. Academics heatedly debated the legitimacy, reasonability, and necessity of "education through labor" (*laojiao*), and the practice of "taking someone in for examination," which goes beyond the Criminal Law and allows those who have

---

141. Pei, "Racing Against Time," p. 42. Pei's figures for successful challenges to administrative sanctions are considerably lower than China's official figures. For an interesting example of a case brought against a government, see Ju Ren, "Wenhua zhuzhang baishi yijie wenren" (The director of a cultural bureau defeated by an intellectual), *Democracy and Legality* 1997, no. 8: 10–12.

142. Xin Chunying, "China's Signing of the Two UN Covenants on Human Rights: Implications for Domestic Legal Reform," seminar, Harvard University, Fairbank Center, Nov. 12, 1999. Xin Chunying is the acting director of the Institute of Law and the Institute of Politics, Chinese Academy of Social Sciences. Xin's conclusion partly contradicts that of Wang Lu, *Baishude qishi*.

143. Guo Daohui, "Shixian fa zhide siyao."

committed minor infractions, those suspected of committing crimes in several places, and many others to be detained for one month, with the possibility of a one to two-month extension. Critics of the state's use of administrative powers argued that disciplinary penalties that restrict personal freedom for a long period of time should be implemented only after a court trial, and that the "take in for examination" practice should be abolished.[144]

Partly in response to some of these arguments for limiting the power of the state to restrict the rights of citizens, in 1996, the Legislative Affairs Commission under the Standing Committee of the National People's Congress moved to further protect individual rights from arbitrary abuse by administrative organs with the promulgation of the Law on Administrative Penalties. The absence of such a law had made such abuses more likely. This law standardizes administrative penalties, provides for punishment of those who violate the laws on administrative management, lays out the penalties for violation, and specifies which departments are responsible for formulating, enforcing, and imposing administrative penalties. In an effort to prevent illegal fines as well as the embezzlement of the money collected through fines, the law stipulates that departments imposing fines be *separate* from those collecting them. To correct still other abuses, the law requires that those receiving administrative penalties be told the legal basis for them. Victims of wrongful punishment may ask for compensation.[145] Since the State Compensation Law was passed in 1994, compensation committees have been set up in all courts above the intermediate level. In 364 (42 percent) of the 870 state compensation cases completed in the period 1994–98, the court ruled that the state agency involved should compensate the plaintiff. During the same period, procuratorial organs awarded compensation for 179 (23 percent) out of 762 requests for compensation by those wrongfully held on criminal charges.[146] Those (accidentally) injured by the police, those mistreated during imprisonment, and, generally, those who have suffered damage because of improper enforcement of the law have also received compensation.[147]

For those individuals sentenced to labor camps, detention, house arrest,

144. Wang Tiancheng, "Zhirenzhe zhi yu fa."
145. "Administrative Penalty Law Hailed," *China Daily*, Oct. 2, 1996, p. 1.
146. Liu Han and Li Lin, "Woguo fazhi jianshe 20 nian chengjiu yu zhanwang."
147. Xu Xun, "State Compensation."

or surveillance by administrative organs, it is difficult to overstate the importance of the 1996 Administrative Penalty Law. Under the administrative law
for "re-education through labor," millions of people had no recourse to the
legal system. Administrative units, including work units and the police,
could determine on their own if a person had violated a law—or merely had
poor attitudes—and should be punished. The decision was made outside
the judicial system and could not be challenged in court. No protections
guaranteed by the Criminal Law, such as the right to a lawyer and a limited
period of detention, were available to those being punished by administrative
organs. "Re-education through labor" is

China's most severe variety of administrative detention, and is intended for those
whose behavior is deemed to fall "between crime and error." Those sentenced to *laojiao* have included vagrants, petty criminals, and some political offenders. Virtually
all are from urban areas. Until 1979, *laojiao* sentences could be open-ended, and
conditions might be as bad as those experienced by regular *laogai* convicts. Since
then, sentences have been more clearly defined and are generally shorter.[148]

Changes in administrative law have been reinforced by the 1997 revisions
of the Criminal Law. That code now states that the degree of criminality
and the sentence, including "reform through labor" (*laogai*),[149] must be according to the law, with the sentence matching the degree of criminality (an
effort to eliminate arbitrariness in punishments) and that all must be treated
as equals before the law (that is, no special treatment for officials and party
members). As with all revisions to the law, they will be meaningless unless
they are respected and enforced, but putting these revisions on the books is
an essential step in inculcating respect for the law and its enforcement.

---

148. James D. Seymour and Richard Anderson, *New Ghosts, Old Ghosts: Prisons and Labor
Reform Camps in China* (Armonk, N.Y.: M. E. Sharpe, 1998); reviewed by June Teufel Dreyer,
"Concentrating on the Camps," in *Free China Review*, Oct. 1998, p. 37. Some Chinese scholars
disagree with these conclusions about *laojiao*. They note that in many cases, the courts have
actually reviewed and ruled against the government's use of *laojiao* (Wang Zhenmin, correspondence, July 2001).

149. *Laogai* is a punishment for criminals and is meted out by the formal judicial system.
This is usually a far more severe punishment than "re-education through labor," but at least it
has the merit of being sanctioned by law rather than imposed by arbitrary administrative or
police decisions.

The Police

There are ongoing efforts to improve administrative procedural law in order to protect plaintiffs' rights.[150] But there are many obstacles in the path of thoroughgoing reform. For example, because the police are paid shockingly low salaries, they often arrest and fine individuals in order to be paid bribes. Internal supervision of the police has failed to curb corruption and abuse. In the summer of 1998, the Campaign of Rectification and Education was launched to ferret out and punish police and judges who were using illegal detention and torture in order to extract confessions. Front-page news articles trumpeted the campaign's success. According to official data, at least 400 cases of police torture occurred each year and resulted in the deaths of many suspects. The government's willingness to publish such data has been an important step forward in dealing with police and judicial abuse.[151] Nevertheless, China's legal culture still gives priority to confession as the main form of evidence. For obvious reasons, systems that rely on confession are more prone to use torture. Creating a preference for forms of evidence other than confession and guaranteeing the right to remain silent and the right against self-incrimination may prove far more difficult than other reforms. This is a good example of the interrelated nature of the reforms— what appear to be significant reforms that will benefit democratization are in fact undermined by other, as-yet-unreformed elements of the system.

Another obstacle to the reform of China's judicial and administrative system is that economic liberalization has spawned a host of semiofficial and even unofficial police units: police guard mines, oil fields, shopping centers, railroads, universities, and factories, as well as hotels, karaoke bars, night-clubs, business executives, and entrepreneurs. Because it is possible to buy the trappings of police uniforms (including epaulets, neckties, tie clips), anyone can pose as a police officer and even pretend to have police powers to detain or search suspects. These private, semiofficial, and fake police are re-

150. Liu Heng, "Xingzheng suquan mianliu de ruogan wenti ji duice" (Some problems faced by administrative legal rights and their solutions), *Xueshu yanjiu* 1997, no. 1: 37–41.

151. Murray Scot Tanner, "The Public Security Bureau," seminar, Harvard University, Fairbank Center, Oct. 21, 1998. This bureau is the Gongan zhu.

sponsible for some 25 percent of the illegal detentions in China today.[152] At this point, they are even more difficult to supervise and punish than the official police, since there is no official chain of command to control them.

Finally, the inability of the legal system to ensure that justice is done in the courts makes it more difficult to carry out effective police reform. Police need to know that if they turn over a criminal to the judicial system, the accused (if found guilty) will be punished—instead of being released because bribes were paid to judicial personnel. Despite the reforms to administrative and criminal law, the police will no doubt continue to both arrest and punish until China has a stronger judicial system.[153] And citizens themselves will continue to engage in vigilante justice against other citizens who they think are guilty of wrongdoing.

Changes to the Criminal Law and the Law of Criminal Procedure

Over the long run, other changes made to the laws are likely to improve the system of criminal justice. For example, in 1996–97, the National People's Congress approved revisions to the 1979 Criminal Law and the Criminal Procedure Law. It replaced the clause that assumed guilt with a presumption of innocence until proven guilty. The right to legal counsel begins as soon as a person is formally charged with a crime by the police rather than immediately prior to trial (although in a number of highly publicized cases, this has not occurred). The National People's Congress also changed the maximum period of administrative detention of suspects from three years to thirty days. The "supervision" of criminal suspects may no longer be interpreted as allowing their "detention." Instead, criminal suspects under supervision cannot leave their residences without permission, and the period of supervision is limited to six months.[154] Court procedures have also changed.

---

152. Ibid. Tanner, an audacious researcher, managed to acquire all the trappings of a police uniform while in Beijing—this in spite of the fact that he is conspicuously not a Chinese policeman!

153. Ibid.

154. Chen Guangzhong, "Guaranteeing Human Rights Is the Distinguishing Feature of the Amended Criminal Procedure Law." Chen is vice president of the Chinese Association of the Science of Law and a professor at the Chinese University of Politics and Law, Beijing. Some liberal democratic countries have issues not entirely different from China's. In France, for example, the "presumption of innocence" is often honored in the breach, and the National Assembly is still trying to strengthen it through new legislation. In the meantime, half of the 55,000 prisoners in France have not been convicted of any crime. The magistrate (from the

In criminal cases, defendants (and their legal counsel) are encouraged to present their own evidence and witnesses in court. In addition, the facts of the case are supposed to be investigated and a determination of guilt made in the court—the proceedings of which are to be open to public scrutiny. This is contrary to the situation in the past, when only the police and procuratorates usually would present evidence and would determine guilt before the case was presented in court.[155]

In addition, in 1997, the National People's Congress eliminated the political category of "counterrevolutionary" crimes. China always insisted that it had no "political criminals," only "counterrevolutionaries," who through their words or actions had threatened the state or its leadership. This category was the one most commonly used to prosecute political cases. The revised Criminal Law specifies more precisely which actions are considered offenses that endanger the security of the state and are therefore criminal.[156] Removing this category opens the way to a "reversal of verdicts" for those whose actions during the 1989 demonstrations in Tiananmen Square had earned them the label of "counterrevolutionary." The revised law eliminates a category open to arbitrary decisions by poorly trained judges who rely on ideology rather than the law in making decisions.[157] This does not mean that the state can no longer arrest individuals it believes to be politically dangerous, since it may still cast the cases in terms of a threat to national security, but the much clearer definition of crimes against the state constricts the scope of criminal prosecution of political dissidents.[158]

---

procuracy) who investigates the case, rather than an independent judge, puts a suspect in custody, and defendants may not see a lawyer until a day after their arrest (see Suzanne Daley, "Expose of Brutal Paris Prison a Jolt to France's Self-Image," *New York Times*, Jan. 28, 2000, pp. A1, A9; the article was inspired by a book on prisons by Veronique Vassuer, chief doctor at La Sante Prison [1999]).

155. Ni Shouming, "Justice, Democracy and High Efficiency"; and Cao Shouye, "The Reforms of Trial Procedures in the Chinese Courts Are in Full Swing."

156. Among other changes made by the Eighth National People's Congress in March 1997 were the criminalization of the activities of underground societies and religious extremists, actions that instigate ethnic hatred, security and stock fraud, and activities that endanger national security (State Council Information Office, "Progress in China's Human Rights Cause in 1996").

157. Seth Faison, "China Updates Criminal Code, and It May Be Harsher," *International Herald Tribune*, Mar. 8, 1997, pp. 1, 2.

158. Human rights groups do not agree with this viewpoint. They argue that those actions previously termed "counterrevolutionary" have simply been renamed as actions "endangering state security." Thus, in essence, political dissidents—especially those with foreign funding—

Legal Reforms and China's Constitution

Legal reforms have gone beyond the boundaries of both the 1982 State Constitution and communist ideology. In spite of this, they have been allowed to stand. For example, China had no concept of property rights at the time of the 1982 Constitution because it was a socialist system. In 1999, however, property rights were codified. Similarly, the Administrative Litigation Law, the Law on State Compensation, the amended Law on Criminal Procedure, as well as the Law on Contracts expand the framework of legal protection for individual rights beyond what the Constitution provided for.[159]

Many proposed laws and regulations may never be promulgated because they too blatantly contradict China's constitution. Constitutional amendments are required to bring China's domestic laws into compliance with certain international agreements and covenants, notably the two U.N. Covenants on Human Rights, which China has signed but not ratified.[160] For example, China's Criminal Law has dozens of articles relating to the death penalty, but Article 6 of the U.N. Covenant on Human Rights supports the right to life. China is not, of course, the only country that needs to amend or abolish national legislation that does not comply with international agreements, treaties, or covenants to which it has agreed.[161]

---

and political separatists (such as those promoting Tibetan independence), are just as vulnerable as before to chargers under the new Criminal Law. See, e.g., Human Rights in China and Human Rights Watch/Asia, "Whose Security?"

159. Xin Chunying, "China's Signing of the Two UN Covenants on Human Rights: Implications for Domestic Legal Reform," seminar, Harvard University, Fairbank Center, Nov. 12, 1999.

160. Ibid.

161. A case in point is Great Britain, which ratified the European Convention on Human Rights in 1951. It was not until 1998, however, that the convention was formally incorporated into domestic law, and the changes necessary to bring domestic legislation into compliance with the European Convention. That meant that individuals complaining of specific encroachments on fundamental rights could not ask British courts to enforce the state's treaty obligations embodied in the convention. Thus, the only remedy available to British subjects was an appeal to the European Court of Human Rights in Strasbourg, France. It was not until 2000 that British citizens gained fundamental human rights enforceable by British courts. If it is found that a law or a policy infringes on these rights, British courts may issue a "declaration of incompatibility." This puts Parliament on notice of being in violation of its treaty obligations. If Parliament, the ultimate lawmaking authority in Britain, refuses to change the law, then the individual will once again be left with the option of seeking relief in Strasbourg (discussions with Michael Tolley, Northeastern University, 2000; see also Sarah Lyall, "Brit-

China's Institute of Law, the National People's Congress, and judicial personnel in other parts of the legal system are now discussing how to bring China's Criminal Law into compliance with the U.N. Covenant on Human Rights. So far, the consensus is that China cannot abolish the death penalty, but that it should be more judicious in its use. In China as elsewhere (including the United States), it is not the government as much as it is society that wants to keep the death penalty. It is also widely believed in China that if the government were to abandon the death penalty, even more people (especially in China's remote villages) would take the law into their own hands and kill those believed to have committed heinous crimes. The concept of "an eye for an eye" is still culturally rooted in much of China.[162]

On the other hand, it is the government, not the people, that has expanded the number of crimes punishable by death. The 1980 Criminal Law listed 28 crimes punishable by death, but by the mid-1990s the number had grown to 70. The result is that more than 35 percent of all criminal offenses are subject to capital punishment. Many of these are nonviolent or economic crimes, including, for example, tax fraud or forgery, the sale of fake invoices or birth control certificates, bribery, the killing of even one tiger or panda, bigamy, blackmail, destruction of or damage to public or private property, the theft of cows, goats, camels, or horses, and "hooliganism" that has "serious consequences"—with no precise definition of what "serious consequences" might be. Another catchall phrase, "other serious endangerment to public security," is also open to arbitrary interpretation and abuse. Throughout the 1990s, the broader use of the death penalty, especially its application to economic crimes and to first-time offenders under the age of 25, has been repeatedly criticized in China's legal journals and books. Its deterrent value has been questioned by many. In the view of China's legal reformers, the use of capital punishment should be more narrowly and clearly defined.[163]

---

ain Quietly Says It's Time to Adopt a Bill of Rights," *New York Times*, Oct. 3, 1999, p. 6, of "Week in Review"). For the chaos created in the Scottish legal system by incorporating the European Convention on Human Rights into British law, see "Human-Rights Law: Alarm Bells in Edinburgh," *Economist*, Nov. 20, 1999, pp. 67–68.

162. Xin Chunying, "China's Signing of the Two UN Covenants on Human Rights: Implications for Domestic Legal Reform," seminar, Harvard University, Fairbank Center, Nov. 12, 1999.

163. Howie, "Chinese Critiques of the Ultimate Penalty."

Traditional values also pose obstacles to legal reforms. In the West, "the right to remain silent" arises from the belief that individuals should not be compelled to testify against themselves, but in China, the emphasis in criminal cases is for individuals to tell the truth, to confess. Thus, it is viewed as potentially harmful in China's legal circles to give the accused the right to remain silent.[164] Even liberal reformers within China's legal community hesitate to accept one of the fundamental principles of the liberal democratic judicial system.

Nevertheless, if one were to ask whether China is making progress toward political liberalism and institutionalizing the protection of individual rights, the answer would have to be yes. In addition to increasingly democratic elections, the creation of new laws to protect individuals,[165] and revisions to the Criminal Law, the Law of Criminal Procedures, and Administrative Law, there is the growing body of commercial and property law. (China's concept of private property rights is, however, still limited). The Law on State Compensation (1994), which provides for compensation to citizens whose legal rights and interests have been infringed by state organs,[166] and the Public Procurators Law and the Judges Law (2001) also accord greater protection to individuals. Altogether, these laws are intended to keep government and party officials, as well as administrative organs, from interfering in the decisions of judges and the investigative branch (the procuratorate)[167] and to give greater protection to individuals.

The existence of these laws does not, however, mean that the Chinese legal and judicial system fully complies with the new legislation and laws or that the protection of individual rights, and especially prisoners' rights, are

---

164. Ibid.

165. In 1988, China signed the Convention Against Torture and Other Cruel, Inhuman or Degrading Treatment or Punishment; and in 1994, China promulgated a Prison Law relating to the protection of prisoners' rights (State Council Information Office, "The Progress of Human Rights in China," pp. 13–14).

166. Ibid., p. 11.

167. Once an individual is arrested, the procuratorate is responsible for investigating the evidence. If there is inadequate evidence, the accused is released. This, incidentally, is one of the reasons why the vast majority of those accused of a crime in court are found guilty: upon procuratorial investigation, those believed to be innocent are released, and only those who are believed guilty actually go on trial. From 1993 to 1997, the procuratorates in China decided not to approve the arrest of 271,629 persons, prosecuted 14,371 persons, and decided not to prosecute 25,638 persons (Liu Han and Li Lin, *Woguo fazhi jianshe 20 nian chengjiu yu zhanwang*, pp. 12–15).

guaranteed in practice. Nor does the codification of new laws prevent the inhumane treatment or torture of prisoners, but it does mean, at least officially, that this is not state policy, that the national government has accepted the values embodied in these laws, and that it believes they should provide new standards for treatment of prisoners. New laws and legislation that enhance the legal rights of individuals against the state (including state-owned enterprises) and clarify the rights of one private individual vis-à-vis another, continue to be promulgated. To the degree they are implemented, China will have a stronger legal foundation on which to erect a more democratic system.

THE GROWING RIGHTS AND POWERS
OF THE LEGISLATIVE BRANCH

Although delegates to the National People's Congress are not elected directly, and it does not necessarily represent the people's interests, this national legislative body is assuming a larger role in democratizing China. As we have seen, the National People's Congress and its Standing Committee have passed many laws to protect China's citizens against the power of the state and to make China's leaders more accountable to the legislature.

The National People's Congress is today far more deeply involved in the legislative process than it was before the reforms began. Since 1979, China has moved away from the old system in which the State Council (the executive branch) would issue policy documents on critical issues as "administrative regulations" or "Party Central Committee documents" (*zhongfa*), and these would then be submitted to the congress as "laws." Gone are the days when the congress merely heard a brief summary of a bill, immediately moved to a vote, and then invariably passed the bill by a unanimous vote. As Murray Scot Tanner has wryly remarked, it has become unexpectedly difficult to "rubber stamp" a law. When bills and laws come before the National People's Congress (or its Standing Committee), "they are subjected to extended, repeated subcommittee review and serious floor debate. Most surprisingly, it is now quite common for the NPC and its Standing Committee to seriously delay, amend, table, or return bills to their drafters and insist on major changes. In recent years, the NPC has from time to time voted down proposed State Council amendments to their own draft laws."[168]

---

168. Tanner, *The Politics of Lawmaking in Post-Mao China*, p. 5.

In the twenty years from 1979 to 1998, besides amending and promulgating the 1982 Constitution and two amendments to the Constitution, the National People's Congress and its Standing Committee made 333 laws and decisions concerning legal issues,[169] and local and provincial people's congresses passed thousands of laws. Western legal doctrines, constructs, and technical terms have heavily influenced the content of the new national laws and even many of the new provincial laws. The promulgation of so many new laws points to the growing importance of China's legislature at the expense of overall control by the Chinese Communist Party and the State Council—but not necessarily against their wishes. Indeed, although one could argue that the Communist Party assigned a succession of important party leaders to head the Congress's Standing Committee in order to ensure continued party control over the legislative branch, this could also be interpreted as an effort by the Party to shift day-to-day responsibility for lawmaking *away from* itself to the Congress, whose central role in lawmaking was reaffirmed in a 1991 directive.[170]

The greater legitimacy and power of the National People's Congress have resulted in a far more proactive role for its delegates. In 1996, 30 percent of the legislators showed their dissatisfaction with the government's law enforcement efforts by voting against, or abstaining from voting on, the report on law enforcement and corruption submitted by China's top prosecutor. (This is one way in which the Chinese legislature challenges the work of the government.) Now legislators even propose legislation for debate, and they debate, amend, and revise laws that the State Council has submitted for approval. The Congress has openly expressed its disapproval of proposed laws submitted by the State Council through vociferous debates and large votes against such legislation as the Enterprise Bankruptcy Law (1986), the Central Bank Law (draft, 1995), and the Education Law (draft, 1995).[171] In the end all three laws passed, but at least one-third of the legislators voted against them. The Standing Committee of the National People's Congress has, however, rejected amendments to the National Highway Law proposed

169. Liu Han and Li Lin, "Woguo fazhi jianshe 20 nian chengjiu yu zhanwang."

170. Pei, "Racing Against Time," pp. 38, 41. The chairpersons of the Standing Committee during the reform period have been, in succession, Ye Jianying, Peng Zhen, Wan Li, Qiao Shi, and Li Peng. Arguably, these appointments merely reflected who held power within the leadership.

171. Ibid., pp. 38–39. For a superb case study of the 1986 Enterprise Bankruptcy Law, see Tanner, *The Politics of Lawmaking in Post-Mao China*, pp. 135–66.

by the State Council. This law would have abolished the "fees" vehicles must pay to provincial governments when they cross their boundaries and replaced them with a national tax on oil. This tax would have gone into the *national* budget, and the provinces would have lost revenues.[172] Thus, the Communist Party and the State Council can no longer count on the National People's Congress to rubber-stamp proposed legislation. "Party discipline"—the ability of a party to insist that its members vote favorably for party-supported legislation—appears to be eroding in China's national legislature.[173]

The National People's Congress and its Standing Committee cannot be considered a truly independent legislative body. Although the Standing Committee meets six times a year and has a workable size of about 150 members, the Congress meets only once a year for two weeks, and its cumbersome size of some 3,000 members means there are few chances for real debate. Members of the Congress hold other jobs, a practice that could, minimally, be described as involving a "conflict of interest" with their role as delegate to the Congress. For example, every provincial governor and mayor of a large city, as well as all provincial party secretaries and party secretaries of large cities are members of the Congress. They have to worry that if they vote against a government bill, their province or city might be punished by being denied resources, or they might be replaced with a more compliant governor or mayor. Although delegates do vote secretly, the governor and provincial party secretary do not usually dare to formally instruct delegates from their unit to vote against the government.[174]

Nevertheless, the National People's Congress is gaining more power. Unwilling to remain a mere ratifier of government bills, it has developed new strategies for lawmaking. Ratification now takes place in multiple stages. Furthermore, a far wider range of individuals and organizations in China try, some quite successfully, to get proposals considered by the Congress. Al-

---

172. Discussions with Chinese colleagues, July 2001.

173. Although the National People's Congress is not a true parliamentary system because there is no genuine opposition party, it is worth noting that in parliamentary systems, party discipline is often very strict. For example, Britain's prime ministers, whether the Conservative Party leader Margaret Thatcher or Labour Party leader Tony Blair, demand party loyalty. Blair, for example, has demanded that Ken Livingstone, a member of the Labour Party and the first elected mayor of London, prove his loyalty to the Labour Party to party leaders ("An Independence Beyond their Ken," *The Economist*, Nov. 20, 1999, p. 69).

174. Discussions with Chinese colleagues, July 2001.

though the vast majority of the hundreds of legislative proposals put forward in each session still originate in the State Council and the ministries under it, an increasing number come from intellectuals, think tanks, the mass media, businesspeople, "mass organizations," and associations.[175]

People's congresses at all levels, from the National People's Congress down to the township people's congresses, have also gained power vis-à-vis the Party through their greatly enhanced role in nominating and approving the selection of key government officials. For example, in 1995, one-third of the deputies in the National People's Congress refused to support the nomination of a vice premier by Jiang Zemin because of the nominee's record of corruption while governor of Shandong province.[176] Several provincial people's congresses have also blocked the nominations of high-level provincial officials and substituted candidates not endorsed by the Party—and the Party has accepted the results.[177]

In spite of setbacks on the broader political stage of China since 1979, the National People's Congress has proven to be a resilient legislature. Surprisingly enough, the launching of three major campaigns[178] that were decidedly antiliberal did not have a negative impact on the Congress's ability to act as a more independent political body. To the contrary, it was able not only to persist, but also to quickly resume its forward momentum as an institution in terms of delegate assertiveness (number of motions submitted), legislative influence, delegate dissent (number of no votes and abstentions), and organizational development (number of staff and committees).[179] The support staff, for example, grew from a mere six in 1978 to more than 2,000 by 1993.[180] Of course, a strictly rubber-stamping congress had little need for staff.

---

175. Tanner, *The Politics of Lawmaking in Post-Mao China*, pp. 209, 211–14, 233.

176. Orville Schell, "China—The End of an Era," *Nation*, July 17, 1995.

177. Pei, "Racing Against Time," p. 39.

178. The Anti-Spiritual Pollution Campaign of 1983–84, the Anti-Bourgeois Liberalization Campaign of 1987, and the repression in the wake of the 1989 crackdown on Tiananmen demonstrations.

179. According to Tanner (*The Politics of Lawmaking in Post-Mao China*, pp. 237–38), even under the chairmanship of the conservative former premier Li Peng since 1997, there has been no reversal of this forward momentum.

180. Michael W. Dowdle, "Transformative Development of Constitutional Institutions: The Role of Parliament—A Chinese Case Study," paper prepared for the Conference on the Changing Meaning of Citizenship in Modern China, Harvard University, Fairbank Center, Oct. 29–31, 1999. Other data, such as whether the Congress has sources of information inde-

Thus, if *institutionalization* is one of the measures of the strength of democratization, then China has made significant progress since 1979. It may still be a weak legislature, but it has many of the procedures, the structure, and the resources, as well as the resilience, to develop in a more independent and democratic direction. If and when direct election of legislative representatives occurs in China, the National People's Congress as a legislative institution will be well positioned to become a truly powerful democratic body.

CONCLUSIONS

This chapter has focused on the institutionalization of democracy: the growth of electoral rights and procedural democracy in urban districts and work units and in rural villages, and the reform of administrative law and the judicial and legislative systems in ways that advance the people's rights. As such, it is concerned with the procedural and civil rights of particular interest to those advocating greater democracy for China.

Electoral rights vary across China's villages and cities. Clearly, the Ministry of Civil Affairs wants to encourage more democratic procedures and thereby increase local self-governance in villages. The question is how far the ministry's writ runs. In the event, the resistance or support of local town and township leaders for elections and local autonomy has been far more decisive than the ministry's wishes in determining the extent of village democratization. Furthermore, whether in urban districts or villages, the preferences of local leaders seem far more important than the level of economic development in determining how much democratization occurs: the more advanced economic areas are *not* necessarily the most democratic. In addition, although the residents of rural areas are generally less well educated than urbanites, the former have been much more deeply involved in the democratic process. As a result, it could be argued that villagers, not the urban middle and working classes, have been at the forefront of political change in China.

Whatever the reasons that led to opening up the electoral process to China's villagers, electoral rights have been steadily refined and made more meaningful since they were first institutionalized in 1987. So have the rights of urban residents and workers to participate in the choice of their leaders.

---

pendent of the Executive Branch, would help to assess how well institutionalized the Congress is becoming.

For this reason, in this area of civil rights, there is a sense of progress in China today. For China's future well-being, however, the growth of procedural rights per se may be less important than whether this growth is simultaneously helping to advance a sense of community and encouraging greater civic participation. These issues are addressed in the following chapters.

Although it would be a stretch to say that China's "socialist democracy" in the pre-reform period could survive the scrutiny of Western liberal democrats, major parts of the institutional framework for democracy was put in place in the 1950s. Though hardly free and fair, China has long had a form of elections, as well as the notion of political parties, judicial, legislative, and executive branches of government, and a well-developed civil service. Changing the content of those institutions to make them truly democratic may be far more complex than merely reforming what is already there, but it does not require a revolution. The changes that are happening in the procedures and role of the National People's Congress, as well as in laws and the judicial system, indicate that reformers have the ability to move China toward a more democratic system.

The steps taken by the government to institutionalize procedural democracy and the legal system are important, but they are inadequate for making public officials both responsive and accountable. Because China's internal auditing and administrative supervisory organs are not under the State Council, it is hard for them to exercise supervision over government organizations. Chinese academics have argued that if supervision were shifted from being top-to-bottom self-supervision and self-restraint within government organs to external, open, frequent, systematic, and legal supervision, by bodies answerable only to the people's congresses and their standing committees, it would be easier to exercise control over the state.[181] This perspective would be endorsed by institutionalists,[182] who argue that controlling state organs and making government officials responsible requires constant vigilance and regular checks on their performance, as well as certain punishment if there are infractions. At the local level of governance, the next election (or a recall) may occur too late to stop irreparable damage. Proponents of institutionalism argue that there should be procedures to guarantee transparency and oversight, such as independent accounting and auditing offices and in-

---

181. Huang Ziyi, "Guanyu zai woguo jianshe shehui zhuyi ya zhi guojia de luogan wenti."
182. For example, North, *Institutions, Institutional Change, and Economic Performance.*

dependent statistical offices. In other words, further institutionalization is necessary to *prevent* the damage rather than trying to repair it after it is done. Good examples would be exorbitant and unauthorized taxes and fees on farmers, wasteful spending on projects, or exorbitant expenditures by cadres on food, transportation, and phones. If transparency and public awareness were guaranteed so that such things could be stopped before they started, officials would be seen as accountable to the public for their actions, and the value of elections would be more obvious. China's 1998 law on village self-governance does require that all village accounts and policies be open to public scrutiny, but compliance is far from universal.[183]

Finally, the emphasis on deliberation in the Chinese political system as a means of reaching consensus could prove to be an important building block for democratization. Consensus building may be limited largely to the elite, but the Chinese system is still more open to democratic resolution of conflicts through discussion than are dictatorial systems, where neither consensus building nor elections are institutionalized. Nevertheless, this stands in contrast to Western liberal democracies, where the focus is on an *electoral* process that leads to a multiparty system.[184] The goal, then, is quite different. In liberal democracies, it is representation, whereas in China, the object thus far has been to reach a consensus and maintain societal order, the "Great Harmony" (*datong*) treasured in traditional Chinese political thought.

---

183. Yang Dali and Su Fubing, "Elections, Governance, and Accountability in Rural China," pp. 231–39. According to one survey, carried out by *China Auditing News (Zhongguo shenji bao)* (Nov. 21, 2000), "90 percent of the villages in the sample don't have formal rules and regulations on accounting. . . . 70 percent of the village accountants are unclear about their responsibilities. . . . And half of the accountants also serve as cashiers." In fact, the accountant is often a relative of the village leader! On top of this, "20 percent of the villages don't even have accounting books and 30 percent of the accountants refuse to pass on their books to their successors" (cited in Yang and Su, p. 237).

184. Discussion by David Strand and Michael Dowdle at the Conference on Changing Meanings of Citizenship in Modern China, Harvard University, Fairbank Center, Oct. 29, 1999.

7   *China's Developing Civil Society:*
     Associations and Interest Groups

Does it matter whether fully autonomous and independent social groups in China
are chipping away at the state's hegemony when so many quasi-autonomous
groups and individuals, all of them heirs to the cultural legacy of late state socialism in the former Soviet bloc, are already doing the job in a "peaceful and evolutionary" way?

—Paul G. Pickowicz

The dilemma of ideology in a reforming Soviet-type regime, then, is not so much
that ideology either cannot change or changes totally, but that ideology has to
change yet the regime cannot afford to change it totally while wishing to maintain
ideological hegemony and political stability.

—Yan Sun

Our vision of the China of the future must not be narrowly confined
to ideas of a political system that resembles our own. Instead, while posit-
ing the need for greater democracy in China, we should envisage a framework for a political system that will provide other essential aspects of
the "good" society—one that is fair, stable, and secure, and provides a decent
life for its citizens. The following analysis examines political parties, associations, and interest groups, which are components of the Western idea
of a democratic system, and asks how their adoption in China might affect efforts to achieve the "good" society. Chapter 8 looks at intellectuals,
who are tied to the state in a clientelist relationship because they
work for and identify with different state-sponsored organizations and
associations.

EPIGRAPHS: Pickowicz, "Velvet Prisons and the Political Economy of Chinese Filmmaking."
Yan Sun, "Ideology and the Demise or Maintenance of Soviet-Type Regimes," p. 336.

Civic associations and the growth of civil society in China are affected by several extraneous factors and their interactions.[1] First, global factors, such as the increasing importance of technology, the arrival of the information age, and the specialization of knowledge and interests, affect most countries regardless of developmental level. Developing countries are also susceptible to global pressures to act in a manner that conforms to global standards. Countries like China, which were formerly isolated from the international system, are now exposed to its values and standards. Now that China is bound by international treaties, covenants, and customary norms of behavior, to what degree has it substituted international standards for internally generated standards as the basis for judging its own institutions and behavior? Second, many developing countries, including China, have experimented with democratization, the decentralization of state control, and economic liberalization. What impact have these processes had on China's formation of the institutions and environment of a civil society? Third, factors specific to China, such as the role of the family and traditional Chinese culture, have influenced society's relationship to the state. To what degree do cultural factors still shape this relationship?

This chapter examines the impact of these three sets of factors on associations in China and looks at the development of associations as both cause and effect of increasing democratization and economic decentralization. It also analyzes how Chinese traditional culture modifies the form and behavior of China's associations, and how the Chinese state attempts not only to tap into the expertise of associations but also to limit their autonomy. We are witnessing a state that, in allowing the proliferation of associations, has exchanged increasingly ineffective methods of control, methods that suppressed the creative energies of society, for ones that, much like capitalist market forces, achieve control and development in part by inspiring freewheeling dynamism and interaction. The degree of power held by society relative to the state, the issue of autonomy versus control, is one of the key questions for China, as it is for all societies.

---

1. A significant part of this chapter was published in an earlier form in my "China's Developing Civil Society."

A MULTIPARTY SYSTEM

Although aware of the problems accompanying the emergence of a multiparty system in former communist party–ruled states, the West continues to advocate the adoption of a multiparty system for China. Yet, there is no guaranteed connection between a multiparty system and the advance of (liberal) democracy. Furthermore, as has happened elsewhere, a multiparty system in China could well turn out to be merely the Chinese Communist Party divided into two or more political parties.[2] The Communist Party leadership would still be there, but the presently existing intraparty factions might acquire different party labels, as has happened in Kazakhstan, Kyrgyzstan, Tajikistan, Rumania, Hungary, and Poland. (Only Russia, of all the former communist party-led states, retained a party called the Communist Party from the very day Communist Party rule collapsed.) New parties might be formed by non-party leaders, but it is not inevitable that they would be able to gain power. Nor is it inevitable that a multiparty parliamentary system will function democratically. Elected presidents have, in the cases of Russia, Rumania, Argentina, Azerbaijan and Tajikistan, simply bypassed their elected multiparty legislative bodies and ruled by presidential decree.[3] Iran's elected parliament harshly restricted basic freedoms of speech and assembly, as well as of dress. Belarus and Kazakstan, under the label of democracy, have functioned as borderline tyrannies. About half of the world's "democratizing" countries may be classified as "illiberal democracies," that is, countries in which democratically elected governments "routinely [ignore] constitutional limits on their power and [deprive] their citizens of basic rights and freedoms."[4] Nationalist parties that come into power commonly try to

---

2. Of course, it could be argued that this would be preferable to having them remain mere factions *within* the Party, where it is impossible for citizens to know who is supporting which policy, much less throw their weight behind one faction or another by means of the ballot box.

3. For example, Romania's National Salvation Party was essentially made up of ex–Communist Party members; and, although the National Salvation Party was dominant in the legislature, President Iliescu (1990–97, 2000–present), himself a member of that party, basically ignored the legislature and ruled as a dictator (discussions with Minton Goldman, 2001).

4. Zakaria, "The Rise of Illiberal Democracy," pp. 22–24. Zakaria bases his estimates on Roger Kaplan, ed., *Freedom Around the World, 1997* (New York: Freedom House, 1997), pp. 21–22. Zakaria was referring to Russian President Boris Yeltsin and Argentinean President Carlos Menem.

suppress the rights of minorities. Majoritarian rule can, in short, be very authoritarian and can even result in tyranny when there are no counterbalancing institutions.

The recent histories of Mexico, Japan, and Taiwan indicate that single-party rule may survive for a significant period even in a multiparty environment. This is partly because the dominant "mainstream" party often hijacks the most popular policy positions of opposition parties on both the left and the right. In Taiwan, for example, the Guomindang (Nationalist Party) incorporated aspects of the platforms of opposition elements both within and outside the party, such as expanded relations with mainland China and greater national autonomy for Taiwan. In doing so, it claimed "the center" of Taiwan's politics. What was once radical thereby became mainstream, and the Nationalist Party was able to retain its dominant position until the presidential elections in 2000.[5]

Similarly, the Chinese Communist Party has shifted ground to accommodate what in a multiparty system would have been the policies of the opposition. For example, the "reformers" under Deng Xiaoping adopted policies formerly condemned as "rightist" (such as the "open door" policy, legal reforms, and greater freedom of the press) and recast them as mainstream policies. This undercut what might have become the political platform for any "liberal democratic" pretenders to power, while simultaneously leaving the "leftists" ("conservatives") opposed to reform on the fringe. Thus, the reformers were attuned to the needs and demands of China's citizens as well as the country's need to develop, even if they were also motivated to reform the political system to increase their political power. In turn, many of the leaders of the conservative wing of the "New Enlightenment movement," who had been the major intellectual and political force behind the Tiananmen demonstrations in 1989, thereafter joined the reform faction and took leading positions within the state structure, including universities and legislative bodies, as technocrats or theorists of modernization. Arguably, this

---

5. The Nationalist Party subsequently lost its dominant position in the legislature in the 2001 elections. The strategy of moving toward the center is hardly limited to political systems dominated by one party. For example, in the United States in 1992, Bill Clinton moved toward the right in order to position the Democratic Party more within the mainstream of American politics, and in Great Britain in 1997, Tony Blair similarly moved away from the more extreme policies of the left in order to claim for the Labour Party the more popular policies associated with the "right."

happened because the reformers shared, or adopted, the same perspectives as these "dissident" intellectuals. From this perspective, 1989 was not an example of civil society confronting the state because the goals of the intellectuals were "completely compatible" with the state's goals.[6]

Perhaps the strongest sign that the Party may be moving to capture the middle, and abandoning the far more extreme policies guided by Marxism, Leninism, and Mao Zedong Thought, is that it is seriously studying the policies and practices of the European leftist parties. It has sent numerous delegations to Western Europe to discuss policies with these parties. (Some of these were founded by individuals who had split off from the communist party in their own country.) And at the celebration of the Party's eightieth anniversary on July 1, 2001, instead of continuing its practice of inviting only other communist party leaders from abroad, it held a special forum for the social democratic party representatives form Western Europe. It is even considering a change in the name of the Party that would reflect this more moderate leftist stance, such as the "social democratic" (*shehui minzhu*) party. Just as important, Jiang Zemin's announcement of the Party's "theory of three representatives" (*san'ge daibiao sixiang*) in 2001 explicitly states the Party's changing nature. The Party's role is to move beyond serving as the "vanguard of the revolution" to affirm the Party's responsibility for governing; the Party will represent the most advanced culture in the world, including modern ideas about politics and governance; and its membership will represent *all* the people's interests, not just those of workers and peasants. This means that the Party will now recruit those who labor with their minds and their money—intellectuals and businessmen, with capitalists no longer viewed as "exploiters" but as "workers." This change reflects the Party's ac-

---

6. The term "New Enlightenment movement" does not describe a truly coherent intellectual movement; rather, it covers "a far-flung and jumbled social trend" comprising a hodgepodge of individuals who are not always in full agreement with one another. What originally united them was "their shared critique of orthodox socialism, a unity forged in the process of their common support for the goals of 'reform,'" including "autonomy and freedom in the economic, political, legal, and cultural spheres." The "movement" began in 1979. The more radical intellectuals in the movement formed a new political opposition, which promoted human rights and liberal democratic political reform. New Enlightenment intellectuals in the more conservative wing would include such figures as Wang Qishan, a vice director of the Chinese People's Bank and director of the China Development Bank, and Professor Li Yining, a vice director in the Chinese People's Consultative Congress's legal department. See Wang Hui, "Contemporary Chinese Thought and the Question of Modernity," pp. 18–21, 40.

knowledgment of reality, especially that many Party members have themselves become entrepreneurs: businessmen are *already* in the Party. It also indicates the Party's awareness that it is China's entrepreneurs and intellectuals who have been responsible for much of China's remarkable development in the past twenty years. Without their support, the Party will not only continue to lose legitimacy but also will lack their input in shaping China's future.

In short, parties can and do change both their ideologies and their profile. They can become more representative and adopt a political platform with broader appeal, in China no less than in other countries. If this happens, one-party rule may not be as anti-democratic in its implications, and stable one-party rule may outperform multiparty rule in its ability both to develop the country and to represent its broad national interest instead of narrower sectoral interests.

THE RELATIVE IMPORTANCE OF PARTIES VERSUS ASSOCIATIONS OR INTEREST GROUPS

A well-functioning pluralistic political system empowers individuals and groups by allowing the expression of multiple perspectives and the balancing of conflicting interests. Apart from political parties, however, there are other institutions and channels that can present political interests and demands. Both in well-established democratic states and in states inching toward democracy, political parties are not necessarily as important as they once were in representing their constituents' interests. This is not to deny that most multiparty systems are preferable to most single-party systems. Aside from everything else, broad-based parties attempt to function as the arbiters of the totality of interests in a society, whereas any particular interest group or association fundamentally represents only one interest.

Nevertheless, even in countries long governed by an authoritarian political system, citizens today tend not to embrace partisan symbols and ideologies and instead prefer to support a more diverse group of interests. In part, this reflects a growing awareness by citizens that they can act collectively without participating in a political party. This is not to say that political parties in the end relinquish control to interest groups, associations, and social movements, since ultimately political parties still represent their various interests in the government, but these groups have far more power to influence parties and to act autonomously than in the past.[7]

In some post-communist states, political parties embody nothing more than narrow sectoral interests or the political ambitions of one individual. For example, in Poland's first fully democratic elections in 1991, 111 "electoral committees" presented party lists; by 1995, there were 250 officially recognized political parties. In Czechoslovakia, there were 79 registered parties by the end of 1991. Hungary had some 120 political parties by 1991, although the number had been whittled down to 34 by 1994.[8] Such a multiplicity of parties indicates that no one party was able to capture the broad public interest because the public identified with numerous narrow, sectoral interests.

The highly specialized legal and technical knowledge required in today's complex world is in large part responsible for this shift in the locus of power to associations and interest groups. In most developed countries, experts not only can be but must be called in to solve problems, and special interest organizations, which become expert in the intricacies of their own issues, are responsible for representing their constituencies' interests on major economic, social, political, and cultural issues. For example, in the United States, many political pressures come from outside political parties and shape their policies. Interest groups, social movements, associations, lobbies, and think tanks have all gained in importance in recent decades. Much of the legislation before Congress is the result of these various groups, not political parties as formal organizations, persuading members of Congress to consider particular policies. Legislators listen to them not just because they represent powerful groups within the society, but also because they understand the highly technical issues involved. In areas as diverse as taxation, roads, dams, medical technology, pollution, banking policies, housing, trade issues, consumer protection, and insurance, legislators need to know both what their constituencies want and how legislation will affect those interests.

Specialized interest groups have, therefore, added their voices to those of government and party officials and are significantly increasing their input into decision-making in those areas that affect them. Given the rapid development of science, technology, commerce, and communication, together

---

7. Schmitter, "Interest Systems and the Consolidation of Democracies," p. 160.

8. James A. Norris and Aie Rie Lee, "Democratic Consolidation Among Mass Publics in East-Central Europe," paper for the annual conference of the Southern Political Science Association, Nov. 3–7, 1999, Savannah, Georgia.

with increasingly complex societal and economic arrangements, party politicians are unable to keep up with the intricacies of the problems their societies face. In a simpler world, party politicians were better positioned to handle the totality of issues facing their country. Today that is hardly the case—and no less so for a rapidly developing and an increasingly complex China than for the more developed countries of the world. Thus, in China, the days of "red over expert" (in which the individual with strong political credentials rather than the knowledgeable person was likely to be in charge) are long gone. The mainstay of the government's policies is no longer rooted in ideology but in pragmatism, and those people rising to the top of organizations must be expert at their increasingly complex and demanding jobs.

China has more than 200,000 interest groups and professional associations at the county, prefectural, and provincial level,[9] and some 1,800 national-level and interprovincial groups.[10] These represent constituencies as diverse as commercial entrepreneurs, lawyers, doctors, women, businesspeople, importers and exporters, accountants, consumers, environmentalists, trade groups, shareholders, parent-teacher associations, artists, sports clubs, television and movie producers, computer groups, *qigong* practitioners, dancers, workers, musical societies, religious groups, retired workers, sportsmen, industries, and anti-tax groups. The state's (ineffective) policy is to prevent these groups from becoming too powerful by discouraging the horizontal organization of nationwide organizations.[11] Indeed, one of the major motivations for the government's insistence on vertical, top-down integration of associations is to prevent the emergence of powerful national organizations based on horizontally integrated grass-roots groups.[12]

There are three categories of associations. First, those officially registered. Second, those nominally affiliated with legally registered associations (including those that have a nominal affiliation with business enterprises—but if and when they register, they are then considered to fall into the first cate-

---

9. All such associations and interest groups are lumped under the label *shehui tuanti* or *shetuan*.

10. Human Rights in China, "China: Social Groups Seek Independence in a Regulatory Cage," pp. 6–7.

11. Shaoguang Wang, "The Politics of Private Time," pp. 168–69, citing Whyte, "Urban China: A Civil Society in the Making?," p. 91.

12. Saich, "Negotiating the State," p. 132.

gory). This group is said to have "one foot in and [the other] foot outside the law." Many *qigong* associations are believed to be in this group. The third category is "illegal" associations, that is, those not officially registered. Often called "salons" or "tribunes" or "clubs," they include many ordinary groups that are commonly found in China's cities and countryside. Examples would be folk-arts societies in a city, and religious and temple fair associations in rural areas. Although they are "illegal," usually the government has no interest in forcing them to register or shutting them down. In today's China, all three categories of associations are generally thriving.[13]

China's interest groups, societies, associations, think tanks, and so on may be further divided into three types: those that assist the state by consulting with it and by regulating their membership to conform to state policies, those that represent their members' interests in a way that challenges state policies or state control, and those that do both. Those that assist the state are less a part of civil society than those that represent their members' interests even when they challenge state policies. But in China, more often than not, associations do both.

Examples of the numerous associations that take on this dual role can be found in areas as diverse as social welfare services, economic regulation, environmental protection, consumer protection, the promotion of science and technology, and specialized organizations for professionals. For example, in 1995, the Ministry of Justice founded a national association for China's 90,000 lawyers: the All-China Lawyers Association. From the perspective of the state, one of the primary functions of this association is to control and regulate lawyers by, among other things, determining qualifications for membership in the profession. Officially, however, it is an autonomous organization, and its members voted to replace the officials appointed by the Ministry of Justice with newly elected officials. They also set up other legal organizations to protect the rights of ordinary citizens believed to have been treated unfairly by government.[14] The All-China Lawyers Association also functions as an interest group. In particular, it tries to protect the legal rights of lawyers from violation by the state. This advocacy role may bring it into a more adversarial relationship with the state. In turn, the state consults the All-China Lawyers Association about legal issues.

---

13. Gao Bingzhong, "The Rise of Associations in China and the Question of Their Legitimacy," pp. 73–74.

14. Pei, "Racing Against Time," p. 43.

In this respect, the association assists the state, presumably for the good of the entire society.[15]

The Ministry of Justice also created the China Law Society to conduct research about criminal matters. When the National People's Congress decided to modify the Criminal Code in 1996, this society researched the draft laws establishing the principle of equality before the law, determining sentencing by law, and abolishing the category of "counterrevolutionary." It then offered advice on these topics to the relevant legislative subcommittees of the National People's Congress. The China Law Society has branches at every level of government, with specialized legal research societies under each branch. For example, the Jurisprudence Society focuses on the basic conditions for the rule of law and the relationship between the rule of law and "socialist spiritual civilization"; the Civil and Economic Law Society on contract laws and laws concerning foreign-invested enterprises; and the Procedural Law Society on improving the criminal and civil procedural law.[16]

Many interest groups are part of associations organized and controlled by the state, such as the All-China Women's Federation and the Communist Youth League. For example, the government program, Women's Images in Media, which is responsible for monitoring how women are presented in the media, conducted a survey in 1997 of television ads depicting women in conjunction with the Women's Studies Institute, which is linked to the Women's Federation. The findings of the survey, which revealed extreme sexism in television advertising (women were almost always portrayed as "helpless, vain, and needing a man"), were published in *China Women's News*. The result was that the State Administration of Industry and Commerce, the Ministry of Radio, Film, and Television, and the Chinese Advertisers Association jointly issued a statement requiring compliance with the Advertising Law. That law (January 1996) states that all advertisements must respect the dignity of women and prohibits the use of those images and words that are "insulting to women."[17] This is another example of how a state-controlled organization can work to promote the interests of a major sector in civil society.

---

15. Zhongguo faxuehui, "Overview of Work by Associations and Societies Under the Ministry of Justice," sect. 9, pp. 623–24.

16. Ibid., pp. 621–22.

17. Xiong Lei, "TV Ads Depict Women as Helpless and Weak," Inter Press Service, Apr. 29, 1997, document 223. Web.lexis-nexis.com.

Some associations are fully interchangeable with government agencies. For example, the All-China Federation of Sports is the same as the State Sports Bureau, except in name. In Chinese jargon, such arrangements are known as "one institution, two labels" (*yitao jigou, liangkuai paizi*), and the same person may even direct both organizations. The same is true for the Environmental Health Association, which is run by a government agency of the same name at every level of government. The Shanghai Municipal Environmental Health Association, for example, has a technical consulting department, and it helps carry out a governmental program to eliminate *matong*, the wooden buckets widely used as toilets in Shanghai.[18]

As with health and consumer protection associations (see Chapter 5), state-organized environmental groups can represent the interests of civil society. This is an example of a concern—environmental protection—in which the interests of state and society usually coincide. Indeed, health, consumer protection, and the environment are areas in which society is asking the state to become *more* involved in advancing the public's interests. One way in which the state has responded is to require state-run media to increase the number of advertisements in newspapers and during prime-time television programs (and on billboards along major roads) dedicated to increasing public awareness of such issues as environmental protection and AIDs.[19] Another approach the state uses is to launch "campaigns" to increase public awareness of, and public compliance with, new policies. Thus, in collaboration with environmental associations, and sometimes under pressure from society at large, the state has also organized, proposed, or at least acquiesced in numerous campaigns for environmental protection, such as the campaign for stringent control of industries using natural resources and the campaign to protect panda bears, tigers, and other endangered species.

Any department or ministry may also establish associations, institutes, and think tanks, to carry out its policies. They are sometimes referred to as "non-governmental organizations" (NGOs) in Western liberal democracies, although many analysts prefer to use the term "government-organized non-

---

18. Ma Yili and Liu Hanbang, *Shanghai shehui tuanti gailai*, p. 142.

19. Since 1996, when the state began its efforts to increase public awareness advertising on a national scale, more than 70,000 ads have been placed on television, in newspapers and magazines, and on billboards ("Media to Promote Ethics, Culture," BBC *Summary of World Broadcasts*, Jan. 15, 2000, document 5. Web.lexis-nexis.com).

governmental organizations" (GONGOs). In the case of China it makes more sense simply to call them associations, institutes, think tanks, foundations, or charities, with the assumption that unless they are not registered, they are in most cases somehow government-organized. Thus, the National Environmental Protection Agency has established the China Environmental Protection Foundation, the China Association of Environmental Protection Industry, and the Chinese Society for Environmental Sciences. Sometimes the relationship between the governmental agency and the association can be quite cozy. The China Social Group Research Society, established by the Ministry of Civil Affairs, sponsors overseas travel by ministry officials as representatives of this society. This pattern of affiliated social groups is replicated at all levels of the bureaucracy and accounts in part for the relatively large number of social groups currently registered in China.[20] When the leadership of an association and a government agency overlap, the government has the institutional means to influence the association, but the association in turn possesses the institutional means to influence the government.[21] In short, the relationship is often symbiotic, and civil society may benefit just as much as the government does.

Funding for associations may come from foreign sources, such as the United Nations, the Republican Institute, the United Nations Development Programme, the Asia Foundation, the Ford Foundation, the European Union, or the British Council; from Chinese corporations and individuals; or from membership fees. Most of the personnel in associations are paid by the government for other jobs, even though the bulk of their time is spent working for the association. The Chinese state is not, however, necessarily willing to permit some organizations and agencies to set up an association, since they are often fronts for profit-making or political activities.[22] Many associations, although organized by the state, are able to carve out an autonomous area of action in which the state does not intervene. This is particularly true of the tens of thousands of associations that represent interests at the local level. The Women's Federation, for example, must oversee more than 3,500 organizations dealing with women's affairs; it is unlikely it can

---

20. Human Rights in China, "China: Social Groups Seek Independence in a Regulatory Cage," pp. 8–9.

21. Zhu Guanglei, *Dangdai Zhongguo zhengfu guocheng*, pp. 191–94.

22. Tony Saich, seminars, Harvard University, Fairbank Center and Asia Center, Oct. 15, 1999; Nov. 12, 1999.

monitor the daily activities of all these organizations.[23] The overall decentralization of control that has accompanied economic liberalization has been responsible for much of the growth in local autonomy.

Ironically, the Chinese Communist Party's penchant for organizing people taught them organizational skills that they now use in the non-government-directed public sphere—and sometimes for the purpose of pressuring the government to change policy.[24] Minimally, individuals with common interests can work through organizations such as associations, interest groups, and think tanks to advance their members' interests within the framework of existing laws and regulations. To put this in the vocabulary of Western social science, the Chinese use organizational skills acquired from training by the state and the Party to articulate their interests and aggregate their demands through associations established by the state. In 1996, for example, urban neighborhood associations in Beijing joined forces to stop local noise pollution from portable stereos blasting on the streets and sidewalks. Women "fan dancing" to the clashing of cymbals, tambourines, gongs, and drums and thousands of Chinese couples learning ballroom dancing from taped music were using some of the few public spaces available to them in a crowded urban environment. Beijingers unable to sleep through the racket worked through neighborhood residents' associations to force the government to pass a noise ordinance that lowered the allowed decibel level on streets. In turn, the fan dancers and the ballroom dancers organized and petitioned local officials to protect their "right" to express themselves through dancing in the streets.[25] In China, these voluntarily organized, informal, unregistered associations can be just as important as formal organizations in expanding the public space of civil society.

The government tries to make the ever-growing number of associations, interest groups, think tanks, charities, and foundations functioning in China

---

23. Saich, "Negotiating the State," p. 134.

24. For an excellent analysis of how the "patterns of protest" in China have replicated the "patterns of daily life," see Wasserstrom and Liu, "Student Associations and Mass Movements," pp. 362–66, 383–86. The authors make the point that the students of Tiananmen Square had learned how to organize, lead, and follow in school. The same was true for workers who participated in the 1989 protests "not as individuals or members of 'autonomous' unions but as members of danwei delegations, which were usually organized with either the direct support or the passive approval of work-group leaders, and which were generally led onto the streets by people carrying flags emblazoned with the name of the unit" (ibid., p. 383).

25. Ogden, notes from living and working in Beijing, 1996–97.

subordinate to government agencies. Most charities in China are appendages of the China Charities Federation, which is itself part of the Ministry of Civil Affairs. As of 1997, there were 59 charities, or federations of charities, under the national federation working in such areas as orphanages, environmental protection, disaster relief, and construction of school buildings and medical facilities. These are formal but not official charities, and usually their funding comes from foreign donors (who tend to be investors in China) or from overseas Chinese businesspeople and charities. Because charities and foundations generally are portrayed as "non-governmental," they are allowed to raise money both domestically and internationally for their programs. Spring Buds, for example, funnels money into programs to provide primary education for poor children; its primary mission is to keep girls from dropping out of school for lack of funds. The China Children's Fund, which directs the Spring Buds program, is a foundation under the All-China Women's Federation.[26] Project Hope, an internationally funded public and private charity that focuses on health education projects, especially children's medical issues, also receives funds from private Chinese citizens and companies.[27] Other charities are springing up in China. In the context of a public used to the state providing all services for the people, charities and charitable giving are not ideas that come easily. International support has sometimes been indispensable. On occasion, the new charities have been confronted by a government office that feels they are stepping on its toes.[28] In some cases, such as international support for orphanages, these efforts have been seen as challenging China's sovereignty.

By no means do all charities receive foreign funds. The government's Family Planning Agency funds the Family Planning Association because the United Nations prohibited the government agency from receiving family planning funds from the United Nations and participating in its population-

---

26. Human Rights in China, "China: Social Groups Seek Independence in a Regulatory Cage," pp. 3, 7–9.

27. The health education projects are led by American physicians and nurses. Project Hope led private efforts to raise funding and build the Shanghai Children's Medical Center, which was dedicated when the Clintons were visiting China in June 1998. The City of Shanghai and Shanghai's Second Medical University collaborated in the effort. See William B. Walsh (President, Project Hope), "Building Public/Private Collaboration in China," *Health Affairs* 17, no. 6 (Nov./Dec. 1998): 6.

28. Pamela Yatsko, "Helping Hands: Private Charities Survive Against the Odds," *Far Eastern Economic Review*, May 7, 1998, p. 14.

planning activities. The Family Planning Association has been a critical force in shaping government policy. This association, which is a GONGO, acts as a proxy for the Chinese government.[29] So does the government-organized China Human Rights Study Society. GONGOs may act autonomously from, or as a proxy for, the Chinese government, for example, by "making public statements to defend official positions domestically and internationally . . . or in implementing government programs."[30] In this respect, they function much like the "transmission-belt" organizations once common in communist states.

Finally, it should be noted that the establishment of NGOs by governments is common to many developing countries, and even to developed Western liberal democratic states. Although the latter are characterized by the existence of a web of associations that are autonomous from the state, "there has also been a tendency for these to become integrated into the state." This is often referred to as "corporatism." But, as Charles Taylor argues, the practice could better be described as "an interweaving of society and government to the point that the distinction no longer expresses an important difference in the basis of power or the dynamics of policy-making. Both governments and associations draw on and are responsive to the same public."[31] When compared to other countries, then, China is not really that unusual in its approach to the creation of associations that represent societal interests. What is distinctive is the sheer number of associations that the state has established since the reform period began in 1979 and the recognition by China's reformers of the need for associations and interest groups. Why did this happen? The answer lies in how reformers redefined society's relationship with the state, the increasing role of pragmatism and expertise at the expense of ideology, and, as discussed earlier, the growing complexity of Chinese society as it became more developed and as economic liberalization led to decentralization.

---

29. Saich, "Negotiating the State:," pp. 136–37.

30. Human Rights in China, "China: Social Groups Seek Independence in a Regulatory Cage," p. 8.

31. Charles Taylor, "Modes of Civil Society," *Public Culture* 3, no. 1 (Fall 1990): 96, 98, quoted in Sullivan and Abed-Kotob, *Islam in Contemporary Egypt*, p. 4. Sullivan and Abed-Kotob (p. 25) note that in Egypt, most analysts prefer not to use the term "NGO" to describe charitable and nonprofit organizations because they are not really independent of the government.

The Chinese Redefinition of Society's
Relationship with the State

By the late 1980s, the notion of "society" as defined by the "class struggle" between "the people" and "the enemy" had been abandoned. "The people" was
no longer a social class representing the total unity of one class's interests,
and the unity of that class's interests with the party-state, in opposition to
another class, "the enemy," in a divided, confrontational society governed by
a state "dictatorship." Instead, "the people" had become virtually synonymous with "society." Society, in turn, came to be viewed as an entity
containing pluralistic interests, which were considered equally legitimate
instead of "contradictions among the people" or potential threats to the state.
Thus, the state no longer had to be a dictatorship in order to control "the
enemy." It could simply "manage public affairs."[32]

As a result, by the late 1980s, a concept of "interest pluralism" (*liyi duoyuan
zhuyi*) had developed. And, whatever the variety of social interests that
may always have existed among "the people" under socialism, economic liberalization was believed to have greatly augmented them—and to have
brought a consciousness of individual rights. In turn, "political pluralization"
(*zhengzhi duoyuanhua*), which mirrored social and economic pluralism in
China, came to be seen as an important part of democratization in China.
The earlier (pre-reform) emphasis on the *unity* of the interests of the people
(society) and of the people with the party-state had made the formation
of different interest groups unnecessary, even illegal. Political pluralization
began the process of legitimizing the expression of diverse and even conflicting interests. "Democracy" took on a new meaning: "a process of interest
accommodation, coordination, and compromise." This was in striking contrast to the process of "class struggle," which had viewed the expression of
different interests as a sign of class conflict.[33] Not only were the interests
of the state and society not identical, but even interests *within* society were
not unified.

---

32. Ding, "Pre- and Post-Tiananmen Conceptual Evolution of Democracy in Intellectual
Circles," pp. 230–32.
33. Ibid., pp. 238–39, 241.

The Increasing Role of Pragmatism and Expertise

The tendency to organize around issues and interests in China today is more than a reflection of the declining role of communist ideology in shaping policy and economic liberalization. It also reflects the state's assertion of highly pragmatic concerns in policymaking and the desire of distinct constituencies to fall in line with, and take advantage of, the state's new approach to issues and policy. Although China has never been homogeneous and uncomplicated, it is considerably more heterogeneous and complicated now than it was before 1980. Because of economic and social development and the growth of social autonomy, there are far more diverse needs and interests to be represented than there were previously, and specialized associations and interest groups have sprung up to articulate these interests.

Another, perhaps more cynical, explanation for the formation of so many associations and interest groups is that a large number of retired or idled cadres still remain energetic and want to retain their social status, as well as their influence over political and economic policies. So they establish, or are appointed to head up, academic, economic, and professional groups, the Chinese equivalent of retired bureaucrats becoming consultants. There have, in fact, been cases in which such an appointment was offered to induce a cadre to retire. As a result, associations sometimes have earned the sobriquet of "old folks homes."[34] It seems unlikely that retired or idled cadres would have as much power or influence as someone who is still in office, but they are nevertheless usually quite effective as leaders of associations. Since those in power today are the former subordinates of these retired cadres, they tend to cater to the leaders of these groups.[35] In short, retired officials may retain powerful connections with those still in power; and they may draw on those connections to benefit the associations they lead.

Interest groups and corporatist associations are arguably more effective instruments for representing a variety of particularistic collective interests

---

34. Human Rights in China, "China: Social Groups Seek Independence in a Regulatory Cage," p. 15.

35. Li Gang, "Deng hou Zhongguode keneng qianjing"; and Zhongguo zhanlüe yu guanli yanjiuhui, Shehui jiu zhuanxing ketizu, "Zhongguo zhuanxingde zhongjinqi qushi yu yinghuan," pp. 10–11. This view is confirmed by Margaret Pearson ("The Janus Face of Business Associations in China," p. 38), who found retired officials on managing boards in her own 1994 study of socialist corporatism in foreign enterprises.

than are political parties in today's world, and China's present pragmatic government continues to seek input from interest groups and professional associations to help shape policy and advance the goals of modernization. China has prohibited the formation of competing political parties, but it has tolerated, even encouraged, interest groups and associations, especially those representing relatively narrow concerns or localized issues. One result of the government's gradual delegation of increasing power to associations since the 1980s is that associations are better positioned to represent their constituents' interests. This sometimes puts them in an adversarial relationship with the government.

The state may also create associations as a way to control people in the context of an inadequate legal system and the destabilization brought about by economic liberalization. Associations that encourage members to obey regulations help the government control society and at the same time protect society from its own worst members. Self-regulation works best through organizations that represent their members' interests. For example, the National Association of Science and Technology established a code of ethics for publications concerning science and technology. Among other things, the code prohibits plagiarism and copyright violations. It is in the interests of the association's members *and the state* to have such regulations, but the state left it to the members of this association to write them.[36]

Whether China has more than one major party may, then, be less important for the development of civil society than the fact that interest groups and associations continue to thrive and to expand their channels for making demands on the government, even as they assist the government in regulating their members. In short, the flourishing of interest groups and associations in China today represents the triumph of pragmatism over ideology and of pluralism if not multiparty rule over a monolithic one-party state.

THE RELEVANCE OF POLITICAL
PARTIES TO DEMOCRACY

This, then, leads to the question, do political parties necessarily serve democracy well? Or are they increasingly vulnerable to co-optation by special interest groups and those who seek patronage opportunities? If China were

36. Jin Zhenrong, "More than 200 Scientific and Technological Journals Signed the Moral Covenant."

to permit a true multiparty system, who would join these parties if "patron-age opportunities, clientelistic advantages, opportunity for corruption, and the like"[37] were not guaranteed to those joining? And, if they were guaran-teed, who would argue that such a multiparty system was promoting the cause of democracy?

It would hardly be surprising if a multiparty system in China fell victim to the same sorts of political evils that have befallen newly formed multiparty systems elsewhere. In many Arab countries, for example, liberalization has allowed political parties to blossom, but they are seldom run democratically. When opposition parties do gain political power, they tend to act in an au-thoritarian manner.[38] In Syria, Egypt, and Tunisia, the parties that have gained power through the electoral system have tended to "crush the life out of the legal opposition."[39] Furthermore, "distrust of party politics is endemic among people for whom 'the party' meant exploitative apparatchiki" and the unquestioning acceptance of Marxist-Leninist principles. Today, in Russia, the Czech Republic, Slovakia, Hungary, and Poland, "political parties lead the list of institutions that [they] distrust."[40]

This is not an argument that China will be better off with the Chinese Communist Party monopolizing power. The fact, however, that so many countries that have adopted a multiparty democratic system in recent dec-ades have not benefited from it either in terms of social stability or economic development has undoubtedly added to the hesitation on the part of both rulers and ruled to abandon one-party rule. Moreover, the serious erosion of the Chinese Communist Party's legitimacy since the 1960s, even if its poli-cies in the past two decades have been successful, has also in the minds of some Chinese diminished interest in creating still more political parties. On the other hand, some Chinese clearly feel a multiparty system would be the best antidote for the Party's problems.

Many Chinese would agree that had the students and intellectuals who participated in the demonstrations in Tiananmen Square in Beijing in 1989 become the leaders of a new ruling party, they would have been just as elitist, authoritarian, and corrupt as the Communist Party leaders they were chal-lenging. Indeed, those student-participants in the Tiananmen Square dem-

---

37. Linz, "Change and Continuity in the Nature of Contemporary Democracies," p. 188.
38. Harik, "Rethinking Civil Society," p. 49.
39. "Arab Autocracy Forever?" *Economist*, June 7, 1997, p. 42.
40. Rose, "Rethinking Civil Society," pp. 19, 25.

onstrations in 1989, such as Wang Dan and Shen Tong, who left China castigated themselves and their fellow demonstrators for many of these same reasons.[41] In early June 1989, just prior to the military crackdown on the demonstrations, the well-known literary critic Liu Xiaobo, the greatly admired pop singer Hou Dejian, and two other young friends began a hunger strike in Tiananmen Square to reignite interest and support for the student movement. Their support for the students did not, however, stop them from issuing an extraordinary indictment of the student movement:

The students' mistakes are mainly manifested in the internal chaos of their organizations and the lack of efficient and democratic procedures. Although their goal is democracy, their means and procedures for achieving democracy are not democratic. . . . Their lack of cooperative spirit and the sectarianism that has caused their forces to neutralize each other have resulted in all their policies coming to naught. More faults can be named: financial chaos; material waste, an excess of emotion and a lack of reason; too much of the attitude that they are privileged, and not enough of the belief in equality.[42]

China's protestors often adopt some of the less attractive aspects of the official organizations they oppose. The demonstrators in Tiananmen Square were, for example, unable to work together across class boundaries because they had internalized the official cultural orthodoxy about social status hierarchies.[43] When disturbing news about the behavior of students and intellectuals who had been leaders of the 1989 demonstrations filtered back to China, those students and intellectuals still in China harshly criticized them. But they also criticized the other former leaders of the movement who had not left China: Had the dissidents won in 1989 and taken control of the country, "things would be much worse today. Perhaps after all, the rebels were themselves products of communism, the students children of Mao, and they

---

41. About a dozen participants attended a conference at Harvard University on June 2–3, 1999, to discuss the meaning of the 1989 Tiananmen Square demonstrations ten years after the event.

42. Liu Xiaobo et al., "A Hunger Strike Manifesto," trans. in Han Minzhu, ed., *Cries for Democracy: Writing and Speeches from the 1989 Democracy Movement*, p. 352.

43. Wasserstrom and Liu, "Student Associations and Mass Movements," pp. 378, 381–82. Chai Ling, the self-declared "Commander of the Square," was highly dictatorial, and Wu Erkaixi, like several other leaders in Tiananmen Square, are now known as much for their corruption as for their challenge to China's leadership. Insights into the student leaders' motivation and their organizational skills are brilliantly exposed in Carma Hinton and Richard Wilson's documentary film *Under the Gate of Heavenly Peace* (released in 1997).

could not but fight for new ideals in the old way, with mass rallies, slogan chanting, factionalism, and corruption."[44]

In short, although some Chinese talk privately about the potential benefits of a multiparty system in limiting corruption and other political evils, many wonder if new parties will differ much if at all from the style of the Communist Party, for they believe they are trapped in the ideas of an entrenched political culture. Even worse, they fear a multiparty system could lead to the type of confusion and turmoil that China experienced before 1949. Rather than generating the sort of institutional checks that would limit corruption, a multiparty system, which would require national elections, might spawn even more corruption. People in China are aware that Taiwan has faced this problem ever since it allowed multiple parties and free elections. Money politics was, in fact, the key domestic issue in the Taiwanese presidential elections in 2000.[45] Candidates throw lavish feasts, make deals with businesspeople, and spread money around in order to get the vote. Equally disturbing to the Taiwanese is the growing amount of election-related violence and the influence of the underworld on the elections.[46] Known as "black and gold politics" (black for criminal, gold for money), corruption is undermining Taiwan's efforts to democratize.[47] It is easy for the Chinese Communist Party to present this widely publicized situation to China's people as reason enough for prohibiting new political parties.

---

44. Zha, *China Pop*, p. 12.

45. Money politics, vote-buying, and general dishonesty, which have plagued all of Taiwan's parties since elections were first held, have burgeoned over the years. This stems in part from the growing importance of elections; see Cal Clark, "Taiwan in the 1990s: Moving Ahead or Back to the Future?" in Joseph, *China Briefing*, p. 206. Even after the Democratic Progressive Party became the ruling party in the 2000 elections, there were allegations of "rampant vote-buying by many party delegates running for the [DPP's] Central Executive Committee" ("DPP Congress Tinged by Accusations of Vote-Buying," *China News Digest*, www.cnd.org, July 18, 2000). And, during soul-searching discussions in Taiwan in January 2001 with a number of Nationalist leaders, most candidly stated that the party's major problem was corruption.

46. Myra Lu, "Crackdown on Vote-Buying Continues," *Free China Journal*, Nov. 27, 1998, p. 2.

47. As the Nationalist Party is the first to admit, it was so busy democratizing Taiwan that it neglected to democratize itself. Because it lost the presidential elections, and then lost control of the Legislative Yuan in the December 2001 elections, it is rethinking its political platform and making efforts to rid itself of serious corruption and elitism (discussions with Shaw Yu-ming, Deputy Secretary General, at Nationalist Party Headquarters, Jan. 2001).

Finally, not all Chinese feel confident that politicians in a multiparty system would represent their interests. The expectation is that most individuals with power try to reap personal benefits. Many Chinese freely admit that were they to have power, they, too, would use it for personal gain.[48] For at least some Chinese, the ideal would be for the Communist Party to become less corrupt but to maintain one-party rule.[49] Moreover, were a political party to come to power with the help, or what appeared to be the help, of a foreign country, most Chinese people would be suspicious of its intentions. Indeed, the easiest way for China's leaders to win the support of the Chinese people against the organizers of a political party (or against any dissidents) who challenge the Party's rule is to link them with a foreign country.

China's State and Society as Interdependent, Not Confrontational

China's state and society are not clearly distinct and autonomous spheres. To the contrary, they are interlinked and often utilize each other to their mutual benefit. In the traditional patriarchal Chinese concept of the empire, a view that has carried over to the present-day conception of the state, the state is responsible for the welfare of its citizens. Familial authority and political authority have not always been clearly differentiated. The foundation of the state is the family, and the state is the ruler's household.[50] The Chinese people *expect* that, in return for their loyalty to the state, it will take care of them: it will find work for them, assign housing to them, provide healthcare and education, and in general attend to their needs. It is a perspective that encourages dependency on a paternalistic state and allows that state to control its citizenry.

The patriarchal state is, in short, a state *responsible* for its citizens. In turn, Chinese citizens have *obligations* (*yiwu*), not as individuals but as members of society: obligations to obey officials and state policies and to take care of

---

48. Discussion with university colleagues from China, 1998. They say that (with the exception of the spring 1989 demonstrations), Chinese people do not normally see corruption as a reason for challenging the government's or the Party's leadership. They assume that anyone in a position of power would act the same way. They also endorse the view that had the students in Tiananmen Square in 1989 successfully overthrown the government, they would have acted in the same manner as many government officials whom they criticized as corrupt.

49. Discussion with Chinese students, 1997.

50. This is discussed at length in Ogden, "Chinese Concepts of the State, Nation, and Sovereignty."

their families. One could say that the result of this political culture has been to make it difficult for the Chinese state and society to function as separate entities; for unlike the West, where civil society preceded the formation of the nation-state, with the latter evolving from the former, a strong centralized state long preceded any efforts to introduce elements of a civil society in China. Thus, China's centralized state is in a better position to shape and even control the development of civil society.

Moreover, as discussed below, the emphasis in Chinese culture on the family interferes from the bottom up with the creation of a public sphere. Both the state's authority and the centrality of the family are, however, being challenged by the economic and political reforms, which have led to the state's partial abdication of its role as caretaker. This erosion of controlling authority at both the top and the bottom, combined with a better-educated youth who are more assertive in demanding their rights, and the creation of a large number of interest groups and associations, has in turn led to the creation of significantly greater public space.

CORPORATISM

The relationship between the state and society in China may be viewed from the perspective of "civil society," in which society is independent of, and even in conflict with, the state. Alternatively, the relationship may be viewed from the perspective of "corporatism," in which dependence and cooperation co-exist.[51] Corporatism seems to better explain the relationship between state and society in China today. This does not mean that China's civil society— that part of human activity that is neither public nor private and is independent of the state—is not developing. To the contrary, whether in spite of or because of the stable relationship between state and society within a corporatist framework, elements of a civil society are emerging. Perhaps B. Michael Frolic's term, "state-led civil society," is the best description of China today: it is composed of "the hundreds of thousands of social organizations and quasi-administrative units created by the state to help it manage a complex and rapidly expanding economy and changing society." This is civil society, Chinese style, and may be seen "as an 'Asian' type of political development, that is, a form of state corporatism or non-Western communitari-

---

51. Ding, "Pre- and Post-Tiananmen Conceptual Evolution of Democracy in Intellectual Circles," p. 250.

anism that differs noticeably from the more conventional civil society of the West."[52]

Corporatism may exist in any system, from a single-party state to a liberal democratic one. This institutional form is chosen by governments that prefer to deal with organized and cooperative interest groups instead of the more competitive and conflictual types found in some liberal democratic states. The corporatist model has emerged in some liberal democratic states such as Japan and Great Britain. "Societal corporatism," the term used to describe the form of corporatism found in these states, suggests that the associations' leaders are responsible to their members rather than the state. The main purpose of "state corporatism" is "a goal-oriented harmony, orchestrated to serve a national mission," such as modernization and economic development. The name implies that the responsibilities of the associations' leaders tilt more in the direction of the state. This is the form of corporatism seen in more authoritarian states, such as Taiwan and South Korea.[53] Corporatism in socialist states, however, might better be described by the term "socialist corporatism" to reflect the modifications made to accommodate a socialist context for corporatism.[54]

In its ideal form, state corporatism is a system wherein the state recognizes only one organization at the national level as representing the interests of all those in the organization's constituency. The state itself establishes almost all these associations, and membership may be compulsory for all those in the relevant constituency. In China (as in Taiwan), however, there are numerous exceptions to compulsory membership, especially for associations and societies that represent hobbies, charities, or support groups. Thus, membership in such groups as the Cooking Association, the Japan Society, the Stamp Collectors' Association, and the Anti-Cancer Support Association is voluntary. Not everyone who collects stamps has to join the Stamp Collectors' Association, but on the other hand, no philatelist can start an organization that competes with the officially organized one.

Another type of exception would be organizations that have strict requirements for membership. For example, membership in the All-China Writers and Artists Federation, which has branches for various fields, such

---

52. Frolic, "State-Led Civil Society," pp. 48–49.
53. Unger and Chan, "China, Corporatism, and the East Asian Model," pp. 31–32; and Unger, "Bridges," pp. 795–96.
54. Pearson, "The Janus Face of Business Associations in China," p. 33.

as drama, literature, and music, is considered a privilege, and certain benefits come with membership, such as travel funds and expedited access to passports. Those who choose not to join may be more independent of the party, but they also do not get the privileges of membership. The Writers and Artists Federation is controlled by the Party, and it reports directly to the Propaganda Department. A member whose writing or artwork is adjudged unacceptable to the association might lose his or her privileges, but rarely more.[55]

The organizations at the provincial, county, and local levels are merely lower branches of the national organization, if one exists. Examples are the national, or "peak," associations for education, wildlife protection, health, religion, various academic disciplines and charitable causes, the business association, the women's federation, the association for children's welfare, and the farmers' association.[56] There are never two competing organizations in one locality representing, say, textile manufacturers or healthcare or photography. This fact should not, however, obscure the point that in large cities such as Shanghai, there may be a photographers' society in every district of the city, and each may have a completely different relationship with the state.

An example of an unofficial, unregistered organization is the group of artists that formed the Beijing Yuanming Garden Arts Village in 1990. The group was banned in 1995. In abandoning the iron rice bowl and household registration to establish an artists' colony in unregistered residences in northwestern Beijing, the members of this group had sought freedom from official control over their artistic expression. At the time the organization was banned, it had 215 members.[57] Organizations suspected of advocating homosexuality have also been shut down, but there are many other ways of limiting the activities of a social organization, including the establishment of a party cell within it.[58] (Gays and lesbians still lack official organizations since homosexual practices are illegal; but in recent years, the state has generally taken a more benign, look-the-other-way approach. Because of the Internet and the proliferation of bars, nightclubs, restaurants, and discos in China's major cities, it is far easier for gays to meet and organize.)

---

55. Discussion with Bonnie S. McDougall, Feb. 1999.
56. Unger, "Bridges," p. 795.
57. Jin Yinong, "1995 yishu cun da taowang toushi."
58. Saich, "Negotiating the State," pp. 132–33.

"Peak" associations maintain a degree of autonomy from the state, but they do not (that is, they are not meant to) challenge the authority of the state. Indeed, they were created in large part to prevent more autonomous groups from arising to capture the interests and the members of a particular sector. The state insists that these associations exercise sufficient control over their members to implement state policies; yet at the same time, they often work with the state to shape policies relevant to their constituencies.[59]

China learned the basics of corporatism from the Soviets, although more recently it has come to understand it theoretically through Western writings.[60] China's national objective of promoting growth, socialism, and security assumed that "leaders and led, management and workers," would share a common mission in one harmonious whole.[61] This vision did not encompass the possibility of a serious conflict of interests between leaders and led or between labor and management. At the time liberalization began in 1978, in fact, there were only 103 national associations. Furthermore, most associations were organized in "politically safe" areas, such as the natural sciences, engineering, health, education, and recreation, and even then, they engaged in few if any activities.[62]

This model seemed to work in the early years of Communist Party control and a command economy, but as a result of the post-1978 economic reforms, which were intended to delegate power and improve productivity, the existing peak associations were inadequate to represent the newly emerging sectoral and private interests. The response of the Chinese government was to create more corporatist associations.

China's 1989 Regulations on the Registration of Social Organizations strictly prohibit more than one national association from representing any one sector. In theory, the state may exercise substantial control over each association—at least at the national level.[63] In 1998, these regulations were revised, and the resulting Provisional Regulations on the Registration of Non-Enterprise Units Established by Society required all associations

---

59. Unger and Chan, "China, Corporatism, and the East Asian Model," p. 30.
60. Zhang Jing, *Fatuan zhuyi.*
61. Unger and Chan, "China, Corporatism, and the East Asian Model," p. 37.
62. Pei, "Chinese Civic Associations," pp. 290–91.
63. China's Regulations on the Registration of Social Organizations are very similar to those in Taiwan, and to Japan's as well until recent years. That is, all social organizations must register, and they must be attached to a state organization in order to be registered (discussion with Tony Saich, Harvard University, Fairbank Center, seminar, Nov. 12, 1999).

to re-register with the Ministry of Civil Affairs.[64] New rules concerning funding from abroad were also promulgated. On the basis of these regulations, the State Council canceled, merged, and/or reorganized many associations,[65] although the reasons for this were not necessarily the result of official disapproval or purposeful efforts to impede the growth of civil society.[66] Nevertheless, out of fear that this was precisely what would happen, many reformers protested the regulations, particularly the requirement that each organization must have a sponsoring agency (*guakao danwei*), or "mother-in-law." They have argued that the sponsorship system wastes a lot of time and is difficult to maintain because the sponsors lack the wherewithal to fulfill their obligations. Their preference is that social organizations should only have to register with the appropriate department in the Ministry of Civil Affairs. Because of opposition by stronger forces within the government, however, these proposals were rejected.[67]

There are many ways in which organizations and interest groups may avoid official registration. One way is to register not as a social organization, for which there are stringent regulations, but as a business, which is very easy (although this is much more difficult since the 1998 regulations went into effect). Or, a group may qualify as a "secondary organization," that is, as part of something else. Thus, a group within a university, such as a research institute, does not have to register with the Ministry of Education. Similarly, a group may register as a "subsidiary" organization within a dormant or shell organization. This is a likely choice if the group has political goals. Finally, many groups, such as those affiliated with clans or local temples, do not register at all. Others organize as "clubs," "salons," or "forums," which, although illegal, are common in urban China.[68]

---

64. Human Rights in China, "China: Social Groups Seek Independence in a Regulatory Cage," p. 14.

65. For an example, see the figures for the merging or termination of civil associations in Guangdong given in Yang Bing and Zheng Yuqing, "Shetuan zhong xin dengji huanzheng."

66. For example, "the group may have run out of money, its members or officers may decide it is no longer needed, it may have been involved in fraudulent or other criminal activities, and so on" (Human Rights in China, "China: Social Groups Seek Independence in a Regulatory Cage," p. 21). This report gives examples of associations shut down precisely because they incurred official disapproval.

67. Saich, "Negotiating the State," pp. 129–31.

68. Ibid., pp. 134–35.

Ideally, associations function as "transmission belts" between state and society, although this more accurately describes the relationship of the state with the old-style, pre-reform "mass" organizations than with the associations of the reform period. The reformist state has delegated control to interest groups and associations, and they may be highly autonomous as long as the state is satisfied with their activities and role. The state's relationship to these groups is not, then, predicated on relinquishing, lessening, or. even strictly speaking, decentralizing control. Instead, the relationship is based on *more effective* control of society through the delegation of authority to associations. This, of course, is where the state faces a dilemma, for in order for civic associations to perform the roles the state has assigned to them, it has to tolerate the aggregation and articulation of members' interests, which may be incompatible with those of the state. For example, an association may propose policies or projects that would require the state to allocate greater resources to it, or a larger percentage of the budget to a particular sector, such as healthcare or education, than it would like; an economic association may want the state to change the tax structure to benefit its members; or an environmental association may want the state to undertake the protection of a species or flora that would interfere with the state's plan for, say, building dams.

Today, China has associations for ever more narrowly defined interest groups: the handicapped, associations for providing support to migrant workers, support groups for divorced women, abused women, and those with terminal illnesses, self-help groups, associations to find children and women who have been abducted, legal aid societies, associations for single people, and thousands of others. The government claims that 200,000 officially registered "social organizations" (*shetuan*) exist, and some believe there are at least that many unregistered associations. In any case, just because an organization is registered does not mean it is a puppet of the state.[69]

A specific example of an autonomous association pursuing interests that conflict with the state appeared in a legal case, in which the Flower Potters' Association sued the Bureau of Forestry, its official "sponsoring organization." The Flower Potters Association was founded in 1983 by a group of retired officials, experts in flower potting, and professors who love flowers and woodlands. It was registered as an independent association under the sponsorship of the Bureau of Forestry. In the case, the judges

---

69. Forney, "China: Voice of the People."

ruled that the Bureau of Forestry was "only the nominal leader of the Flower Potters' Association" and that the director of the bureau had violated the rights of this social organization by taking over the ownership and assets of the profitable *Potted Flower and Trees Magazine*, which was started by the association. The courts ordered the bureau to return the account books, funds, and administration of the magazine to the association.[70]

The autonomy of associations is also illustrated by the many women's groups that have sprung up at the local level to help women deal with the decline in their social position and economic opportunities that has occurred as fallout from the sexism accompanying China's economic liberalization. These groups run counseling services, telephone hotlines, and job retraining and job creation programs at the local level (as does the All-China Federation of Trade Unions). In doing so, they cut into the territory of the All-China Women's Federation, which is at the national level and more under the control of the state.[71]

The fact that China limits any particular sector or interest group to forming only one national association makes the rapid growth of associations since 1978 even more phenomenal, for it reflects just how diverse China has become. Or one could argue that it reflects how the Chinese are redefining themselves. Instead of seeing themselves as divided up into a mere hundred or so national associations as they did in 1978, liberalization has allowed them to see themselves as so complex that they need hundreds more national associations.

The membership of the associations may be just as important as their autonomy when measuring the strength of civil society. As Pei Minxin has concluded from his study of Chinese civic associations, those with a high

---

70. Unfortunately, although the courts' ruling was clear, within a few hours of issuing its "Notice of Implementation," the court received an oral notice from one leader in the provincial high court not to implement the ruling. This is really a commentary on the problems of implementation of judicial decisions, but in this case it obviously limited the rights of a social organization. See Hua Shi, "Yi quan kang fa qingfan shetuan liyi, liangji fayuan panjue wunai yiwei tingzhang" (Two court rulings can do nothing about a bureau director who violated the interests of a social organization and obstructed law with power), *Yanhuang chunqiu*, no. 71 (Feb. 1998): 38–40.

71. Gordon White et al., *In Search of Civil Society*; and Human Rights in China, "China: Social Groups Seek Independence in a Regulatory Cage," p. 8. Economic liberalization in most countries leads to a stronger position for women and less sexism, but in China's case, it has allowed an escape from policies that tried to enforce equal treatment of the sexes, a policy that was at odds with China's traditional culture.

percentage of corporate members (largely state-owned units) may have a lower degree of "civic density" because such associations are most concerned with the interests of their large group members, not the "civic needs" of individual members. At the national level, certain types of associations, such as business and trade associations, tend to have more group members, but at each successive lower level (moving down to the provincial, municipal, and county or district associations), individual memberships become increasingly dominant. Associations in the arts, education, and health, on the other hand, tend to have largely, or exclusively, individual members.[72]

State Control Versus Autonomy

Associations in China span the range from state-controlled to fairly autonomous. Although initially each association was assigned to the control of the relevant bureaucracy, over time associations have increasingly come to act "as sectoral representatives somewhat separate from the state."[73] The result is organizations that are at least minimally, and sometimes almost completely, independent of state control.[74] Moreover, the state itself encourages substantial autonomy, in part because the state already has its hands full and in part because most associations do not threaten the state. One exception is the trade unions, which, before they were brought under the state's control in the 1950s and again since the rise of Solidarity in Poland in the 1980s, have been seen as a potential threat to Chinese Communist Party rule. But the state views trade unions in certain types of enterprises (such as foreign-funded ones) as contributing to its stability and strength.

Regional and local branches of national associations also tend to push for greater autonomy in order to promote their own local interests, regardless of the preferences of the national association. The leaders of these lower-level associations are under significant pressure from the enterprises and constituencies they oversee to lobby on their behalf at both the local and the national level. Furthermore, their predilection is to protect regional and local resources from appropriation by the state above, but at the same time they have to prevent resources from being destroyed by the enterprises under

---

72. Pei, "Chinese Civic Associations," pp. 296–98, 306–7.

73. Unger and Chan, "China, Corporatism, and the East Asian Model," pp. 38–89.

74. Vivienne Shue, "State Power and Social Organization in China"; and Pearson, "The Janus Face of Business Associations in China." See also Pearson, *China's New Business Elite.*

their control. In this respect, China's state corporatist associations are slowly developing into societal corporatist associations.[75]

Where there is collusion, including corruption, between elements of civil society and local government officials for mutual benefit, it is sometimes referred to as "local corporatism." The ambivalent relationship between associations and the state exists in part because local government officials sit on the boards of local associations. Local officials often see it in their interest to promote local entrepreneurs in order to enhance economic development, even though they may pollute the environment,[76] produce dangerous or defective products, destroy scarce resources, or do little to fulfill the state's objectives. The end result is that private actors, such as businesses, work in an alliance with the state at the *local* level in order to enhance their autonomy vis-à-vis the *central* state.[77] The growing autonomy of "civil society," then, reflects the increasing ability of private citizens or enterprises to collude with the lower levels of the state bureaucracy to promote their interests in opposition to the upper levels of the state. In all too many cases, this greater autonomy has actually harmed the overall interests of the community while enriching the few.

In short, much like the gentry of imperial China, who aided the central government in local governance, the leaders of associations have divided loyalties. They may be officials of the Party or the state, but they are also members of the local community. They must live with the results of their policies, and they know that they are the ones who have to bear the brunt of their constituents' frustrations and anger. To do otherwise can mean that the local membership of an association neither respects nor obeys its leaders. Such an association therefore does not effectively perform its role of either representing or regulating its members.

A good example of an organization whose leaders are torn between loyalty to the center and the interests of the association is the Self-Employed Laborers' Association (SELA; Geti laodongzhe xiehui). SELA was estab-

---

75. Unger and Chan, "China, Corporatism, and the East Asian Model," pp. 48, 50, 52.

76. According to Professor Qu Geping, chair of the Environment Committee in the National People's Congress, the town and village enterprises, in which 140 million people are involved, account for 50 percent of overall industrial production in China, but also for much of the pollution. By 1999, the Ministry of the Environment had shut down over 60,000 of these enterprises (Qu Geping, Harvard University Committee on Environment: China Project Seminar, Apr. 16, 1999).

77. Wank, "Private Business, Bureaucracy, and Political Alliance in a Chinese City," p. 70.

lished by the government in 1986 and is strictly controlled by the Bureau for Industry and Commerce. The leaders of the organization are picked by the government, and its operations are heavily subsidized by the government.[78] Membership is compulsory and enrollment in the organization is automatic for every individual petty entrepreneur (*getihu*) who obtains a business permit. This includes the operators of stalls or pushcarts, as well as the owners of small family craft or service businesses such as repair shops and small restaurants. By the end of 1992, SELA had close to 25 million members, all of whom were officially licensed.[79] (Many small entrepreneurs operate without a permit and thus do not join the association. This no doubt reflects the questionable legality of their enterprises as much as, or perhaps more than, it does a desire to escape government control.)

Some Chinese argue that associations that not only represent the interests of small business owners but also control them are essential if society is to be even partially protected against the more rapacious entrepreneurs. Whether it is entrepreneurs who acquire marble for sale by blasting the side of a mountain into thousands of useless fragments or those who whip up cosmetics in the kitchen sink that cause serious rashes, sell defective or illegal or falsely labeled products, use old and very polluting technology, divert water from rivers and cause them to dry up, or dynamite streams to kill all the fish, including thousands that are too small to eat—all too many simply do not obey the law. In short, however useful associations may be for aggregating and articulating public (and private) interests, they also protect society against the worst abuses of the unharnessed individual. Associations do more than help expand the "public space" of civil society; they also help control those who really need to be controlled.

Associations such as SELA promote social order, but they also articulate the interests of individual entrepreneurs to higher authorities, thereby serving the interests of both civil society and the state. SELA officials do want the petty entrepreneurs in their organization to do well, for the growth of the private sector under their supervision enhances their official status and simultaneously increases financial support for the local government. For the many petty entrepreneurs and workers from the countryside who have re-

---

78. Unger and Chan, "China, Corporatism, and the East Asian Model," pp. 39–40. They note that this is the same way in which associations are set up in Taiwan.

79. Pearson, "The Janus Face of Business Associations in China," pp. 44–45; and Unger, "Bridges," pp. 796–98.

cently migrated to the cities and lack *guanxi*, SELA supplies a sort of ready-made organizational *guanxi*.[80] (Unofficial associations of people from the same province or locality are well established in the cities. Although migrant entrepreneurs are often exploited by these mafia-like organizations, they also provide the essential *guanxi* to get them started in a new city.) Somewhat ironically, China's entrepreneurs must deal with local government officials much more frequently than those living in the cocoon of the state-owned *danwei*; for they lack the state support offered by the *danwei* and need to pay taxes and apply for licenses and permits. More so than members of *danwei*, they have to rely on the services provided by the state sector directly to their enterprises and themselves (security, sanitation, transportation, and so on). These constant interactions with the bureaucracy have made entrepreneurs far more politically active. Indeed, although it was the government that insisted that all entrepreneurs and independent businessmen join SELA, the association has become a powerful lobby representing the collective interests of China's new entrepreneurial class. An even more important membership benefit is the access the association offers to "the vertical, informal clientelism embedded in these associations"—channels through which SELA members "can develop or draw on existing *guanxi*."[81]

Paradoxically, then, business entrepreneurs—who can claim considerable autonomy vis-à-vis the state—have done little to assert that independence. Instead, they view officials as essential to their success, not a hindrance to it, and "try to *rebuild* informal ties to the state."[82] Much like the employees of a *danwei*, they find that developing ties with local officials through banqueting, the provision of goods and services, and gift-giving is essential to their success.[83] In short, clientelism coexists with corporatism and is, in fact, an essential part of it.

The state's purpose in establishing SELA was not, of course, to encourage entrepreneurs to make trouble but to link enterprises to the state. The assumption is that both state and society benefit from this link: the association will represent its members' interests, but it will also help enforce mem-

---

80. Unger, "Bridges," p. 801; Nevitt, "Private Business Associations in China," pp. 35, 37–38; and Oi, "Fiscal Reform and the Economic Foundations of Local State Corporatism in China."

81. Pearson, *China's New Business Elite*, p. 135.

82. Ibid., pp. 4, 113.

83. Shi, *Political Participation in Beijing*.

bers' compliance with government regulations. Although at times the state's control may seem to outbalance the association's autonomy, the general trend seems to be toward autonomy. Local SELA branches tend to support their members' objectives, such as the demand for benefits like those available to workers in state-owned *danwei*, a better wholesaling network, broader access to municipal services, or protection from unregistered entrepreneurs; they may even defend members against the higher levels of the state.[84]

The balance between control and autonomy shifts even more in favor of the latter in smaller cities and towns, where there are fewer powerful state officials in charge of associations than in a city like Beijing. The same is true of associations whose members are powerful in their own right, such as the All-China Federation of Industry and Commerce. Its members are large, wealthy, and powerful businesspeople and businesses who *voluntarily* join the federation, and the Federation's board consists of businesspeople, not officials.[85]

How much autonomy any given association achieves depends on many factors. Perhaps the most important are its leaders and their political connections. Retired cadres, if they still have significant ties with those in power, and politically influential cadres are more likely to increase the power and autonomy of the associations they lead. The China Disabled Persons' Federation, for example, probably owes much of its success in pushing for the rights of the disabled to the fact that it is headed by Deng Xiaoping's son, Deng Pufang.[86]

It is not necessary, however, to see all association leaders as torn in their loyalties. In many respects the government wants them to be responsive toward the members of the organizations they head. This was the state's purpose in establishing the two federations of associations that replaced China's industrial ministries when they were abolished in 1993 and the fourteen corporatist industrial associations that replaced Shanghai's fourteen industrial bureaus when they were abolished in 1992. By replacing ministries and bureaus with corporatist associations, the state hoped to focus on the concerns

---

84. Unger, "Bridges," pp. 801–11.

85. Ibid., pp. 802–11. In a study of the All-China Federation of Industry and Commerce in Tianjin, Nevitt ("Private Business Associations in China," pp. 30–31) arrived at similar conclusions but felt that the SELA did little to advance the interests of the petty entrepreneurs.

86. Human Rights in China, "China: Social Groups Seek Independence in a Regulatory Cage," p. 10.

of a privatized sphere within each industrial sector, thereby undermining top-down state control.[87] The state went even further with the National Association of Light Industries, which it broke into some fifty corporate associations that represent the specialized interests of industrial groups. As these and other associations become even more specialized and divided into sub-associations, they move further from state control.

Civil Society and Work Units, Associations, and the Government

In China, the same corporatist institutional relationships prevail between urban work units and the state as between associations and the state. When these two corporatist structures—associations and work units—meet, however, they do little to enhance each other's autonomy against the state. According to Tianjian Shi, in a system still based largely on the work unit, associations, including trade unions, find it difficult to band together across work units to pursue common interests. Workers identify with their own work unit, not with broader categories of people in their same position, such as would be represented in an association or interest group. This is because the government allocates resources to the work unit. Were textile workers to band together *across* work units to gain more resources for their profession, the results would not necessarily benefit the specific work unit of any particular participant. Even if the employees of one unit were to lobby the government for more resources, the individual employees who had pressured the government for those resources would not necessarily benefit; for once the resources are allocated to a specific work unit, it is still up to its officials to distribute them as they see fit. Thus, it is more rational for employees to focus their efforts on the officials of their own work unit.[88]

The work unit's finite pool of resources and its inability to increase that pool creates a zero-sum situation: once the unit's officials distribute resources to one employee, they are no longer available for others. A group-based strategy for articulating interests is therefore not rational. As a result, employees act as individuals in competition with other employees: if one employee successfully cultivates *guanxi* with an official and gets a two-bedroom apartment, that resource is no longer available to others. This puts pressure on other members of the unit to similarly give gifts, entertain, and

---

87. Unger and Chan, "China, Corporatism, and the East Asian Model," pp. 42–43.
88. Shi, *Political Participation in Beijing*.

exchange favors with work unit officials so as to stake a claim on the limited available goods. This work unit–based "patron-client" strategy is highly personalized, can become increasingly expensive, and easily slides into corrupt behavior. Political participation is affected by an institutional design that builds bribery into this top-down redistributional system. In addition, rather than encouraging cooperation with others in the work unit to aggregate and articulate broader collective concerns, it sets employees against each other. In this sense, political participation in the work units is inherently anti-democratic. Nevertheless, Shi concluded from his study of political participation that workers in Beijing had a strong sense of efficacy, at least at the local level of the work unit. Since most decisions important in their daily lives are taken at this level, this sense of political efficacy is very important.[89]

Reforms have, however, led to the closing of many state-owned enterprises and the dissolution of their associated work units. The market and the government have taken over the distribution of benefits that were once the prerogative of work-unit officials. The knock-on effect has been the elimination of the power of work-unit officials and, along with this, the elimination of a major source of corruption. This structural change allowed people's interests to be organized in more modern, cross-sectional groups.[90] This could be a major impetus for the growth of civil society.

Cultural Constraints on the Growth of Civil Society

Because civil society is made up of that part of society which is both non-governmental *and* non-familial, its development in China has been impaired by the continued emphasis within society on the family. Indeed, most of China's self-employed are running *family* businesses. As in southern Italy[91] and so many developing countries, the preference in China is for businesses based on family ties, especially in the countryside. In the cities, businesses may be extended beyond the family on the basis of *guanxi*, personalistic relationships that are themselves often based on family ties. As noted in Chapter 4, it is rare for a business to move beyond personal ties based on "trust" to

---

89. Ibid.; and Tang and Parish, *Chinese Urban Life Under Reform.*
90. Shi, *Political Participation in Beijing;* and Tang and Parish, *Chinese Urban Life Under Reform.*
91. Putnam, *Making Democracy Work.*

employ outsiders, which, along with regulations limiting size, has kept Chinese businesses small by comparison with those in much of the West.

Neither communist ideology nor an authoritarian state can explain why China prefers personal and corporatist relationships to those of a "civil society." What is missing from the explanation is China's culture, with its strongly authoritarian strains. Culture is deeply embedded in China's institutions, and it is not easy for business associations to escape its hold.

Each half of the clientelism-corporatism marriage has a deeply rooted legacy in China. The use of informal personal ties existed not only prior to 1949, but has also pervaded the post-1949 context in conjunction with the formal authority relations of neo-traditionalism. The Janus-like pattern that underlies socialist corporatism is rooted in a long history of merchant-government ties. Indeed, the post-Mao government's corporatist strategy can be conceived of as an attempt to have business serve the same function—aiding economic development while controlling the political role of merchants—as it did in the Qing period, and as the state-sponsored guilds did in the Nationalist era.[92]

Culture is also deeply rooted in the family, whose members tend to be distrustful of those outside the family and who favor the promotion of family members above all others, regardless of competence, fairness, or even legality.

Chinese Confucianism . . . does not legitimate deference to the authority of an all-powerful state that leaves no scope for the development of an independent civil society. If civil society is weak in China, that weakness is due not to a statist ideology, but rather to the strong familism that is basic to Chinese culture, and the consequent reluctance of the Chinese to trust people outside of their kinship groups.[93]

Those who think political reform alone will bring democracy to China are, therefore, overlooking the critical role of the family and culture in maintaining an authoritarian and patriarchal system.

Whereas interference by the state through corporatism may cut into civil society from the top down, the family's closing in on civil society from the bottom up may be just as important; for families, in order to protect their business from intervention by the state, cultivate what are, or verge on, corrupt relationships with officials; officials become rent-seekers (that is, they essentially steal resources generated in the public sector, such as oil, electric-

---

92. Pearson, *China's New Business Elite*, pp. 142–43.
93. Fukuyama, "Confucianism and Democracy," p. 28.

ity, water, former communal property, or the property of former state-owned enterprises). For the right price, officials pass these on to individuals in the private sector. Alternatively, families and clans may even resort to forming underground ("black") societies and use illegal methods, as well as violence, to protect and advance their interests.[94]

Because of the distorted manner in which the central role of the family plays out in China and because of the culture's emphasis on the authority and dominant role of the state, Chinese culture hinders the development of civil society. Until associations can prove they are effective in protecting the interests of their individual members, family-run enterprises will continue to count on the culturally reliable technique of influencing officials to get what they want. (Of course, much of what happens in clientelist relationships is not technically illegal, for the laws are not entirely clear, and the culture condones it.[95] Hence, to label the relationship between businessmen or families and officials "corrupt" is not necessarily correct.)

One final cultural dimension to the problems faced in creating consensual groups that have the power to confront the state with their demands has been the tendency of Chinese to fight among themselves and to coalesce in personalistic factions that promote their own individual interests.[96] This tendency was no doubt exacerbated by decades of repeated "struggle sessions," "criticism/self-criticism sessions," "anti-rightist campaigns," and "class struggle"—all of which aggravated the predisposition not to trust those outside a small circle of friends, family, and others tied in by *guanxi*. It explains why clientelism has been favored over corporatism as a protective strategy as well as a strategy for personal advancement.

---

94. Xiao, "Reconstructing China's Civil Society," pp. 6–7. An investigation by a consumer organization of a gang in Hei'an County, Fujian, found that the gang was threatening local people's property and lives; the investigation led to their arrest (see Xiong Fenxi, "Analysis of Consumer Complaints in 1998 Received by This Periodical").

95. For example, *guandao*—official profiteering—was not regarded as corrupt in the early reform period. Further, nepotism is rife in China, in spite of the promulgation of laws in 1996 to regulate it. Sometimes, the percentage of staff in a ministry or provincial agency who are related in some fashion to one another is as high as 75 percent (Xiaobo Lu, *Cadres and Corruption*, pp. 180–82, 202).

96. Friedman, *The Politics of Democratization*, p. 29. Friedman is pointing to the lack of a national consensus, or an even more narrowly defined community consensus, as the basis for people working together in groups.

Trade Unions

The proposition that the dismantling of the institutions of a command economy may help create a favorable environment for the growth of civil society is aptly illustrated in China's labor sector.[97] The government's willingness to negotiate with more autonomous workers' associations arose from changes in the labor market due to economic decentralization. The state has created associations to represent independent, self-employed entrepreneurs coping with the developing, non-state-owned, market economy, but it has also encouraged trade unions to harness *unorganized*, and potentially dangerous, workers. The greater autonomy accorded trade unions, however, illustrates the need for the state both to negotiate with and to control *organized*, and potentially dangerous, workers in the state-owned sector.

Trade unions in China exemplify the complex relationship evolving between the state and the growing associational society. Before the reform period, the interests of workers were seen as identical to those of the party-state; workers in state-owned enterprises, it was held, did not need autonomous organizations to represent their interests vis-à-vis state-appointed management. By the 1990s, that view had changed, and the state was gradually relaxing its control over labor unions. Unions could "negotiate"[98] for improved working conditions and welfare benefits. In fact, workers felt they had to fight for their rights because, with economic reform, managers signed contracts with the state that pressured them to increase productivity and profits even at the workers' expense. Faced with the end of the iron rice bowl, and with it the possibility of unemployment and the elimination of pensions, workers began to demand greater organizational autonomy. The state was caught in a bind: it wanted profitable enterprises, but it could not risk millions of workers taking to the streets to protest working conditions. The re-

----

97. Rose, "Rethinking Civil Society," p. 23.

98. My use of the term "negotiate" is not meant to imply that China's trade unions come to the bargaining table with independent status and power in some sense equivalent with the government's. Rather, the government has had to make concessions to the trade unions because of its need to placate disgruntled workers who threaten to strike, demonstrate, and cause major societal upheaval unless some of their demands are met. Because of the extraordinarily large numbers of workers angered by the negative effects of economic liberalization, the government cannot simply use force to maintain order. It must also make concessions. Hence "negotiations."

sult was that the state turned to the trade unions to resolve the conflicts between workers and management.[99]

The government also realized, as a result of workers' efforts to create autonomous unions during and after the Tiananmen Square demonstrations of 1989, that it needed to accede to some of the demands of an increasingly anxious and unhappy workforce to avoid greater labor unrest. In short, the Party needed the support of the unions as well as a means to control them.[100] After 1989, the Party and the unions developed a symbiotic relationship—the trade unions continued to support the Party in exchange for greater input into policymaking and greater negotiating power in the enterprise.[101]

From the perspective of the All-China Federation of Trade Unions (ACFTU), the economic reforms that threatened the workers' well-being brought it into conflict with the state. Under pressure from the workers, the ACFTU sought to represent their interests and to attain organizational autonomy by confronting the state. The ACFTU's bargaining on behalf of the workers should be viewed as a pragmatic policy to maintain its power as a major national peak association. It was created by the state yet bargains on the workers' behalf "against" the state.[102]

Both workers and their unions are increasingly successful in confrontations with management. Individual workers who use arbitration to settle a grievance have a better than 50:50 chance of winning a case against a state enterprise.[103] Factory trade unions can improve their chances of negotiating successfully with the state, a state-owned enterprise, or even a privately owned factory if they apply for and receive independent corporate legal status. This newly available status makes unions legally equivalent to factories: a factory may not, for example, appropriate the trade union's fund as

---

99. Yunqiu Zhang, "From State Corporatism to Social Representation," pp. 128, 133–34.

100. Ironically, the 1989 demonstrations illustrate the frequent overlap between the official and the unofficial that makes it difficult to discern to what degree an association is truly autonomous from the state. For example, during the demonstrations, the Beijing Workers Autonomous Union required those workers who wanted to join it to be regular employees of one of the city's state-controlled work units—this in spite of the fact that the whole purpose of developing an independent unit was to protest to, if not against, the state. The same was true for the more than twenty autonomous workers associations that sprouted in nineteen of China's provinces at that time (Perry, "Labor's Battle for Political Space," p. 317).

101. Ng and Warner, China's Trade Unions and Management, pp. 57–58.

102. Jiang Kaiwen, "Gonghui yu dang-guojiade chongtu."

103. Ng and Warner, China's Trade Unions and Management, table 4.1: "Settlement of Labour Disputes Accepted and Handled by Labour Arbitration Committees in the PRC."

part of the factory's property. The willingness of trade unions to use laws passed by the National People's Congress to bring suits against management[104] is another indication of the growing power of organized workers vis-à-vis the state—and the willingness of the state to negotiate with workers who have been treated unfairly within a legal framework that the state itself created. In short, the state has recognized the power that workers have to challenge the party-state, and it is trying to work with the associations that represent workers to avoid conflict and maintain stability.

On the other hand, the power of a trade union in a factory that the state is planning to, or already has sold, to the collective or private sector, or that the state has declared bankrupt, is virtually nil. This is in part because the ACFTU agreed to layoffs of redundant workers necessitated by economic reforms as part of a quid pro quo for other state concessions to workers, including the 1994 Labor Law, which took the ACFTU ten years to negotiate with the state and led to the initiation of the five-day work week in 1995. Other results of the shifting relationship between the state and the ACFTU were the Regulation of the Minimum Wage in Enterprises and improvement of mine safety.[105]

The Labor Law gave trade unions the right to oversee labor contracts within their respective enterprises and to intervene to protect workers' interests if employers cancel or break contracts without justification. Additionally, trade unions represent workers in negotiations and dispute mediation over wages, vacations, and labor safety, as well as in such matters as workmen's compensation and insurance.[106] The Labor Law also gave workers the right not to work (essentially, to go on strike) if their safety was at risk and required that foreign-owned enterprises allow trade unions to be established.[107]

Thus, in the 1990s, the ACFTU changed from a top-down transmission belt focused on control to a two-way transmission belt. Although it still carries out state-assigned objectives, it pushes for its own independently deter-

---

104. Other regulations, such as the Regulation of Minimum Wages in Enterprises, also now provide a basis for workers bringing legal action; see Qin, "How Can the Funds of a Trade Union Be Forcibly Transferred?"; and State Council Information Office, "Progress in the China's Human Rights' Cause in 1996."

105. State Council Information Office, "Progress in China's Human Rights' Cause in 1996."

106. Yunqiu Zhang, "From State Corporatism to Social Representation," p. 140.

107. Howell, "Trade Unions in China," pp. 161–62.

mined objectives. Economic reforms have, moreover, forced the ACFTU, like so many organizations in China that had been dependent on state funding and (inadequate) membership dues, to find new financing. As a result, the ACFTU has become involved in raising money to pay for the increased welfare benefits it promised to workers. Trade unions at lower levels within the ACFTU now run their own enterprises to raise money. By the end of 1995, 138,000 ACFTU-run enterprises were generating a significant amount of income to fund the ACFTU's activities.[108] This has produced the paradoxical situation in which worker unions have become *managers* of workers. A reputedly state-run organization, the ACFTU, which was originally created in order that the party-state could control the workers, now runs its own enterprises, which are neither state-owned nor state-controlled. Overall, the ACFTU has gained greater autonomy from the state as a result of its greater financial independence.

Equally important is the increased control that members of some local trade unions now exercise over their own officials. For example, in many of the trade unions at the enterprise level in the city of Qingdao, enterprise trade union presidents are no longer appointed. Instead, they are directly elected by workers in the enterprise. Furthermore, because the management-responsibility system has removed the Party from administrative affairs, and because workers are interested almost solely in material benefits, not ideology, the leaders of Communist Party committees are essentially ignored.[109]

As the government has steadily decentralized and rationalized administration, bureau-level trade unions have been eliminated in some cities. Federations of local-level trade unions in enterprises within the same industrial sector have emerged in their place in such broad sectors as chemicals, light industry, textiles, and heavy machinery. These federations are far more independent than were their smaller predecessors. And, of course, their larger size makes them far more powerful vis-à-vis both enterprise management and the state.[110]

---

108. Ng and Warner, *China's Trade Unions and Management*, pp. 57–58; and data from p. 40, which are based on ACFTU statistics published in 1996. See also Howell, "Trade Unions in China," p. 164.

109. Yunqiu Zhang, "From State Corporatism to Social Representation," pp. 138–39.

110. Based on Yunqiu Zhang's (ibid., p. 139) study of labor unions in the two cities of Weifang and Chanzhou.

Trade union federations are among the many associations that have used the "transmission belt" to their advantage: the party-state needs them to mobilize their members to carry out its goals, particularly because it cannot count on local governments to carry out its policies.[111] As a result, these associations can negotiate trade-offs with the state in exchange for compliance.

Trade Unions in Foreign-Funded Enterprises

Economic liberalization led not only to dramatic changes in the forms of ownership but also to new categories of workers in China: migrant laborers, workers in foreign enterprises (joint ventures), and town and village enterprise workers were added to the existing categories of peasants and workers in state-owned enterprises. At the beginning of liberalization, however, no organization represented these new categories of laborers.[112] For example, some 20 million new workers in village and township enterprises were until recently peasants tilling the soil, and some 15 million workers formerly employed in state-owned enterprises are now employed by foreign-funded and private enterprises. Many have been angered by their treatment and have resorted to industrial actions. Typical of the problems they face are late payments of wages, job insecurity (most are hired on short-term contracts), appalling working conditions, and inadequate housing.[113]

Some of China's workers in non-state-owned enterprises where no trade unions exist have joined unofficial or underground workers' organizations, as have those who have been laid off because of economic reforms; but they also may join if they feel they are being exploited. The latter is the case with workers in many of the foreign-run companies in the Free Enterprise Zones in the coastal areas. Underground workers organizations have even hired gangsters to take care of their grievances with exploitative managers. They use far cruder tactics than the branches of the ACFTU—including violence against employers and destruction of employers' property.[114] Finally, unofficial and underground unions are even organizing workers to protest against economic reforms that adversely affect workers' benefits in state enterprises.

---

111. Saich, "Negotiating the State," p. 140.
112. Howell, "Trade Unions in China," p. 152.
113. Ng and Warner, *China's Trade Unions and Management*, p. 53.
114. Gordon White, "Chinese Trade Unions in the Transition from Socialism," pp. 29–32.

The desire of local governments to attract foreign investment has tended to outweigh any concerns local officials might have to protect and advance workers' interests. The last thing they want is for workers to make demands that will drive foreign investment away. Foreign businesspeople (most of whom are from Hong Kong or Taiwan) may introduce efficient capitalist-style management, but their enterprises are often little more than sweatshops. Workers in these enterprises are, in fact, far more likely to suffer from exploitative labor practices than the workers in China's state-owned enterprises. A study of foreign-funded enterprises in Qingdao, for example, noted that they did not pay overtime, did not provide safety equipment, did not sign contracts that specified terms of employment, and had even revived once-common practices of corporal punishment and personal humiliation (including strip searches) as methods to control workers. Since foreign-funded enterprises have no party committees to discipline workers, labor militancy in response to these conditions is more common in them than in state-owned enterprises. Thus, it was in the state's interest to set up trade unions to act as mediators in foreign-funded companies.[115]

In part, the success of trade unions in the foreign-funded sector may be attributed to the fact that over time their leaders have come to be elected on an annual basis by union members. Because these unions no longer have party committees and can sometimes enlist the support of the local government in disputes with management, they have gained significant autonomy to negotiate with management. This does not worry the state, since it helps stabilize labor-management relations in the potentially explosive foreign-funded sector.[116]

In short, even the development of almost completely autonomous associations in the labor sector has not necessarily led to confrontation with the state. Indeed, the state sees their development as essential to cope with the problems introduced with economic liberalization and has viewed this advance of civil society as a non-zero-sum game, in which both the state and the society win.

---

115. Yunqiu Zhang, "From State Corporatism to Social Representation," p. 142; Howell, "Trade Unions in China," p. 150.

116. Zhang, "From State Corporatism to Social Representation," pp. 143–45.

Associations for Enterprises with Foreign Investment

In addition to establishing trade unions in some foreign-funded enterprises, in 1987 the Chinese government established the China Association for Enterprises with Foreign Investment (CAEFI) as a national or peak association, with 40 subassociations below the national level. Members usually represent groups (the enterprises), not individuals; most individual members are Chinese, not foreign. They function much like chambers of commerce in a capitalist state. (Indeed, the American Chamber of Commerce, located in China's largest cities, no doubt serves as a model.) At the national level, CAEFI has deep ties with the Chinese state, especially with the Ministry of Foreign Trade and Economic Relations. At lower levels, it is often local officials who have founded the associations. At both the national and local levels, the association is mainly self-funding, although this does not necessarily translate into greater autonomy. Furthermore, at both the national and branch levels, CAEFI has an "interlocking directorate" of serving or retired officials from the ministry and CAEFI managers. This arrangement may interfere with CAEFI's ability to redress problems, but these personnel links with the government do facilitate CAEFI's ability to achieve such objectives as attracting more foreign investment.[117]

CAEFI associations do, moreover, thwart many of the state's attempts to interfere with the operations of foreign-funded enterprises, especially at the local level where the enterprises are actually located. Nevertheless, because the CAEFI associations are made up of businesspersons who benefit from many of the state's policies to promote a strong business environment, they are in general not "anti-statist."[118] In short, the efforts of CAEFI associations to become more autonomous do not necessarily put it in conflict with the state.

Through new types of trade unions, then, China's workers have gradually gained the right to negotiate with their employers, whether they are private, collective, foreign-invested, or state firms. Their success has no doubt contributed to the rapidly growing number of labor disputes.[119] In turn, China's new types of employers—private, collective, foreign-invested, and town and

---

117. Pearson, "The Janus Face of Business Associations in China," pp. 37–38.
118. Ibid., pp. 39–42.
119. In 1993, China had a reported 12,358 labor disputes, an increase of 50 percent over 1992 (Pei, "Racing Against Time," p. 20).

village enterprises—have also gained more autonomy from the state through participation in associations. Like the workers, the employers' associational relationship with the state is often one of mutual advantage.

DEMOCRACY AND A MULTIPLICITY
OF ASSOCIATIONS

The proliferation of interest groups is not necessarily a sign of the growth of a civil society or a more democratic society. The autonomy of associations in civil society must have limits:

A hyperactive, confrontational, and relentlessly rent-seeking civil society can overwhelm a weak, penetrated state with the diversity and magnitude of its demands, leaving little in the way of a truly "public" sector concerned with the overall welfare of society. [Civil society] must be autonomous from the state, but not alienated from it. It must be watchful but respectful of state authority.[120]

George Soros adopts the same perspective in his *Crisis of Global Capitalism: Open Society Endangered*, which was translated into Chinese and widely read by intellectuals concerned with reforming China. Soros argued that there is no guarantee that the "collapse of a closed society" will lead "to the establishment of an open society; on the contrary, it may lead to the breakdown of authority and the disintegration of society. A weak state may be as much of a threat to an open society as an authoritarian state."[121] To focus exclusively on the development of interest groups or associational pluralism may, then, distort our understanding of democratic change in China. It is arguably more important to consider whether these groups, even as they are proliferating and growing in autonomy, are also weakening the state to the point at which it can no longer effectively govern.

---

120. Diamond, "Rethinking Civil Society," pp. 5, 14–15.

121. George Soros, *The Crisis of Global Capitalism: Open Society Endangered* (New York: Public Affairs Press, 1998), pp. 69–70; quoted in Cheng Li, "Promises and Pitfalls of Reform," pp. 126–27. As Marie-Claire Bergère concludes in *The Golden Age of the Chinese Bourgeoisie* (Cambridge, Eng.: Cambridge University Press, 1989), the attempt of Shanghai's bourgeoisie in the early twentieth century to turn increased associational autonomy "into a viable civil society" failed as much because of "the weakness of the central state" as it did because of their own weakness as a class (as cited in Davis, "Introduction: Urban China," in idem et al., *Urban Spaces in Contemporary China*, p. 17*n*28).

The view that a weak state is not the best breeding ground for a strong civil society is exemplified by the Soviet Union, where the rapid weakening of the Soviet party-state at first appeared to advance the creation of a civil society significantly. It quickly became evident, however, that civil society could not survive the collapse of party-state institutions.[122] The seventy-year-old legacy of socialism and the replacement of a fairly strong state with a web of interpersonal networks dedicated to their own interests and not to those of society at large proved detrimental to the development of a civil society and thus of democracy.

The presence of a decrepit state structure—one whose offices can be bought or co-opted by private interests—engenders patterns of interest organization that deviate sharply from those associated with a normal civil society. . . . The organizations of civil society must enjoy independence from the state in order to function normally, but state institutions also must possess a degree of autonomy if they are to respond to demands in a manner that encourages pluralist competition.[123]

In short, a multiplication of interest groups does not necessarily add up to a strong civil society. The state may be weakened by them, but not in a way that benefits society as a whole. And because the most powerful interest groups are likely to be funded by the wealthier segments of society (or large numbers of not so wealthy people, such as retired persons or trade union members), the interests of individuals unable to organize into a powerful association tend to be neglected. Moreover, individuals and groups burdened by the practices and institutions of an authoritarian society, which require negotiating complex bureaucracies in order to obtain licenses, permissions, resources, and access, may find it difficult to participate effectively in an emerging pluralistic society. For them, "informal collusion" or clientelism may be a better tactic than organizing interest groups and associations.[124]

---

122. On comparisons of China and the Soviet Union (and Russia), see Nolan, *China's Rise, Russia's Fall*, pp. 236–41.

123. Fish, "Rethinking Civil Society," pp. 33–34. As Fish (p. 41) notes, "Unfortunately, those actors who are best equipped to forge civil-societal organizations—from the president in Moscow to activists on the local level—have often proven more effective as orators and pamphleteers than as organizers. Xenophobes, nationalist demagogues, religious fanatics, criminal bosses, and other champions of anticivil parochialization have, at least since the downfall of communism, taken problems of organization and mobilization far more seriously."

124. Schmitter, "Interest Systems and the Consolidation of Democracies," pp. 169, 172. Illiya Harik ("Rethinking Civil Society," p. 48) notes that in Arab countries, their "most 'mod-

In the absence of strong state institutions to protect collective societal interests, the development of too many associations, each fighting for its own interests, may hinder China's democratic development. If competing associations have no loyalty to the state as a collective whole, only a strong state can avoid the corrosive impact of the uncontrolled expression of their narrowly based self-interests. On the other hand, a strong state (which is willing to relinquish strong centralized control over the society) can protect weaker associations and unorganized societal elements against more powerful associations, thereby maintaining some degree of social equilibrium and order. In China's case, its state institutions may be disintegrating faster than new ones are being constructed to replace them, with the result that society is becoming increasingly ungovernable.[125] And, the less able the government is to control China, the less likely it will tolerate the growth of more autonomous associations that threaten its control. Nevertheless, the state may still have enough residual control to give China a better long-term chance of developing democracy than Russia and the former Soviet republics have had.

Whereas individuals and members of small organizations are still inclined to rely on family ties and patron-client relationships, Chinese associations with large memberships are becoming increasingly effective in using political means to achieve their goals. Furthermore, interest groups and associations are being forced to turn increasingly to private financing; and this necessarily gives the wealthier organizations more clout. For example, in conflicts between environmentalists and private entrepreneurs in business associations, the power of the purse often favors business. The problem is aggravated by the fact that local leaders responsible for both business development and for implementation of environmental controls tend to favor business because of the tax revenues generated by business. In some cases, however, pressures from environmentalists on the government have led to serious action, such as the shutting down since 1996 of hundreds of small paper factories that had proliferated as a result of economic liberalization.[126]

---

ern' associations—business groups, labor unions, professional and intellectual societies—*show little or no interest in democratization*" (italics added).

125. Pei, "Racing Against Time," p. 48.

126. Zheng Zhixiao, "Kezhixu fazhan zonghengtan."

The International System and the Growth of Associations

International NGOs and funding agencies have been keenly interested in establishing a foothold in China, and Chinese interested in promoting policies in certain sectors often look to such international groups because of the need for funding from sources other than the government. These international associations work through, and with, the Chinese government to promote their interests. Again, the relationship tends to be advantageous both to the state and to the development of civil society. The Ford Foundation's work with the Ministry of Civil Affairs to help establish a democratic electoral system and the Republican Institute's work with lower-level officials on rural self-governance are good examples of the dual benefits to society and the state. Another is the Harvard School of Public Health, which in conjunction with UNESCO, has funded studies of healthcare in China over the past twenty years. It also helped create a think tank appended to the Ministry of Health and is now working on a new one for the Ministry of Labor and Social Security.[127] Like domestic associations and interest groups, international NGOs working in China are supposed to be attached to, or "hang from," a government department, and their programs are supposed to be approved by it.[128] Nevertheless, even though the Chinese government has created an organization to register international organizations (CANGO, or Chinese Association for NGOs), many do not register.[129]

The number of international development agencies, international NGOs, and international funding agencies operating in China has grown dramatically. Today, about 180 international NGOs are estimated to be working in China. These include the Save the Children Fund, Project Hope, Oxfam International, The Smile Train, Yale-China Association, SOAR Foundation, Worldwide Fund for Nature (China Program Office), the Wetlands Association, Lions Club, Handicap International, Health Unlimited, Tibet Pov-

---

127. William Xiao, Harvard School of Public Health, discussion, April 2001.

128. Human Rights in China, "China: Social Groups Seek Independence in a Regulatory Cage," pp. 3, 7–8. Friends of Nature, an international NGO which acts with remarkable independence in China, chose not to register under the National Environment Protection Agency because it felt it was being asked to do too much, namely, to represent the interests of all Chinese people. So in 1994, it registered as an organization with the Academy of Chinese Culture, where its organizer, Liang Congjie, is a professor and vice-president (Saich, "Negotiating the State," p. 131).

129. David Zweig, Harvard University, New England China Seminar, Jan. 25, 2001.

erty Alleviation Fund, the John D. and Catherine T. MacArthur Fund, Helen Keller International, and Médecins sans Frontières. In addition, there are some 70 advocacy groups such as international human rights or environmental groups, about 150 church-based charitable groups that raise money for projects in China, and seventy or so smaller grant-making foundations. Since the 1990s, international NGOs and foundations have channeled an estimated US$100 million every year to projects in China. This sum is equal to all the funding China receives through UN agencies, such as WHO, UNESCO, UNICEF, and UNDP.[130]

China today is an integral part of a highly complex international system, in which all sorts of associations and social movements are active. Under these circumstances, the formation of new political parties is not the only way to articulate societal demands. Moreover, many associations that are outside the control of the party-state are supported by constituencies from abroad as well as within China.[131] In fact, their work with their international counterparts has already introduced many values of the international community into China.

This is the case, for example, with Friends of Nature, an NGO in China whose financial resources come almost entirely from the international community. The propagation by China's official mass media of "green" ideas from the international environmental movement has led some Chinese citizens to become environmental activists. China's environmentalists must still work under the direction of the government, but the relationship is not always adversarial. Given the near crisis-level conditions in the environment caused by China's rapid economic development, the government is quite willing to allow activism by citizen environmental groups. Except for such controversial projects as the Three Gorges Dam on the Yangtze River, which has caused considerable concern within China (even within the government) as well as among certain international environmental groups and organizations, citizen action groups look to the government, more than to the international community, to provide the resources and policies to address serious environmental issues.[132]

---

130. Nick Young, "Introduction," in Ku, *2000 Directory of International NGOs Supporting Work in China*, p. i.

131. Davis, "Introduction: Urban China," in idem et al., *Urban Space in Contemporary China*, p. 18.

132. Qi, "From Concept to Social Action," pp. 42–43.

Chinese trade unions would no doubt welcome international support for higher wages and more benefits, but the Chinese government has limited their involvement with international organizations for fear that it might lead to demands for increased wages and benefits from state-run enterprises that would make China's exports more expensive and less competitive. Even so, the ACFTU has benefited from greater contact with the International Labor Organization (ILO). Perhaps of greatest value has been the increased exposure to the variety and style of industrial relations practices in other countries, such as collective bargaining, which ACFTU officials have received thanks to ILO funding for overseas trips, conferences, and research.[133]

Normally, international NGOs and funding agencies manage to work in China without threatening the state's interests, but their involvement in potential public-relations disasters such as certain healthcare issues (like AIDs) or orphanages may lead to serious problems for an association. Frequently the international NGO is no longer permitted to campaign for its cause within China. Foreign involvement is, moreover, not always beneficial to the development of a civil society, whether in China or elsewhere, and may aid the growth of rent-seeking behavior and other forms of corruption (as is alleged to have happened with Project Hope).

As with Russia and its former republics, China's economic liberalization has led to a "conflation of political and economic elites" (and their families), who participate directly in the international economy and act as agents for large industries. Marketization and the enmeshing of China in the globalization of capital have in some cases hindered rather than supported the development of autonomous associations and a democratic-minded middle class and led to the emergence of a rent-seeking class (albeit a middle class) that controls both domestic capital and political power.[134] As countries move away from socialism and the public ownership of resources and industries, they are naturally confronted with the basic issue of whether it is even legitimate to privatize public resources. China is thus caught in a bind: to become an integral part of the international economic community, which is run on capitalist principles of efficiency and profit, it must privatize most public resources and unprofitable state-owned enterprises; yet in doing so,

---

133. Howell, "Trade Unions in China," p. 163.

134. Wang Hui, "Contemporary Chinese Thought and the Question of Modernity," pp. 32, 37.

China exposes itself to the risk of rent-seeking behavior. China's policymakers need only compare the figures for the growth in GDP per capita in China to those of the Russian Federation from 1975 to 1998 (an average 7.5 percent annual growth rate for China compared to –0.8 percent for the Russian Federation) to conclude that a more gradual, incremental approach is better for economic development.[135]

In the case of China, then, the development of a middle class will not necessarily lead to democratization. Consisting largely of entrepreneurs, the middle class would prefer that the government keep many of its regulations and controls, including its control over trade unions. Thus far, the middle class has been the beneficiary of government policies and is more inclined to cooperate with, rather than challenge, the state.[136] And, apart from being the product of entrepreneurial successes, the middle class has also been greatly enlarged by state policies that have allowed rent-seeking to occur.

Thus, neither marketization nor the emergence of a middle class nor foreign involvement nor the proliferation of associations guarantees democratization. Chinese intellectuals are wrong to believe that "'opening' in and of itself will result in China drawing closer to the West, thereby resolving the problem of democracy." This is because "the integration of Chinese economic activity with international capital" has exacerbated political corruption, which has antidemocratic implications. Still, although marketization and global capitalism may not lead to a civil society, and may even have thwarted its emergence in some respects, they have at least constrained the near-dictatorial power of China's formerly highly centralized state.[137]

---

135. United Nations Development Programme, *Human Development Report 2000*, p. 183. World Bank employees say that those who have worked on China are always far more cautious and conservative in their advocacy of changing economic and political institutions than others (discussions with World Bank employees, May 2001). Similarly, Nolan (*China's Rise, Russia's Fall*, p. 174) notes that in the World Bank, almost all those who had worked on China took on a far more pragmatic approach to reform than those who had not.

136. David Zweig, Harvard University, New England China Seminar, Jan. 25, 2001.

137. Wang Hui, "Contemporary Chinese Thought and the Question of Modernity," p. 34, and note 33.

Associations and the Development of Civil Society

The Chinese government still maintains controls over associations and interest groups and has retained adequate power to resist their demands if they push beyond their narrow sectoral interests to challenge overall state control. But as long as they do not publicly oppose the government in their activities or statements, the state generally seems not to preoccupy itself with the details of their activities. Indeed, the state even sponsors efforts by associations to address problems created by economic reform, especially in the modern enterprise sector, in which entire ministries have been transformed into associations. Various economic sectors, such as automobile manufacturing and banking and finance, have likewise been encouraged to join together into horizontal associations.[138]

The language still used by both the government and associations and interest groups is, of course, that the associations are advancing the interests of their own clientele in order to serve the goals of the Party and state. Thus Shanghai's Brain Olympics Association was established to "advance the four modernizations" by training students for the International Brain Olympics Contest. Shanghai's Cooking Association was established to "support reform and the open door policy," and "abiding by China's laws," to unify all the city's cooks in spreading the art of Chinese cooking abroad. It also publishes a bimonthly magazine and sponsors exhibits and workshops. The Rural Enterprises Association promotes "spiritual civilization" by supporting basketball, soccer, chess, films, singing, and karaoke among its members. The mission statements of groups as diverse as the Futurology, Family Planning, Qigong, Fishing Economics, Food Therapy, and *The Dream of the Red Chamber* research associations, as well as the Playwrights, Musicians, Film Producers, and Calligraphers associations pledge to "support the four principles," "the open door policy," and "the two 100's."[139] The Leprosy Prevention Association "upholds the four basic principles" by aiming to eliminate leprosy. And the Association for Eliminating the Four Pests (mice, mosquitoes, flies, and cockroaches) also exists "to uphold the four basic principles" by uniting, organizing, and coordinating all technical forces and

---

138. Li Yongzeng, "Rise of Horizontal Business Associations."

139. A reference to "Let a hundred flowers blossom, let a hundred schools of thought contend," an ancient slogan.

contributing to the "four modernizations" by safeguarding people's health.[140] The jargon notwithstanding, the importance of these changes for civil society are real. As Christopher Nevitt concluded from his study of associations for entrepreneurs and businesses in Tianjin:

> It seems that in the Chinese context a civil society may not develop separate from and in opposition to the state but rather in the niches and spaces that the state leaves open, and that it will grow in response to opportunities deliberately engineered or accidentally created by the state. And, in turn, such a civil society may make demands upon the state—not to undermine or weaken it but to constrain its behavior in some circumstances and to endorse and support it in others.[141]

In summary, the Chinese government may officially reject "peaceful evolution" toward civil society[142] or, perhaps better stated, toward "associational" or "interest pluralism," yet this appears to be what is happening—and with the support of the state. To the degree that the political and social system can tolerate this dramatic challenge to its control structure, the development of these many associations and the creation of a civil society will benefit the Chinese people and advance democracy. Although China's interest groups and associations are not fully autonomous, this may turn out to be far less important to the development of democracy than the extent to which these corporatist associations contribute to stability or instability.

CONCLUSIONS: ASSOCIATIONAL OR INTEREST PLURALISM IN CHINA

Many Western scholars say the term "civil society" is a Western notion that cannot be applied to non-Western societies because "non-Westerners simply cannot develop along European trajectories." But this really reflects the limits of Western social philosophy, which lacks the frameworks and concepts to account for social groups and how they function in non-Western

---

140. In 1982, this association established a company in Pudong District (the Shanghai Health and Pest Prevention Company) that provides consulting, processing, and marketing services and sells pesticides. It is, in short, the moneymaking arm of the association. See Ma Yili and Liu Hanbang, *Shanghai shehui tuanti gailan*, pp. 108–74.

141. Nevitt, "Private Business Associations in China," p. 43.

142. The party-state dismisses the idea that democratization in China may occur through what they term "peaceful evolution" (*heping yanbian*) that is, that it cannot stop the democratization process.

societies.[143] As I hope the preceding has made clear, any simplistic view of "civil society," in which individuals and associations are seen as fully independent of and even in opposition to the state, ignores the subtle and complex intertwinings found in China. "Quasi-autonomous groups and individuals" in China are eroding the state's control—without embarking on a devastating revolution.[144] This includes intellectuals as well as labor unions, student clubs[145] as well as *qigong* associations.[146] In Elizabeth Perry's words,

the binary opposition between "state" and "society" implied by the term "civil society" obfuscates the peculiar blend of private, public, and state involvement that characterizes associational activity in contemporary China. . . . Our Western social science habit of viewing state-society relations as a zero-sum game, in which society's gain is the state's loss, does not shed much light on a China where private ties, public associations, and state agents are so thoroughly intertwined.[147]

Economic liberalization in the past twenty years has created a new role for associations and a friendlier environment for the evolution of civil society. Ultimately, it has turned out to be in the state's interests to create still more associations and to give greater autonomy to certain associations while maintaining tight control over others that have the potential to undermine the state's power. Yet the state's control is being eroded by other forces set in motion by economic liberalization—forces whose interests are not aggregated and articulated by official associations, and forces that do not always serve the best interests of a developing civil society. Examples include the polarization of wealth, massive internal migration, and the increasing amount of criminal activity.

---

143. Sullivan and Abed-Kotob, *Islam in Contemporary Egypt*, p. 3.

144. Pickowicz, "Velvet Prisons and the Political Economy of Chinese Filmmaking," p. 220.

145. Students have become extremely interested in participating in various environmental protection campaigns; see Wong Koon-kwai, "The Environmental Awareness of University Students in Beijing, China," table 10.

146. China's 200 million *qigong* practitioners are affiliated with thousands of *qigong* associations. Some of these are "officially sanctioned bureaucratic organizations," and some are not, particularly those led by charismatic masters. Sometimes they even overlap, with illegal healing by the same *qigong* master who is the head of an official qigong organization. See Elizabeth J. Perry, "Introduction" to Part III: Urban Associations, in Davis et al., *Urban Spaces in Contemporary China*, p. 298.

147. Ibid., pp. 297, 301.

There is no easy formula for judging just how much state control is good for the development of China's public sphere. Like all societies, China continues to wrestle with the proper balance between autonomy and control. If associations become deeply institutionalized, the state may not be able to confer and retract their power and responsibilities at will. If, however, competing interest groups and associations occur in the context of a weak state and further destabilize society, this would hardly promote the growth of civil society.

If we define political pluralism in terms of a multiparty system and the sort of civil society found in liberal democracies, we will miss the significance of what is going on in China today. The tens of thousands of associations and interest groups that have sprouted over the past twenty years and the development of social autonomy and corporatism are, in comparison to the situation in pre-reform China, a great leap forward in the direction of democracy. So is the greater tolerance for different viewpoints on policy and ideology that is emerging both within and outside the Chinese Communist Party (a topic covered in the next chapter). Charges of "ideological deviation" against one's opponents (whether political leaders or intellectual dissidents) are far less likely today than at any other time since 1949—and disagreements with the official line are far less likely to incur serious political costs.[148] The fact that Deng Liqun and ten other retired high-ranking party members could publish a statement on the Internet denouncing Jiang Zemin's "theory of three representatives" without having it censored is testimony to the leadership's growing tolerance for a diversity of opinions.[149]

Among China's leaders, from the State Council and Politburo and Central Committee to the grass roots, there is a diversity of opinion. As mentioned above, were a multiparty system to be declared, it would probably

---

148. "The emergence of a widely shared consensus over the tremendous harm of a single interpretation of a broadly shared ideology was a crucial step in the repudiation of Hua Guofeng's whateverism and the unfolding of the subsequent reassessment in the post-Mao era" (Yan Sun, *The Chinese Reassessment of Socialism*, pp. 269, 271).

149. They have accused the party of betraying its purpose, which is to act as "the vanguard of the proletarian class," and taking the party down the road to "social democracy" (Feng Chongyi, "The Party-State, Liberalism and Social Democracy," p. 24). Deng Liqun had served as the all-powerful director of the Party's Propaganda Department. Although all the signatories are retired and perhaps have little to lose, that they even dared to challenge Jiang's idea of bringing capitalists into the Party and that the Party did not bother to censor the Internet statement is remarkable.

consist largely of the same people who now rule China. Instead of belonging to factions *within* the Chinese Communist Party, however, they would belong to different parties. Even more likely is that today's reformist leaders would provide the leadership for the winning party; for unlike those intellectuals or dissidents who might run for public office and despite the serious corruption within the Party's ranks, the reformers can point to success in providing the framework for economic growth, stability, and political liberalization. Andrew Nathan shares this viewpoint: if "elections were extended to the provincial and national levels, the reform faction could win, *whatever name it ran under.*"[150]

One serious obstacle to the growth of new parties is that thus far, because the regime has not permitted a legal political opposition, there has been no training ground for new leaders. Nor has an underground dissident movement been able to develop such leaders. A new leadership from outside the Communist Party could, however, arise from within China's many associations, which are providing numerous opportunities to their members to develop skills in managing and leading organizations.

Finally, it should be kept in mind that the desire of many urban and well-educated Chinese to have a greater autonomous input into governmental decisions and an interest on the part of corporatist associations to have a greater say over political and economic reforms that benefit their own constituencies are not the same as a longing for democracy—certainly not in the sense of one-man, one-vote. A system that enfranchised the entire population to participate in national elections would put China's government into the hands of its peasantry, who still constitute close to 70 percent of the population. Generally speaking, neither urban workers nor intellectuals favor turning power over to China's villagers,[151] whom they consider to be less educated and less "civilized" in their behavior and viewpoints. The real fear is, of course, that their less civilized country cousins might vote for a more rural orientation in social policy and to constrain their exploitation by the cities. Whatever the Party's failings in the eyes of China's urbanites and intellectuals, at least its policies have been almost unreservedly biased toward the cities.[152]

---

150. Nathan, "China's Path from Communism," p. 40.

151. Kelliher, "Keeping Democracy Safe from the Masses," p. 381.

152. The findings of the Gallup Organization's Third Survey of Consumer Attitudes and Lifestyles in the PRC, conducted in 1999, indicate that China's urbanites, who constitute only

The picture that emerges, then, is of a steadily larger and more complex chessboard of associations, which, even if they are not fully autonomous, press for the collective interests of their constituents. As in any civil society, China's associations pursue public interests through the aggregation and articulation of their needs, ideas, and concerns, but they are simultaneously satisfying private interests by relying on personalistic ties and are frequently motivated by opportunities for profitmaking, if not outright corruption.[153] This is conspicuously true of businesspeople and workers, but it may also be true of, say, environmentalists[154] or consumers' rights groups.[155] And, as noted above, some of the sectoral interests pursued by the newly emerging associations and interest groups may be in serious conflict with the overall good of the society. Thus, without appropriate limits to the ability of any one association to pursue its own interests, the public's interests may be adversely affected.

The amount of residual state control over China's associations leaves something to be desired, but even in Western society, associations and interest groups face this issue. As Benjamin Barber notes, "By definition all private associations necessarily had private ends. Schools became interest groups for people with children (parents) rather than the forgers of a free society; churches became . . . special interest groups pursuing separate agendas rather than sources of moral fiber for the larger society . . . ; voluntary associations became a variation on private lobbies." Even environmental groups were necessarily just another "special interest group" pursuing their own special interests "in competition with the special interests of polluters."[156]

---

30 percent of the population, own or benefit from 70 percent of the country's wealth. Mean annual household income in the cities is more than $2,500, compared to $870 in rural areas (Palmer, "What the Chinese Want," p. 230).

153. Zhongguo zhanlüe yu guanli yanjiuhui, Shehui jiu zhuanxing ketizu, "Zhongguo zhuanxingde zhongjinqi qushi yu yinghuan," pp. 10–11.

154. *Wenhui bao* (Shanghai), Jan. 26, 1999.

155. Xiong Fenxi, "Analysis of Consumer Complaints in 1998 Received by this Periodical." The name of the magazine, *Zhongguo zhiliang wan li xing* (Quest for product quality in China), is also the name of the consumer rights organization, which is very influential in China. It sends out teams to investigate consumer complaints concerning product and service quality and also deals with broader issues of criminality, such as swindling.

156. Benjamin R. Barber, "Jihad vs. McWorld," from idem, *Jihad vs. McWorld*, pp. 281–287; quoted in Myers and Parsekian, *Democracy Is a Discussion*, p. 28.

Still, China's broad collection of official and unofficial associations at the national, regional, and local levels are providing an increasingly strong institutional framework for representation of constituencies and specialized interests that are different from those of the state. They are seeking "concessions, benefits, policy changes, relief, redress, or accountability" from the state. In doing so, they are steadily eroding the heavy hand of the centralized state.[157] As in other civil societies, moreover, at the same time that they are chipping away at the state's authority, they are not standing in opposition to it. Especially at the local level, associations provide the Chinese people with opportunities to influence the state. And, in so doing, associations provide them with an alternative both to political parties and to personalistic ties for disseminating new ideas and for articulating, aggregating, and advancing their interests. In short, if we can enlarge our understanding of a civil society to encompass one that is not *against* the state but works with the state in many areas, we can gain a better appreciation of the dynamics of the relationship between associations and interest groups and the state in China. As Anthony Saich has noted, even the term "corporatism" as a description of the state-led nature of control over associations and interest groups in China today risks oversimplifying and ignoring the benefits that these organizations and their members receive from top-down governance, including the ability to affect policymaking far more than if they were truly autonomous. Indeed, with both state and society in transition, a number of models of state-society are operating simultaneously in China.

Each social organization in China has negotiated with the state its own niche that derives from a complex interaction of institutional, economic and individual factors. In some cases, the outcome may be a close "embedded" relationship with the state, in others it may entail formal compliance while operating strategies of evasion and circumnavigation of the state. . . . It is not mere expediency that causes new social formations or organizations to tie their fortunes to the existing state structures, especially at the local level, but it is strategically optimal for them. It can enable them to manipulate the official and semi-official institutions for their own advantage.[158]

Is it possible, then, that the strengthening of civil society in China, or at least of associational pluralism, has strengthened the ability of the Chinese Communist Party to remain in power and that state control of associations

---

157. Diamond, "Rethinking Civil Society," pp. 6–8, 10–11.
158. Saich, "Negotiating the State," pp. 138–39.

is not necessarily against the wishes of society as a whole? To assume that the party-state is in a confrontational relationship with society is to miss their complex and interdependent relationship. It is also to miss the point that control, like freedom, is subjective, and has to be interpreted within a Chinese context.

8   *The Clientelist Relationship*
     of Intellectuals with the Party-State
     and the Capitalist Class

In looking for the emergence of civil society, we can make three assumptions: that there is a Western/Chinese mix of values and ideology that is producing a Chinese variant of civil society, that disengagement from authoritarian Leninist structures and norms will be slower than expected, and that nascent civil society should not be confused with the imminent democratization of China. We should also remember that civil society is about culture, values, and attitudes, which change slowly. When millennia of traditions still count, it is too much to think that fundamental transformation can occur within a single generation.

—B. Michael Frolic

Who are China's intellectuals? Many observers in the West assume that the classification "intellectuals" refers only to university professors, writers and artists in the cultural sphere, and researchers or policy specialists in the Chinese Academy of Social Sciences, the Chinese Academy of Sciences, and think tanks. And the often unstated assumption is that China's intellectuals are by definition dissidents.[1] Indeed, Western scholars tend to assume that "since the Chinese regime is communist, any opposition to that system, such as the 1989 Tiananmen movement, is unquestionably. . . democratic."[2] Those intellectuals who are not openly challenging the mainstream ideas of the Chinese state are often assumed to be toadies of the state or to have been silenced. Such assumptions distort our understanding of China's intellectuals.

EPIGRAPH: Frolic, "State-Led Civil Society," p. 49.

    1. The term "dissidents" tends to be reserved for intellectuals; workers and peasants who disagree with the regime are usually referred to as "protesters" or "demonstrators."

    2. Cheng Li, "Promises and Pitfalls of Reform," p. 126.

Like so many terms, the concept of "intellectuals" is a social construct, and no more so than in the People's Republic of China. In the days of Mao Zedong's rule, a high school graduate might be termed an "intellectual" (*zhishi fenzi*). Usually, those who had at least this level of education occupied the higher positions of the state institution in which they worked. They tended to be the teachers, professors, technocrats, journalists, and managers. They were often called "experts"—in contrast to those who were "red." During the Cultural Revolution, they were classified as the "stinking ninth category," a classification based largely on their level of education, and were persecuted for their expertise.

Today, the significant difference is that those classified as "intellectuals" are likely to have an advanced degree (with many exceptions, especially for those not formally educated during the Cultural Revolution), but they still constitute a broad, heterogeneous group: "experts, scholars, managers, and technocrats [who] are subjected to the same relentless process of stratification as everyone else in Chinese society."[3] Intellectuals who are engaged with matters of the mind, rather than serving as propagandists, managers, or technocrats, often do not like to be described as *zhishi fenzi*. They would prefer to be referred to as *xuezhe*, or "scholars," because it conveys the sense that they are engaged in independent thought and the creative life of the mind, rather than working to promote societal values endorsed by the state.[4]

Perhaps most important in understanding the role that Chinese intellectuals play is to realize that their position within Chinese society, and their role in shaping China's history, values, and ideas, is more like that of French intellectuals than, say, American intellectuals. That is, Chinese intellectuals have played an important role in China's history, and so what they say and do matters. They take themselves—and are taken—seriously, both as individuals and as members of China's intellectual elite. This is precisely the reason that Chinese rulers, from pre-imperial times through the present, have been concerned about what Chinese intellectuals say and has tried to control them.

This is in stunning contrast to intellectuals in the United States, who as a "class" hardly matter at all. It would be difficult to imagine the vast majority

3. Wang Hui, "Contemporary Chinese Thought and the Question of Modernity," p. 27.

4. The term *xuezhe* conveys a meaning closer to that of the intellectuals who studied classics in imperial China and who were referred to as *wenren* (Elizabeth Perry and Gloria Davies, discussion during the workshop "Chinese Intellectuals Between the State and the Market," Harvard University, Fairbank Center, June 30, 2001).

of American intellectuals sitting around and self-consciously discussing who they are and what their role is in shaping American values, ideas, and the country's future—or that either the public or the government would care what they thought. Only a handful of public intellectuals, such as William Buckley, Gore Vidal, Gloria Steinem, Susan Sontag, or Paul Krugman, would imagine that their ideas and values might be taken seriously by the broad public—and would have guaranteed access to a public platform.

As was the case in imperial China, intellectuals today generally serve the state, yet they are divorced from the common people in their concerns. Their lack of sensitivity to the issues of ordinary people is exacerbated by the fact that intellectuals tend not to interact with the common people or understand their problems. They rarely make more than brief visits to the countryside, and in the cities they rarely have factory workers as neighbors. Apart from everything else, intellectuals are usually housed together, in work units isolated from ordinary workers and dedicated to intellectual pursuits (or at least work units that require a high level of education), such as the Academy of Social Sciences, universities, the media, and the various ministries. They have tended to be interested more in their own issues as intellectuals than in democratization for the masses, even if they have been required to write about their issues.[5] Intellectuals work for many types of state institutions, from the mass media and cultural institutions to state ministries and agencies. Their relationship with the state depends on the institution with which they are connected, as well as their status within that organization. The relationship is fluid, however, and as the institution changes, so does the relationship. Although most intellectuals are part of the party-state apparatus, their connections vary from minimal and distant to complex and deep. Usually, but not always, intellectuals have a "clientelist" relationship with sponsors within party-state institutions.[6]

---

5. Kelliher, "Keeping Democracy Safe from the Masses." Kelliher's conclusions are based on an examination of three major protest movements in China since the reforms began: 1978–79, 1986–87, and 1989. The major division between the intellectual elite and the masses was the intellectuals' emphasis on rights such as freedom of speech and the press, at the expense of any interest in promoting popular sovereignty, democratic participation of the masses, and institutional change that advanced democratization. China's intellectuals have steadfastly held that intellectual freedom must come first and that democracy must be postponed until the masses have become adequately educated and "civilized."

6. Cheek and Hamrin, *China's Establishment Intellectuals*; Goldman, *China's Intellectuals*; idem, *Sowing the Seeds of Democracy in China*; Goldman et al., *China's Intellectuals and the State*.

In short, Chinese intellectuals come in all shapes and sizes. To simplify, they can be broken down into five major groups in terms of gradations of their closeness to the party-state.[7] First are those who serve as a mouthpiece of the party-state, or "those who write with their pens" (*bi gan zi*), and have no ideas of their own. Next are those intellectuals in "think tanks" (*zhinang-tuan*), who do think and do research. The party-state assigns them a research topic, but they have promoted some of the most important reforms. Being assigned a topic does not necessarily confine them at all. It just means they are addressing an issue that someone else thinks important.

Further away from the party-state is the third group, pure academics (*chun xuezhe*) who engage in scholarly and usually apolitical research. They are followed by "public intellectuals" (*gonggong zhishi fenzi*), who debate topics of public concern, such as liberalism and conservatism. They are part of the party-state and are usually employed by universities or the Chinese Academy of Social Sciences. Although they are not dissidents, they try to maintain a distance from the government. Finally, "dissidents" (*yiyi fenzi*) are engaged in a discourse that has emerged over the past twenty years and are independent from the state. They engage in debate over the issues with public intellectuals.

Most of those trained in the social sciences or humanities would like to be part of the state "intellectual power elite," which is located in the universities, the Chinese Academy of Social Sciences, media and publishing houses, and the state's research centers.[8] So would cultural intellectuals—artists, musicians, poets, and novelists. Even "dissident" intellectuals, who appear to the outside world to be confronting the state and may indeed detest the state's policy, work for a party-state institution or *danwei*. In effect, they are "dissidents" only because their party-state sponsors are not the dominant faction in control of policy formation at the moment.[9] Those who disagree with current policy are attempting to get the state to reshape itself through political reforms rather than trying to overthrow the state. The "neo-

---

7. Discussions with Lin Tongji, 2001.
8. Wang Hui, "Contemporary Chinese Thought and the Question of Modernity," p. 27.
9. One well-known exception to such a conclusion would be Fang Lizhi, China's prominent dissident physicist, who, even after his patron was removed from power, continued to speak out against the Communist Party. However, as Shu-yun Ma ("Clientelism, Foreign Attention, and Chinese Intellectual Autonomy") argues, the only reason Fang was still "protected" was because he became the client of a new patron, the United States.

authoritarianism" espoused by certain intellectuals in the late 1980s thus called for a "modified authoritarianism, not for democracy."[10]

Most intellectuals prefer to be part of the establishment because the party-state controls and disperses the resources they covet. Even political scientists, sociologists, and economists, who form one of the most likely pools for dissidents, usually hope to serve as advisers to the leadership.[11] This is in the tradition of China's intellectuals, who, since the earliest times in Chinese history, have been pragmatic and primarily interested in governance. Indeed, one of the major preoccupations of social scientists and cultural intellectuals alike has been to establish patron-client ties with high-ranking officials and climb the ladder of success within the party-state. In their efforts to restructure state-society relations, they have tended to adopt a cooperative approach, rather than a confrontational one that pits civil society against the party-state.[12] Intellectuals avoid moving beyond the boundaries of allowable dissent set by the Chinese Communist Party's dominant faction. Otherwise, they risk losing state approval of their activities and access to officially sponsored publications and performance venues—and perhaps even their jobs.

These tendencies and attitudes do not meet with universal approval. Some well-known dissidents now living abroad (such as the journalist Liu Binyan) imply that intellectuals in China who do not push radical ideas to the point where they are in danger of being demoted, fired, or even imprisoned have sold out. They criticize their compatriots for pandering to the establishment in order to improve their status and all that status can bring: trips abroad, honorary positions in the National People's Congress, a better job, better housing. In their view, those intellectuals who have these things want to keep them and those who do not want to get them.[13] They decry the

---

10. Frolic, "State-Led Civil Society," p. 51.

11. Gu, "Plural Institutionalism," p. 299. The political involvement of many Fudan University faculty members begins with advising the Shanghai municipal government. Faculty in Beijing's leading universities likewise often seek to become advisers to leaders of the party-state at both the city and the national level.

12. Gu, "Cultural Intellectuals and the Politics of the Cultural Public Space," pp. 390, 397.

13. Liu Binyan, "Criticizing Chinese Liberal Intellectuals," seminar, Harvard University, Fairbank Center, Apr. 27, 2000. Liu Binyan, one of China's pre-eminent intellectuals and famous for his reportage, left for the United States in the late 1980s. Apart from everything else, beginning with the Anti-Rightist Campaign of 1957, he was imprisoned for the better part of twenty years; he was thrown out of the Party for his liberal views in the mid-1980s.

fact that China's intellectuals rarely criticize the leadership directly.[14] Western scholars, such as Arif Dirlik, even criticize China's new Confucians for their efforts to revive Confucianism as "oriental 'Orientalism.' It is at best a conspiracy between the state and freeloading intellectuals—a foremost instance . . . of intellectual discourse creating its object."[15]

Liu Junning, a leading PRC scholar of China's politics and an outspoken "liberal," also contends that China's intellectuals favor the tangible rewards of status and power over the right to free speech. They do not pursue knowledge for its own sake or for the sake of criticizing the government, says Liu. Rather, China's intellectuals strive to excel academically in order to become government officials, bureaucrats, or experts in fields such as law, the sciences, engineering, industry, or medicine or to become experts on whom officials rely for their knowledge, such as economists and sociologists. Intellectuals in history, political theory, and the social sciences are particularly eager to publish articles analyzing, and praising, each new party or government idea or policy, such as the theory of "the primary stage of socialism," or the theory of "socialism with Chinese characteristics." China's intellectuals prefer status and power over political protest against the state. They would, says Liu, rather spend their lives kowtowing to the state than be powerless but have freedom.[16]

These harsh critiques hardly give many of China's intellectuals the credit they deserve for their relentless efforts to expand the parameters of acceptable debate into unchartered and potentially dangerous topics—even if they

---

14. Some intellectuals do, of course, take a chance and publicly challenge the party-state. For example, Li Shenzhi, former vice chair of the Chinese Academy of Social Sciences, lost his job after signing a petition defending students. In 2000, Li published an article entitled "The Spreading of the Peking University Liberal Tradition" ("Hongyang beida de ziyou chuantong") in a book edited by Liu Junning: *The Peking University Tradition and Modern China* (*Beida chuantong yu jindai Zhongguo*). Li's foremost target was Jiang Zemin, whom he accused of sweeping away all the tragedies China has endured since the Communist victory in 1949 by celebrating the first 50 years of the Party's rule. Another exception would be Mo Lo, whose book, *Record of Shame* (*Shi ruje shouji*), targets Chinese culture and the Chinese people themselves for all the tragedies of the past 50 years and calls on them to face their shame for what they have done to each other and to their country (Liu Binyan "Criticizing Chinese Liberal Intellectuals," seminar, Harvard University, Fairbank Center, Apr. 27, 2000; and Liu Junning, "The Revival of Liberalism in Contemporary China," seminar, Harvard University, Fairbank Center, Oct. 3, 2000).

15. Arif Dirlik, "Confucianism in the Borderlands: Global Capitalism and the Reinvention of Confucianism," *Boundary* 2 (1995), pp. 238, 242; cited in Ames, "New Confucianism," p. 26.

16. Liu Junning, "Shichang jingji yu youxian zhengfu," pp. 65–69.

do not eagerly court punishment for their views. Today punishment is unlikely to result in imprisonment, but those who dare challenge the implied or stated boundaries of criticism may well lose their jobs[17] or, in the case of cultural intellectuals, have their work banned.[18]

China's intellectuals are hardly unique in being opportunistic and trying to advance their careers. But they also are very much in the tradition of Chinese intellectuals from imperial times on. In imperial China, the greatest desire of Chinese scholars was to act as the emperor's teacher (*wei wangzhe shi*). Present-day scholars who crave the role of advisor to China's leaders should be seen as part of the grand tradition rather than the result of either the communist system or a market-orientation.[19]

Under the People's Republic, China's intellectuals have been plagued by an inability to achieve a consensus about political reforms beyond abstractions such as freedom and democracy. This is in part because, for both political and institutional reasons, they are a fragmented force. The party-state is itself fragmented, with conflicting interests between and within branches of government at all levels. Not surprisingly, intellectuals, and especially the new-left and liberal camps, accuse each other "of collaborating with the party-state, because each side sees a different part or different side of the party-state."[20] In addition, the organization of work life into *danwei* interferes with the formation of broadly based associations of intellectuals to pur-

---

17. For example, in June 2001 several editors and journalists lost their job: Ma Yunlong, the deputy editor-in-chief of *Dahe News* in Zhengzhou, Henan, was dismissed because, according to Ma, he had approved the publication of articles exposing corruption among business regulators, health insurance officials, and drug companies, and because he had allowed the publication of a Xinhua News Agency (which is government controlled) article that discussed complaints made by foreign investors about the graft and obstruction of Henan officials. (A member of the Henan Propaganda Department denied, however, that anyone at *Dahe News* had been penalized.) Two editors at *Southern Weekend* were also dismissed in June 2001, and other journalists and newspaper editors have been warned to observe the Party's limits on coverage. One analyst believes that the government is worried about the power of independent reporting to "fan resentment over rising unemployment and official corruption. Many also want to muzzle the media to prevent them from joining in power struggles as China begins a transition to a new generation of top leaders next year" (Christopher Bodeen, "China Cracking Down on Media," *Boston Globe*, June 19, 2001, p. A8).

18. For example, the eventual bannings of Zhou Weihui's novel *Shanghai Baby* and of Jia Pingwa's *Abandoned Capital* and the suspension of Wang Shuo's television series (discussed below).

19. Discussions with Chinese scholars, Aug. 2001.

20. Chongyi Feng, "The Party-State, Liberalism and Social Democracy," p. 23.

sue common interests. Instead, they are drawn into patron-client relations, which tend to be based on the work unit.[21] Thus, intellectuals work for, and identify with, different institutions, each of which has its own organizational culture and political preferences. Intellectuals, and the "public spaces" they create, are, in short, factionalized intellectually and organizationally along the same lines as the party-state. "Every faction or circle or group has its own identity, its own way of consensus-mobilization and its own manner of membership selection."[22]

Yet many of China's intellectuals have struggled successfully to overcome such problems, and in spite of, or because of, their interdependent, nonconfrontational relationship with the state, they have managed to play a key role in reform and liberalization. The contributions of some members of think tanks and research groups to the cause of reform are undeniable. The now-defunct Research Group on Problems of China's Rural Development, for example, began as a non-state-sponsored organization. It became a state-sponsored group when it helped the reformers of the mid-1980s (including the Party General Secretary Zhao Ziyang and the chair of the Standing Committee of the National People's Congress, Wan Li) win a policy dispute on the implementation of the household responsibility system. Other groups have similar nonconfrontational relationships with the state; for example, those involved with editing series of books, such as the editorial committee of the *Towards the Future* series published in the 1980s;[23] and nonofficial "people-managed" (*minban*) institutions and academies, such as the non-governmental organization called the Beijing Social and Economic Sciences Institute (BSESI), and the International Academy of Chinese Culture. Both BSESI and the International Academy engaged in "independent academic research in cultural studies."[24] BSESI also advocated legal reform and the expansion of human rights as part of political reform.[25]

These groups are not, however, totally outside the state. The leaders of the Research Group, even when it was a non-state-sponsored association,

---

21. Shi Tianjian, *Political Participation in Beijing.*

22. Gu, "Plural Institutionalism," pp. 295, 301.

23. This included many books written by Western social scientists and translated into Chinese. For more detail about the Future Group, including a list of the books it published, see Gu, "Cultural Intellectuals and the Politics of the Cultural Public Space," pp. 399–408.

24. Gu, "Plural Institutionalism," p. 278. For more detail on both these groups, see Gu, "Cultural Intellectuals and the Politics of the Cultural Public Space," pp. 407–13.

25. Frolic, "State-Led Civil Society," p. 50.

were members of the Communist Party. And in spite of financial independence, groups such as the BSESI are not completely autonomous from the state; for even unofficial or "people-managed" institutions must be registered and be attached to and dependent on (*guakao*) a party-state organization. Nevertheless, the dependency suggested by such registration appears in most cases to be fictional, since the party-state organization rarely intervenes in the activities of the *minban* institutes. Further, since the mid-1980s, even though *minban* research institutes must still be registered as "pendant and dependent" on a state-party organization, the state has not permitted them to receive financial support from the state.[26] In general, the state pays less attention to those organizations that it does not fund, and therefore, intellectuals in them have more autonomy.

Being a part of the party-state and yet a critic of it has come to characterize many of China's most important public intellectuals—that is, those intellectuals whose opinion on almost any topic is valued by the public. For example, both editors of the influential book series *China's Problems* (or *Contemporary China's Problems*), which critiques the reforms, are themselves part of the establishment: Dong Yuyu is a senior editor of *Guangming Daily*; and Shi Binghai is senior editor of the *China Economic Times*. Wang Huning, who was a political science professor at Fudan University and is now the top political adviser to Jiang Zemin, contributed to *Political China: Facing the Era of Choosing a New Structure*, a highly controversial volume in the series, which discusses many of the most politically sensitive issues surrounding political reform. Among the other 32 contributors to the volume were journalists, former officials who had been dismissed for being too sympathetic toward democratization, and government officials still in office.[27]

Many of China's investigative journalists are likewise members of the establishment, and those who act independent of the Party are not numerous. They tend to serve as the Party's watchdogs, advocate state objectives, and offer social commentaries on "unhealthy" social trends. Even freelancers must get their articles published in order to earn money, and those who write articles on forbidden topics are unlikely to see them in print. In spite of their market-orientation, the media are still usually subsidiaries of major party organs. As media commercialization has deepened, moreover, all too many journalists accept bribes in exchange for publishing stories about

---

26. Gu, "Plural Institutionalism," pp. 286–87, 289.
27. Cheng Li, "Promises and Pitfalls of Reform," p. 134.

commercial products as if it were "news." Some have become mouthpieces for China's new economic elite, creating clientelistic relations with this elite. And some journalists even extort money from businesses by threatening to publish damaging stories about them. Whether it is the party or the market—or both—then, journalists seem beholden to forces other than a free press. They have become "one of the most readily and easily co-opted intellectual groups." Still, China's investigative and muckraking journalists have, especially in stories involving official corruption or incompetence, often brazenly pushed beyond the boundaries of permissible challenges to the power structure in search of the truth and in defense of victims of the abuse of power. Some of these reform-oriented journalists travel to "the darkest corners of Chinese society, places, in the words of a villager in a remote area, 'even ghosts will not go.'"[28]

A good example of the symbiotic relationship between Chinese intellectuals and the state is the journal *Reading (Dushu)*, "the standard-bearer of free thinking." Since it was published by a state publishing house and administered by the Bureau of Journalism and Publications, it was hardly an unofficial publication beyond the reach of the state. By the late 1990s, it was replaced in its role as China's major liberal publication on politics and economic issues by *Res Publica (Gonggong lun)*, which has a circulation of 10,000. Since its inception in 1994, it has been allowed to flourish.[29]

The leadership can have few illusions about the nature of the writings in *Res Publica*, which is funded by the Ford Foundation and whose chief editor was until recently Liu Junning.[30] It is an open secret, for example, that Shen Tong (who was forced into permanent exile after 1989) and other dissidents have written several articles for it. In article after article, it argues for liberalism as an *alternative* to the existing (if nearly defunct) ideology of Marxism-Leninism and insists that China's political culture is liberalizing.[31] Since the state publishing house must submit the table of contents of each issue to the

---

28. Yuezhi Zhao, "Underdogs, Lapdogs, Watchdogs, and Other Breeds," pp. 8–19.

29. Wang Hui, "Contemporary Chinese Thought and the Question of Modernity," pp. 32–33. Wang Hui has been a joint editor-in-chief of *Dushu* since 1996. China's "neo-liberals" denounce him as a "neo-leftist," with all the negative connotations that the word "leftist" has in China today.

30. Liu Junning was, however, forced to resign as editor of *Res Publica* in 2000 and was fired from his position in the Chinese Academy of Social Sciences.

31. Liu Junning, "The Revival of Liberalism in Contemporary China," seminar, Harvard University, Fairbank Center, Oct. 3, 2000.

Party's Propaganda Department for approval prior to publication, the party-state is hardly ignorant of its content, but it has chosen not to shut it down—or even censor the articles. Shen Tong attributes the hands-off attitude of the party-state to the meticulous care the journal's editors take to keep the articles within acceptable limits. Thus, the articles discuss the meaning of democracy and liberalization and ways to improve the political system, but they never directly criticize China's present leaders.[32] Liu Junning himself believes that the market economy has promoted many sorts of freedom, including freedom of the press. When the government stopped subsidizing the press and left newspapers and journals either to make a profit or to collapse, journalists and editors had to publish more appealing newspapers in order to attract advertising. And who was advertising? Joint ventures, private entrepreneurs, and even state enterprises. Hence the market economy, by generating entrepreneurship and greater wealth, promoted the expansion of freedom of the press.[33]

At the same time, of course, many questions arise as to whether this "free market" of the press has not curtailed press freedom much as party censorship did. "Yesterday's state-subsidized Party [media] organs have mutated into today's Party-controlled and advertising-supported media conglomerates." Ironically, market mechanisms seem to perform a censorship role of their own, which is not necessarily at odds with Party propaganda. Rather, they "have actually helped neutralize dissent at a time when the bottom line is the party line." This illustrates the shared interests of the Party and business elites, and China's urban middle class. As members of China's urban middle class, journalists likewise benefit from political stability and the integration of China into the global economy.[34]

Nevertheless, in "independent" journals such as *Reading, Res Publica,* and others,[35] intellectuals do not hesitate to take on some of the most sensitive

---

32. Discussion with Shen Tong, Harvard University, Apr. 28, 1999.

33. Liu Junning, "The Revival of Liberalism in Contemporary China," seminar, Harvard University, Fairbank Center, Oct. 3, 2000.

34. Yuezhi Zhao, "Underdogs, Lapdogs, Watchdogs, and Other Breeds," pp. 32–33, 35.

35. Other "independent" journals established after 1989 include *Xueren* (The scholar), *Zhongguo shehui kexue jikan* (Chinese social science quarterly), *Yuan dao* (Inquiry into the way), and *Gonggong luncong* (Public forum) (Wang Hui, "Contemporary Chinese Thought and the Question of Modernity," p. 32).

political topics in China today. They may be on the state's payroll,[36] but concerns that they might lose their job no longer deter them from voicing an extraordinary range of opinions about political reform in China. Their purpose is as much to influence the direction of policy and the shaping of political culture and values as it is to critique the government. In one book published by the Chinese Academy of Social Sciences, for example, the writers took on the delicate topic of how to democratize society and the political system while maintaining stability. Among other points, they argued that the Party's proposals for the supervision of senior leaders are weak because of the highly centralized political and economic system. The overcentralized administrative system needs to be reformed in order to enhance socialist democracy and socialist legality and thereby to fight corruption. Self-supervision has not worked. Senior leaders will not be adequately supervised until there is a separation of powers, with one institution's power balancing the power of another institution (and its leaders).[37]

Articles written in more liberal journals, which are also published by official presses, frequently express attitudes that implicitly criticize the Chinese Communist Party:

If a party's or a faction's interest is different from and even opposed to the people's interest, democracy is often sacrificed in favor of protecting the party's or the faction's interest. When the party or faction interest is granted superior status, only those aspects of democracy that are beneficial to the party or faction interest will be preserved. Other aspects of democracy . . . will be discarded. In such a case, democracy is relegated to being an ornament that can be toyed with by the party or faction. Because democracy has its logical starting point in the people's interests, it is resented by those who favor one party or one faction.[38]

Others have gone even further. Books and articles do not hesitate to challenge the system of one-party rule and to suggest reforms. For example, Cao

---

36. Liu Junning is, for example, a member of the Academy of Chinese Culture, one of many independent groups, which Tony Saich calls "orphans," that are under the aegis of the Chinese Academy of Social Sciences.

37. "Society and Politics: To Form a Combined Force and Progress While Maintaining Stability," chap. 2 in Weng Jieming et al., *Zhongguo fazhan baogao shu:1996–1997*, pp. 31–39.

38. Liu Jinxi, "Minzhu xin lun," p. 84. The journal in which this appeared, *Xuexi yu tansuo* (Study and exploration), is published by the Heilongjiang Provincial Academy of Social Sciences.

Siyuan, a consultant on bankruptcy issues and president of the Beijing Research Center for Social Sciences (a private organization), proposed a series of political reforms for the National People's Congress, the government itself, and the Chinese Communist Party "to adapt China's political infrastructure to its economic reality." First, the National People's Congress and People's Political Consultative Conference should be reformed to make them like the U.S. House of Representatives and Senate, respectively, a transformation that could be implemented "without much difficulty." Then, the government should be reformed, not just streamlined, in order to have a system of checks and balances and separation of powers among the executive, legislative, and judicial branches. Finally, the Communist Party should be reformed so that it represents "China's current social and economic reality." Cao even proposed that the party change its name to the Chinese Socialist Party, that the party raise its revenue from membership fees and public donations instead of the government, that it carry out competitive elections for positions within the Party, and that China's constitution be revised and a multiparty system adopted during the Sixteenth Party Congress in October 2002.[39]

Similar demands for political reform are expressed in a book about the fall of the Soviet Union. The authors, from the Russian Studies Center in the Chinese Academy of Social Sciences, argue that the lessons are that China must press forward with political and economic reforms to address the likely causes of such a collapse, namely, "political autocracy, economic dogmatism, and ethnic chauvinism." The authors conclude that China should not go as far as Gorbachev did because China is not ready for a multiparty system, but they do propose the gradual introduction of elections above the village level, an enhanced role for the National People's Congress, and further reform of the legal system.[40]

Why has the party-state allowed intellectuals, especially those in the media, to expose the down-side of the reforms, to offer social commentaries on the decline of socialist values, to write articles challenging state policies, and

---

39. "Well-known Political Scientist Proposes Political Reform," *China News Digest*, Mar. 15, 2001, based on a report in *South China Morning Post*, Mar. 15, 2001; www.cnd.com. Cao published these ideas in the May 2001 issue of *Zhongguo guoqing guoli* (China's national essense and strength) (Beijing: State Statistical Bureau), and in the March 2001 issue of a journal that has restricted circulation and is published by a Beijing think tank (*Economist*, June 30, 2001, p. 23).

40. Xu Xin, Chen Lianbi, Pan Deli, and Jiang Yi, *Collapse of a Superpower* (2001); cited in Philip P. Pan, Washington Post Foreign Service, Aug. 20, 2001, p. A10.

to track down corrupt officials? One possibility is that, in the face of increasing social tensions, the Party has come to see media exposure and critiques by intellectuals as playing the role of a social safety valve. Not only does silence on the part of the media do nothing to assuage public anger, but it is also more likely to mean the perpetuation of horrendous situations and to encourage corruption, precisely the sources of social instability. Even if the media would just as soon not speak up, China's aggrieved citizens, those who have crowded into CCTV headquarters, swamped newspapers with letters to the Editor, jammed phone lines to radio call-in shows, and cajoled journalists to investigate their complaints, have caused the Party to believe that allowing the media to serve as a social safety valve is necessary if it wants to remain in power.[41]

THE DIVERSITY OF PERSPECTIVES AMONG INTELLECTUALS

During the reform period, a wide variety of perspectives have arisen within the intellectual community, from realist, conservative (*baoshoupai*), and neo-conservative (sometimes referred to as "cultural nationalists") to liberal (*ziyoupai*), radical reformer,[42] modern radical, neo-authoritarian, internationalist, nationalist, "Old Left,"[43] and "New Left."[44] The New Left is subdivided into those who have been to the West and returned and those who have not traveled outside China. There have also been numerous shifts among these groups. For example, the magazine *Zhanlüe yu guanli* (Strategy and management), which used to be a stronghold for the conservatives, now champions the liberals. One indication of China's growing pluralization in the realm of ideas is that both liberalism and conservatism have been gaining strength. Liberalism in particular has enjoyed a spectacular growth in popularity. Before 1998, liberalism was considered a dirty word. Since then, intellectuals

---

41. Yuezhi Zhao, "Underdogs, Lapdogs, Watchdogs, and Other Breeds," pp. 19–20.

42. Radical reformers believe that too much emphasis on Chinese tradition and "Chinese-ness" interferes with efforts to modernize.

43. The Old Left wants to strengthen the Communist Party and restore the principles of socialism, Marxism, Leninism, and Mao Zedong Thought.

44. The New Left borrows ideas from the West such as neo-Marxism and post-modernism, yet is anti-Western and anti-institutionalist.

have been proud to identify themselves as liberals and write and publish articles *as liberals*.[45]

Liu Junning argues that liberalism, even though it is not a part of Chinese political culture and did not accompany economic reforms, will prevail in China because of the common concerns for private property and freedom of speech. Not everyone shares his opinion, however. Liberalism is under attack both from the Old and the New Left, which promotes communitarianism, populism,[46] and post-modernism (ideas that Liu believes are too difficult for most Chinese to grasp), and from the Party's Propaganda Department, which does its best to stop ordinary people from being exposed to "non-nationalistic liberalism."[47] Indeed, this is a frequent criticism on the Internet, where Chinese liberals are regularly upbraided for ignoring the nationalistic sentiments of the Chinese people.[48]

Nationalism in China, captured in an extreme form in the 1996 book *China Can Say No*,[49] is an abiding undercurrent. In recent years, nationalism has been spurred by the bombing of the Chinese Embassy in Belgrade,

---

45. Zhang Zhuhua, "Nationalism, Liberalism, and Conservatism in China Today," seminar, Harvard University, Fairbank Center, June 7, 1999. Zhang says that the pivotal event was the appearance of the article "1998: Liberalism Surfaces" in *Southern Weekend*. Zhang Zhuhua was a member of the Standing Committee of the Chinese Youth League of the Chinese University of Law and Politics, but because he signed a petition to bring a lawsuit against Premier Li Peng for his role in the military crackdown on Tiananmen Square demonstrators in 1989, he lost all his positions. He is now in the "private" sector and advises state-run enterprises on the legalities of becoming privately run enterprises. See also Zheng Yongnian, *Discovering Chinese Nationalism in China*.

46. Populist books call for social justice for the common people, particularly for the millions of unemployed workers, while China carries out reforms. One such book is Liang Xiaoshen's *Zhongguo shehui gejieceng fenxi* (Social-level analysis of Chinese society) (Beijing: Jingji ribao chubanshe, 1997). Another is *Scales of Justice*, published by a Tsinghua University professor. One that reflects extreme populism is *China's Problems* (*Zhongguo de wenti*), a book series co-authored by Dong Yuyu and Shi Binghai, which is required reading for party cadres (Zhang Zhuhua, "Nationalism, Liberalism, and Conservatism in China Today," seminar, Harvard University, Fairbank Center, June 7, 1999).

47. Liu Junning, "The Revival of Liberalism in Contemporary China," seminar, Harvard University, Fairbank Center, Oct. 3, 2000. Zhang Zhuhua ("Nationalism, Liberalism, and Conservatism in China Today," seminar, Harvard University, Fairbank Center, June 7, 1999) also made the point that the ideas of the New Left were problematic, because the ideas were too advanced for China's conditions. China is not, for example, a "post-modern" society.

48. Discussions with Gu Xin, 2000; and Zhao Yuezhi, July 2001.

49. Song et al., *Zhongguo keyi shuo bu*.

China's prolonged application for membership in the World Trade Organization, its efforts to be named the site of the 2008 Olympics, the crash of a Chinese jet and the emergency landing of a U.S. spy plane on Chinese soil in 2001, and American interference in Beijing's efforts to bring Taiwan under its control. In the post-Tiananmen period, popular nationalism has taken on a life of its own, undeterred by official efforts to restrain it and not necessarily reflecting the official line about the proper form of "nationalism."

Intellectuals have not been immune to these trends. Nationalistic sentiments are expressed by intellectuals across a wide spectrum of political perspectives. The fear is that rapid democratization could lead to national disintegration as in the former Soviet Union and Yugoslavia. Rejection of Western ideas in favor of a newfound pride in China's own past and values is also a factor in the growth of nationalism among China's intellectuals. Although it may have emerged independently of official propaganda on the need to embrace China's traditional culture and patriotism,[50] the overlapping of the discourses on this profoundly important issue has brought many intellectuals closer to the party-state.[51]

China's broad variety of intellectual schools has allowed remarkably diverse opinions to be expressed in the debates now raging. Ironically, many of those Chinese intellectuals advocating cultural nationalism received their training in the West. They have used the intellectual tools of the West, including postcolonialism, postmodernism, post-Marxism, and Orientalism, to attack Western culture. To wit, they "have chosen as their weapons the language, concepts, and style of Western discourses," with the result that their own discourses on nationalism are so full of Western jargon that anyone unfamiliar with it would find it difficult to comprehend "these erudite exponents of Chinese nationalistic writ-

---

50. The patriotic education campaign, which began in 1992, emerged in the wake of the Tiananmen crackdown and the crisis of legitimacy it created for the regime.

51. The propaganda network tends to use the term "patriotism" (*aiguozhuyi*) because the term "nationalism" (*minzuzhuyi*) has strong racial overtones. "In the PRC official discourse, the terms 'nationalism' and 'chauvinism' referred to parochial and reactionary attachments to nationalities, whereas 'patriotism' was love and support for China, always indistinguishable from the Chinese state and the Communist Party." To criticize the party was, in effect, to be unpatriotic (Suisheng Zhao, "We Are Patriots First and Democrats Second," pp. 23, 27, 30–31, 37).

ings."[52] The following lists only a few of the more widely discussed and contentious issues.[53]

1. Nationalism, external threats to China, and China as a threat to others;

2. Modernizing the Chinese state, and whether it should follow the Western model of modernization; the decentralization of economic, fiscal, and political power and its implications for the state's "extractive capacity" and even for the dissolution of the state.

3. Ways to build a strong state without returning to a totalitarian regime, including the "third way"—"social democracy" (*sheyui minzhu zhuyi*) or "democratic socialism" (*minzhu shehui zhuyi*), as exemplified by Western European governments;

4. The appropriate symbols for China's new nationalism and how to differentiate between Chinese and Western civilization;

5. The effect of China's traditional culture and a culturally fueled nationalism on efforts to democratize;

6. Whether social disintegration is more of a threat than social stagnation;

7. China's ties with the international system and the degree to which it should accept established international norms and rules,[54] even though its own role in creating them was minimal;

---

52. Ibid., p. 38. According to Suisheng Zhao, after Deng Xiaoping's southern China tour in 1992, ideas that challenged the rigid conservative version of communism emerged, including some neo-authoritarian arguments relabeled as neo-conservatism. The emphasis in neo-conservatism is on stability and control and the restoration of a Confucian-based morality to replace Marxism-Leninism, which has failed to mobilize loyalty to the state. In short, they argue for Chinese nationalism and the need for a powerful state to keep China strong and united. He Xin, as a major proponent of neo-conservatism, strongly supported the government slogan "stability above everything" (ibid., pp. 33–34).

53. Many of the following topics on nationalism are discussed in Zheng Yongnian, *Discovering Chinese Nationalism in China*; Gong Nanxiang, "Make Nationalism a Constructive Force for Democratization"; and Zhu Muqun, "Chinese Nationalism in the Post-Deng Era." They are also discussed in a special issue of *China Studies* (*Zhongguo yanjiu*), 2000, no. 6, dedicated to the issue of nationalism. On the discussion of traditional Chinese values and their relationship to individual rights, as well as of China's traditional values and modernization generally, also see Gu, "Cultural Intellectuals and the Politics of the Cultural Public Space."

54. Li Shenzhi, a well-known liberal intellectual, argues that China should accept internationalization and the rules of the international system. He believes an emphasis on Chinese

8. The degree to which the state should relinquish Chinese traditions and "Chineseness" and accept more "universal" values such as those prevalent in the West;[55]

9. The degree to which Westernization-oriented government policies should guide China's domestic development;[56]

10. The role of ideology in maintaining national identity;

11. The relationship between Confucian-based ethnic nationalism and modern nationalism;

12. The superiority of Chinese civilization; must a "patriot" support China's traditional cultural values and oppose Western liberalization?;

13. The tensions between national identity and internationalization, and between a national cultural identity and cultural invasion from abroad;[57]

14. Samuel Huntington's portrayal of the post–Cold War period and future conflicts in his book *The Clash of Civilizations and the Remaking of World Order.*

The arguments among Chinese intellectuals over the contrary ideas of Huntington and Francis Fukuyama[58] have engendered a debate even more rowdy than the intellectual debate their ideas generated in the West. An increasingly large number of China's intellectuals have come to the conclusion that ideology has, in the post–Cold War period, been replaced by a desire on the part of individual nation-states to sharpen their own national identity and interests. Confrontations will thus arise "between different nation-states, understood as cultures, but under the banner of nationalism."[59]

---

nationalism would harm China. For a list of Li's articles, see Gong Nanxiang, "Make Nationalism a Constructive Force for Democratization," pp. 25–26n1.

55. Ji Xianling, a well-known liberal Chinese scholar, believes that much can be learned from ancient Chinese culture that would be beneficial to the post-modern world and that nationalism should be channeled into positive international cultural exchanges (ibid., pp. 26–27n2).

56. He Xin, a "conservative" intellectual and neo-nationalist, opposes any form of Westernization (Zhu Muqun, "Chinese Nationalism in the Post-Deng Era," pp. 58–59nn1–2).

57. Gong Gang, "National Identity and Cultural Resistance."

58. Fukuyama, *The End of History and the Last Man.*

59. Suisheng Zhao, "We Are Patriots First and Democrats Second," p. 34. For Chinese discussions of Huntington's and Fukuyama's ideas, see Yi, "Minzuzhuyi yu xiandai jingji fazhan"; and Wang Jisi, *Wenming yu guoji zhengzhi.* Wang Jisi is director of the Institute of American Studies in the Chinese Academy of Social Sciences.

More specifically in the arena of democratization, China's intellectuals have, among numerous other topics,

1. Debated the role of law in maintaining the balance between governmental power and citizens' rights;[60]
2. Discussed the relationship between private property rights and individualism;
3. Discussed gay and lesbian issues and what "rights" gays and lesbians have;
4. Urged the expansion of the rule of law to protect an individual's "private space," including the right of individuals to express ideas freely without being accused of violating the law;[61] and,
5. Urged the passage of laws to protect freedom of the press, arguing that all too often the news media have served as the mouthpiece of various sectors of the party-state. Greater freedom of the press would, they contend, serve as a safety valve by exposing social problems and letting the public know the government is addressing rather than ignoring these problems; allow for the exchange of information and safeguard citizens' rights to get information and express opinions; and facilitate supervision of the resolution of social problems by public opinion rather than judicial, legislative, or administrative supervision.[62]

China's intellectuals have also debated numerous international economic and political issues relating directly or indirectly to democracy and modernization, such as:

1. Theories of international circulation, comparative advantage, and export-led strategies;
2. "Market rationality," international interdependence, and whether globalization has benefited wealthier countries at the expense of China and other developing countries;
3. Deliberative versus economic democracy;
4. Whether there is an appropriate Western model for democratizing China;[63]

---

60. Zhou and Huang, "Lun fa zhengfu quanli he gongmin quanlide pingheng."
61. Wang Yan, "Cujin guojia zhengzhi shenghuode fazhihua."
62. Zhang Ximing, "Xinwen fazhi yu shehui fazhan."
63. Yongnian Zheng, *Discovering Chinese Nationalism in China.*

5. The degree to which a commitment to egalitarianism continues to distort income distribution;[64]

6. Whether the polarization of wealth is acceptable and necessary for development or is instead causing major social upheaval;[65]

7. Whether the claim of "humanitarian intervention" as a reason to meddle in a sovereign state's affairs (as in Yugoslavia concerning Kosovo) is a mere pretext for advancing national interests rather than human rights.

In the post–Cold War, post-Tiananmen era, the debates over most of these issues, as well as those among cultural intellectuals (discussed below), have been deeply affected both by the growing knowledge about and "fever" for Western culture, values, and theories (*xixue re*)—and by the rejection of the same by many Chinese intellectuals, who in the 1990s have (out of a belief that Western ideas were not relevant or useful for modernizing China) embraced Chinese (including Confucian) culture and values (*guoxue re*) to counter both Western values and communism. Thus, even though the resurgence of cultural nationalism among China's intellectuals coincided with the state's campaign since 1992 for patriotic education in China's schools and universities, it emerged largely independently of the state-led campaign. Ironically, many of those steeped in Western theories and values have done an abrupt about-face, becoming cultural nationalists and using Western theories and values to critique the West.[66] Their growing cynicism "about the moral superiority of the West" and their increasing resentment of "Western arrogance" have spurred them to challenge Western ideologies and values.[67]

Finally, many of China's public intellectuals have done more than participate in the debate over China's policies and problems. They have also become activists in social movements: promoting women's rights and opposing

---

64. Li Yining, "Zhongguo jingji tizhi gaigede lunli xue sikao." Li Yining is a professor at Beijing University.

65. Zhu Guanglei argues that economic development cannot happen without the polarization of wealth; others, such as Hu An'gang, Yang Fan, and He Qinglian, say the polarization of wealth is not acceptable, that the reforms are responsible for it, and that the government must do something about it (Cheng Li, "Promises and Pitfalls of Reform," pp. 140–46).

66. Suisheng Zhao, "We Are Patriots First and Democrats Second," pp. 35–37.

67. Xu Jilin, "Qimeng de mingyun: ershinian lai de Zhongguo sixiang jie" (The fate of enlightenment: the Chinese intelligentsia during the past two decades), *Ershi shiji*, no. 50 (Dec. 12, 1998): 4–13: cited in Cheng Li, "Promises and Pitfalls of Reform," p. 138.

domestic violence, defending the rights of gays and lesbians, joining in the movement to protect the rights of migrant workers, and becoming leaders of the environmental movement.[68] Although the numbers of intellectual-activists may not be large, the very fact that they are now fighting for the common man, the common woman, and even the uncommon man/woman, is a remarkable breakthrough for an intellectual elite grounded in inegalitarian assumptions.

CULTURAL INTELLECTUALS AND
STATE PATRONAGE

In the cultural sphere as well, intellectuals are normally dependent on the state. They rely on government patronage, and when that patronage has been withdrawn, they have found themselves unable to pursue noncommercial artistic creativity. In today's commercialized culture, this means that their energies must be plowed into making a living by producing commercially viable works with a broad public appeal.[69] In a liberalizing China, intellectuals in the cultural arena are threatened with the vulgarity of the marketplace, which demands popular cultural products, not sophisticated or experimental ones. This has been as true for poets and musicians as for playwrights and artists. They have had to continue to seek state sponsorship because of their own lack of entrepreneurial skills and the public's lack of interest in elite intellectual culture.[70]

The sad irony for China's intellectuals, as for former Soviet intellectuals, is that now that they have the freedom to express themselves more creatively, and even to write dissident plays, novels, or poetry, the public is not interested.[71] The majority of new publications have been pulp fiction and books,

---

68. Cheng Li, "Promises and Pitfalls of Reform," p. 139.

69. Sylvia Chan, "Building a 'Socialist Culture with Chinese Characteristics'?," p. 2. Statistical information from China indicates that there has been a steady decline in real terms of the government's funds that are allocated to culture, with many state-run cultural institutions receiving even less than they need to pay their employees' salaries.

70. Kraus, "China's Artists Between Plan and Market," pp. 181–84.

71. At a conference at Northeastern University in Boston in 1992, Russian dissident intellectuals, adored by the public under the old system of tight censorship, complained bitterly about the impact of economic reforms. Before the collapse of the Communist Party's system of censorship and of state support for artists, people would clamor to hear them read poetry, see their plays, and read their books. Now, economic reforms require all cultural organiza-

magazines, and tabloids pandering to popular taste. They have already made such heavy inroads into mainstream culture that serious literary and academic works, even those by the country's best writers and scholars, are being edged out of the market. Writers and academics whose works are thought not to have much market value often have to pay not only publication costs but also for the right to publish.[72] Of course, there are exceptions, and some cultural intellectuals have proved highly entrepreneurial and commercially successful since the market reforms were introduced. After the "golden decade for the revival of Chinese intellectual life" (1979 to 1989), they joined China's rapidly developing pop culture, producing soap operas, tabloid newspapers, mass-market books, action movies, sitcoms, pop music, and radio talk shows.

Elite intellectual discourse with its lofty idealism, critical energy, and highbrow aspirations dominated China's cultural landscape in the 1980s. Popular culture existed only in the margins during that period. It lacked legitimate production and distribution venues, since the state still held firm financial and political control of the mass media and cultural production. . . . The potential of popular culture remained latent, and to most Chinese intellectuals, it was simply a blind spot.[73]

The Maoist state had transformed popular culture into a medium that reflected correct political values. With the reforms that began in 1979, elite intellectual culture flourished. Tiananmen was the turning point that, ironically, led to a renaissance in popular culture. After the initial vicious purge of the cultural and political spheres, the party-state became torn by "ideological schizophrenia, administrative laxity, realpolitik, and simple incompetence." Although the party-state wanted to maintain central control over culture, economic reform demanded greater investment from Hong Kong, Taiwan, and elsewhere, and this required not scaring away foreign investors.[74] As a result, popular culture has been able to thrive "in the cracks between political

---

tions, and intellectuals, to support themselves with cultural products that have market appeal, and it turns out that dissident political literature in an open society has little. See also ibid., pp. 191–92.

72. Apart from other costs, state-run publishing houses control the issuing of legally required book numbers (ISBNs) and charge an author several thousand yuan to get one. When they become scarce and unaffordable, "Hong Kong publishers move in with their inexhaustible supply of ISBNs at cheaper prices" (Sylvia Chan, "Building a 'Socialist Culture with Chinese Characteristics'," p. 8).

73. Zha, "China's Popular Culture in the 1990s," pp. 109, 112, 113.

74. Barme, *In the Red*. p. 188.

repression and economic opening, between old-style elite culture and official censorship and recent international influences." It has helped shape a new generation interested in lifestyle not revolution and led to the expansion of "personal expression, debate over social issues, and development of mass entertainment."[75]

Those intellectuals and associations that were part of the "oppositional cultural scene" of the 1980s (but who were paid by the state) remain ambivalent about the new popular culture of the 1990s because it caters to popular tastes and the market and spurns high-brow but (to the masses) uninteresting ideas. Instead of bowing to the marketplace, they continue to solicit subsidies from the state in order to produce what they believe to be intellectually or artistically honest work,[76] a situation common to Western liberal democratic states. Yet the state seems determined to make China's culture industry profit-oriented and has essentially pushed cultural intellectuals out of the party-state's nest. Most can no longer live behind a "velvet curtain," where they could become "self-censoring non-critics" in exchange for room and board.[77]

Thus the paradox of artistic freedom is that cultural intellectuals who are not supported by the state may have less opportunity to be creative, for they must pander to the market; whereas those supported by the state must pander to the Party. In return for an assured livelihood, travel abroad, special privileges, and high salaries, cultural intellectuals must maintain a degree of loyalty to the state. They may express non-Marxist viewpoints but not anti-Marxist ones.[78]

---

75. Zha, "China's Popular Culture in the 1990s," p. 109.

76. Julia F. Andrews and Gao Minglu, "The Avant-garde's Challenge to Official Art," in Davis et al., *Urban Spaces in Contemporary China*, p. 278; and Zha, "China's Popular Culture in the 1990s," p. 121.

77. See Richard Kraus, Review of Geremie R. Barme, *In the Red: On Contemporary Chinese Culture*, China Journal, no. 44 (July 2000): 157–58.

78. Miklos Haraszti has referred to artists in the socialist states as being placed in "velvet prisons" by the state. "Artists sold out to the state in droves and deceived themselves by calling it progress. Some even convinced themselves that they had achieved independence or autonomy. In reality, they enjoyed the power and the comforts, and were unlikely to do anything to jeopardize their new status. Although few admitted it, the vast majority of artists collaborated with the socialist state in the post-Stalin era. . . . Their art was an art of complicity that legitimized and perpetuated the hegemony of the state. All artists were on the state payroll. If they were not on the state payroll, by definition they were not artists. As loyal professionals, artists benefited from lavish state funding for the arts. Indeed, they became addicted

The same sort of clientelistic relationship characterizes television and film directors: they do not stand in opposition to the state. In many respects, in fact, they actively collude with the state. No member of the "Fifth Generation" (post-Cultural Revolution) of television script writers and film directors, for example, has ever turned down state funds.[79] China's best-known television writer in the 1990s, Wang Shuo (who is also a novelist), is funded by the state, even though his soap operas deal with the seamy side of Chinese society (infidelity, crime, social fragmentation, corruption, alienation). Nevertheless, he has not given air time to what the government would call dissident themes.[80] His messages are politically ambivalent, and his mocking of the pretensions of intellectuals and high culture no doubt has made him acceptable to the Party. Even so, he has had problems. His constant harping on the defects and evils of Chinese society in his soap operas led the authorities to suspend the televising of his programs in 1997. This gadfly of the cultural establishment was told to focus on more positive themes.[81]

Did ordinary Chinese people protest this censoring of a favorite program? Whether the government is simply good at getting its values and messages across, or whether the people embrace these values because they are traditional values, the results are the same: many ordinary Chinese seemed to agree with the government's decision to take Wang Shuo's programs off television because he was providing negative models of behavior. They believe that Wang Shuo has *an obligation* to provide positive models for the Chinese people to follow and that he has been too cynical and critical for their tastes.[82] Even one of China's leading public intellectuals and himself a critic of the regime, Liu Zhifeng, "criticized Wang Shuo for profaning litera-

---

to state funding." Given dependency on state support, artists engaged in "self-censorship" (Miklos Haraszti, *The Velvet Prison: Artists under State Socialism* [NY: Noonday Press, 1989]; cited in Pickowicz, "Velvet Prisons and the Political Economy of Chinese Filmmaking," pp. 194–95).

79. Pickowicz, "Velvet Prisons and the Political Economy of Chinese Filmmaking," p. 205.

80. Ibid., p. 206. According to Zha Jianying (*China Pop*, p. 110), Wang Shuo is very cautious in dealing with any question about human rights. Zha Jianying also disputes the view that Wang is funded by the state, stating that, unlike most of China's educated elite, "he earns a living on his own."

81. The Chinese are hardly unique in this concern. See Chapter 1 above on Plato, the U.S. Congress, and New York Mayor Rudolph Giuliani, all of whom have argued that art must be uplifting and provide good role models.

82. Discussions with Chinese students, colleagues, taxi drivers, and friends in Beijing, 1996–97; and with Chinese students in the United States, 1998.

ture and decency." Liu also criticized Wang Meng, a novelist and former minister of culture and himself a public intellectual "for surrendering his 'intellectual soul in the name of cultural pluralism and tolerance.'" [83] Here again is an example of Chinese society perceiving the state as the *guardian* of its interests, not its oppressor, and framing the issue in terms of protecting societal interests, not in terms of "freedom of the press" or individual rights versus state rights.

The same is true of CCTV's talk show *Speak Honestly*. According to its producer, Yang Dongping, the program was criticized by the authorities for not "giving more guidance to public opinion." He was told to curb his open-ended style, which he had chosen because he felt many of the problems presented on the show did not have definite answers. He wanted the programs to stimulate public discussion. The authorities insisted, however, that the program give a definite, clear-cut answer to the audience: it should be *this* way, not *that* way.[84] But, Yang added, ordinary viewers criticized the program for the same reason. Especially the middle-aged and elderly listeners found talk-show hosts too flippant and, for this reason, objectionable. Chinese producers have been willing to sacrifice some measure of acerbity and the freedom to say whatever they wanted because, Yang said, the survival of the "talk show" was at this point more important than its content.[85]

Thus, the individual artist and the intellectual, the ballet troupes and the symphony orchestras, the novelist and the poet, the theaters and the actors—all have a complex relationship with the state. It is not a case of individuals and autonomous associations—civil society—making demands *against* the state. To the contrary, many ordinary Chinese believe that the role of China's intellectuals is to serve them, the country, and the Commu-

---

83. Liu Zhifeng, editor, *Daode Zhongguo: dangdai Zhongguo daode lunli de shencong yousi* (Moral China: deep concerns and thinking about ethics and morality in today's China) (Beijing: Zhongguo shehui kexue chubanshe, 1999), pp. 13–15; cited in Cheng Li, "Promises and Pitfalls of Reform," p. 155. Wang Meng defended the "Wang Shuo phenomenon," saying that in post-Mao China, Chinese literature "was actually a critical response to hypocrisy and other ugly human behaviors of the Cultural Revolution" (ibid., p. 156).

84. It has been my experience in teaching Chinese students both at Northeastern University and in the Foreign Affairs College in Beijing that, in response to my sophisticated, elegant lectures on the multiple theories proffered to explain an international event, they—and only they—will come up after class and ask me to tell them which one is "correct."

85. Zhang Weiguo, "Tuokuoxiu zai Zhongguo," pp. 3–4.

nist Party by providing appropriate values and role models in their works.[86] Of course, not everyone feels the same way. In a 1995 *Beijing Youth Daily* survey, for example, 47.1 percent of the respondents over sixteen years of age said they would like the paper to "increase its criticism of the dark side of the society."[87] Surveys of Chinese youth have indicated they believe the role of literature is, in fact, to expose society's shortcomings. In response to the statement "Literature should not excessively expose the seamy side of society," fully 43.6 percent disagreed, and 31.7 percent "only somewhat agreed."[88] (In the same surveys of Chinese youth, however, there seemed to be strong agreement [51.9 percent] with the statement "Freedom of speech does not mean allowing the publishing of reactionary speech.")[89]

Whatever Chinese youth said in surveys, the popularity of Jia Pingwa's darkly critical (and pornographic) 1993 novel, *The Abandoned Capital* (*Feidu*), suggests that many people are eager to read about the bribery, depravity, greed, and moral turpitude of Chinese characters. But their interest may have been aroused less by Jia's realistic portrayals of the seamy side of society than by the salacious scenes of sexual debauchery.[90] Regardless of the reason for its popularity, critics felt that *The Abandoned Capital*, written by an author who had heretofore written only high-brow literary fiction, was one more piece of evidence that "serious writers were now prepared to 'kowtow to the vulgar, *meisu*,' for the sake of fame and gain." It was also evidence of the slack standards for publication that had emerged by 1993—the result of officials caught between a sclerotic political ideology and the new commercialism.[91]

---

86. Discussions with Chinese students in United States, fall 1997.

87. "Beijing People Are Reading the Newspaper," *Beijing qingnian bao*, Oct. 4, 1995, sect. 7.

88. Zhongguo shehui kexue yuan, Shehuixue yanjiusuo, Zhuanxing ketizu, *Zhongguo qingniande toushi*, p. 107.

89. The wording of this survey is a bit ambiguous, at least to a Westerner: it is not clear whether this is a statement of fact (Reactionary speech is not permitted under the present conception of freedom of speech by the state) or a statement of opinion about the meaning of freedom of speech. The survey, done only in 1988, had as its other responses "agree somewhat" (24.3 percent), "agree only a little" (12.8 percent), and "disagree" (7.7 percent) (ibid., p. 144).

90. Published by Beijing Publishing House in 1993, more than a million copies were sold within the first year of publication (Zha, *China Pop*, pp. 129–39).

91. The official response was slow, and the book was banned only in late 1993, half a year after it was first published. The Party's Department of Propaganda claimed it really had to ban it because it had received so many letters from parents concerned about the effects of the book on their adolescent children (Barmé, *In the Red*, p. 185).

In response to the Party's call to beef up China's "spiritual construction," since the mid-1990s China's film and television writers have created a number of movies and TV programs that tell stories both acceptable to the Party and popular with television viewers.[92] The vast majority of China's intellectuals seem willing to accept responsibility for promoting societal values endorsed by the state rather than insisting on art for art's sake. They are realists in their work.

China's famous film producers Zhang Yimou and Chen Kaige are good examples. Many of their films are foreign funded,[93] they occasionally get into trouble with the authorities, and they promote themselves as "political renegades." In truth, however, they have actually been "highly privileged insiders who are closely connected to and enjoy good working relations with the cultural establishment."[94] Geremie Barme asserts that Chen Kaige "provided a role model for his juniors on how to exploit the system" when he abandoned his earlier "cultural sincerity" for "designer veneer." Barme writes of witnessing "famous critics of the party reach accommodation with the authorities in private while putting on the brave face of the dissident to foreign journalists and scholars." Following their co-optation by the state, they become "official artists," "negotiated dissidents," and "market weathervanes."[95] Yet, if what Chinese intellectuals want is greater artistic and intellectual freedom, why should intellectuals like Chen, who have pushed back the boundaries of control, be criticized? Even if Chen Kaige's films might serve the state's purpose of promoting nationalism in China, they have also advanced Chen's own objective of re-creating a Confucian culture in China.[96] Like most intellectuals, Chen is pursuing his interests by doing things the Chinese way, through cultivating relationships. Chen and Zhang do not, moreover, challenge the establishment by producing what would be called "dissident cinema." Instead,

---

92. Domestically produced movies include *Red River Valley*, *Kong Fansen*, and *Red Cherry*. Television programs include *Yearning*, *Great Turning Point*, *The Heavens Above*, *Oriental Time and Space*, and *Our Dad and Mom*.

93. For example, Zhang Yimou's *Judou* and *Raise the Red Lantern* were both foreign funded, as was Chen Kaige's *Farewell My Concubine*.

94. Pickowicz, "Velvet Prisons and the Political Economy of Chinese Filmmaking," pp. 212–13.

95. Barme, *In the Red*. pp. xiii, xvii, 194.

96. Zha, *China Pop*, p. 102. For more on Chen Kaige and Zhang Yimou, see ibid., pp. 79–104.

they produce more finely textured and nuanced films than most other directors in the state-run film industry. Foreign funding also allows them a degree of independence from internal control.[97]

Still, some of China's cultural intellectuals do try to gain the attention of the international community (especially the press and human rights groups) by portraying themselves as "dissidents." (And some of them actually are dissidents.) This almost assures the success of their work (especially for "independent" film makers) and may enhance their reputation within China— even when the work is mediocre. This "symbiotic relationship between dissidents and the foreign media" provides the latter with the material they need to manufacture international opinion about China and its dissidents.[98] And, because the classification of Chinese intellectuals is so broad, it is easier to portray anyone pushing the boundaries or criticizing the reforms as a dissident, a label that gains them immediate sympathy in the West.

It is possible, then, that the international community might unwittingly be playing a role in creating "dissidents" who do not actually exist, as well as creating undeserved success for some. The fact that the international community pays more attention to "dissident" intellectuals is regrettable. First, the party-state's reasons for banning a creative work or closing a magazine or journal may have little to do with the expression of an anti-regime sentiment, as the term "dissident" might suggest. Although some intellectuals have indeed expressed political opinions unacceptable to the party-state, others, such as, Zhou Weihui (*Shanghai Baby*) and Jia Pingwa (*Abandoned Capital*) have crossed other boundaries, particularly moral boundaries that many governments might also find unacceptable. Even in liberal democratic states, the moral boundaries on freedom of speech today are still being contested. In the case of China, such restrictions reflect the puritanical standards of traditional Chinese culture as much, if not more so, than the party-state's effort to squelch dissident thought.

---

97. Early on, Chen Kaige and Zhang Yimou collaborated (with Zhang Yimou as cinematographer) on highly successful films, such as *Yellow Earth* and *The Big Parade*, without foreign funding. Some films, however, have been shot without official approval: for example, Zhang Yuan's *Beijing Bastards*, which won the Critics Circle Award at the 1993 Lucarno Film Festival, and *The Blue Kite*, produced by Tian Zhuangzhuang in 1993, which was financed by Hong Kong interests and smuggled abroad. It won the top award at the Tokyo Film Festival (Pickowicz, "Velvet Prisons and the Political Economy of Chinese Filmmaking," p. 219).

98. Barme, *In the Red*, pp. 191–92.

Second, observers of China miss the complexity of China's intellectual scene if they hone in on the curtailment of intellectual and artistic freedom for "dissidents" while ignoring the growth of greater freedom of expression for those intellectuals not labeled "dissidents." In the post-Mao reassessment of socialism, the party-state has recognized the harm done by insisting on a single interpretation of socialism. By permitting a "pluralistic conception and interpretation of official doctrine," it has relinquished its ideological monopoly and "made it more difficult to characterize opponents in political and ideological disputes as guilty of ideological deviation."[99]

Equally important to its willingness to accept contending interpretations of socialism has been the party-state's growing preoccupation with corruption and the side-effects of reforms—at the expense of its earlier fixation on ideology. In any event, statements by China's top leaders have repeatedly indicated an ideological thaw. Although some may dismiss them as meaningless, most Chinese intellectuals would—minimally—see them as a sign of which way the wind is blowing. Thus, many have taken heart from a speech before the Central Committee by President Jiang Zemin, in which he stated that to strengthen the Party's internal discipline and the nation's ideology, five kinds of "spirit" were necessary: "ideological emancipation, seeking truth from facts, and being bold and creative, hard-working, and practical and self-less."[100] Hardly kindling for the next book burning.

Third, since the mid-1990s, a new breed of public intellectual has emerged in China. This group consists of intellectuals who are both part of "the establishment" and critics of it. Many of these participants in the broad debate about China's reforms, values, and goals were trained in the West or exposed to theories from the West, and they tend to be more concerned with issues than ideology. They are frequently joined by Chinese scholars residing abroad and debate with others in electronic magazines on the Internet. Their bold and even daring critiques are aimed at challenging the government to address China's problems in an appropriate manner. It is truly an open debate, in which intellectuals from all persuasions weigh in and even government leaders participate. Those public intellectuals involved are no longer necessarily employed by the state, although some do work in the gov-

---

99. Yan Sun, *The Chinese Reassessment of Socialism*, p. 269.

100. "Jiang Zemin Outlines Party Ideological Blueprint," *China News Digest*, Feb. 18, 2001, on line. As reported by SCMPost. www.cnd.

ernment's think tanks and even for "mouthpieces of the CCP" such as *People's Daily*.[101] No one should accuse them of being toadies of the party-state.

He Qinglian, a trained economist and senior correspondent of the newspaper *Shenzhen Legal News*, is a good example of China's courageous new intellectuals. Although employed by the state, she is the author of *China's Pitfall (Zhongguo de xianjing)*, which was published in both Beijing and Hong Kong in 1998 and is a thoroughgoing critique of the bad side of China's reforms. Among other challenges to the ruling regime, she castigates China's leaders for moving China away from an authoritarian system with a planned economy to "a country run by corrupt bureaucratic capitalists"; they are, she charges, making the same mistake as some other post-communist regimes. Like George Soros, she notes that there is no guarantee that society will evolve from a closed society to a pluralistic civil society with a market economy. She is in turn criticized by other public intellectuals, who point out what they consider to be her errors in analysis. As Cheng Li notes, "What makes this moment in the reform process truly extraordinary and this emerging generation of public intellectuals particularly remarkable, is the fact that problems and pitfalls are so frequently and so feverishly debated."[102]

If we adopt Barme's vocabulary and label many of the political and cultural ideas that are not supported by the ruling faction at the time they are expounded as "nonmainstream" instead of "dissident," we can realize how much vibrancy and strength there is within the intellectual community—regardless of who pays for room and board. Furthermore, China's nonmainstream culture is evolving within the context of a socialist state that is itself undergoing a remarkable transformation. "Both have matured together and used each other, feeding each other's needs and developing ever new coalitions, understandings, and compromises."[103]

The government has, then, had to trade control over intellectuals in the cultural sphere for responsiveness to the market, and control over intellectu-

---

101. Cheng Li, "Promises and Pitfalls of Reform," pp. 124–34. Zhao Yuezhi ("Media and Elusive Democracy in China") suggests, however, that the very fact that these intellectuals confine their debates to the Internet and small, elite journals allows them to be elitist in their discourse and to ignore the concerns of Chinese peasants and workers.

102. Cheng Li, "Promises and Pitfalls of Reform," pp. 126–28. Unfortunately, in July 2001, He Qinglian suddenly fled China because she was concerned that she was about to be arrested or somehow punished for her work.

103. Barme, *In the Red*, p. xv.

als in the social sciences and media for a societal safety valve and for their expertise and ability to offer policy alternatives. It has decentralized the management of intellectuals and their associations, relaxed its former "rigid political control on the content and forms of cultural products," and promoted greater diversity within China's culture.[104] Finally, by encouraging foreign investment and opening China's doors to international influence, China's leadership has set in motion powerful forces for social, cultural, economic, and political change.

THE CONTRIBUTION OF INTELLECTUALS
TO CIVIL SOCIETY

What, then, are the limits on freedom of speech for Chinese intellectuals? Have they benefited from an expanding definition of freedom of speech? Have they been able and willing to extract themselves from a clientelistic relationship with the state so that they can help shape a civil society, only to fall into a clientelist relationship with China's new bourgeoisie? Are they yet at a point where they see full autonomy of a civil society from the state as an essential goal? Or do they believe that ending their clientelist relationship with the state is not necessary for them to exercise significant freedom of speech and to achieve the broad ends and level of democratization that they think is appropriate to Chinese conditions and culture? In short, do we demean the important role of Chinese intellectuals when we insist that a civil society must be confrontational with the state? And, finally, how much does either the market, or the desire to become a public intellectual with widespread public recognition and significant commercial value, or the desire to serve as an adviser to the government, affect what an intellectual says and does?

It is easy to forget that intellectuals everywhere are products of their own culture and institutions. We cannot assume that just because intellectuals do not challenge a government or do not engage in open dissidence that they are mere sycophants, or alternatively, that they are miserable because they so long to speak out. In fact, it could be argued that there is a more cooperative and more symbiotic relationship between the China's intellectuals and the state's leaders than between intellectuals and the common people. The elite-

---

104. Sylvia Chan, "Building a 'Socialist Culture with Chinese Characteristics'?," p. 2.

mass conflict and the anti-egalitarian perspective of China's intellectuals (especially toward country people) have undercut efforts to achieve democratization—even when both sides supported the same causes.[105]

In this period of rapid political, cultural, and social flux, it is hard to know what proportion of China's intellectuals truly feel "oppressed" by the system, what proportion feel they must accommodate or be ruined, and what proportion feel they are thriving and have a remarkable amount of freedom of expression in spite of the party-state and in spite of the new commercialism. Certainly those cultural intellectuals who do not incorporate explicit political content into their work are less likely to feel pressure from the party-state. But it is interesting to contemplate the dismay felt by Chinese literary figures, before 2000, at the fact that no Chinese author had won the Nobel Prize for Literature.[106] What did they blame for this national, and personal, affront? They blamed poor translations of their works into Western languages[107] or the lack of translations, which left them inaccessible to members of the Nobel Prize Committee. They did not blame an oppressive party-state—perhaps because they did not really feel it was to blame, and perhaps because they did not believe it was a lack of the right to

---

105. Kelliher, "Keeping Democracy Safe from the Masses." As noted above, China's intellectuals have insisted that intellectual freedom must precede democratization for the masses, which can only occur when the masses have become adequately educated and "civilized."

106. The prize was awarded to Gao Xingjian in 2000. Unfortunately for the Chinese sense of pride, he was a writer whose work had been banned in China in the 1980s, and he has lived in Paris since 1987. Wounded feelings have not been assuaged by the fact that the Nobel is not given to a country but to a person. Further, there was an assumption in 2000 that the prize had to go to a Chinese. This is probably a correct assumption, as the Nobel Prize Committee on Literature has for many years been deeply criticized for ignoring Chinese writing.

Although Chinese intellectuals take pride in the fact that Gao was born and raised in China and that much of the work cited as the basis for the prize was written while he was still in China, many may well feel the award was a calculated political affront to China, part of the "anti-China" stance of the West. Why else select out someone whose work is banned rather than someone whose work is not, or at least someone who continues to live and work in China rather than abroad? This response is more common among those cultural intellectuals who believe China had far more impressive writers, including the novelist Ba Jin and dissident poet Bei Dao. Of course, this may well be dismissed as sour grapes, but there appear to be a number of Western authorities on Chinese literature who do not believe Gao was the most deserving Chinese writer. On the other hand, others whose work has been banned or at least criticized may somehow feel vindicated.

107. Barme, *In the Red*, p. ix.

express themselves freely that kept this prize beyond their reach. Such attitudes suggest the complexity of the clientelist relationship between China's intellectuals and the party-state. Clientelism is in some senses a non-zero-sum game, in which both sides win and lose together.

On the other hand, the furor caused by the 2000 Cheong Kong *Reading (Dushu)* awards suggests that the awarding of *any* prize is likely to cause controversy among Chinese intellectuals. This is perhaps in part because of the suspicion that it is indeed a clientelist relationship between the Party and the award-givers and winners that is involved. The venomous debate over the *Reading* awards occurred largely out of the public eye, on a website inaugurated by *Dushu* on June 18, 2000, and named *Zhonghua dushu* (The Chinese reader). The vituperative, polemical, and *ad hominem* denunciations of the prizewinners as "neo-leftists"—a term with peculiarly negative connotations in post-leftist China—was apparently motivated as much by professional jealousy of the international jet-setting winners and the enhanced social capital and publishability they would garner from winning the prize, as by a belief that the Hong Kong businessman funding the prize wanted to ingratiate himself with the Party and that the prizes were fixed. (Its winners were all closely associated with *Dushu*. The primary winner, Wang Hui, was *Dushu's* joint editor-in-chief.)[108] Perhaps the viciousness of the critiques was also affected by the attack mentality groomed during the class struggle of the preceding era.

In any event, as the Chinese state moves away from the heavily authoritarian relationship with Chinese citizens that characterized the period of Mao Zedong's rule to an authoritarian system with inklings of democracy, it appears that the regime will continue to allow Chinese intellectuals, whether liberal or conservative, neo-Marxist or populist, to speak their piece as long as they do not openly challenge the regime.[109] Indeed, those who now most openly challenge Chinese Communist Party rule are not intellectuals, or students, but unemployed workers, rural migrants, disgruntled peasants, and followers of Falungong.

Today, liberals are no longer necessarily perceived as enemies of the party-state. Indeed, there seem to be a fair number of liberals within the

---

108. Barme and Davies, "Have We Been Noticed Yet?," pp. 11–37.

109. Zhang Zhuhua, "Nationalism, Liberalism, and Conservatism in China Today," seminar, Harvard University, Fairbank Center, June 7, 1999; Yuan Yue, director, Horizon (Lingdian) Polling Company, Harvard University, Fairbank Center, Sept. 27, 2000.

leadership of the party-state who are pushing for political and economic lib-eralization in general, and such policies as accelerated privatization, the full legalization of private property, the termination of government involvement in enterprises, and increased marketization.[110]

Nevertheless, it is common for regimes moving from "hard" authoritari-anism to "soft" authoritarianism, to concentrate their limited resources on a few political dissidents who dare to challenge the party-state openly while according considerable freedom to those who do not. This was precisely the style of the Deng Xiaoping–led party-state, which abandoned the Maoist style of massive crackdowns on intellectuals and instead used selective re-pression. Unfortunately, the international media's tendency to focus on the high-profile dissidents who are the targets of such repression creates the im-pression that the regime engages in broad political repression.[111] In fact, party-state officials do not really want to catch the "small potatoes" and tend to ignore them. Officials in charge of watching them are often sympathetic to their ideas, while others lack an understanding of what they are saying, since the Chinese quickly translate Western works into Chinese and pick up the sometimes incomprehensible Western style of discourse. In general, China's intellectuals believe it is not *what* they say but *how* they say it (and where they publish it) that can protect them from censorship.[112]

Outright opposition to the regime has not been the style of China's intel-lectuals, but this hardly means they have lacked influence over the course of Chinese politics or that they hesitate to critique the regime's policies. To the contrary, they have played a pivotal role through their positions within gov-ernment ministries, agencies, academies, universities, and think tanks, their writings in books and journals, and their production of movies, television

---

110. Chongyi Feng, "The Party-State, Liberalism and Social Democracy," p. 24, who on this point refers for details to Zhang Wenmian, et al., eds., *Zhongguo jingji da lunzhan* (Controversies on the Chinese economy), vols. 1–5 (Jingji guanli chubanshe, 1996–2000).

111. Pei, "China's Evolution Toward Soft Authoritarianism," pp. 75–76. Pei bases his con-clusions on studies of the percentage of China's political prisoners classified as "counterrevo-lutionaries," the only criminal classification for political dissidents, and the number of coun-terrevolutionaries who were arrested and tried annually. His study indicates that the percentage of counterrevolutionaries in China's prisons fell from 13.35 percent in 1980 to 0.51 percent in 1989; and that the number of counterrevolutionary cases prosecuted in China fell from 358 in 1987 to 271 in 1997. During the post-Tiananmen crackdown from 1989 to 1990, there was a spike in the number of such cases, from 208 in 1988 to 448 in 1989 to 728 in 1990 (ibid., p. 78).

112. Discussions with Lin Tongji, Oct. 2001.

programs, and cultural events. To decry their clientelist relationship with the state as self-aggrandizement and pandering to those in power is to miss how effective intellectuals have been in using this approach to achieve greater pluralization, if not outright democratization, of the political system. It is a subtler approach to political change than intellectuals in a liberal democratic system would normally take, but it has worked exceedingly well during China's reform period. Debates over a remarkable range of social, political, cultural, and economic ideas and policies do take place, even if the limits to this debate are still decidedly narrower than some would like.

Finally, even if we conclude that the relationship between intellectuals and the state is more along the lines of "socialist corporatism" than "civil society," Chinese intellectuals today still enjoy a position of far greater autonomy and influence than they had before the reform period. For that relationship to evolve, intellectuals may have to step not only beyond the boundaries of residual socialist culture and socialist institutions but also beyond the constraints of Chinese culture.

9 Fair and Consistent Standards for Evaluating Freedom and Democracy in China

[The political systems of China, Singapore, and Japan] suggest the real possibility, in the late modern context, of regimes that clearly meet the test of the minimum universal content of morality, and do as well or better than liberal states on other criteria relevant to human flourishing, without adopting liberal institutions or social norms and without converging on the universal civilization anticipated in the Enlightenment philosophy of history. These regimes . . . are examples of the successful adoption of Western technologies by flourishing non-Occidental cultures that remain deeply resistant to Western values.

—John Gray

When we undertake a critique of rights and democracy in China, we are obliged to ask the kinds of questions we would ask ourselves when restrictions on individual rights and incursions on democracy occur in a liberal democracy: Does a problem reflect a basic conflict between the political ideas and practices of liberal democracy on the one hand and an illiberal culture on the other? Does the problem arise because of a failure to implement liberal democracy fully? Or is it the result of a defect in the institutions of democratic liberalism? Or in the process of implementation? Or in the implementers? Or in social conditions? In short, before we issue a wholesale indictment of China's political system, we need to understand its ideological and cultural roots, as well as the factors that constrain its performance.

It is particularly difficult to make definitive statements about China because it has many of the trappings of civil society and democracy, if not of

EPIGRAPH: Gray, *Enlightenment's Wake*, p. 83.

liberalism. The National People's Congress and legislatures at each level from the provinces to the townships discuss policy and pass laws to implement it. The system is underpinned by a system of elections to villagers' committees and indirect elections to county-level people's congresses. The legal system is based on a constitution and laws passed by the National People's Congress, as well as a judicial system featuring courts, lawyers, judges, jurors, and investigators. And even if China currently outlaws the creation of new political parties and the Chinese Communist Party controls the handful of so-called democratic parties, at least China has an institutional precedent for a multiparty system.

These institutions might be dismissed as tools of an authoritarian system, institutions that in practice may be cynically manipulated to serve the purposes of the state; but China appears to be an authoritarian system that is democratizing, and these institutions could well form the framework of a democratic system if the processes and practices of these institutions continue to develop along some of their present trajectories. They have, in fact, already evolved to a point where they are far more democratic than at any time in Chinese history. Perhaps most important for a people who throughout history have had to worry about the potential consequences of criticizing their rulers, people today can openly disagree with the party line, mock their leaders, ridicule communist ideas in public,[1] and vigorously attack the corruption of government and party officials without fear of being condemned as "enemies of the people," as long as they do not publicly and directly question the legitimacy of Chinese Communist Party rule. The government has come to tolerate and even encourage far more criticism through "official channels," such as surveys of people's concerns, public opinion polls, official complaint bureaus, letters to the editors, and discussions in work unit meetings.

This is not to say that the road to greater freedom and democracy is unobstructed. Social conditions—the enormous size and diversity of the population and the country, poverty and the disaffection it generates, as well as

---

1. For example, one of China's more irreverent directors, Meng Jinghui, in his staging of Vladimir Mayakowsky's play *The Bedbug*, had choral refrains like "Work! Unite! Create! Struggle!" delivered with comical flair. Actors spoke about using a hammer to pound socialism into their heads. At least the Shanghai audience seemed to think it a comical take on socialism (Sheila Melvin, "Chinese Welcome a Break from Old-Style Drama," *New York Times*, June 10, 2001, sect. 2, pp. 1, 31).

the erosion of the Chinese Communist Party's legitimacy, and greater expo-sure to foreign influence—make *control* a critical issue for the government. Control over the people and land has been a central issue in China for mil-lennia, and many of the methods used to ensure control, order, and stability were used long before the Communists came to power in 1949—and are likely to continue. China's wide variety of social and economic conditions means that policies beneficial to one part of the population or section of the country often do not benefit other segments or regions, and that policies supported by one group may be opposed by others.[2] As the experiences of ex-communist regimes in the former Soviet Union and Central Europe indi-cate, a democratic political system consisting of a multitude of small parties, each representing a narrow constituency, may exacerbate the fracturing of society, making control difficult and consensus impossible.

Finally, political institutions do not exist in a cultural vacuum; they are embedded in a particular environment and function and develop as part of that environment. The nature of China's culture and how it does and does not support the institutionalization of greater democracy and freedom are discussed at length in the preceding chapters. Here it need only be remarked that cultures can and do evolve and that it will take time to overcome the

---

2. This is evident in China's major cities, where policies established to benefit urban resi-dents with a proper household residency registration (*hukou*) purposefully exclude the mil-lions of rural migrants now in cities from benefits such as health care and education. For an in-depth look at the registration system as the basis for institutional exclusion, see Wang Fei-ling, "The Roots of an Institutional Exclusion." Similarly, the international controversy that erupted in 1999 over the World Bank's funding ($40 million) of China's resettlement of hun-dreds of thousands of people from the arid, desolate plateau of eastern Qinghai to western Qinghai (the population is 23 percent Tibetan) is an example of the complicated social condi-tions China faces in making policy. If we are to believe Western press reports from journalists who have interviewed some of the peasants involved, "the people tapped for relocation are barely surviving, and . . . the few peasants already resettled in the west have gained a better life. Three times as many people have applied to move [from eastern to western Qinghai] as will be able to do so if China receives its funding." But those outside China who are concerned about the survival of Tibetan culture in China proper contend that this is merely a plot by the Chinese government to further dilute the Tibetan population. They also contend that China will use prison labor in building the resettlements, which the government denies. But, "poli-tics and prisoners are far from the minds of most people in the villages. . . . In eastern Qinghai, the talk was all about survival" (Indira A. R. Lakshmanan, "China's Long March: Newton Man Becomes Pawn in Debate on Resettlement," *Boston Globe*, Aug. 22, 1999, pp. A1, A22). In 2000, in the face of extensive lobbying by activists for the Campaign for a Free Tibet, the World Bank decided not to fund the project, but China went ahead with it anyway.

cultural obstacles to democratization. The formidable weight of China's culture, as well as the social and demographic conditions under which cultural change must occur, impede a rapid transformation in this area. The Chinese may be unable to abandon certain deeply rooted Confucian elements and aspects of the political culture that are integral to China's present institutions and policies. But whether Confucianist values are viewed as pro-, anti-, or a-democratic, they now exist alongside of (and, minimally, are being reshaped by) the more democratic and modern values accompanying development and internationalization. The fact that China's citizens increasingly rely on laws and associations rather than personalistic relationships to advance their interests, and that the state itself now justifies its actions through reference to laws instead of to its moral legitimacy provides evidence of change in China's political culture.

Yet, as is also noted in the preceding chapters, many of the democratizing steps introduced since the reform period began in 1979 may have enhanced the ability of the Chinese Communist Party to remain in power. For example, the decision of the party-state to provide outlets for ordinary people to express grievances, the proliferation of associations that serve as transmission belts in both directions and give their members a vested interest in supporting the system that empowers them, and reforms that have enriched the country and given people many more rights—all have helped to keep the Chinese Communist Party in power (so far).

An evaluation of freedom and democracy in China must make assumptions that are consistent, correct and fair. If they are, such an evaluation can be used for comparative analysis. This might, for example, require that an assessment of the state of democracy and freedom in China extend beyond political institutions to include the quality of life that the state is providing for the people. Criteria for fairness might also include a review of the trajectory of political institutions and political change: Are they moving in the direction of greater freedom and democracy? Do the Chinese themselves feel optimistic about their future?

How, then, do we develop fair and consistent standards for evaluating rights and democracy in China? This book uses both an "internal critique" and an "external critique." External critiques are, of course, applicable to any country, regardless of ideology and type of government. An "internal critique," however, judges a society by its own standards, not by the standards of other societies. If China meets its own standards for democracy or at least for justice and fairness to its people as set by its own government, and if the Chinese population as a whole seems satisfied with these standards, then negative external assessments matter less. But if the Chinese government cannot meet the standards for democracy, justice, and fairness established by its own leaders, if the people are dissatisfied with their lives and have little hope that things will get better in the future, then others are on more solid ground in criticizing the Chinese government's failings.

A methodological preference for an internal critique is less an embrace of cultural relativism and more a rejection of the imposition of ethnocentric and ideologically motivated concepts of democracy by individuals and governments outside the polity being studied, concepts that, for example, in the case of China conflate democracy with an anti-communist ideology. (Nothing, however, prevents one from applying an external critique to one's own polity. Some Chinese intellectuals use Western ideas, values, and theories to think about China. On the other hand, China's cultural nationalists are performing an internal critique of China by using Chinese values, while using Western values and theories to critique the West.) Another advantage of the internal critique is that it leaves in place the nearly utopian objectives and standards the Chinese Communist Party has often used for evaluating its own success. In the 1990s, Chinese intellectuals, the media, and even the National People's Congress and officials of the party-state became far more critical of the government's failure to meet its own goals and of the many devastating side-effects of the economic reforms. Furthermore, although not all the participants in the "Wither China?" debate argue that more democracy will lead to less corruption (many in fact point out that greater democracy in Taiwan has spawned a ferocious form of corruption),[3] they frequently link greater crime and corruption with economic liberalization.

---

3. China's leaders and intelligentsia are fully aware that charges of corruption were rife during the campaign for Taiwan's presidential elections in 2000. In fact, the most daunting domestic task facing Chen Sui-bian, elected as president in 2000, has been to address the issue of money politics. For example, criminal syndicates take advantage of the Nationalist Party's willingness to pay enormous sums to gain the support of local political bosses. According to a January 4, 2000, editorial in the *Taipei Times*, "In the process of Taiwan's democratization, many people with organized crime backgrounds 'bleached' themselves in elections and became politicians. According to statistics, two-thirds of the gangs in Taiwan have lawmakers running on their behalf in the legislature, while one-quarter of elected public representatives have criminal records." The public in 2000 was deeply concerned about corruption and did not feel the situation was improving. They were particularly angry that the

Although not endorsing blind cultural relativism, I do stress the importance of culture to democratization, for one critical reason: the Chinese approach to rights and democracy is inspired at least as much by culture as it is by ideology. Many of the practices and policies adopted by the Chinese Communists after 1949 are rooted in culture and will not necessarily disappear if the Communist Party's rule collapses. What we are seeing may not be communism but modernization, not ideology but culture, elements of which are being hijacked by cultural nationalists and by the regime for their own purposes. Indeed, it is not the withering away of communism but cultural changes and institutional, social, and economic modernization—themselves affected by such factors as China's position within the international community, economic and social conditions, decentralization, and economic liberalization—that will more deeply challenge China's undemocratic practices and policies. This is one more reason for thinking about China in as nonideological a manner as possible.

An alternative approach to understanding the issue of freedom and democracy in China is to develop fair and consistent standards for comparing China with other countries by using not just nonideological but even noncultural categories of thinking. This approach would ask questions such as "Does the government treat its people justly?" And, regardless of our presuppositions about how socialist societies function, do the Chinese people perceive their society as just? Do they feel the society is less just under policies of economic and social liberalization than it was under the earlier, more authoritarian policies? And if so, is this because the government is doing less to provide for the fundamental needs of its people and instead relinquishing its responsibility to the market? In the eyes of the Chinese people, has the freedom of economic exchange encouraged by economic liberalization decreased egalitarianism? Do Chinese citizens, many of whom suffered from the overemphasis on equality during the Maoist years, view equality as an element of a just society? If the people feel that society is less just than it was

---

Nationalist Party had business assets worth US$2.6 billion, which are used to influence the political system (Shelley Rigger, "Taiwan Rides the Democratic Dragon," *Washington Quarterly*, Spring 2000, pp. 112–13).

For articles in the Western press on corruption, or "black gold," in Taiwan, see "Mob Rule," *The Economist*, Nov. 30, 1996, p. 34; and Julian Baum's series of articles: "Sin City," *Far Eastern Economic Review* 159, no. 4 (Jan. 25, 1996): 16; "Price of Progress," *Far Eastern Economic Review* 159, no. 20 (May 16, 1996): 16–20; and "Perilous Politics," *Far Eastern Economic Review* 160, no. 18 (May 1, 1997): 18.

before the introduction of economic liberalization, is that because their expectations of the government's responsibility to them has changed? Finally, do the Chinese conflate "justice" and "fairness" with the "good society," regardless of the form of government? And, does a country that has provided a more materially prosperous life to its people also seem, in the eyes of its people, to be more just and fair? Such a utilitarian perspective is valuable for judging China's success in developing a fair and just society, with or without liberal democratic institutions and processes.

Amartya Sen, although he has reservations about full-fledged utilitarianism, believes that a modified utilitarianism offers important insights. It asks that when judging social arrangements, we pay attention to their *results* and to the *well-being* of the people involved. Utilitarians, or "consequentialists," believe that the value of, say, the right to private property, must be judged on the grounds of whether its consequences are positive (such as its role in promoting economic expansion) or negative (such as environmental degradation or the immiseration of those without property). If the right to free speech leads to the articulation of ethnic hatred, which in turn leads to ethnic violence, it is not an unmitigated good. By contrast, those who prefer an emphasis on rights and liberties often neglect their consequences. Those who emphasize personal liberties or property rights, such as Robert Nozick or John Rawls, believe that such rights should have "*absolute priority*" because they are "constitutive of individual independence" and that the procedures for guaranteeing those rights "are to be accepted no matter what consequences follow from them." The uncompromising priority of libertarian rights can be particularly problematic since the actual consequences of the operation of these entitlements can, quite possibly, include rather terrible results. It can, in particular, lead to the violation of the substantive freedom of other citizens to achieve those things to which they attach great importance, such as escaping avoidable mortality, being well nourished and healthy, being able to read, write, and count, and so on. The importance of these freedoms cannot be ignored on grounds of the "priority of liberty."[4]

---

4. Sen, *Development as Freedom*, p. 66. Sen is, of course, interested in civil rights and political freedom and believes the utilitarians could attach more value to them while not ignoring their consequences for the substantive freedoms (literacy and so on) already possessed by the people. For his other concerns about the limitations of utilitarianism, see ibid., pp. 60–66. Sen is referring to John Rawls, *A Theory of Justice* (Cambridge, Mass.: Harvard University Press, 1971); and Robert Nozick, *Anarchy, State, and Utopia* (New York: Basic Books, 1974), as well as Nozick, *The Examined Life* (New York: Simon & Schuster, 1989).

An international survey of 41 countries, both developed and developing, based on the utilitarian emphasis of a people's well-being as perceived by the people themselves, suggests that in comparison with the citizens of the other countries surveyed, a significantly greater proportion of Chinese evaluate their own standard of living positively.

Self-evaluation of living standards as	Percentage of respondents in the world as a whole[5]	China
Better than average	24%	26%
Average	46	57
Below average	30	18

In this same study, 7 percent of urban inhabitants worldwide responded that they lived in poverty, versus 3 percent in China.[6]

Similarly, a study conducted in the city of Guangzhou asked respondents to evaluate their own social position. They were given a continuum of five classes to choose from, although the standards urban residents used to determine their own class are unclear. The results were as follows:[7]

Self-evaluation as	Percentage of respondents
Upper class	1.2%
Upper-middle class	3.2
Middle class	40.7
Lower-middle class	28.4
Lower class	19.6

A 1998 survey that asked urban residents to evaluate their satisfaction with life likewise indicated a high level of satisfaction (6.8 percent were "very satisfied," and 63.6 percent were "satisfied"), as well as optimism that life would be even better for their children.[8]

---

5. The percentages used treat the 41 countries as if they were "the world"; i.e., as if the 41 countries were one unit. Thus, 24 percent = 24 percent of all people in all 41 countries.

6. "Zhongguo renmin dui guojia fazhan congman xinxin" (Worldwide survey shows chinese people's full confidence in the country's development), Beijing qingnian bao, Sept. 12, 1995, sect. 7. The Lingdian Survey Company did the sample in China.

7. K. K. Choi, "System factors, Living Quality and Status," paper presented at the Conference on Social Class Structure in Chinese Societies, Chinese University of Hong Kong (Dec. 1993); cited in Ho Suk-ching, "The Emergence of Consumer Power in China," p. 16.

8. "1998 shenghuo ganshou." The study was conducted by the private survey company, Horizon (Lingdian). There were 5,673 adult urban resident respondents from eleven cities.

Another study found that China's local elites expressed greater satisfaction with their lot and more hope for the future than similar elites in three Western liberal democratic countries.[9] Such a conclusion is reinforced by the results of a 1998 Gallup poll: Chinese of all ages throughout the country not only said that their lives had improved over the preceding five years but also expect that "their lives will be better five years from now."[10] These data are at least suggestive of how fairly and equitably the Chinese believe they are treated under their system of governance, regardless of objective measurements (by objective international standards, a far larger percentage live in poverty) or the opinions of those living in liberal democratic countries.[11]

As we enter the twenty-first century, can we thrust a developing country's government into the moral arena of liberal democratic governments, most of which govern within the context of a far higher level of development and are themselves still debating the meaning of morality and fairness, the "just" society, democracy, and freedom in the context of a rapidly changing world? Why not judge China by the standards of the liberal democratic countries of the 1960s or even the 1940s? Or, why not judge China by the standards, or the satisfaction, of its own people?

---

9. Shen and Eldersveld, "Problem Perceptions of Chinese Local Cadres and Masses," pp. 53–54. The three Western countries are the United States, the Netherlands, and Sweden. Shen Mingming is director of the Social Science Research Center for Contemporary China at Beijing University. The study's authors note that conditions in the Western countries in the survey are indeed worse than they were 20–30 years ago and that the Chinese counties studied are in fact better off than they were 20–30 years ago. Thus, the responses of China's local elites seem quite realistic. Still, the study's authors believe that China's local elites "are just not as disturbed about their problems, and do not see them as 'serious' as in the West" (p. 53).

10. This is based on the Gallup Organization's Third Survey of Consumer Attitudes and Lifestyles in the People's Republic of China (1998); see Palmer, "What the Chinese Want," p. 232. For a more detailed and nuanced presentation of urban optimism, see Tang and Parish, Chinese Urban Life Under Reform.

11. Perhaps "objective" data would suggest that the Chinese are not as poor as we might think. For example, one study categorized China's "urban households according to their ownership of financial assets (cash, bank savings, and stocks)." The study chose five classifications for wealth: super-rich, 1%; rich, 6%; well-to-do, 55%; sufficiency, 34%; poor, 4%. The study, "Widening Gap Between the Rich and Poor," was reported in the Hong Kong Economic Times, June 14, 1995, p. A14; cited by Ho Suk-ching, "The Emergence of Consumer Power in China," pp. 16–17. Without seeing the original study, it is hard to know all the issues involved. Of course, people from the wealthier countries might find these classifications of urban Chinese preposterous.

The idea that there is or ever has been a universal standard of morality concerning justice, democracy, and freedom, for all times and all places, is fallacious. In this century, it will certainly be harder to assert such a universal standard, for the conflicts in which liberal societies and states become enmeshed will most likely not possess the "moral simplicity" of conflicts in the twentieth century "between Western liberalism and National Socialism and Soviet Communism. They will be conflicts in which at least some non-liberal regimes and cultural forms possess genuine virtues and harbour authentic excellences that are weak, or lacking, in liberal regimes." Moreover, just because liberalism has contributed to the well-being of those individuals living in liberal societies does not mean it constitutes a valid argument for the adoption of liberalism by *all* societies.[12]

This is equally true of the issue of human rights, which is still heatedly debated in the international community. Even in countries in which, for example, the right to a fair trial is held up as an ideal, the practice is all too frequently far from perfect: for the poor, there is no real guarantee of a fair trial in the United States, where it is acknowledged that the wealthy can buy "justice" by hiring better lawyers and that both judges and juries are often racist in their assumptions and verdicts. Torture is still used (and only acknowledged if caught) even in developed democratic countries such as Great Britain (against suspected Irish terrorists) and Israel (against suspected Palestinian terrorists) and is publicly justified by the need to gain information to protect national security or save people's lives. In 1999, close to half of France's 55,000 prisoners had never been convicted of a crime.[13] The death penalty is still used in the United States and Japan.

Many states place limits on the exercise of religious freedom. In the United States, the "separation of church and state" is a frequently contested constitutional issue that affects the rights of citizens to practice religion where and how they want to. Heresy and blasphemy have provided grounds for prosecution in Great Britain. The Church of England enjoys legal protection from "scurrilous, abusive or offensive" attacks, a protection denied other churches. Foreign nationals with ties to the Church of Scientology have been denied entrance to the country. The protection of freedom of re-

---

12. Gray, *Enlightenment's Wake*, pp. 84, 86.

13. Suzanne Daley, "Expose of Brutal Paris Prison a Jolt to France's Self-Image," *New York Times*, Jan. 28, 2000, pp. A1, A9. The article was inspired by the book *Chief Doctor at La Sante Prison*, by Veronique Vasseur (1999).

ligion was institutionalized in Great Britain only in October 2000, with the implementation of the 1998 European Human Rights Convention, but even at this late date, a study of religious discrimination (largely against Muslims but also against Catholics) at work, in school, and throughout society in England concluded that there is a "link between the Church of England and the state as the source of much of the religious discrimination in British society today."[14]

In addition, both Great Britain and the European Community have embraced human rights with reservations that would seem to allow the suspension of rights at the convenience of the government. According to the European Convention on Human Rights, the right to freedom of expression

may be subject to such formalities, conditions, restrictions or penalties as are prescribed by law and are necessary in a democratic society, in the interests of national security, territorial integrity or public safety, for the prevention of disorder or crime, for the protection of health or morals, for the protection of the reputation or rights of others, for preventing the disclosure of information received in confidence, or for maintaining the authority and impartiality of the judiciary.[15]

Liberal democratic countries that engage in war against other countries in the name of defending democracy or virtually exterminate native peoples (or help other governments do so) nevertheless have not been reluctant to apply their own ideals of freedom, democracy, and human rights to China. In short, they judge themselves and their allies differently from the way they judge China. But the point here is not to decry abuses of human rights or undemocratic practices in liberal democratic states. Rather, it is to find standards for assessing a state's progress toward a better, more just society.

If we judge governments by their success in according "rights" that provide for the good life and justice, which are arguably two of the main reasons peoples want freedom and democracy, then we can look across all cultures

---

14. Michael C. Tolley, "Religion and the State: Great Britain," paper presented at the Annual Meeting of the American Political Science Association, Washington, D.C., Aug. 31–Sept. 3, 2000, pp. 8–10, 16. The study, conducted by a research team at the University of Derby, was entitled the Derby Report.

15. This is from Britain's Human Rights Act 1998, chap. 42, which adopts the rights and freedoms of the European Convention on Human Rights, with certain reservations. Michael Tolley, seminar, Northeastern University, Department of Political Science, Dec. 5, 2000. Based on Tolley, *Freedom, Rule of Law, and Democracy in the United States and Britain.*

and political systems to evaluate how well China has performed in a comparative context. Erik Allardt, suggests an index based on "having, loving, being."[16] Building on his ideas, the following criteria for evaluating the freedom to live and *choose* a decent life in China could be considered:

Having: the right to housing, health care, food, and clothing and the right to acquire wealth;

Being: the right to be a participant in decision-making, the right to (and choice of) leisure, the right to live in a peaceful and secure environment, and the right to good health;

Doing: the right to work (including the right for women to work and advance in the workplace) and create, the right to humane working conditions, including acceptable work hours, vacation time, and protection from industrial accidents, and the right to wages sufficient for living a decent life;

Knowing: the right to education, knowledge, and information, so that individuals may make meaningful choices in life, choices that are enriching, fulfilling, and provide hope for the future;

Loving: the right to have a meaningful role in the community, to belong to a community that gives one dignity, and to enjoy one's family and friends.

The "human capabilities" criteria promoted by the United Nations Development Programme provide another standard for judging whether a government has accorded sufficient "rights" to individuals for them to have the substantive freedom necessary to live that good life. Most of these rights fall into the category of *distributive* rights—those concerned with social and economic justice. These are often dismissed as "secondary" or "welfare" rights, but developing countries like China believe they are more important as a first step to a just society than are *procedural* rights, which emphasize civil and political justice. Indeed, distributive rights have been advocated by some

---

16. "Having refers to those material conditions which are necessary for survival and for avoidance of misery . . . nutrition, air, water." It also includes economic resources, the income and wealth available to a people, as well as housing, working conditions, health, and education. Loving refers to attachments to the local community, family, friendship, and relationships with co-workers. And being refers to "the need for integration into society and to live in harmony with nature," that is, personal growth, involvement in decision making, and political activities (Erik Allardt, "Having, Loving, Being: An Alternative to the Swedish Model of Welfare Research," in Nussbaum and Sen, *The Quality of Life*, pp. 89–91).

Chinese familiar with Western political thought since the early twentieth century. Sun Yat-sen, for example, advocated distributive rights, as did many other early reformers and revolutionaries. They voiced the belief that freedom of speech and thought are preconditioned on the existence of "life capabilities."[17]

The problem is the basic incompatibility of these two types of rights—the one in pursuit of freedom, the other in pursuit of equality (see Chapter 2). As Henry Rosemont has argued, "liberty and justice for all" is an ideal that is far from being realized in most societies because of the difficulty of "extending the concept of basic human rights from the civil and political realm—where it originated—to the social and economic." That is, no matter how free, a person still has no *right* to demand a job or health care or education. So far, no one has been able to make a logical connection between the fundamental principle that each person is a free and independent individual and the conclusion that each person has a right to be employed. No one has yet shown "how I can demand that other human beings create these goods for me without them surrendering the 'first generation' or civil and political rights which accrue to them by virtue of their being free, autonomous individuals."[18]

The United Nations is itself moving toward a new definition of human rights and social justice. It declared the 1990s the "UN Decade for the Eradication of Extreme Poverty" and has condemned acute poverty as a violation of human rights.[19] Since the *Human Development Report* was first published by the United Nations Development Programme in 1990, it "has defined human development as the process of enlarging people's choices."[20] In the absence of a choice, the freedom to choose is meaningless. Therefore individuals must have not only the freedom of choice but a (growing) number of alternatives to choose from. This often requires that the government make choices available through various programs or by increasing the level of de-

---

17. Gao Yihan, "Sheng xianfa zhong de minquan wenti" (The question of people's rights in the provincial constitutions), *Xin qingnian* 9, no. 5 (1921): 5–7; trans. in Angle and Svensson, "On Rights and Human Rights," p. 62.

18. Rosemont, "Human Rights: A Bill of Worries," p. 57.

19. The European Union has reframed the issue of poverty to include "social exclusion," notably, long-term unemployment. France has promulgated a new comprehensive law to protect people from extreme poverty and social exclusion.

20. United Nations Development Programme, *Human Development Report, 1997*, p. 15.

velopment.[21] According to Sen, if we evaluate societies on the basis of "functionings" and rights such as those listed above that allow an individual to attain well-being, we can judge whether a person really has the "capability" or "substantive freedom" to make genuine choices and, therefore, "how good a 'deal' a person has in the society."[22] Sen's ideas are reflected in the *Human Development Report*: "In the capability concept the focus is on the functionings that a person can or cannot achieve, given the opportunities she has. Functionings refer to the various valuable things a person can do or be, such as living long, being healthy, being well nourished, mixing well with others in the community, and so on."[23]

In adopting a utilitarian perspective, this book has argued that the consequences of China's institutions, policies, and processes for distributive justice—largely social and economic benefits—are at least as important as their impact on the liberties necessary for procedural justice. In assessing the progress China has made toward procedural justice and liberty, I have contended that assumptions about how oppressed individual Chinese feel based on how *we* might feel under similar levels of governmental control are misleading and, moreover, that even along the dimension of procedural rights, the Chinese are making significant progress.

In its "human development index" (HDI) as well as in its "human poverty index" (HPI), the UN Development Programme evaluates China, as it does all countries, largely on utilitarian grounds. These are standards that are neither Western nor Chinese. The HDI is not predicated on either communist, anticommunist, pro-Western, religious, or liberal democratic values. Instead, it attempts to measure the *quality* of a life within each country. As such, it is at least partly a measure of the willingness and ability of a country's government, regardless of its form, to address the needs and development of its citizens.

The HDI, "measures the overall achievements in a country in three basic dimensions of human development—longevity, knowledge and a decent standard of living." The measurements for these three dimensions are "life expectancy, educational attainment (adult literacy and combined primary,

---

21. This is a point also made by some Chinese academics. See, e.g., Liu Jinxi, "Minzhu xin lun," pp. 83–84.

22. Sen, *Inequality Re-examined*, pp. 40–41. A person's "functionings" are those "things a person may value doing or being"; a person's "capabilities" are "a kind of freedom . . . the freedom to achieve various lifestyles." Poverty can thus be seen as "capability deprivation" (Sen, *Development as Freedom*, pp. 75, 87).

23. United Nations Development Programme, *Human Development Report, 1997*, p. 16.

secondary and tertiary enrollment) and adjusted income." The HDI "measures progress in a community or country as a whole. The HPI measures the extent of deprivation, the proportion of people in the community who are left out of progress." In other words, the HPI measures the unequal distribution of poverty, that is, the percentage of the population who are deprived of human development.[24]

These standards provide "an alternative to the view of development equated exclusively with economic growth"[25] and help us understand that poverty is really "the deprivation of basic capabilities rather than merely . . . lowness of incomes."[26] Although HDI rank is deceptive in some cases, since an unusually high GDP per capita can distort the overall HDI value, it certainly provides a better measurement of human welfare than do the GDP figures.[27] According to the 1998 UNDP data, a country like Kuwait with a high GDP per capita drops by 31 places if the HDI (ranked number 36 in the world) rather than GDP per capita (ranked number 5) is used, whereas Cuba advances by 40 places in the ordinal ranking.

Intercountry comparisons reveal that the correlation of, say, increased longevity with increased GDP per capita only exists when GDP has an impact on the incomes of the poor and on increased government spending on health care. In other words, if the gains in GDP are not used to remove poverty and improve health care, there is no necessary correlation between increases in GDP per capita and increases in life expectancy.[28] Hence the discrepancies in the relative HDI and GDP per capita rankings of countries are indicative of their commitment or lack thereof to developing the fundamental capabilities of their citizens. In China, the "state-led" process of reducing mortality by providing basic health care as opposed to waiting until the country had a larger GDP to address health care, was a choice made by an authoritative party-state, not by a procedural democracy.

---

24. United Nations Development Programme, *Human Development Report, 1998*, pp. 15, 25–26. Data are provided to the UNDP by a variety of organizations, NGOs, and statistical agencies, but their data often come at least in part from the governments themselves. Because collection methods may vary from country to county, comparisons can be difficult. Although not perfect, UNDP data are generally considered the most reliable available. For further discussion of the data's reliability, see http://www.undp.org/hdro/response.html.

25. Ibid., p. 16.

26. Sen, *Development as Freedom*, p. 87.

27. Rogers et al., *Measuring Environmental Quality in Asia*, pp. 36–37.

28. Sudhir Anand and Martin Ravallion; cited in Sen, *Development as Freedom*, p. 44n7.

Within the category of "developing countries," which includes govern-ments that are communist, socialist, democratic, fascist, Islamic, and/or dic-tatorial, China has been one of the most successful in providing its people with the capabilities and "functionings" essential to human development. According to 1998 data, among the 85 developing countries (with lower numbers being better), China's HPI rank was 30, Indonesia's 46, Egypt's 55, and India's 58 (to compare four developing states with large populations).[29] Among all 174 countries ranked (including the most developed), China's HDI rank was 99, Indonesia's 109, Egypt's 119, and India's 128.[30] From one perspective, the measures of human development and well-being embodied in these indices (longevity, knowledge, and a decent standard of living) in-clude some of the most basic "rights" that people living in a liberal democratic system hope to gain and maintain through their freedom to vote and choose their leaders.

These same four countries ranked in the same order in the gender-related development index (GDI), which measures gender inequality in achieve-ment (in education and income). Among the 143 ranked countries, China was number 79, Indonesia 90, Egypt 99, and India 108.[31]

Comparison of China and India is particularly relevant. Both are large, developing countries with huge populations. India has been under multi-party, democratic rule for all but a few years of the period since independ-ence in 1947. China has been under one-party rule since 1949. They have

---

29. United Nations Development Programme, *Human Development Report, 2000*, p. 151.

30. Ibid., pp. 149, 157–60. These are, however, ordinal rankings, which may give the im-pression of larger differences between countries than may exist in terms of the percentage val-ues of the separate "human development" rankings for each category or the combined "human development index value," which is also given in the reports. The highest "HDI value" possi-ble is 1.00. In 1998, the highest HDI value achieved by any country was Canada's 0.935, and the lowest was Sierra Leone's 0.252. China's HDI value ranking was 0.706, and India's was 0.563. This is a significant spread (of 0.143) and is about the same spread in the HDI (in the other direction) as that between China and the Republic of Korea (0.854) and the Czech Re-public (0.843). Basically, the HDI value is generated by adding the indices for life expectancy, education, and GDP per capita (expressed in purchasing price parity dollars) for each country and applying the Atkinson formula. This formula takes income elasticity into account and reflects "the diminishing value of additional income." For an explanation and critique of the computation of the HDI value, see Rogers et al., *Measuring Environmental Quality in Asia*, pp. 36–38. For a technical note on how the indices were computed, see United Nations Devel-opment Programme, *Human Development Report, 2000*, pp. 269–73.

31. United Nations Development Programme, *Human Development Report, 2000*, pp. 154, 161–64.

thus had about the same amount of time to test the validity of their respective political systems in terms of providing for human development. Although each has complex internal conditions and cultural issues that have affected the development of human capabilities, it would be hard to argue that India faced more difficulties than China. Yet New Delhi was unwilling or unable to undertake policies to address or ameliorate social problems, such as mandating a national language (India still has fifteen official languages) or truly ending the caste system. By almost every measurement used in the United Nations Development Programme's *Human Development Report, 2000,* China has been far more successful in providing for the human development of its people than has India.[32]

As noted above, China ranked number 30 on the HPI among the 85 developing countries, and India 58. The HPI, which measures the unequal distribution of poverty in developing countries and is based on measurements of deprivation in three key dimensions of human development (longevity, knowledge, and a decent standard of living),[33] such as the following (indicated as a percentage of population):

Longevity[34]
Underweight children under age 5 (1990–98)
  China: 16%
  India: 53%
Population not expected to survive until age 40
(as of 1998)
  China: 7.7%
  India: 15.8%
Population not expected to survive until age 60
(1995–2000 data)
  China: 18.0%
  India: 29.7%
Infant mortality rate (per 1,000 live births):
  China: 38
  India: 69

---

32. Ibid., pp. 157–60.

33. The fourth dimension, social exclusion (which refers largely to unemployment), is measured only for the developed countries.

34. United Nations Development Programme, *Human Development Report, 2000,* pp. 169–71, 187–88.

Mortality rate for those under age 5
(per 1,000 live births):
    China: 47
    India: 105
Knowledge
Adult illiteracy rate (age 15 and above;
as of 1998)
    China: 17.2%
    India: 44.3%
Decent Standard of Living
Population below income poverty line
(1989–94)[35]
    China: 29.4%
    India: 52.5%
Population below national poverty line
(1987–1997)[36]
    China: 6.0%
    India: 35.0%
Real GDP per capita (1980–94)[37]
    China's poorest 20%: $722
    India's poorest 20%: $527
    China's richest 20%: $5,114
    India's richest 20%: $2,641
Growth in GDP per capita[38]

	1975	1998	Growth
China	$138	$727	500%
India	$222	$444	200%

---

35. In purchasing price parity dollars (1993 PPP US$) and assuming a requirement of $1 a day to be at or above the poverty line. Such data were not available for China in the most recent UNDP (2000) report. See United Nations Development Programme, *Human Development Report, 1998*, pp. 146–47.

36. United Nations Development Programme, *Human Development Report, 2000*, p. 170.

37. In purchasing price parity dollars (PPP$).

38. Based on 1995 US$. United Nations Development Programme, *Human Development Report, 2000*, pp. 179–80.

Gender-Related Development Index (1998)[39]
China's rank: 79
India's rank: 108
Gender empowerment measure[40]
China's rank: 33
India's rank: 95
Women's participation in economic and
political life (as percentage of male rate,
as of 1995)[41]
China: 82%
India: 46%

These figures capture the value and meaning of life in these two countries. They also suggest that democratic institutions *per se* do not necessarily translate into greater success in providing for basic human needs and human capabilities to be free to make meaningful choices; an authoritarian government with a policy commitment to eradicating the root causes of poverty may well be more successful. The stark difference in success between China's and India's population control policies is a good example of how a more authoritarian government may at times be more capable of carrying out a policy that is better for the society as a whole. Similarly, China's commitment to strong economic development is in startling contrast to the Indian government's commitment until recently to "the Hindu 3 percent rate of growth"—the speed at which the Brahmin class felt India could develop without endangering its privileged elite position.

Finally, out of the 174 countries whose human development capabilities were correlated with economic growth from 1975 to 1998, China's average annual rate of change (in reducing the shortfall in the human development

---

39. This index is based on comparative male-female data on longevity, knowledge, and standard of living. It includes data on the share of earned income of females and males. Ibid., pp. 162–64.

40. This includes data on percentage of seats in parliament held by women, female administrators and managers, female professional and technical workers, and women's share of earned income. See United Nations Development Programme, *Human Development Report, 1998*, pp. 134–36. This information was not available for China or India in the report issued in 2000.

41. Ibid., pp. 154–55. This information on China and India was not available in the report issued in 2000.

index) was one of the fastest, 7.5 percent per year. This compares with figures of 4.1 percent for Indonesia, 3.5 percent for Egypt, 3.0 percent for India,
and a shocking -0.8 percent for Russia. Only Malta (8.3 percent, with an
HDI ranking of 27) and Equatorial Guinea (8.8 percent, HDI ranking of 131)
were reducing the shortfall in the human development index at a faster
rate.[42] These data provide strong evidence that China's government, if measured on a (utilitarian) scale of "effectiveness," is doing considerably better
than other countries of commensurate size and level of development.

But how does the form of government relate to the development of human capabilities and to freedom itself? Amartya Sen, who has pondered the
connection between development and freedom for many years, argues, for
example, there is a social and political dimension to every famine and that
every famine is in part the result of human intervention. Famines do not
happen just because of bad weather. Sen has often been quoted as saying
that "no famine has ever taken place in the history of the world in a
functioning democracy."[43] He rightly decries the authoritarian rule in China
that led to the Great Leap Forward in 1958 and resulted in millions of deaths
from starvation and malnourishment,[44] and he notes that since independence in 1947 India has never had a famine. Those who cite Sen on this point,
however, rarely if ever acknowledge that this is only a part of his much larger
argument that although India has not experienced famine, it has not been
able to eliminate persistent malnourishment, not to mention high levels of
illiteracy or the inequalities in gender relations that result in higher mortality
rates and inequitable access to social and economic goods and political
power for women, as well as an inability to reduce fertility rates. Although
India's political parties have always recognized the importance of preventing
starvation and famine, Sen denounces the opposition parties for allowing

---

42. UNDP, *Human Development Report 2000*, pp. 182–85. Of course, if like Canada or the
United States, a country's HDI value and rank are already very high (Canada's rank is 1, the
United States' is 3), it is harder to raise the HDI value by a percentage as large as those coun-
tries with very low HDI rankings in 1975. It also takes a significantly greater decline in the
HDI value for it to show up as a marked decline, such as the Russian Federation's did.

43. Sen, *Development as Freedom*, p. 16. Sen qualifies this view later in this work, noting that
since independence, "India has been *relatively free* . . . of famine" (ibid., p. 103; italics added).

44. Sen has accepted the figure of 20 to 30 million deaths uncritically. The figure is really
an estimate of shortfall in expected births, which doubles the figure of the dead by including
people who were never born! (correspondence from an anonymous reviewer, based on an on-
line Indian source, Utsa Patnaik, "Experimenting with Market Socialism," *Frontline*, 16, no. 21
[Oct. 9–22, 1999]). Even at half the number, however, the level of starvation was still shocking.

successive governments to "get away with unconscionable neglect of these vital matters of public policy."[45]

Sen is indicting not just the opposition parties but also the democratically elected government of India, which has chosen to ignore problems critical to the development of a fair and just society. As Henry Shue argues, if illiteracy, high mortality rates, or malnutrition occur as the result of decisions not to prevent them, then these policy decisions are, in effect, the cause (at least in part) of their existence.[46] And, Sen admits, it is China's government, not India's, that has made policy decisions to address these issues.[47] As a result, China has done better than India in terms of human development and therefore in terms of creating a fair and just society.

Unfortunately, some of the human development capabilities ensured by the Chinese government before 1979 are now being eroded by policies of economic liberalization. This is especially true for China's poorest workers and farmers, the very people for whom the revolution was fought in 1949.[48] The phasing out of the "right" to a job—virtually guaranteed before economic liberalization began—has had a devastating impact on social stability and on the sense of well-being among the millions of unemployed. Many Chinese are now more concerned that they, too, may lose the right to employment than they are about any other right, political or otherwise.[49] Further, although the official data for the entire country indicate a substantial rise in educational levels,[50] other reports indicate that a decline in both edu-

---

45. Sen, *Development as Freedom*, pp. 156, 154, 102–3, 189–203.

46. Henry Shue, *Basic Rights*, p. 98.

47. Sen, *Development as Freedom*, pp. 186–188.

48. For a series of articles on the growing inequality in income distribution and its impact, see Riskin et al., *China's Retreat from Equality*; Khan and Riskin, *Inequality and Poverty in China in the Age of Globalization*; and World Bank, *Sharing Rising Incomes: Disparities in China*.

49. In 1995 and 1996, social stability had been the primary concern of adult urban residents in eleven cities. In 1997 and 1998, unemployment became the number one concern. See "1998 shenghuo ganshou."

50. In December 1999, the Chinese Civil Education 2000 supervisory group, together with the Ministry of Education and UNESCO, announced that 98.9 percent of all children were enrolled in primary school, with the vast majority (87.3 percent) going on to secondary school. This is a substantial increase over the 71.4 percent who went on to middle schools in 1990 ("UN Report Says China's Illiteracy Rate Down in the 90s," *China News Digest*, Dec. 13, 1999). Again, however, these figures probably exclude the children of rural immigrants living without a *hukou* or residency permit in the cities. The March 2001 World Bank report on China indicated that 15 percent of China's regions have not yet attained the nine-year compulsory education target, although the report does note that China is allocating more resources to de-

cation and health care in the countryside has accompanied policies of economic liberalization and decollectivization. These policies have allowed the market and crony capitalism to substitute for the state in determining the distribution of goods,[51] as the state has withdrawn from its heavy commitment to social welfare and intervention in the lives of its citizens. The decline of personal security and law and order and the widespread return of crime, banditry, and sects involved in illegal activities have been the unfortunate companions to the withering away of state control. The increased polarization of wealth between coastal areas and the hinterlands, within the countryside, and between the rural and urban areas,[52] is largely the result of the economic policies of the reform period, which favor freedom of opportunity and encourage the accumulation of wealth, at the expense of policies that distributed wealth more equally. Furthermore, with decentralization, the state's capacity for redistribution has weakened.[53] These are the trade-offs for and byproducts of other rights gained in the 1980s and 1990s.

If measured in terms of human development and the right to have a decent life, then, economic liberalization has not been an unqualified success— nor has it gained the unqualified endorsement of the Chinese people. As noted in Chapter 5, in a 1999 survey that asked urban families to list the issues of greatest concern to them, fully 80 percent of the respondents

---

veloping the impoverished Western region. It also notes, however, that whereas primary school education in the countryside in many areas is not faring well, the state continues to fund education in the urban sector. For example, beginning in 2001, senior secondary schools and junior secondary schools in major cities will include information technology courses as part of their academic requirements. The report concludes that "too much of the burden for spending on education has been shifted to the households, thus putting poor families at a disadvantage" (World Bank, *China: Macroeconomic Update* [Washington D.C.: World Bank, March 2001]; online at worldbank.org). So, data on the issue of education are in conflict.

51. He Qinglian has referred to the phenomenon as a "simulated market" in which there is political not economic competition, and in which the government colludes with a mafia to rob China's citizens of its resources (cited in Cheng Li, "Promises and Pitfalls of Reform," p. 147). He Qinglian is a mainland economist best known for her devastating critique of China's reforms in her book, *Zhongguo de xianjing* (China's pitfall) (Hong Kong: Mingjing, 1998; also published in Beijing).

52. Wang Xinyi, "Shouru fenpei helihua you laiyu jianchuan jizhi."

53. Thomas Bernstein and Xiaobo Lu, "Taxation Without Representation in China," Harvard University, New England China Seminar, Apr. 16, 2001.

mentioned the increasing polarization of wealth.[54] Although some of the participants in the debate over the reforms feel that polarization is inevitable, and even essential, to development, others vehemently disagree (see Chapter 8).

Nevertheless, economic liberalization and the increase in wealth have allowed a substantial majority of the Chinese people to experience a genuine right to choose from among a variety of goods, services, and jobs and to enjoy better food and housing and increased leisure. The party-state remains committed to enhancing human development. In the 1990s, for example, it adopted legislation making nine years of education compulsory and made efforts to alleviate rural poverty (that is, the "absolute poverty" of those falling below the poverty line of $1.00 per day [expressed in purchasing price parity dollars]). The 8-7 Poverty Reduction Program (the 8 refers to "the 80 million people living in income poverty, the 7 for the program's seven-year period" from 1994 to 2000) required a significant financial commitment by the government.[55] Although China did not achieve this goal by 2000, the policy has continued into the twenty-first century.[56] Finally, the party-state continues to carry out economic, financial, and structural reforms that make institutions more transparent and allow greater public oversight. These reforms have helped open China to the outside world. China's willingness to

---

54. "Survey Indicates Dismay About Falling Socialist Values," *China News Digest*, Jan. 4, 2000, item 3. www.cnd.org This is a dramatic change from the popular attitudes revealed in polls done in 1988 and 1990, when close to 75 percent of urban youth (aged 16–35), disagreed with the statement "The big pot is better than polarization" (Zhongguo shehui kexue yuan, Shehuixue yanjiusuo, Zhuanxing ketizu, *Zhongguo qingniande toushi*, table 4-10, p. 177). But, of course, the question asked was quite different (the image of "the big pot" evoking images of the devastating impact of extreme egalitarianism during the Cultural Revolution), as were the respondents in the more recent survey. Compare a 1994 survey, in which fully 92.9 percent of the 1,443 respondents were concerned with an excessively large income gap (Social Psychological Attitude Research Project Team, "Zhuanxin shiqi de Shanghai shimin shehui xintai diaocha," p. 82).

55. United Nations Development Programme, "Profile of Human Poverty," in idem, *Human Development Report, 1997*, p.50.

56. Arthur Holcombe, president, Tibet Poverty Alleviation Fund, "Contemporary Tibet: Leading Social and Economic Development Issues," seminar, Harvard University, Asia Center, Feb. 4, 2000. Holcombe stated that poverty alleviation policies are definitely being carried out in China's western provinces and Tibet. This, he stated, was in contrast to rural India, where government policies are not addressing the deteriorating situation in much of India's rural area.

undertake painful reforms in order to join the World Trade Organization in 2001 is further evidence of its commitment to improving the well-being of its citizenry.[57]

Information in liberal democratic societies is controlled and packaged. Even if it is done to a lesser degree than in authoritarian societies, it still affects a citizenry's perceptions. The Western view of China has been shaped by information that has been selectively chosen and interpreted to portray China's development in a negative way—often for domestic political reasons.[58] This book offers another interpretation by its presentation of a broad spectrum of China's democratic inklings. As we moved from one topic to another, it became increasingly obvious that the democratization process itself cannot focus on one area in isolation. One area may progress while other areas sit still, but distortions are bound to result. The legal system, for example, has become increasingly equitable in its laws and processes, but the inability to implement court verdicts continues to make much of this irrelevant. For implementation to occur, serious changes in Chinese culture must happen, such as increased respect for the judiciary system's judgments and for law and a decrease in the culturally embedded reliance on relationships, which in turn requires rethinking millennia-old hierarchical and familial relationships.

Because democratization is fluid and encompasses the complicated interrelationships of countless factors, the effect of any one change in the system on its other parts must be considered. This study has dealt with some of the major elements involved with democratization (or the lack thereof) in China: history and culture, the media, economic and welfare policies, intellectuals, elections, individual rights, associations and interest groups, development, law, and the National People's Congress. But it could also have looked at a myriad of other seemingly minor policy and procedural changes that in their totality are having a dramatic impact on democratization in China.

Democratic systems are more likely to guarantee that officials are accountable to the public, but their leaders must be dedicated to the public

---

57. This is not to suggest that carrying out the reforms demanded by the World Trade Organization will indeed lead to improvement, as many people both inside and outside China are predicting catastrophe; but the intent is to improve people's lives.

58. Stapleton Roy, "The Challenge of Comprehending China." Charles Neuhauser Memorial Lecture, Harvard University, Nov. 14, 2001.

good (and have the resources and tools required) to make accountability meaningful. Accountability matters little if a state's leaders have been elected to serve narrow sectoral interests instead of the collective good of the community. The citizens of liberal democracies, moreover, often use the political system to assert their own self-interests at the expense of community interests. All too often democratic institutions allow the powerful and the wealthy to manipulate the system to serve their own interests, just as economic entrepreneurs and powerful corporations often use a capitalist economic system to exploit workers and damage the environment in order to increase profits. In some cases, the most vocal (and best-funded) proponents of policies in democratic states support policies that harm the interests of the population as a whole. Majoritarian governments can behave in a tyrannical manner toward minority interests; and a multiparty system has not necessarily been able to guarantee the advancement of the collective good.

By contrast, the Chinese have had to rely on their leaders to make policies that benefit the entire country instead of narrow sectoral interests or classes in a system in which for decades accountability seems to have been primarily to other leaders behind closed doors. Regardless of good intentions, the blame for the "twenty bad years" from 1957 to 1976 falls squarely on a system that lacked true accountability to the people.[59] China's socialist system may have generally been able to put good people into power, but it has not been able to get bad people out of power in a routine predictable manner. Its preferred methods of party rectifications, mass campaigns, and class struggle have often had devastating effects on society and government.

Nevertheless, since the reform era began in 1979, Chinese leaders' untempered zeal for developing China and making it a country that commands respect from the international community has been accompanied by political reforms that have made local leaders more accountable to the people, by the introduction of a market economy and reforms that have undercut centralized control of the country, and by a greater reliance on expertise in both management and the government. Compared to most large developing countries classified as democratic, since 1979 China appears to have had a more competent leadership, a more effective governmental administrative apparatus, and a greater willingness to carry out policies that advance human de-

---

59. This period includes anti-rightist movements, party rectifications, the disastrous Great Leap Forward in 1958 and the following "three bad years," and the Great Proletarian Cultural Revolution from 1966 to 1976.

velopment. This gives us still other dimensions for assessing the performance of China's government. That is, rather than judging China's government along moral or ideological lines as "good" or "bad," it can be compared
to other governments along lines such as "more" or "less" government, competent or incompetent, strong or weak, effective or ineffective.

China's leaders have become almost obsessively cautious, for good reason.[60] They know what has failed in the past—rapid change and inadequate
experimentation. Moreover, the leadership remains divided over the precise
goals of reform, and a cautious approach makes it easier for the pro-reform
group to pull the conservative (reform-resistant) group within the leadership
into a consensus. An acute awareness of the political disintegration that occurred in the Soviet Union with the collapse of communism and remem-
brances of things past like the haste of the Great Leap Forward have further
convinced China's leaders of the correctness of their policy of controlling political change.[61] As Deng Xiaoping once said, China developed so slowly because it tried to go so fast. The problem remains that China's leaders know
what has not worked in the past, but they do not know what will work in
the future.

In spite of its cautious approach, China's government appears to be losing
control over—that is, the ability to govern—the population. Greater freedom and democracy for the Chinese people may, in fact, undermine the very
conditions that are, at least for a large developing country, best for human
development, and ultimately, for the advancement of a civil society. Just how
much state control is good for the development of China's public sphere and
the proper balance between autonomy and control are issues that the Chinese government must address. A developing China armed with a more
comprehensive legal system, strong economic development, peace, and prosperity may be better able to contend with the challenges to stability and order that accompany economic liberalization and democratization.

The fact that reforms in social and organizational control have been so
widely debated in both the mass media and work units and that so many reforms have already been implemented may make the transition to a more

---

60. See, e.g., Fan Gang, "Tebiede fangshi yu texude wenti." Fan Gang is a member of the
Chinese Academy of Social Sciences.
61. Nolan, *China's Rise, Russia's Fall*, pp. 5, 168–71.

pluralistic and more democratic society smoother.[62] "Peaceful evolution" toward democracy and toward civil society (or at least toward "associational pluralism") is occurring in China, both with and without the support of the state. The same may be said of the expansion of social and economic rights, and even legal, civil, and political rights. To the degree that the political and social system can tolerate this dramatic challenge to its structure of control, these changes in the relationship between society and the state will benefit the Chinese people and advance democracy.

China's political culture, its level of development, and the many other economic, political, social, demographic, and international factors discussed in this book will affect the rate and depth of democratization in China. Yet no factors—foreign involvement, marketization, the emergence of a middle class, or economic development—can guarantee democratization. Even the growth of fully autonomous associations and institutions and the development of broader political rights may turn out to be far less important to China's democratic development than whether the Chinese state can maintain stability while undergoing relentless and rapid economic and social change.

Although some observers assert that China is moving too slowly toward democracy, it could easily be argued that the pace is actually too fast, and hence too destabilizing, for the long-run health of a democratizing authoritarian society. China's political system may never resemble that of a Western European liberal democratic regime, but it has made substantial progress in the same direction as some of the more advanced democratizing societies in East Asia such as South Korea and Taiwan. China is moving at a fair pace along the continuum from an "authoritarian" to a "democratic" regime, and its leaders appear determined to continue to make China into a fairer and more just society.

---

62. Victor Shaw (*Social Control in China*, p. 272) argues that the public is in fact prepared for a transformation in social and organizational control.

Appendix

Appendix
Surveys Conducted
in China

Social scientists, marketers, and government policy analysts in China have in the past twenty years turned increasingly to quantitative methods, especially statistical analysis of survey research data. With the increased power and availability of computers, this trend has become even more evident. In a changed political environment, with decreasing emphasis on ideology and more on profits and successful strategies for enriching China, those responsible for market and government policy decisions want to collect as much data as possible.

For social scientists, who are often as interested in value orientation as in policy, there is an even more compelling reason: for 30 years, China's social scientists were treated as if they were mere propagandists, as they usually were. Their role was to rationalize and validate the Party's policies and values. They were not encouraged, or even allowed, to do research independent of direction from the Party.

With the changed emphasis since 1979, social scientists have been encouraged to put aside the quest for "redness" and to become "experts." Using social science research surveys or polls and employing quantitative analysis, China's social scientists have published a growing number of articles based on hard data. But the industry is frequently criticized. As one senior researcher at the Institute of Sociology of the Chinese Academy of Social Sciences in Beijing put it, often the figures used are "absurd," results are "far-fetched," or even "rubbish." "Some studies pass on erroneous information, others lead young people astray." Even worse, if "certain foreign colleagues . . . can get hold of a floppy disk of data, they can stuff China's numbers into a theoretical framework, and thus complete a 'sinological' treatise."[1] This, I want to assure the reader, is not what I have done.

Nor does this negative assessment necessarily apply to most of the growing number of polling and survey research organizations in China. Since polling began in 1982, public opinion polls and survey research carried out by Chinese institutions have addressed a variety of questions, such as whether the Chinese people believe that cultural openness will undermine community and whether they believe that free speech and pluralism will lead to the erosion of law and order. Other studies have traced the reasons for changes in public opinion. The polls are conducted by a variety of methods: standardized questionnaires, interviews, focus groups, participatory observation, and phone and mail surveys.[2]

In China as in the West, surveys of public opinion do not always use proper methodology. Sometimes terms are not defined for the respondents, and the questions are poorly worded. An added problem for those who want to analyze the data is that the polling methods used in the surveys are not always explained. Since this type of research has been done on a broad scale only for a short time in China, however, we can expect surveys to become more methodologically sound as the pollsters and survey researchers gain expertise.

In spite of the fact that we do not know how much pressure Chinese respondents feel to supply the expected or the socially acceptable answer or how much the survey researchers manipulate the data to show more impressive findings than actually exist (problems common to survey research in *all* countries), the data are still useful and revealing. Minimally, they give us a glimpse into Chinese thinking. Even the types of questions asked and the manner in which they are framed by Chinese social scientists reveal cultural values and orientation.[3] And they show what types of questions Chinese so-

---

1. Chen Yiyun, "Out of the Traditional Halls of Academe," p. 70.

2. In China, the most effective type of survey is an interview at home, but it is the least acceptable type of survey to the general public. See "Gongzhong zui yuanyi jieshou baokan diaocha: woguo diaochaye ziwo shenshi zhisi" (The public is most willing to be surveyed by newspapers and magazines: The self-reflection of China's survey industry), pt. 4, *Zhongguo qingnian bao*, Feb. 1, 1997, p. 8.

3. Traditional sayings and statements about values are often used on questionnaires. They are made as statements, and respondents are asked to agree or disagree. Examples are "If one does not live for himself, he will be killed by heaven and earth"; "Small rivers will be dry if there is no water in big rivers"; "Selfishness is the source of all evils"; "People are afraid to be

cial scientists think it important to ask.[4] Many questions are those a West-ern social scientist who wanted to understand public sentiment might ask.[5] On the other hand, some surveys have been unsuccessful because the ques-tions made no sense to the Chinese who were polled, as has happened when an international organization or multinational corporation conducting re-search has, in an effort to be scientific, asked the same questions in every country in the survey.[6]

The results of some surveys are published in journals and in newspapers. Instead of controlling polling firms directly, the Chinese Communist Party's Propaganda Department controls the news media. If it does not want a poll's findings released, the media will probably not publicize them, but it generally does not say the firm cannot do the study in the first place.[7] Al-though we may question some of the politics behind the types of questions that are asked in surveys, it would make little sense for organizations to go to the expense and trouble of polling if it were not providing useful information. There is, moreover, a sufficient breadth of organizations doing research to provide checks on the data generated.

Polling and survey research companies are classified as "unofficial" (that is, private, for-profit firms not under the aegis of a state-run body), semi-official (for-profit groups that operate separately from the official body that established them), or official organizations. Among the official and semi-official agencies, there are joint-venture agencies and agencies established by academic and media institutions. By 1998, there were more than 800 licensed

---

famous as pigs are afraid to be fat"; and "One cannot be rich and kind." See Zhongguo shehui kexue yuan, Shehuixue yanjiusuo, Zhuanxing ketizu, *Zhongguo qingnia de toushi*, pp. 64, 65, 106, 107.

4. For example, "Literature should not expose the seamy side of society too much"; "Im-ported movies should be censored"; and "Rank the most 'uncivilized' behaviors from top to bottom" (the leading response was lack of filial piety; ibid., pp. 107, 108).

5. For example, one survey asked, "How should national decisions be made?" (possible an-swers were the leadership should decide; the people's representatives should discuss and de-cide; after everyone has discussed, the leadership should decide; and experts should propose regulations, and the leaders should decide). Another question asked to what degree the respondent agreed with the statement "Reform is the business of leaders, and it is useless for ordinary people to become involved" (ibid., pp. 142, 144).

6. Victor Yuan (Yuan Yue), "Public Opinion Polling in China: Development and Its Problems," Harvard University, seminar, Fairbank Center for East Asian Research, Sept. 27, 2000.

7. Ibid.

market survey and polling agencies in China. About half of them are located in Beijing. As of 1998, this rapidly growing industry was already taking in annual revenues of about US$100 million.[8]

Many of these companies sell their data. Their customers are both public and private groups. Some firms do surveys for government ministries and bureaus so that they can construct appropriate policies, make more money, or better understand the social, political, and economic concerns of the Chinese people.[9] Other organizations help newspapers and television and radio stations assess their audiences for programming as well as marketing purposes. The majority of those paying for survey and polling are foreign-invested enterprises and overseas customers who want market surveys.[10] Among the organizations conducting surveys are:[11]

various institutes under the Chinese Academy of Social Sciences;
Investigatory Group under the Beijing News Organization;[12]
People's University Public Opinion Research Institution;[13]
Chinese Institute of Societal Investigation;[14]
China's State Statistical Bureau's Urban and Rural Sampling Investigatory Team;[15]
China's Statistical Information Consulting Service Center;[16]
China Societal Investigation Center;[17]

---

8. Ling Yue. "Zhongguo zhuanye shichang diaocha jigou zai jing jushou."

9. One survey asked about the respondents' perception of societal conditions, on a five-point scale of responses from top to bottom: How much social order is there (from turbulent to stable)? Is there conflict among nationalities in China? Do the respondents perceive gender equality / gender inequality? Is social morality decayed or in a good state? Are legal conditions good or not so good? Evaluate the government on the issue of corruption. Is there equality of opportunity to develop or not? etc. (State Statistical Bureau, Statistics Division; and Chinese Research Center for the Promotion and Development of Science and Technology, *Zhongguo shehui fazhan ziliao*).

10. Ling Yue. "Zhongguo zhuanye shichang diaocha jigou zai jing jushou."

11. Except where otherwise indicated, the following list is taken from Chen Tsun-shan, "Zhongguo dalu de minyi diaocha."

12. Founded in 1982; first such unofficial group doing public opinion polling.

13. Unofficial organization; established in 1986.

14. Unofficial organization; founded in 1986. It has branches in cities throughout China.

15. Official organization; established in 1984.

16. Established in 1984; this is an "official" organization, but it charges for its information.

17. An official organization established in 1987 by China Economic System Reform Research Institute. It conducts public opinion polls on a regular basis.

Guangzhou Societal Situation and Public Opinion Research Center;[18]

China Broadcast and Television Association Audience Research Committee;[19]

Beijing Broadcast Institute;

Beijing Market Research Consultancy;

a variety of public opinion investigation organizations under institutes of higher education, science and research organizations, and advertising companies;

Center for Social Science Research on Contemporary China at Beijing University (headed by Shen Mingming and partially funded by the Ford Foundation);

Lingdian diaocha gongsi (Horizon Survey Company).[20]

By 1998, there were 800 registered research and polling firms in China. Among the leading ones, some are joint ventures: A. C. Nielsen (U.S.), Gallup (U.S.), Market Facts (U.S.), Tailor Nelsen (U.K.), Research International China (U.K.), and AMI (Hong Kong); a few are state-owned (Pan-Asia, All-China, Mainland, CCSV, and New Horizon); one is affiliated with an academy (SSI of Beijing Broadcasting Institute); and a few are private Chinese firms (Horizon, Diagaid, White Horse, and Zhilian).[21] It is illegal for foreign polling firms to conduct polling in China. Most polling is therefore done by their joint venture Chinese partners or by Chinese firms, notably, Lingdian (Horizon), People's University Public Opinion Research Institution, the China Research Center of Economic Variation, the State Statistical Bureau, the Social Survey Center of *Chinese Youth Newspaper*, and Mainland. Since January 2000, local firms studying social issues with funding from foreign sources have to submit their proposals, data bases, questionnaires, contracts, and proposals to the State Statistical Bureau.[22]

---

18. A semiofficial organization established by the Guangzhou Economic and Social Development Research Center and Guangzhou Mingxin Pharmacy Factory. It has an internal publication called *Public Opinion Internal Reference*.

19. Established in 1991, it has 26 organizations under it.

20. Horizon was established in 1992 by Yuan Yue (also known as Victor Yuan).

21. Victor Yuan (Yuan Yue), "Public Opinion Polling in China: Development and Its Problems," seminar, Harvard University, Fairbank Center for East Asian Research, Sept. 27, 2000.

22. According to Yuan (ibid.), almost all applications are approved, usually within a few days.

Joint ventures earn 50–55 percent of the total research revenue generated by surveys and polling in China; privately owned firms account for 20–25 percent. The largest clients using the research firms are manufacturers of consumer goods (28 percent), the news media (19 percent), and ad agencies (17.5 percent).[23]

Lingdian (the Horizon Survey Company, also known as the Horizon Research Group), a privately owned and operated company, is a good example of a major Chinese firm that conducts market research for enterprises and public opinion polling on major social issues in China. According to its founder, Yuan Yue, Lingdian and other polling organizations are free to research most social issues, such as public security, problems associated with the floating rural labor force, migrant workers, beggars, the handicapped, the public's major concerns, the public's attitudes toward the government's policies and government offices at the local level, and the public's assessment of social welfare policies and quality of life issues.[24] They may also conduct polls on the impact of government policies on the lifestyles of urban socio-economic groups or the impact of implementing a specific law. Perhaps even more important, Lingdian has been asked by official work units to survey public attitudes. The results have been used to help officials shape policy in such areas as education and the law. Lingdian earns 70 percent of its revenues from studies for manufacturers of consumer goods, 18 percent from public opinion polls, and 7 percent from policy analyses.[25]

There are, according to Yuan Yue, only four major areas that are out of bounds: the performance of current state leaders, Deng Xiaoping's historical status (compared to that of other leaders), attitudes toward the student movement in 1989, and opinions about Taiwan's independence. Lingdian, like most other organizations in China that want to be free of state censorship, engages in enough self-censorship to keep the state out of its affairs.[26]

---

23. Ibid.

24. This includes the public's rating of such factors as professional satisfaction (job stability, pay, promotion, and so on), tolerance of inflation, expectation of reform, and perception of adequacy of public security.

25. *Lingdian diaocha* (Horizon research; company pamphlet), Beijing 2000; Victor Yuan (Yuan Yue), "Public Opinion Polling in China: Development and Its Problems," seminar, Harvard University, Fairbank Center for East Asian Research, Sept. 27, 2000.

26. Ibid.

What types of surveys and polls have I used? First, because I am dealing with a broad topic here, and the questions of how "democratic" China's political culture already is and how Chinese view their government constitute only a part of that topic, I am not as concerned as I might otherwise be with examining data sets, interview techniques, measurement techniques, confidentiality, and so on. I am interested simply in getting a sense of the attitudes of the Chinese people and how these attitudes might relate to China's progress toward democracy. There are, in any event, so many surveys and polls conducted in China, some in collaboration with international survey and polling organizations, that it would be foolish to ignore the information they provide.

Second, some of the surveys and polls I draw on were not intended by those who designed them to make any of the points I do or to support any of the conclusions I reach. Although much else can be wrong with surveys and polling done in China, it is unlikely that the Chinese would purposefully distort the results of these particular surveys and polls in order to make Chinese attitudes appear either more or less "democratic." Most of them had other purposes.

Third, as noted above, Chinese surveys are done by a broad range of institutions: official, semiofficial, and unofficial or private. Chinese organizations or enterprises that need reliable information in order to make policies or sell products are increasingly hiring the for-profit semiofficial and private organizations. For-profit private commercial enterprises such as the Horizon Company do surveys to obtain a correct assessment of the market in terms of such things as gender, age, income, and education-related interests and attitudes. These surveys and opinion polls, as well as the survey research sponsored by official and semiofficial institutions, would be a waste of the limited funds available if the results were faked. Although the state may certainly find it in its interest to announce a poll or survey that shows strong support, say, for the government's policy of law and order or for holding the Olympics in Beijing (and to prohibit the publication of polls and surveys whose results the government does not like), in general, there would be no need to conduct the hundreds of surveys and polls published each year if the party-state intended to supply false data. So, although it is entirely possible that some surveys are unscientifically or fraudulently conducted in order to produce the desired results, it is unlikely that *most* opinion polls and survey research, even when conducted by official or semiofficial organizations (such as news organizations), are intentionally fraudulent. Nevertheless, surveys by these organizations should be taken with a grain of salt.

Fourth, the polls and surveys are intended for Chinese audiences. Although those conducting them may have entertained the possibility that certain foreigners might be interested in their results, in most of the surveys cited in this book, it was probably not their major concern. In short, it is improbable that the Chinese would distort the results of polls and surveys primarily in order to give a favorable impression to foreigners.

Finally, the results of research conducted by Western social scientists or Western organizations in China, especially research that has political implications, are not necessarily more reliable and indeed may be more suspect than those conducted by Chinese organizations. For example, Western survey researchers have discovered that the various members of a work unit will frequently get together to discuss a questionnaire handed out by the researcher and decide how to respond.[27] And some pollsters sent out to the field have been found to fill in the results themselves to save time—a problem for those hiring pollsters anywhere in the world.

Because of government restrictions, it is still very difficult for Western social scientists to carry out social science research in China. The few who have managed to conduct their own social science research surveys in China on issues related to authority, freedom, participation, and democracy encountered tremendous costs and bureaucratic complications for their Chinese partners. In addition, Chinese officials (as well as ordinary people) remain sensitive to the types of probing questions foreigners like to ask.[28] When, for example, I went to China in September 1999 to do research on the results of village elections, I was told that if I wanted to use a formal questionnaire, every question would have to be approved in advance by the

---

27. Shi Tianjian, Andrew Nathan, M. Kent Jennings, William Parish, Andrew Walder, Martin Whyte, and Stanley Rosen, among others, have, however, done carefully controlled social science research in China, and I have referred to some of their survey findings in this book.

28. Shen Mingming, who heads the Center for Social Science Research on Contemporary China at Beijing University and who was trained at the University of Michigan, lamented the skyrocketing costs and bureaucratic difficulties incurred once foreigners become involved in research in China. Approval from various levels of bureaucrats, including since 1999 the State Statistical Bureau, which is now in charge of approving and supervising any foreign-funded research, may hold up research projects indefinitely, as well as force the survey researchers to drop certain questions and reshape others (discussion with Shen Mingming, Beijing University, Sept. 1999).

State Statistical Bureau. Those not approved could not be asked; and those asked had to be asked exactly in the form submitted. Given the limited time I had available, and the possibility of having my project completely rejected, I resorted to open-ended interviews which, as it turned out, proved extremely useful.

In any event, to add at least a veneer of scientific objectivity, I have included the results of some surveys, many of which are as interesting for the Chinese values reflected in the questions as much as for the answers. These are, of course, only a tiny part of the evidence I have for drawing conclusions about democratization in China, and I am fully aware that even the choice of which surveys or polls to use was not done scientifically. For me, Chinese politics, history and culture, the media, conversations with Chinese people over many years, and what is subjectively observable through living and working in China were more reliable sources for understanding the political process and Chinese values concerning democratization.

Minimally, the willingness of the Chinese government to carry out or to permit nonofficial organizations to carry out surveys of public opinion implies a belief on their part that it is important to take public opinion into consideration when making policy. Just because China does not have a multiparty system or a democratically elected national parliament does not mean it ignores, or can afford to ignore, the voices of its people.

Reference Matter

Bibliography

Alford, William P. "Double-Edged Swords Cut Both Ways: Law and Legitimacy in the People's Republic of China." In Tu Wei-ming, ed., *China in Transformation*, pp. 45–70. Cambridge, Mass.: Harvard University Press, 1994.

———. "Making a Goddess of Democracy from Loose Sand: Thoughts on Human Rights in the People's Republic of China." In Abdullahi An Na'im, ed., *Human Rights in Cross-Cultural Perspectives: A Quest for Consensus*. Philadelphia: University of Pennsylvania Press, 1992.

Almond, Gabriel A., and Sidney Verba. *Civic Culture: Political Attitudes and Democracy in Five Nations*. Princeton: Princeton University Press, 1963.

Alter, Jonathan. "Society: Communism Is Dead, Crony Capitalism Lives." *Newsweek*, June 29, 1998, pp. 30–31.

Ames, Roger T. "New Confucianism: A Native Response to Western Philosophy." *China Studies (Zhongguo yanjiu)*, no. 5 (1999): 23–51.

An Yunqi. "Changing Political and Social Attitudes of Chinese Workers: Surveys of Chinese Workers Since 1982." *Modern Currents of Thoughts (Dangdai sichao)* 1997, no. 2 (Apr. 20): 15–23. From http://www.chinabulletin.com/e/surveys.txt.

Angier, Natalie. "On Human Nature and the Evolution of Culture." *New York Times*, Oct. 10, 2000, pp. D1, D2.

Angle, Stephen C., and Marina Svensson, guest eds. Special issue: "On Rights and Human Rights: A Contested and Evolving Chinese Discourse, 1900–1949." *Contemporary Chinese Thought* 31, no. 1 (Fall 1999).

Barber, Benjamin R. *Jihad Vs. McWorld*. New York: Random House, 1995.

Barlow, Tani E., ed. *Gender Politics in Modern China: Writing and Feminism*. Durham, N.C.: Duke University Press, 1993.

Barme, Geremie R. *In the Red: On Contemporary Chinese Culture*. New York: Columbia University Press, 1999.

Barme, Geremie R., and Gloria Davies. "Have We Been Noticed Yet?—Intellectual Contestation and the Chinese Web." Paper for the workshop "Chinese Intellectuals Between the State and Market," Fairbank Center for East Asian Studies, Harvard University, June 30–July 1, 2001.

Barnathan, Joyce, et al. "China: Is Prosperity Creating a Freer Society? *Business Week*, June 6, 1994, pp. 94–99.

Beijing qingnian bao (Beijing youth newspaper). A number of articles based on surveys are from *BQB*; not listed separately.

Benewick, Robert; Jude Howell; and Irene Tong. "Self-Governance and Community: A Preliminary Comparison of Villagers' Committees and Urban Community Councils." Collection of English papers presented at "The International Symposium on Villager Self-Government & Rural Social Development in China," Beijing: Ministry of Civil Affairs and the Carter Center, Sept. 2001, pp. 2–11.

Berger, Peter L., and Thomas Luckmann. *The Social Construction of Reality*. Garden City, N.Y.: Doubleday, 1967.

Biersteker, Thomas, and Cynthia Weber, eds. *State Sovereignty as Social Construct*. Cambridge, Eng.: Cambridge University Press, 1996.

Bond, George C., and Angela Giliam, eds. *Social Construction of the Past*. New York: Routledge, 1994.

Brook, Timothy, and B. Michael Frolic, eds. *Civil Society in China*. Armonk, N.Y.: M. E. Sharpe, 1997.

Buchanan, Allen E. *Marx and Justice: The Radical Critique of Liberalism*. London: Methuen, 1982.

Butterworths Asia, in cooperation with China Law and Culture Publishers; Sino–Hong Kong–Taiwan Legal Consultancy Holding, trans. *China Law Reports, 1991*. Hong Kong: Utopia Press, 1995.

Campbell, Angus; Philip E. Converse; Warren E. Miller; and Donald E. Stokes. *The American Voter*. New York: John Wiley & Sons, 1964.

Cao Shouye. "The Reforms of Trial Procedures in the Chinese Courts Are in Full Swing." *China Law*, no. 1 (Jan. 1997): 64–65.

Carter Center. "The Carter Center Report on Chinese Elections: Observation of Village Elections in Fujian and the Conference to Revise *The National Procedures on Villager Committee Elections*." Working Paper Series. Atlanta: Emory University, Carter Center, 2001.

————. *The Carter Center Report on Chinese Elections: Observations on the Township People's Congress Elections and Cooperative Activities with the Ministry of Civil Affairs, August 1, 1998–January 15, 1999*. Atlanta: Carter Center, 1999.

Chan, Anita. "The Emerging Pattern of Industrial Relations in China and the Rise of the Two New Labour Movements." *China Information: A Quarterly Journal* 9, no. 1 (1995): 36–59.

————. "Revolution or Corporatism? Workers and Unions in Post-Mao China." *Australian Journal of Chinese Affairs*, no. 29 (1993): 31–61.

Chan, Sylvia. "Building a 'Socialist Culture with Chinese Characteristics'? The Case of the Pearl River Delta." *Issues and Studies: A Journal of Chinese Studies and International Affairs* 31, no. 5 (May 1995): 1–24.

Cheek, Timothy, and Carol Lee Hamrin, eds. *China's Establishment Intellectuals.* Armonk, N.Y.: M. E. Sharpe, 1986.

Chen Erjin, *China, Crossroad Socialism: An Unofficial Manifesto for Proletarian Democracy.* London: Verso Editions, 1984.

Chen Guangzhong. "Guaranteeing Human Rights Is the Distinguishing Feature of the Amended Criminal Procedure Law." *China Law*, no. 2 (1996): 68–69.

Chen Tsun-shan. "Zhongguo dalude minyi diaocha" (Public opinion polling in Mainland China). *Xinwenxue yanjiu* 47 (June 1993): 17–34.

Chen Yiyun. "Out of the Traditional Halls of Academe: Exploring New Avenues for Research on Women." In Christina K. Gilmartin, Gail Hershatter, Lisa Rofel, Tyrene White, eds., *Engendering China: Women, Culture, and the State*, pp. 69–79. Cambridge, Mass.: Harvard University Press, 1994.

China Rural Villagers Self-Government Research Group and China Research Society of Basic-Level Government. *Study on the Election of Villagers Committees in Rural China.* Beijing: Ministry of Civil Affairs, with support of Ford Foundation, 1993.

Chu, Leonard L. "Continuity and Change in China's Media Reform." *Journal of Communication* 44, no. 3 (Summer 1994): 4–21.

Clarke, Donald C. "Dispute Resolution in China." *Journal of Chinese Law* 5, no. 2 (Fall 1991): 245–96.

———. "One Step Back Permits Two Steps Forward: Legal Authority Expands Through Administrative Fiat in the Recent Law Reforms." *China Rights Forum* (Fall 1996): http://www.igc.org/hric/crf/english/96fall/pp. 1–6.

Cohen, Paul A. *Discovering History in China: American Historical Writing on the Recent Chinese Past.* New York: Columbia University Press, 1984.

Davis, Deborah S., ed., *The Consumer Revolution in Urban China.* Berkeley: University of California, 2000.

Davis, Deborah S.; Richard Kraus; Barry Naughton; and Elizabeth J. Perry, eds. *Urban Spaces in Contemporary China: The Potential for Autonomy and Community in Post-Mao China.* Cambridge, Eng.: Cambridge University Press and Woodrow Wilson Center Press, 1995.

de Bary, Wm. Theodore. *Asian Values and Human Rights: A Confucian Communitarian Perspective.* Cambridge, Mass.: Harvard University Press, 1998.

———. *The Liberal Tradition in China.* New York: Columbia University Press, 1983.

de Bary, Wm. Theodore, ed. *Sources of Chinese Tradition.* 2 vols. New York: Columbia University Press, 1960, 1964.

de Bary, Wm. Theodore, and Tu Weiming, eds. *Confucianism and Human Rights.* New York: Columbia University Press, 1998.

DeGolyer, Michael E., et al. *The Hong Kong Transition Project, 1982–2007, Reform: Hong Kong's Version of "One Country, Two Systems" and China's Path to Unification.* Hong Kong: Hong Kong Baptist University, Government & International Studies, 2000.

Diamond, Larry. "Economic Development and Democracy Reconsidered." In Gary Marks and Larry Diamond, eds., *Reexamining Democracy: Essays in Honor of Seymour Martin Lipset,* pp. 93–139. London: Sage Publications, 1992.

———. "Rethinking Civil Society: Toward Democratic Consolidation." *Journal of Democracy* 5, no. 3 (July 1994): 4–17.

Diamond, Larry, ed. *Political Culture and Democracy in Developing Countries.* Boulder, Colo.: Lynne Rienner Publishers, 1993.

"Diannao shidaide Beijing zhongxuesheng: Beijing zhongxuesheng keji yizhi diaocha baogao" (Beijing middle school students in an age of computers: investigative report on awareness of science and technology among Beijing middle school students). *Zhongguo qingnian bao (China Youth Daily),* Nov. 9, 1996, p. 4.

Ding, Yijiang. "Pre- and Post-Tiananmen Conceptual Evolution of Democracy in Intellectual Circles: Rethinking of State and Society." *Journal of Contemporary China* 7, no. 18 (July 1998): 229–56.

Dittmer, Lowell, and Samuel S. Kim. *China's Search for National Identity.* Ithaca: Cornell University Press, 1993.

Dittmer, Lowell, and Lu Xiaobo. "Structural Tranformation of the Chinese Danwei: Macropolitical Implications of Micropolitical Change." *China Studies (Zhongguo yanjiu),* no. 3 (Spring 1997): 113–43.

Dong Yuyu and Shi Binhai, eds. *Zhengzhi Zhongguo: mianxiang xintizhi xuanzede shidai* (Political China: facing the era of choosing a new structure). Beijing: Jinri Zhongguo chubanshe, 1998.

Dowd, Daniel V.; Allen Carlson; and Shen Mingming. "The Prospects for Democratization in the People's Republic of China: Evidence from the 1995 Beijing Area Study. *Journal of Contemporary China.* 8, no. 22 (Nov. 1999): 365–80.

Drakulic, Slavenka (Yugo). *How We Survived Communism and Even Laughed.* New York: Norton, 1991.

Dunn, John. "Conclusion." In idem, ed., *Democracy: The Unfinished Journey, 508 BC to AD 1993,* pp. 239–66. Oxford: Oxford University Press, 1992.

———. *Modern Revolutions: An Introduction to the Analysis of a Political Phenomenon.* 2d ed. Cambridge, Eng.: Cambridge University Press, 1989.

———. *Political Obligation in Its Historical Context.* Cambridge, Eng.: Cambridge University Press, 1980.

Ehrlich, Paul R. *Human Natures: Genes, Cultures and the Human Prospect.* Washington, D.C.: Island Press, 2000.

Eldersveld, Samuel J.; John E. Jackson; M. Kent Jennings; Kenneth Lieberthal; Melanie Manion; Michael Oksenberg; Zhefu Chen; Hefeng He; Mingming Shen; Qingkui Xie; Ming Yang; and Fengchun Yang. *Four-County Study of Chinese Local Government and Political Economy, 1990.* Published by University of Michigan and Beijing University in 1994; distributed by Inter-university Consortium for Political and Social Research, Computer file, Study no. 6805, 1996.

Etzioni, Amitai. "On the Place of Virtues in a Pluralistic Democracy." In Gary Marks and Larry Diamond, eds., *Reexamining Democracy: Essays in Honor of Seymour Martin Lipset,* pp. 70–78. London: Sage Publications, 1992.

Fan Baojun, ed. *Zhongguo shehui tuanti dacidian* (A comprehensive handbook of Chinese civil associations). Beijing: Zhongguo jingguan jiaoyu chubanshe, 1995.

Fan Gang. "Tebiede fangshi yu texude wenti—Zhongguo gaigede mogan tezhengde lilun fenxi" (Special approaches to special problems: a theoretical analysis of some characteristics of China's reform). *Zhongguo yanjiu,* no. 1 (Autumn 1995): 27–47.

Fan Lei. "1995 nian Beijing shimin zhengzhi xintai diaocha" (Investigation of Beijing citizens' political-psychological attitudes in 1995). *Beijing jingji liaowang* 1996, no. 1, pp. 6–10. Reprinted in *Renda fujin ciliao.*

Fan Yu and Dong Min. "Guomin falü yishi diaocha" (A survey of people's awareness of the law). *Zhongguo qingnian bao,* Jan. 18, 1997, p. 8.

Feng Chongyi. *Luosu yu Zhongguo* (Russell and China). Beijing: Sanlian shudian, 1994.

———. "The Party-State, Liberalism and Social Democracy: The Debate on China's Future." Paper presented at the workshop "Chinese Intellectuals Between the State and the Market." Fairbank Center for East Asian Studies, Harvard University, June 30–July 1, 2001.

Fish, M. Steven. "Rethinking Civil Society: Russia's Fourth Transition." *Journal of Democracy* 5, no. 3 (July 1994): 31–42.

Fisher, Roger, and William Ury. *Getting to Yes: Negotiating Agreement Without Giving In.* Boston: Houghton-Mifflin, 1981.

Forney, Matt. "China: Voice of the People." *Far Eastern Economic Review,* May 7, 1998, pp. 10–11.

Foulis, Patrick. "Taking the Mickey out of Mao." *Varsity* (Cambridge University), Jan. 19, 1996, p. 10.

Friedman, Edward. *The Politics of Democratization: Generalizing East Asian Experiences.* Boulder, Colo.: Westview Press, 1994.

Friedman, Edward, and Barrett L. McCormick, eds. *What If China Doesn't Democratize?* Armonk, N.Y.: M. E. Sharpe, 2000.

Frolic, B. Michael. "State-Led Civil Society." In Timothy Brook and B. Michael Frolic, eds., *Civil Society in China,* pp. 46–67. Armonk, N.Y.: M. E. Sharpe, 1997.

Fukuyama, Francis. "Confucianism and Democracy." *Journal of Democracy*, Apr. 1995, pp. 20–33.

———. *The End of History and the Last Man*. New York: Free Press, 1992.

———. *Trust: The Social Virtues and the Creation of Prosperity*. London: ⌐enguin Books, 1996.

Gadsden, Amy. "Grassroots Elections, Grassroots Challenges." Collection of English papers presented at "The International Symposium on Villager Self-Government & Rural Social Development in China," Beijing: Ministry of Civil Affairs and the Carter Center, Sept. 2001, pp. 42–52.

Gamer, Robert E., and Shou Huisheng, "Township Elections and the Transformation of Local Power Structures." Collection of English papers presented at "The International Symposium on Villager Self-Government & Rural Social Development in China," Beijing: Ministry of Civil Affairs and the Carter Center, Sept. 2001, pp. 53–72.

Gao Bingzhong. "The Rise of Associations in China and the Question of Their Legitimacy." *Social Sciences in China*, no. 1 (2001): 73–87.

Gibson, James L. "The Political Consequences of Intolerance: Cultural Conformity and Political Freedom." *American Political Science Review* 86, no. 2 (June 1992): 338–56.

Gilley, Bruce. "Whatever You Say: Survey Shows Surprising Support for the Government." *Far Eastern Economic Review* 158, no. 49 (Dec. 7, 1995): 35–36.

Goldman, Merle. *China's Intellectuals: Advise and Dissent*. Cambridge, Mass.: Harvard University Press, 1981.

———. *Sowing the Seeds of Democracy in China: Political Reform in the Deng Xiaoping Era*. Cambridge, Mass.: Harvard University Press, 1994.

Goldman, Merle; Timothy Cheek; and Carol Lee Hamrin, eds. *China's Intellectuals and the State: In Search of a New Relationship*. Cambridge, Mass.: Harvard University Press, 1987.

Gong Gang. "National Identity and Cultural Resistance: A Commentary on Zhang Chengzhi's Cultural Sociology." *China Studies (Zhongguo yanjiu)*, no. 5 (1999): 129–45.

Gong Nanxiang. "Make Nationalism a Constructive Force for Democratization." *China Strategic Review* 2, no. 2 (Mar./Apr. 1997): 14–30.

"Gongzhong zui yuanyi jieshou baokan diaocha: woguo diaochaye ziwo shenshi zisi" (The public is most willing to be surveyed by newspapers and magazines: the self-reflection of China's survey industry), pt. 4. *Zhongguo qingnian bao*, Feb. 1, 1997, p. 8.

Goode, Erica. "How Culture Molds Habits of Thought." *New York Times*, Aug. 8, 2000, pp. D1, D4.

Goodman, David S. G. *Beijing Street Voices: The Poetry and Politics of China's Democracy Movement.* London: Marion Boyars, 1981.

Gray, John. *Enlightenment's Wake: Politics and Culture at the Close of the Modern Age.* London: Routledge, 1995.

Grieder, Jerome B. *Hu Shih and the Chinese Renaissance: Liberalism in the Chinese Revolution, 1917–1937.* Cambridge, Mass.: Harvard University Press, 1970.

Gu, Edward X. (Gu Xin). "Cultural Intellectuals and the Politics of the Cultural Public Space in Communist China (1979–1989): A Case Study of Three Intellectual Groups." *Journal of Asian Studies* 58, no. 2 (May 1999): 389–431.

————. "Plural Institutionalism and the Emergence of Intellectual Public Spaces in Contemporary China: Four Relational Patterns and Four Organizational Forms." *Journal of Contemporary China* 7, no. 8 (July 1998): 271–301.

Guo Daohui. "Shixian fa zhide siyao" (The "four musts' in realizing the rule of law). *Falü kexue* 1996, no. 3: 3–4.

Guowuyuan fazhan yanjiu zhongxin. "The Characteristics of Psychological Changes of Our Nation's Urban Residents and Analysis of Reform and Society Situations—An Analytical Report for 1994 by the State System Reform Commission for Societal Investigation." *Guanli shijie* 1995, no. 4: 130–36.

Guthrie, Doug. *Dragon in a Three-Piece Suit: The Emergence of Capitalism in China.* Princeton: Princeton Unviersity Press, 1999.

Hachigian, Nina. "China's Cyber-Strategy." *Foreign Affairs*, Mar./Apr. 2001, pp. 118–33.

Han Minzhu, ed. *Cries for Democracy: Writings and Speeches from the 1989 Chinese Democracy Movement.* Princeton: Princeton University Press, 1990.

Harding, Neil. "The Marxist-Leninist Detour." In John Dunn, ed., *Democracy: The Unfinished Journey, 508 BC to AD 1993*, pp. 155–87. Oxford: Oxford University Press, 1992.

Harik, Iliya. "Rethinking Civil Society: Pluralism in the Arab World." *Journal of Democracy* 5, no. 3 (July 1994): 43–56.

Harvard Law School, East Asian Legal Studies Program and Human Rights Program. "Human Rights and Foreign Policy: A Symposium." Cambridge, Mass.: Harvard Law School and Human Rights Program, 1994.

Ho, Suk-ching. "The Emergence of Consumer Power in China." *Business Horizons*, Sept.–Oct. 1997, pp. 15–21.

Hoston, Germaine A. *The State, Identity, and the National Question in China and Japan.* Princeton: Princeton University Press, 1994.

Howell, Jude. "Trade Unions in China: The Challenge of Foreign Capital." In Greg O'Leary, ed., *Adjusting to Capitalism: Chinese Workers and the State*, pp. 150–72. Armonk, N.Y.: M. E. Sharpe, 1998.

Howie, C. "Chinese Critiques of the Ultimate Penalty." *China Rights Forum*, Fall 1996, www.igc.org//hric/crf/english/96fall.

Hua, Shiping. *Scientism and Humanism: Two Cultures in Post-Mao China*. Albany: SUNY Press, 1995.

Huang, Sung-k'ang. *Lu Hsun and the New Culture Movement of Modern China*. Amsterdam: Djambatan, 1957.

Huang Ziyi. "Guanyu zai woguo jianshe shehui zhuyi ya zhi guojia de luogan wenti" (Some issues on establishing the socialist rule of law in our country). *Falü kexue* 1996, no. 4: 6–12.

Human Rights in China. "China: Social Groups Seek Independence in a Regulatory Cage." Report, Apr. 1998, http://www.igc.org/hric/reports/freedom.html.

Human Rights in China and Human Rights Watch/Asia. "Whose Security? 'State Security' in China's New Criminal Code." *China Rights Forum*, Summer 1997, http//www.hric.org/crf/english/97summer.

Huntington, Samuel P. *American Politics: The Promise of Disharmony*. Cambridge, Mass.: Harvard University Press, 1981.

————. "The Clash of Civilizations?" *Foreign Affairs*, Summer 1993, pp. 22–49.

————. *The Clash of Civilizations and the Remaking of World Order*. New York: Simon & Schuster, 1996.

————. *The Third Wave: Democratization in the Late Twentieth Century*. Norman, Okla.: University of Oklahoma Press, 1991.

Huntington, Samuel P., and Joan M. Nelson. *No Easy Choice: Political Participation in Developing Countries*. Cambridge, Mass.: Harvard University Press, 1976.

Jennings, M. Kent. "Political Participation in the Chinese Countryside." *American Political Science Review* 91, no. 2 (June 1997): 361–72.

Jernow, Allison Liu. "China: The Tight Leash Loosens." *CJR*, Jan./Feb. 1994.

Jiang Kaiwen. "Gonghui yu dang-guojiade chongtu: bashi niandai yilaide Zhongguo gonghui gaige" (The conflicts between trade unions and the party-state: the reform of Chinese trade unions since the 1980s). *Xianggong shehui kexue xuebao*, no. 8 (Autumn 1996): 121–58.

Jiang Liu, Lu Xueyi, and Shan Tianlun, eds. *1993–1994 nian: Zhongguo shehui xingshi fenxi yu yuce* (Analysis and predictions of social conditions in China, 1993–94). Beijing: Shehui kexue wenxian chubanshe, 1994.

————. *1995–96 nian Zhongguo shehui xingshi fenxi yu yuce* (Analysis and predictions of social conditions in China, 1995–96). Beijing: Shehui kexue wenxian chubanshe, 1996.

————. *1996–1997 nian: Zhongguo shehui xingshi fenxi yu yuce* (Analysis and predictions of social conditions in China, 1995–96). Beijing: Shehui kexue wenxian chubanshe, 1997.

Jin Yinong. "1995 yishu cun da taowang toushi" (Perspectives on the failure of the Fine Arts Village in 1995). *Ershi yi shiji xuan yuekan*, no. 33 (Feb. 1996): 72–80.

Jin Zhenrong. "More than 200 Scientific and Technological Journals Signed the Moral Covenant." *Guangming Ribao*, Feb. 2, 1999. From http://www.gmdaily.com.cn.

Johnson, Chalmers. "What's Wrong with Chinese Studies?" *Asian Survey*, no. 10 (Oct. 1982): 919–33.

Joseph, William A., ed. *China Briefing: The Contradictions of Change*. Armonk, N.Y.: M. E. Sharpe, 1997.

Kelliher, Daniel. "The Chinese Debate over Village Self-Government." *China Journal*, no. 37 (Jan. 1997): 63–86.

———. "Keeping Democracy Safe from the Masses." *Comparative Politics* 25, no. 4 (July 1993): 379–96.

Khan, Zizur Rahman, and Carl Riskin. *Inequality and Poverty in China in the Age of Globalization*. Oxford: Oxford University Press, 2001.

Koo, George. "The Real China: A Firsthand Perspective on Human Rights in Today's China." *Harvard International Review*, Summer 1998, pp. 68–71. Reprinted in Suzanne Ogden, ed., *Global Studies: China*, pp. 159–62. Sluice Dock, Conn.: Dushkin / McGraw Hill, 1999.

Kraus, Richard. "China's Artists Between Plan and Market." In Deborah S. Davis, Richard Kraus, Barry Naughton, Elizabeth J. Perry, eds., *Urban Spaces in Contemporary China: The Potential for Autonomy and Community in Post-Mao China*, pp. 173–92. Cambridge, Eng.: Cambridge University Press and Woodrow Wilson Center Press, 1995.

Ku, Fong, comp. and ed. *2000 Directory of International NGOs Supporting Work in China*. Hong Kong: China Development Research Services, 1999.

Kuhn, Thomas. *The Structure of Scientific Revolutions*. Chicago: University of Chicago Press, 1962.

Kwong, Julia. "Ideological Crisis Among China's Youths." *British Journal of Sociology* 45, no. 2 (June 1994): 247–63.

Lang, Olga. *Pa Chin and His Writings*. Cambridge, Mass.: Harvard University Press, 1967.

Laski, Harold J. "Democracy." In Edwin R. A. Seligman, ed., *Encyclopaedia of the Social Sciences*, vol. 4, s.v. New York: Macmillan, 1959 [1931].

Lawrence, Susan V. "China: Excising the Cancer." *Far Eastern Economic Review*, Aug. 20, 1998: 10–13. Reprinted in Suzanne Ogden, ed., *Global Studies: China*, pp. 108–11. Sluice Dock, Conn.: Dushkin / McGraw Hill, 1999.

———. "Democracy, Chinese Style." *Australian Journal of Chinese Affairs*, no. 32 (July 1994): 61–68.

Lee, Teng-hui. "Confucian Democracy: Modernization, Culture, and the State in East Asia." *Harvard International Review*, Fall 1999, pp. 16–18.

Lee, Paul Siu-nam. "Mass Communication and National Development in China: Media Roles Reconsidered." *Journal of Communication*, Summer 1994, pp. 22–37.

Levenson, Joseph R. *Liang Ch'i-ch'ao and the Mind of Modern China.* Berkeley: University of California Press, 1967.

Levin, Michael. *The Spectre of Democracy: The Rise of Modern Democracy as Seen by Its Critics.* London: Macmillan, 1992.

Li Buyun. "Lun geren renquan yu jiti renquan" (On individual human rights and collective human rights). *Zhongguo shehui kexueyuan yanjiu shengyuan xuebao* (Beijing) 1994, no. 6: 19–26.

Li, Cheng. "Promises and Pitfalls of Reform: New Thinking in Post-Deng China." In Tyrene White, ed., *China Briefing 2000: The Continuing Transformation*, pp. 123–57. Armonk, N.Y.: M. E. Sharpe, 2000.

Li Gang. "Deng hou Zhongguode keneng qianjing" (Prospects for post-Deng China). *Dangdai Zhongguo yanjiu* 1997, no. 1: 29–46.

Li Kang. "Zhengtong renhe zhi yu jichen shequ—Ningxia nongcun qianren chou-yang diaocha fenxi" (Successful governance relies on grassroots community—an investigation and analysis of Ningxia Village). In Li Xueju, Wang Zhengyao, and Tang Jinsu, eds., *Zhongguo xiangzhen zhengguande xianzhuang yu gaige* (Current conditions in and reforms of Chinese township government), pp. 275–97. Beijing: Zhongguo shehui chuban, 1994.

Li Lianjiang. "The Two-Ballot System in Shanxi Province: Subjecting Village Party Secretaries to a Popular Vote." *China Journal*, no. 42 (July 1999): 103–18.

Li Yining. "Zhongguo jingji tizhi gaigede lunlixue sikao" (Reflections on the ethics of China's economic reform). *Zhongguo yanjiu*, no. 1 (Autumn 1995): 3–26.

Li, Yongzeng. "Rise of Horizontal Associations." *Beijing Review*, no. 15 (Apr. 13, 1987): 23–25.

Li, Zhisui. *The Private Life of Chairman Mao.* New York: Random House, 1994.

Liang Zhiping. "Cong lizhi dao fazhi" (From rule of *li* to rule of law). *Kaifang shidai* 126 (Jan. 1999): 78–85.

Lin Zhun and Ma Yuan, eds. *Guojia peichangfa wenti yanjiu* (Studies on the issue of the State Compensation Law). Beijing: Renmin fayuan chubanshe, 1992.

Ling Yue. "Diaochaye pingzao qing quan" (Survey industry has repeatedly suffered infringement of rights). *Beijing qingnian bao*, Jan. 15, 1997, p. 8.

———. "Zhongguo zhuanye shichang diaocha jigou zai jing jushou" (Chinese professional market survey agencies meet in Beijing). *Sohu-Lingdian zhuangshang diaocha* (Soho-Horizon joint internet survey) 40, Sept. 21, 1998, http://www.itc.cn.net/survey/repo921-2.html.

Lingdian shichang diaocha yu fenxi gongsi. "1993–1994 nian: zhongxin chengshi wending xing fenxi yu yuce" (Analysis and prediction of stability in central cities). In Jiang Liu, Lu Xueyi, and Shan Tianlun, eds., *1993–1994 nian: Zhongguo shehui xingshi fenxi yu yuce* (Analysis and predictions of social conditions in China, 1993–94), pp. 58–68. Beijing: Shehui kexue wenxian chubanshe, 1994.

Linz, Juan J. "Change and Continuity in the Nature of Contemporary Democracies." In Gary Marks and Larry Diamond, eds., *Reexamining Democracy: Essays in Honor of Seymour Martin Lipset*, pp. 182–207. London: Sage Publications, 1992.

Liu, Alan P. L. *Mass Politics in the People's Republic: State and Society in Contemporary China.* Boulder, Colo.: Westview, 1996.

Liu Han and Li Lin. "Woguo fazhi jianshe 20 nian chengjiu yu zhanwang" (Our country's accomplishments in legal construction over the past 20 years and the outlook for the future). *Qiu shi* 1998, no. 23: 12–15.

Liu Jinxi. "Minzhu xin lun" (New arguments on democracy). *Xuexi yu tansuo*, 1998, no. 3: 81–85.

Liu Junning. "Shichang jingji yu youxian zhengfu" (The market economy and limited government). In *Xue wen Zhongguo* (Studies on the problems of China), pp. 50–93. Nanchang: Jiangxi chubanshe, 1998.

Liu, X. Drew. "A Harbinger of Democracy: Grassroot Elections in Rural China." *China Strategic Review* 2, no. 3 (May/June, 1997): 50–75.

Liu Xinghua. "Youxian touzi yu jichu jiaoyu" (Give priority to investment in basic education). *Qiu shi* 1997, no. 7 (1997): 41–43.

Lu Jianhua, Yang Guodong, and Tu Qing. "1995–1996 nian shehui xingshi: zhuanjia wenzhuan diaocha zonghe fenxi" ("Social Conditions in 1995–1996: Comprehensive Analyses of Survey of Experts). In Jiang Liu, Lu Xueyi, and Shan Tianlun, eds., *1995–1996 nian Zhongguo: shehui xingshi fenxi yu yuce* (China in 1995–96: analysis and predictions of social conditions), pp. 35–44. Beijing: Shehui kexue wenxian chubanshe, 1996.

Lu Ning. *The Dynamics of Foreign Policy Decisionmaking.* 2d ed. Boulder, Colo.: Westview Press, 2000.

Lu, Xiaobo. *Cadres and Corruption: The Organizational Involution of the Chinese Communist Party.* Stanford: Stanford University Press, 2000.

Lu Xin, Lu Xueyi, Shan Tianlun. *1998 nian: Zhongguo shehui xingshi fenxi yu yuce* (1998: analysis and predictions of China's social conditions). Beijing: Shehui kexue wenxian chubanshe, 1998.

Lu Xueyi and Li Peilin. *Zhongguo xin shiqi shehui fazhan baogao (1991–1995)* (Report on development in China in a new period, 1991–95.) Liaoning: Liaoning renmin chubanshe, 1997.

Lubman, Stanley B. *Bird in a Cage: Legal Reform After Mao.* Stanford: Stanford University Press, 1999.

Lull, James. *China Turned on: Television, Reform, and Resistance*. London: Routledge, 1992.

Lum, Thomas. *Problems of Democratization in China*. New York: Garland Publishing, 2000.

Lynch, David C. *After the Propaganda State: Media, Politics, and "Thought Work" in Reformed China*. Stanford: Stanford University Press, 1999.

Ma, Shu-yun. "Clientelism, Foreign Attention, and Chinese Intellectual Autonomy." *Modern China* 24, no. 4 (Oct. 1998): 445–71.

Ma Yili and Liu Hanbang. *Shanghai shehui tuanti gailan* (Overview of Shanghai's societal organizations). Shanghai: Shanghai renmin chubanshe, 1993.

Madsen, Richard. *China and the American Dream: A Moral Inquiry*. Berkeley: University of California Press, 1995.

Maier, Charles. "Democracy Since the French Revolution." In John Dunn ed., *Democracy: The Unfinished Journey, 508 BC to AD 1993*, pp. 125–53. Oxford: Oxford University Press, 1992.

Manion, Malanie. "The Electoral Connection in the Chinese Countryside." *American Political Science Review*, no. 90 (Dec. 1996): 736–48.

Marcus, George, and John Sullivan. *Political Tolerance in American Democracy*. Chicago: University of Chicago Press, 1983.

McCormick, Barrett L. *Political Reform in Post-Mao China: Democracy and Bureaucracy in a Leninist State*. Berkeley: University of California Press, 1990.

McDonagh, Eileen L. "The 'Welfare Rights State' and the 'Civil Rights State': Policy Paradox and State Building in the Progressive Era." *Studies in America Political Development*, no. 7 (Fall 1993): 225–74.

Meisner, Maurice. *Li Ta-chao and the Origins of Chinese Marxism*. Cambridge, Mass.: Harvard University Press, 1968.

Mufson, Steven. "It Looks Like Spring Again in China." *Washington Post National Weekly Edition*, Apr. 27, 1998. Reprinted in Suzanne Ogden, author and ed., *Global Studies: China*, pp. 113–14. Guilford, Conn.: Dushkin / McGraw Hill, 1999.

———. "A New Day in China? Beijing's Baby Boomer Generation Builds Democracy One Village at a Time." *Washington Post National Weekly Edition*, June 29, 1998. Reprinted in Suzanne Ogden, author and ed., *Global Studies: China*, pp. 153–56. Guilford, Conn.: Dushkin / McGraw Hill, 1999.

Myers, Sondra, and Penny Parsekian, eds., *Democracy Is a Discussion: The Handbook*. New London: Connecticut College, Toor Cummings Center for International Studies and the Liberal Arts, 1996.

Nathan, Andrew J. "China's Path from Communism." *Journal of Democracy* 4, no. 2 (Apr. 1993): 30–42.

———. *Chinese Democracy*. New York: Alfred A. Knopf, 1985.

Nathan, Andrew J., and Shi Tianjian. "Cultural Requisites for Democracy in China: Findings from a Survey." In Tu Wei-ming, ed., *China in Transformation*, pp. 95–123. Cambridge, Mass.: Harvard University Press, 1994.

Nevitt, Christopher Earle. "Private Business Associations in China: Evidence of Civil Society or Local State Power?" *China Journal*, no. 36 (July 1996): 25–43.

Ng, Hong, and Malcolm Warner. *China's Trade Unions and Management.* London: Macmillan, 1997.

Ni Shouming. "Justice, Democracy and High Efficiency: China Reforms Its Judicial Style." *China Law* 1998, no. 2 (June 30): 67–69.

Nietzsche, Friedrich. *Zarathustra's Discourses.* Penguin's 60 Classics. London: Penguin Books, 1961.

Nodia, Ghia. "Nationalism and Democracy." *Journal of Democracy* 3, no. 4 (Oct. 1992): 3–22.

Nolan, Peter. *China's Rise, Russia's Fall: Politics, Economics and Planning in the Transition from Stalinism.* New York: St. Martin's Press, 1995.

North, Douglass. *Institutions, Institutional Change, and Economic Performance.* New York: Cambridge University Press, 1990.

Nussbaum, Martha, and Amartya Sen, eds. *The Quality of Life.* Oxford: Clarendon Press, 1993.

Ogden, Suzanne. "China's Developing Civil Society: Interest Groups, Trade Unions and Associational Pluralism." In Malcolm Warner, ed., *Changing Workplace Relations in the Chinese Economy*, pp. 263–97. London: Macmillan, 2000.

———. *China's Unresolved Issues: Politics, Development and Culture.* 3d ed. Englewood Cliffs, N.J.: Prentice Hall, 1995.

———. "The Chinese Communist Party: Agent of Pluralism and the Free Market?" *SAIS Review: A Journal of International Affairs* 13, no. 2 (Summer/Fall 1993): 107–25.

———. "Chinese Concepts of the State, Nation, and Sovereignty." Ph.D. diss., Brown University, 1974.

———. "Field Notes and Interviews, China, 1996–1997."

———. "Field Research Notes on Impact of China's Village Elections and Reforms." Sept. 1999.

———. "The Sage in the Inkpot: Bertrand Russell's Influence on Social Reconstruction in China in the 1920's." *Modern Asian Studies* 16, no. 3 (Oct. 1982): 353–424.

Ogden, Suzanne, author and ed. *Global Studies: China.* 8th ed. Guilford, Conn.: Dushkin / McGraw Hill, 1999.

Ogden, Suzanne; Kathleen Hartford; Lawrence Sullivan; and David Zweig, authors and eds. *China's Search for Democracy: The Student and Mass Movement of 1989.* Armonk, N.Y.: M. E. Sharpe, 1992.

Oi, Jean C. "Fiscal Reform and the Economic Foundations of Local State Corporatism in China." *World Politics* 45, no. 1 (Oct. 1992): 99–126.

Oi, Jean C., and Scott Rozelle. "Elections and Power: The Locus of Decision-Making in Chinese Villages." *China Quarterly*, no. 162 (June 2000): 513–39.

O'Leary, Greg, ed. *Adjusting to Capitalism: Chinese Workers and the State*. Armonk, N.Y.: M. E. Sharpe, 1998.

Paine, Lynn W. "Making Schools Modern: Paradoxes of Educational Reform." In Andrew G. Walder, ed., *Zouping in Transition: The Process of Reform in Rural North China*, pp. 205–36. Cambridge, Mass.: Harvard University Press, 1998.

Palmer, Brian. "What the Chinese Want." *Fortune*, Oct. 11, 1999, pp. 229–33.

Pearson, Margaret M. *China's New Business Elite: The Political Consequences of Economic Reform*. Berkeley: University of California Press, 1997.

———. "The Janus Face of Business Associations in China: Socialist Corporatism in Foreign Enterprises." *Australian Journal of Chinese Affairs*, no. 31 (Jan. 1994): 25–46.

Pei, Minxin. "China's Evolution Toward Soft Authoritarianism." In Edward Friedman and Barrett L. McCormick, eds., *What If China Doesn't Democratize*, pp. 74–98. Armonk, N.Y.: M. E. Sharpe, 2000.

———. "Chinese Civic Associations: An Empirical Analysis." *Modern China* 24, no. 3 (July 1998): 285–318.

———. *From Reform to Revolution: The Demise of Communism in China and the Soviet Union*. Cambridge, Mass.: Harvard University Press, 1994.

———. "Is China Democratizing?" *Foreign Affairs*, Jan./Feb. 1998, pp. 68–82.

———. "Racing Against Time: Institutional Decay and Renewal in China." In William A. Joseph, ed., *China Briefing: The Contradictions of Change*, pp. 11–49. Armonk, N.Y.: M. E. Sharpe, 1997.

———. "Rights and Resistance: The Changing Contexts of the Dissident Movement." In Elizabeth J. Perry and Mark Selden, eds., *Chinese Society: Change, Conflict and Resistance*, pp. 20–40. New York: Routledge, 2000.

Peng, Yali. "Democracy and Chinese Political Discourses." *Modern China* 24, no. 4 (Oct. 1998): 408–44.

Perry, Elizabeth J. "Labor's Battle for Political Space: The Role of Worker Associations in Contemporary China." In Deborah S. Davis, Richard Kraus, Barry Naughton, and Elizabeth J. Perry, eds., *Urban Spaces in Contemporary China: The Potential for Autonomy and Community in Post-Mao China*, pp. 302–25. Cambridge, Eng.: Cambridge University Press and Woodrow Wilson Center Press, 1995.

Pickowicz, Paul G. "Velvet Prisons and the Political Economy of Chinese Filmmaking." In Deborah S. Davis, Richard Kraus, Barry Naughton, Elizabeth J. Perry, eds., *Urban Spaces in Contemporary China: The Potential for Autonomy and Community in Post-Mao China*, pp. 193–220. Cambridge, Eng.: Cambridge University Press and Woodrow Wilson Center Press, 1995.

Plato. *The Republic of Plato*. Trans., with an introduction and notes, Francis Mac-Donald Cornford. London: Oxford University Press, 1941.

Przeworski, Adam. *Democracy and the Market: Political and Economic Reforms in Eastern Europe and Latin America*. Cambridge, Eng.: Cambridge University Press, 1991.

Putnam, Robert D. *Bowling Alone: The Collapse of American Community*. New York: Simon and Schuster, 2000.

———. *Making Democracy Work: Civic Traditions in Modern Italy*. Princeton: Princeton University Press, 1993.

Qi, Hancheng. "From Concept to Social Action: The Green Movement in China." *China Strategic Review* 2, no. 3 (May/June 1997): 39–49.

Qin Xianchun. "How Can the Funds of a Trade Union Be Forcibly Transferred?" *Legal Herald (Fazhi daokan)* 1997, no. 5: 30–31.

"Regulate Various Social Relationships in Accordance with the Law: China Launches Legal Service Telephone Line." *Shidai chao*, no. 27 (Jan. 1999).

Renmin fayuan nianjian 1992 (People's court yearbook, 1992). Beijing: Renmin fayuan chubanshe, 1995.

Research Group on the System of Village Self-Government in China and the China Research Society of Basic-Level Governance. *Legal System of Village Committees in China*. Beijing: Ministry of Civil Affairs, with support of Ford Foundation, 1995.

Riskin, Carl; Zhao Renwei; and Li Shi, eds. *China's Retreat from Equality: Income Distribution and Economic Transition*. Armonk, N.Y.: M. E. Sharpe, 2001.

Rofel, Lisa B. "'Yearnings': Televisual Love and Melodramatic Politics in Contemporary China." *American Ethnologist*, no. 21 (1994): 700–722.

Rogers, Peter P.; Kazi F. Jalal; Bindu N. Lohani; Gene M. Owens; Chang-ching Yu; Christian M. Dufournaud; and Jun Bi. *Measuring Environmental Quality in Asia*. Cambridge, Mass.: Harvard University, Division of Engineering and Applied Sciences, and Asian Development Bank, 1997.

Rose, Richard. "Rethinking Civil Society: Postcommunism and the Problem of Trust." *Journal of Democracy* 5, no. 3 (July 1994): 18–30.

Rosemont, Henry. "Human Rights: A Bill of Worries." In Wm. Theodore de Bary and Tu Weiming, eds., *Confucianism and Human Rights*, pp. 54–66. New York: Columbia University Press, 1998.

Ross, James R. *Escape to Shanghai: A Jewish Community in China*. New York: Free Press, 1994.

Sabine, George H. "The Two Democratic Traditions." *Philosophical Review* 61 (Oct. 1952): 451–74.

Saich, Tony. "Negotiating the State: The Development of Socialist Organizations in China." *China Quarterly*, no. 161 (Mar. 2000): 124–41.

Saich, Tony, and Hans Van de Ven, eds. *New Perspective on the Chinese Communist Revolution*. Armonk, N.Y.: M. E. Sharpe, 1995.

Said, Edward W. *Orientalism*. New York: Vintage Books, 1979.

Saint-Exupery, Antoine de. *Wartime Writings, 1939–1944*. New York: Harcourt, Brace, Jovanovich, 1986.

Sartori, Giovanni. "How Far Can Free Government Travel?" *Journal of Democracy* 6, no. 3 (July 1995): 101–11.

Scanlon, Thomas M. "Fear of Relativism." In Rosalind Hursthouse, Gavin Lawrence, and Warren Quinn, eds., *Virtues and Reasons: Philippa Foot and Moral Theory. Essays in Honour of Philippa Foot*, pp. 219–45. Oxford: Clarendon Press, 1995.

Schell, Orville. "Maoism vs. Media in the Market." *Media Studies Journal* 9, no. 3 (Summer 1995): 33–42.

Schell, Orville, and David Shambaugh, eds. *The China Reader: The Reform Era*. New York: Vintage Books, 1999.

Schmitter, Philippe C. "Interest Systems and the Consolidation of Democracies." In Gary Marks and Larry Diamond, eds., *Reexamining Democracy: Essays in Honor of Seymour Martin Lipset*, pp. 156–81. London: Sage Publications, 1992.

Schoenhals, Michael. *The Paradox of Power in a People's Republic Middle School*. Armonk, N.Y.: M. E. Sharpe, 1993.

Schwartz, Benjamin I. *Chinese Communism and the Rise of Mao*. Cambridge, Mass.: Harvard University Press, 1964.

———. *In Search of Wealth and Power: Yen Fu and the West*. New York: Harper & Row, 1968.

Sen, Amartya. "Beyond Liberalization: Social Opportunity and Human Capability." Pamphlet. London School of Economics, Development Economics Research Programme, Nov. 1994.

———. *Development as Freedom*. New York: Alfred A. Knopf, 1999.

———. *Inequality Re-examined*. Oxford: Oxford University Press, 1992.

Sharman, Lyon. *Sun Yat-sen: His Life and Its Meaning*. Stanford: Stanford University Press, 1968.

Shaw, Victor N. *Social Control in China: A Study of Chinese Work Units*. Westport, Conn.: Praeger, 1996.

Shen Mingming and Samuel Eldersveld. "Problem Perceptions of Chinese Local Cadres and Masses: An Empirical Study." *China Studies* 1997, no. 3: 45–68.

Shi, Tianjian. *Political Participation in Beijing: A Survey Study*. Cambridge, Mass.: Harvard University Press, 1997.

Shi Xiuyin. "Zhongguoren shehui xinli 90 niandai jincheng" (The Chinese mentality in the 1990s). *Kaifang shidai*, no. 117 (Sept.–Oct. 1997): 12–22.

Shu Tinghai. *An jing zhongyang* (Cases that alarmed the central government). Beijing: Guoji wenhua chubanshe, 1996.

Shue, Henry. *Basic Rights: Susbsistence, Affluence, and U.S. Foreign Policy.* Princeton: Princeton University Press, 1996.

Shue, Vivienne. "State Power and Social Organization in China." In Joel Migdal, Atul Kohli, and Vivienne Shue, eds., *State Power and Social Forces: Domination and Transformation in the Third World*, pp. 65–88. New York: Cambridge University Press, 1994.

Skocpol, Theda. *States and Social Revolutions.* Cambridge, Eng.: Cambridge University Press, 1979.

Skocpol, Theda, and Ellen Kay Trimberger. "Revolutions and the World-Historical Development of Capitalism." In Theda Skocpol, *Social Revolutions in the Modern World*, pp. 120–32. Cambridge, Eng.: Cambridge University Press, 1994.

Social Psychological Attitude Research Project Team. "Zhuanxin shiqi de Shanghai shimin shehui xintai diaocha he duice yanjiu" (Investigation of the social psychological attitudes of residents of Shanghai during the period of transition and strategy research). *Shehuixue yanjiu*, 1994, no. 3: 19–25.

"Sohu diaocha tongji jieguo fankui" (Feedback from survey statistical results by Sohu). Feb. 23, 1999, pp. 1–12. From the Internet: http://168.160.224.208/cgi-bin/survey/sohu0212.

Solinger, Dorothy J. "The Floating Population in the Cities: Chances for Assimilation?" In Deborah S. Davis, Richard Kraus, Barry Naughton, and Elizabeth J. Perry, eds., *Urban Spaces in Contemporary China: The Potential for Autonomy and Community in Post-Mao China*, pp. 113–39. Cambridge, Eng.: Cambridge University Press and Woodrow Wilson Center Press, 1995.

———. "Urban Enterpreneurs and the State: The Merger of State and Society." In Arthur Lewis Rosenbaum, ed., *State and Society in China: The Consequences of Reform*, pp. 121–41. Boulder, Colo.: Westview Press, 1992.

Song Qiang, Zhang Zangzang, and Qiao Bian, eds. *Zhongguo keyi shuo bu* (The China that can say no). Beijing: Zhonghua gongshang lianhe chubanshe, 1996.

State Council Information Office. "Progress in China's Human Rights' Cause in 1996." *Xinhua yuebao* (*New China Monthly*) 1997, no. 5: 33–34.

———. "The Progress of Human Rights in China." Special Issue. *Beijing Review*, Dec. 1995.

State Statistical Bureau, Statistics Division; and Chinese Research Center for the Promotion and Development of Science and Technology, comps. *Zhongguo shehui fazhan ziliao: zhiguan, keguan he guoji bijiao* (Data on the development of Chinese society: subjective, objective, and international comparisons). Beijing: Zhongguo chouyang chubanshe, 1992.

Sullivan, Denis J., and Sana Abed-Kotob. *Islam in Contemporary Egypt: Civil Society vs. the State.* Boulder, Colo.: Lynne Rienner, 1999.

Sun Jiaming. *Guannian diaocha—zhuanxing shehuide beijing, 1991–1994* (The generation gap in ideas—background of a society in transition, 1991–94). Shanghai: Shehui kexue chubanshe, 1997.

Sun Li. "1997–1998 nian woguo chengzhen jumin shehui jiben xintai diaocha fenxi" (Survey of urban residents' public opinion in 1997–98). In Lu Xin, Lu Xueyi, Shan Tianlun, *1998 nian: Zhongguo shehui xingshi fenxi yu yuce* (1998: analysis and predictions of China's social conditions), pp. 149–65. Beijing: Shehui kexue wenxian chubanshe, 1998.

———. "Qiu wen duoyu qiu fu" (Seek stability more than riches). *Zhongguo qingnian bao*, July 6, 1996, p. 3.

Sun Peiwu. "Dalu zhengzhi zixia ershangde tiaozhang jixiang" (Signs of challenges from the bottom up in Mainland Chinese politics). *Zhonggong yanjiu* (Taipei) 32, no. 6 (June 1998): 85–93.

Sun, Yan. *The Chinese Reassessment of Socialism, 1976–1992*. Princeton: Princeton University Press, 1995.

———. "Ideology and the Demise or Maintenance of Soviet-Type Regimes: Perspectives on the Chinese Case." *Communist and Post-Communist Studies* 28, no. 3 (1995): 319–38.

Tang, Wenfang, and William L. Parish. *Chinese Urban Life Under Reform: The Changing Social Contract*. Cambridge, Eng.: Cambridge University Press, 2000.

Tanner, Murray Scot. *The Politics of Lawmaking in Post-Mao China: Institutions, Processes, and Democratic Prospects*. Oxford: Clarendon Press, 1999.

Taylor, Charles. *Philosophy and the Human Sciences: Philosophical Papers*, vol. 2. Cambridge, Eng.: Cambridge University Press, 1985.

Thorgensen, Stig. "Cultural Life and Cultural Control in Rural China: Where Is the Party?" *China Journal*, no. 44 (July 2000): 129–41.

Tolley, Michael. *Freedom, Rule of Law, and Democracy in the United States and Britain*. Aldershot, U.K.: Dartmouth Publishing, forthcoming.

Unger, Jonathan. "'Bridges': Private Business, the Chinese Government and the Rise of New Associations." *China Quarterly*, no. 147 (Sept. 1996): 795–819.

Unger, Jonathan, and Anita Chan. "China, Corporatism, and the East Asian Model." *Australian Journal of Chinese Affairs*, no. 33 (Jan. 1995): 29–53.

United Nations Development Programme. *Human Development Report, 1997*. New York: Oxford University Press, 1997.

———. *Human Development Report, 1998*. New York: Oxford University Press, 1998.

———. *Human Development Report, 2000*. New York: Oxford University Press, 2000.

Verba, Sidney; Norma H. Nie; and Jae-on Kim. *Participation and Political Equality: A Seven Nation Comparison*. Cambridge, Eng.: Cambridge University Press, 1978.

Walder, Andrew G., ed. *Zouping in Transition: The Process of Reform in Rural North China*. Cambridge, Mass.: Harvard University Press, 1998.

Waley, Arthur, trans. *The Analects of Confucius*. New York: Random House, 1938.

Walzer, Michael. *Interpretation and Social Criticism*. Cambridge, Mass.: Harvard University Press, 1987.

———. *Spheres of Justice: A Defense of Pluralism and Equality*. New York, Basic Books, 1983.

Wang Binglu. "Yingxiang xiangzhen ganbu falü yishi xingchengde zhuyao yinsu" (Major factors influencing the development of awareness of law among town and township cadres). *Zhongguo nongcun guancha* 1999, no. 1: 60–64.

Wang Fei-ling, "The Roots of an Institutional Exclusion: Sources of Legitimacy of China's *Hukou* System." Paper presented at the 1998 Annual Meeting of the American Political Science Association, Sept. 10, 1998.

Wang Gungwu. "Power, Rights, and Duties in Chinese History." Reprinted in idem, *The Chineseness of China: Selected Essays*, pp. 165–87. Hong Kong: Oxford University Press, 1991.

———. "To Reform a Revolution: Under the Righteous Mandate." In Tu Weiming, ed., *China in Transformation*, pp. 71–94. Cambridge, Mass.: Harvard University Press, 1994.

Wang Hui. "Contemporary Chinese Thought and the Question of Modernity." *Social Text* 55, 16, no. 2 (Summer 1998): 9–44.

Wang Jisi, ed. *Wenming yu guoji zhengzhi: Zhongguo xuezhe ping Huntington de "Wenming chungtulun"* (Civilization and international politics: Chinese scholars critique Huntington's *Clash of Civilizations*). Shanghai: Shanghai renmin chubanshe, 1995.

Wang Lu, series editor-in-chief. *Baishude qishi—xingzheng jiguan baishu baili shuping* (A detailed description of 100 cases that administrative organizations lost). Beijing: Zhongguo zuoyue chuban, 1990.

Wang, Shaoguang. "The Politics of Private Time: Changing Leisure Patterns in Urban China." In Deborah S. Davis, Richard Kraus, Barry Naughton, and Elizabeth J. Perry, eds., *Urban Spaces in Contemporary China: The Potential for Autonomy and Community in Post-Mao China*, pp. 149–72. Cambridge, Eng.: Cambridge University Press and Woodrow Wilson Center Press, 1995.

Wang Tiancheng. "Zhirenzhe zhi yu fa: xingzhengfa yu renquan" (Those who govern should be governed by law: administrative law and human rights). *Zhongwai faxue*, no. 5 (1992), pp. 29–36.

Wang Xinyi. "Shouru fenpei helihua you laiyu jianchuan jizhi" (An equitable income distribution relies on improvement of mechanisms). *Qiu shi* 1997, no. 7: 30–32.

Wang Yan."Cujin guojia zhengzhi shenghuode fazhihua" (Promote the legalization of political life). *Fangfa*, no. 78 (Mar. 1998): 7–8.

Wang Zhenmin. "The Developing Rule of Law in China." *Harvard Asia Quarterly* 4, no. 4 (Autumn 2000): 35–39.

———. "The Evolution of the Chinese Constitution in the 20th Century." Unpublished paper, 2001.

———. "The Recent Constitutional Amendments in China." Paper presented at the Fifth World Congress of the International Association of Constitutional Law, Rotterdam, July 12–26, 1999.

Wang Zhenmin and Li Zhenghui. "The Developing Human Rights and Rule of Law in Legal Philosophy and Political Practice in China, 1978–2000." In Danilo Zolo, ed., *The Rule of Law, Theory, History, and Criticism*, pp. 791–812. New York: Continuum International, 2002.

Wank, David L. "Private Business, Bureaucracy, and Political Alliance in a Chinese City." *Australian Journal of Chinese Affairs*, no. 33 (Jan. 1995): 55–71.

Wasserstrom, Jeffrey N., and Liu Xinyong. "Student Associations and Mass Movements." In Deborah S. Davis, Richard Kraus, Barry Naughton, and Elizabeth J. Perry, eds., *Urban Spaces in Contemporary China: The Potential for Autonomy and Community in Post-Mao China*, pp. 362–93. Cambridge, Eng.: Cambridge University Press and Woodrow Wilson Center Press, 1995.

Watson, Burton, trans. *Han Fei Tzu: Basic Writings*. New York: Columbia University Press, 1964.

———. *Mo Tzu: Basic Writings*. New York: Columbia University Press, 1963.

Weinstock, Daniel M. "The Political Theory of Strong Evaluation." In James Tully, ed., *Philosophy in an Age of Pluralism: The Philosophy of Charles Taylor in Question*, pp. 171–93. Cambridge, Eng.: Cambridge University Press, 1994.

Weng Jieming, Zhang Tiao, An Zhiming, Zhang Ximing, and Liu Jinghua, eds. *Zhongguo fazhan baogao shu: 1994–1995 nian Zhongguo fazhan zhuangkuang yu qushi* (Developing conditions and trends in China, 1994–95). Beijing: Zhongguo shehui kexue chubanshe, 1995.

Weng Jieming, Zhang Ximing, Zhang Tao, and Qu Kemin, eds. *Zhongguo fazhan baogao shu: 1996–1997 nian Zhongguo fazhan zhuangkuang yu qushi* (Developing conditions and trends in China, 1996–97). Beijing: Zhongguo shehui kexue chubanshe, 1997.

———. *Zhongguo fazhan baogao shu: 1998 nian Zhongguo fazhan zhuangkuang yu qushi* (Development conditions and trends in China, 1998). Beijing: Zhonggong zhongyang dangxiao chubanshe, 1998.

White, Gordon. "Chinese Trade Unions in the Transition from Socialism: The Emergence of Civil Society or the Road to Corporatism?" Working Paper no. 18. University of Sussex, Institute of Development Studies, 1995.

White, Gordon; Jude Howell; and Shang Xiaoyuan, *In Search of Civil Society: Market Reform and Social Change in Contemporary China*. Oxford: Clarendon Press, 1996.

White, Tyrene. "Village Elections: Democracy from the Bottom Up?" *Current History*, Sept. 1998, pp. 263–67.

White, Tyrene, ed. *China Briefing 2000: The Continuing Transformation.* Armonk, N.Y.: M. E. Sharpe, 2000.

Whyte, Martin K. "Urban China: A Civil Society in the Making?" In Arthur Lewis Rosenbaum, ed., *State and Society in China: The Consequences of Reform*, pp. 77–101. Boulder, Colo.: Westview, 1992.

Woodside, Alexander. "Lost Modernities." Harvard University, Reischauer Memorial Lecture, Mar. 7, 2001.

"Woguo diaochaye renzhong daoyuan: woguo diaochaye ziwo shenshi zhi liu" (China's survey industry faces heavy task: the self-reflection of China's survey industry), pt. 6. *Zhongguo qingnian bao*, Feb. 1, 1997, p. 8.

Wong Koon-kwai. "The Environmental Awareness of University Students in Beijing, China." *Journal of Contemporary China*, forthcoming 2002.

World Bank. *Sharing Rising Incomes: Disparities in China.* Washington, D.C.: World Bank, 1997.

Wu Luping. "The USA in the Eyes of Chinese Youth." *Zhongguo qingnian bao*, May 1, 1996, p. 4.

Xia Yong. "Renquan zexue san ti" (Three topics on the philosophy of human rights). *Zhongguo shehui kexue jikan* 2, no. 3 (May 1993): 51–59.

Xiang Jiquan. "Zhongguo cunminde gonggong canyu—Nanjie, Xianggao, Fanjiaquan san cunde kaocha fenxi" (Chinese villagers' public participation: investigation and analysis of three villages—Nanjie, Xianggao, and Fanjiaquan). *Zhongguo nongcun guancha*, Feb. 1998, pp. 40–47.

Xiao Suihan. "Reconstructing China's Civil Society." Unpublished paper. Zhongnan University of Finance and Economics, Wuhan, 1998.

Xiong Fenxi. "Analysis of Consumer Complaints in 1998 Received by This Periodical." *Zhongguo zhiliang wan li xing*, no. 73 (Jan. 1999).

Xu Wang. "Xiangcun Zhongguode jichen minzhi: guojia yu shehuide quanli huqiang" (Grassroots democracy in rural China: the mutual empowerment between state and society). *Ershiyi shiji* 1997, no. 4: 147–57.

Xu Xun. "State Compensation—Three Years Experience with the Law in China," *China Law* 1998, no. 1 (Mar. 15):. 60–62.

Yang Bing and Zheng Yuqing. "Shetuan zhong xin dengji huanzheng" (Civic associations required to re-register). *Nanfang Daily*, Feb. 2, 1999, http://www.nanfangdaily.com.cn.

Yang Dali and Su Fubing. "Elections, Governance, and Accountability in Rural China." Collection of English papers presented at The International Symposium on Villager Self-Government & Rural Social Development in China, Beijing: Ministry of Civil Affairs and the Carter Center, September 2001, pp. 229–43.

Yang Gan. "A Critique of Chinese Conservatism in the 1990s." *Social Text* 55, 16, no. 2 (Summer 1998): 45–66.

Yi Baoyun. "Minzuzhuyi yu xiandai jingji fazhan" (Nationalism and modern economic development). *Zhanlüe yu guanli* 1994, no. 3.

"1998 [Yijiujiuba] shenghuo ganshou" (Perceptions of life in 1998), online at sohu.com, Dec. 10, 1998, http://www.itc.cn.net/survey/reports05.htm.

Yong Zhong and Zhongding Yang. "A Mass Medium or a Master's Medium: An Observation and Case Study of the Communication Model Adopted by Chinese Television Talk Shows." *Hong Kong Journal of Social Sciences*, no. 12 (Autumn 1998): 67–81.

Yu, Anthony C. "Confucianism and Human Rights." Lecture, Harvard University, China Humanities Seminar, Oct. 12, 2000.

———. "Enduring Change: Confucianism and the Prospect of Human Rights." *Lingnan Journal of Chinese Studies* (Hong Kong) 2 (Dec. 2000): 27–70.

Yu Guoming. "Beijingren hai guanxin zhengzhi ma? 'Beijingshi jumin shehui zhengzhi wenhua' chouyang diaocha baogao" (Do people in Beijing still care about politics? The sampling investigation report entitled "The Social Political Culture of Beijing Citizens"). *Zhongguo qingnian bao*, Sept. 28, 1996, p. 4.

Yuan Yue. "1995–1996 nian Zhongguo chengshi shehui wending yu gongzhong xintai" (Stability and the psychological attitudes of the public in Chinese cities in 1995–96). In Jiang Liu, Lu Xueyi, and Shan Tianlun, eds., *1995–1996 nian Zhongguo: shehui xingshi fenxi yu yuce* (China in 1995–1996: analysis and predictions of social conditions), pp. 112–24. Beijing: Zhongguo shehui kexue yuan chubanshe, 1996.

Zakaria, Fareed. "The Rise of Illiberal Democracy." *Foreign Affairs*, Nov./Dec. 1997, pp. 22–43.

Zha, Jianying. *China Pop: How Soap Operas, Tabloids, and Bestsellers Are Transforming a Culture.* New York: New Press, 1995.

———. "China's Popular Culture in the 1990s." In William A. Joseph, ed., *China Briefing: The Contradictions of Change*, pp. 109–50. Armonk, N.Y.: M. E. Sharpe, 1997.

Zhang Jing. *Fatuan zhuyi: jiqi yu duoyuan zhuyide zhuyao fenqi* (Corporatism and its major differences with pluralism). Beijing: Zhongguo shehui kexue chubanshe, 1998.

Zhang Mingshu. *Zhongguo zhengzhi ren* (Chinese political persons). Beijing: Zhongguo shehui kexue chuban she, 1994.

Zhang Weiguo. "No Central Authority for TV." *China Monthly*, no. 50 (1996–97): 2. From www.chinamz.org/50issue/50gfbq1.htm.

———. "Tuokuoxiu zai Zhongguo" (Talkshows in China). *Minzhu Zhongguo*, no. 50 (1996): 1–4. From www.chinamz.org/50issue/50gfbq2.htm.

Zhang Ximing. "Xinwen fazhi yu shehui fazhan" (Rule of law in press and social development). *Fangfa*, no. 78 (Mar. 1998): 4–5.

Zhang, Yunqiu. "From State Corporatism to Social Representation: Local Trade Unions in the Reform Years." In Timothy Brook and B. Michael Frolic, eds., *Civil Society in China*, pp. 124–48. Armonk, N.Y.: M. E. Sharpe, 1997.

Zhao, Suisheng. "We Are Patriots First and Democrats Second: The Rise of Chinese Nationalism in the 1990s." In Edward Friedman and Barrett L. McCormick, eds. *What If China Doesn't Democratize?* pp. 21–48. Armonk, N.Y.: M. E. Sharpe, 2000.

Zhao, Yuezhi. "Media and Elusive Democracy in China." *Javnost / The Public* 8, no. 2 (June 2001): 21–44.

———. *Media, Market, and Democracy in China: Between the Party Line and the Bottom Line*. Urbana: University of Illinois Press, 1998.

———. "Underdogs, Lapdogs, Watchdogs, and Other Breeds: Journalists and the Post-1989 Chinese Public Sphere." Paper for Chinese Intellectuals Between the State and Market, workshop, Harvard University, Fairbank Center for East Asian Studies, June 30–July 1, 2001.

Zheng, Shiping. "Paths to Democracy: Theoretical Hypotheses and Chinese Experience." Unpublished paper, 1999.

Zheng, Yongnian. *Discovering Chinese Nationalism in China: Modernization, Identity, and International Relations*. Cambridge, Eng.: Cambridge University Press, 1999.

———. "Xiangcun minzhu he Zhongguo zhengzhi jingcheng" (Rural democracy and China's political process). *Ershiyi shiji*, no. 35 (June 1996): 24–33.

Zheng Zhixiao. "Kezhixu fazhan zonghengtan" (Analysis of sustainable development). *Qiu shi* 1997, no. 7: 15–21.

Zhong, Yang; Jie Chen; and John M. Scheb II. "Political Views from Below: A Survey of Beijing Residents." *PS: Political Science and Politics* 30, no. 3 (Sept. 1997): 474–82.

Zhongguo faxuehui. "Overview of Work by Associations and Societies Under the Ministry of Justice." In *Zhongguo xingzheng sifa nianjian, 1997* (China judicial administration yearbook, 1997), pp. 621–29. Beijing: Zhongguo falü chubanshe, 1998.

Zhongguo qingnian bao (China youth daily). A number of articles based on surveys are from ZQB; not listed separately.

"Zhongguo renmin dui guojia fazhan congman xinxin" (Worldwide survey shows Chinese people's full confidence in the country's development). *Beijing qingnian bao*, Sept. 12, 1995, sect. 7.

Zhongguo shehui kexue yuan, Shehuixue yanjiusuo, Zhuanxing ketizu (Chinese Academy of Social Sciences, Institute of Sociology, Project Team on the Change of Values of Contemporary Chinese Youth). *Zhongguo qingniande toushi: Guanyu yidairende jiazhiguan yanbian yanjiu* (A perspective on Chinese youth: research on one generation's changing values). Beijing: Beijing chubanshe, 1993.

Zhongguo xinwen nianjian (The Chinese journalism yearbook). Beijing: Zhongguo shehui kexue chubanshe, 1991.

Zhongguo zhanlüe yu guanli yanjiuhui, Shehui jiu zhuanxing ketizu. "Zhongguo zhuanxingde zhongjinqi qushi yu yinghuan" (Medium and short-term trends and problems in the structural transition of Chinese society). *Zhanlüe yu guanli*, 1998, no. 30 (May): 1–17.

Zhou Shizhong and Huang Zhusheng. "Lun fa zhengfu quanli he gongmin quanlide pingheng" (On the balance maintained by law between governmental power and citizens' rights). *Shehui kexuejia* 1995, no. 5: 58–62.

Zhu Guanglei. *Dangdai Zhongguo zhengfu guocheng* (Government processes in contemporary China). Tianjin: Tianjin renmin chubanshe, 1997.

Zhu Guanglei, ed. *Da fenhua, da zhuhe dangdai Zhongguo shehui gejieceng fenxi* (Analysis of every stratification in contemporary China). Tianjin: Tianjin renmin chubanshe, 1994.

Zhu, Muqun. "Chinese Nationalism in the Post-Deng Era." *China Strategic Review* 2, no. 2 (Mar./Apr. 1997): 57–86.

Glossary of Terms

associations = *xiehui* 协会

"backdoor" = *houmen* 后门

"black" societies = *hei shehui* 黑社会

civilized = *wenming* 文明

civil rights = *minquan* 民权

democracy = *minzhu zhuyi* or *minquan zhuyi* 民主主义 / 民权主义

dissidents = *yiyifenzi* 异议分子

equality = *pingdeng* 平等

freedom = *ziyou* 自由

great harmony = *da tong* 大同

household registration = *hukou* 户口

human rights = *renquan* 人权

"humaneness" = *ren* 仁

interest pluralism = *liyi duoyuan zhuyi* 利益多元主义

Mandate of Heaven = *tianming* 天命

mass organizations = *qunzhong tuanti* 群众团体

morality = *daoli* 道理

mouthpiece of the party-state = *biganzi* 笔杆子

national essence = *guoqing* 国情

non-action = *wuwei* 无为

non-governmental organization = *minjian xiehui* 民间协会

"one institution, two names" = *yitao jigou, liangkuai paizi* 一套机构，两块牌子

parent-official = *fumu guan* 父母官

peaceful evolution = *heping yanbian* 和平演变

personalistic relationships = *guanxi* 关系

political pluralism = *zhengzhi duoyuanhua* 政治多元化

privately run = *minban* 民办

"propriety" or "rites" = *li* 礼

public intellectuals = *gonggong zhishi fenzi* 公共知识分子

pure academic (scholar) = *chun xuezhe* 純学者

reaching the standard = *dabiao* 达标

rebel = *qiyi* 起义

"relationships" = *guanxi* 关系

(neighborhood) residents' committee = *jumin weiyuan hui* 居民委员会

revolt = *zaofan* 造反

revolution = *geming* (lit. "to cut off the mandate") 革命

righteousness = *yi* 义

rights = *quanli* 权利

rites = *li* 礼

rule by virtue = *yi de zhi guo* 以德治国

"sea" elections = *haixuan* 海选

social organizations = *shetuan* 社团 (short for *shehui tuanti* 社会团体)

sponsoring unit = *guakao danwei* 挂靠单位

state-controlled mass organizations = *qunzhong xiehui* 群众协会

theory of three representatives = *sange daibiao sixiang* 三个代表思想

think tank = *zhinangtuan* 智囊团

virtue = *de* 德

the "way" = *dao* 道

work unit = *danwei* 单位

Index

Harvard East Asian Monographs
(* out-of-print)

Harvard East Asian Monographs

Harvard East Asian Monographs

Harvard East Asian Monographs

Harvard East Asian Monographs

Harvard East Asian Monographs

Harvard East Asian Monographs

163. Constantine Nomikos Vaporis, *Breaking Barriers: Travel and the State in Early Modern Japan*

164. Irmela Hijiya-Kirschnereit, *Rituals of Self-Revelation: Shishōsetsu as Literary Genre and Socio-Cultural Phenomenon*

165. James C. Baxter, *The Meiji Unification through the Lens of Ishikawa Prefecture*

166. Thomas R. H. Havens, *Architects of Affluence: The Tsutsumi Family and the Seibu-Saison Enterprises in Twentieth-Century Japan*

167. Anthony Hood Chambers, *The Secret Window: Ideal Worlds in Tanizaki's Fiction*

168. Steven J. Ericson, *The Sound of the Whistle: Railroads and the State in Meiji Japan*

169. Andrew Edmund Goble, *Kenmu: Go-Daigo's Revolution*

170. Denise Potrzeba Lett, *In Pursuit of Status: The Making of South Korea's "New" Urban Middle Class*

171. Mimi Hall Yiengpruksawan, *Hiraizumi: Buddhist Art and Regional Politics in Twelfth-Century Japan*

172. Charles Shirō Inouye, *The Similitude of Blossoms: A Critical Biography of Izumi Kyōka (1873–1939), Japanese Novelist and Playwright*

173. Aviad E. Raz, *Riding the Black Ship: Japan and Tokyo Disneyland*

174. Deborah J. Milly, *Poverty, Equality, and Growth: The Politics of Economic Need in Postwar Japan*

175. See Heng Teow, *Japan's Cultural Policy Toward China, 1918–1931: A Comparative Perspective*

176. Michael A. Fuller, *An Introduction to Literary Chinese*

177. Frederick R. Dickinson, *War and National Reinvention: Japan in the Great War, 1914–1919*

178. John Solt, *Shredding the Tapestry of Meaning: The Poetry and Poetics of Kitasono Katue (1902–1978)*

179. Edward Pratt, *Japan's Protoindustrial Elite: The Economic Foundations of the Gōnō*

180. Atsuko Sakaki, *Recontextualizing Texts: Narrative Performance in Modern Japanese Fiction*

181. Soon-Won Park, *Colonial Industrialization and Labor in Korea: The Onoda Cement Factory*

182. JaHyun Kim Haboush and Martina Deuchler, *Culture and the State in Late Chosŏn Korea*

183. John W. Chaffee, *Branches of Heaven: A History of the Imperial Clan of Sung China*

184. Gi-Wook Shin and Michael Robinson, eds., *Colonial Modernity in Korea*

185. Nam-lin Hur, *Prayer and Play in Late Tokugawa Japan: Asakusa Sensōji and Edo Society*

186. Kristin Stapleton, *Civilizing Chengdu: Chinese Urban Reform, 1895–1937*

187. Hyung Il Pai, *Constructing "Korean" Origins: A Critical Review of Archaeology, Historiography, and Racial Myth in Korean State-Formation Theories*

188. Brian D. Ruppert, *Jewel in the Ashes: Buddha Relics and Power in Early Medieval Japan*

189. Susan Daruvala, *Zhou Zuoren and an Alternative Chinese Response to Modernity*

Harvard East Asian Monographs